Principles of American Government

SECOND EDITION

Kenneth Prewitt
UNIVERSITY OF CHICAGO
Sidney Verba
HARVARD UNIVERSITY

PRINCIPLES OF AMERICAN GOVERNMENT

Second Edition

Harper & Row, Publishers
NEW YORK HAGERSTOWN SAN FRANCISCO LONDON

Sponsoring Editor: Dale Tharp
Project Editor: Lois Lombardo
Designer: Ben Kann
Production Supervisor: Will C. Jomarrón
Photo Researcher: Myra Schachne
Compositor: Progressive Typographers, Inc.
Printer and Binder: The Murray Printing Company
Art Studio: Eric G. Hieber E. H. Technical Services

Photograph Credits

Photo Trends, APF, 112, *Beckwith Studios,* 14; *Marion Bernstein,* 54; *Culver,* 29; *DPI: Blanche,* 5, *Caplin,* 20, *Laping,* 217; *EPA: McKinney,* 193, *Sachs,* 333, *FreeVision: Combs,* 3, 56; *George Gardner,* 11, 43, 63, 115, 149, 163, 275; *Charles Gatewood,* 27, 47; *Joel Gordon,* 259; *Jeroboam: Optic Nerve,* 129, *Powers,* 143; *Stock, Boston: Brody,* 297, *Gross,* 304, *Herwig,* 8, *Southwick,* 154(*top*), *Sweezy,* 25; *UPI,* 1, 36, 72, 73, 82, 89, 116, 133, 167, 183, 204, 209, 235, 278, 299, 332, 336; *Catherine Ursillo,* 100; *Wide World,* 17, 19, 51, 61, 77, 87, 102, 107, 135, 141, 154(*bottom*), 166, 171, 174, 179, 180, 215, 221, 239, 247, 249, 251, 253, 265, 266, 271, 286, 287, 291, 316, 320.

PRINCIPLES OF AMERICAN GOVERNMENT, *Second Edition*

 For information address Harper & Row, Publishers, Inc., 10 East 53rd Street, New York, N.Y. 10022.

Library of Congress Cataloging in Publication Data

Prewitt, Kenneth.
Principles of American government.

"A shortened and completely rewritten version of An introduction to American politics, second edition."

Includes bibliographical references and index.

1. United States—Politics and government—Handbooks, manuals, etc. I. Verba, Sidney, joint author. II. Title.
JK274.P76 1977 320.9'73 76-54707
ISBN 0-06-045282-X

Contents

CONGRESS 9

THE PRESIDENCY 10

THE SUPREME COURT 11

SEPARATION OF POWERS 12

Preface

Principles of American Government, Second Edition, presents an overview of the major features of politics in the United States. It is impossible to deal thoroughly with all aspects of American politics in a short book of this nature. Rather, we have focused on those recurring patterns of American government and politics that will enable the student to make sense out of the complex day-to-day rush of political life. This is not a book on current events—although we try to illustrate the principles of American government with current material—but a book that should enable the student to see current events in context.

Principles of American Government is a shortened and completely rewritten version of *An Introduction to American Politics, Second Edition.* It should be useful in introductory American politics courses that are shorter than the regular semester or in courses where a shorter overview of American politics is desired as background for further study. We have tried to make the presentation simple enough for students with little exposure to such materials. The reading level is intended to make the book widely accessible. Difficult abstract concepts are not used or, if necessary, are thoroughly explained. Our goal is to teach the student to see the underlying general patterns of politics, but to do this by moving gradually from the more immediately understandable facts of politics to a more general level.

In this version of our text, we have continued various features of our larger book: We present no single theory of American politics, neither elite theory, nor pluralist theory, nor any other all-encompassing theory. Although we believe theory is important in helping us understand politics, we do not know of any overall theory into which one can fit the reality of American politics without distorting that reality. However, we do draw on many of the theoretical interpretations of American politics and have tried in each section of the book to use those that seem most appropriate and to make them accessible to the student.

Just as we have no all-encompassing theory, we have no particular political axe to grind. This is not a "point of view" book. It is our purpose neither to praise nor to condemn the American political system. Our stance toward American politics is critical, but in the strict sense of the word: We try to be objective so as to locate both strengths and weaknesses. The result is that we cannot present *the* interpretation of American politics based on this year's intellectual (or political) trend. We stress *alternative* interpretations. In fact, the theme of controversy is central to the book. At the end of most chapters we raise a controversial issue in which we explore alternative interpretations of American politics. If at times the student is uncertain as to which interpretation is correct, he or she will have gotten our message. Uncertainty is not a comfortable feeling with which to leave an introductory text, but it is healthier than a false certainty.

We have tried to base this book on the latest research in political science, but it is not a compilation of research findings. We use the research to make the political process more understandable to the student who has no technical training. When we do base material on contemporary research, we have taken on the explicit burden of making its meaning and relevance accessible to the student. We do not limit ourselves only to recent research. It is important for the student to know about the arguments in *The Federalist Papers* as well as current research on elections.

In each section of the book we attempt to make an argument, using facts about American politics to clarify the political process. But we also want the student to learn the basic structural facts of American politics. Therefore, we have provided separate "nuts and bolts" sections, in question-and-answer format, describing how some key institutions work—for instance, how cases come before the Supreme Court, the procedures for replacing the President, and how a bill becomes a law.

We begin with a pair of chapters dealing with the fundamental basis of American politics: a particular economic system and a particular constitutional structure. The first chapter deals with the nature of the American economy and how it interrelates with the political process. We do not believe economics explains all, but given the overlap between politics and economics, we feel that one cannot begin without an understanding of how they interrelate. The second chapter traces the historical evolution of the constitutional structure, followed by a chapter tying the separate themes of the first two together—the nature of citizenship in America, focusing on how economic and political inequalities relate to each other.

The next chapter deals with the way in which citizens are linked to the political process: the ways citizens participate in and attempt to influence politics and the process by which political leaders are recruited. Chapter 5 outlines the basic political beliefs of Americans and shows how these beliefs affect the political process. In Chapter 6 we focus on a fundamental question, What is political conflict all about? Here we present and analyze the various kinds of divisions in American society that form the basis for political conflict.

The first six chapters provide the basis for considering the major institutions of American political life. The two chapters that follow discuss the institutions linking the citizen to the political process. Chapter 7 deals with the role of interest groups and Chapter 8 with that of political parties.

In Chapters 9 through 12 we consider the major institutions of the federal government: Chapter 9, Congress; Chapter 10, The Presidency; and Chapter 11, The Supreme Court. Chapter 12 deals with the complex interaction among these three branches of the government and the general principles of the separation of powers.

Having provided a thorough grounding in the workings of the federal government, we turn, in Chapter 13, to an analysis of the relationship between the government and the individual and in Chapter 14 between the federal government and the state and local governments.

Chapter 15 attempts to tie together the previous chapters by looking at the way public policy is actually made. A special section, following the postscript, places in historical perspective the 1976 Presidential Election that sent Jimmy Carter to the White House.

Carolyn Smith carried out the exacting work of revision and condensation. She has a remarkable ability to tell things in simple language without oversimplifying a point.

We owe a special debt to Robert Gamage for tireless and imaginative assistance and to Professor Kay Schlozman, Boston College, who has been a close collaborator and constructive critic.

K. P.
S. V.

Principles of American Government

SECOND EDITION

Introduction

Why Government?

We don't often ask why we have government, because we're used to it and take it for granted. But government makes us do things—pay taxes, drive at certain speeds, stay off of other people's property, serve on juries, and so on. What's more, we *have* to do these things; if we don't, we're likely to be punished. Thus by forcing citizens to do things, government limits individual freedom. If we agree that individual freedom is good, then the case against government is strong. So why do people put up with it?

LAW AND ORDER

We need government to provide law and order. If people were allowed to do whatever they wanted, civilized life would be impossible. We support government because it provides the orderly society in which a citizen can raise a family, work at a job, get an education, and plan for the future.

Economic activities, for example, depend on contracts. But some guarantee is needed to make sure people don't back out on their contracts—to make sure that car buyers don't stop making their payments, that employers don't decide not to pay their employees, and that the bank doesn't close its doors and keep its customers' savings. Such contracts are backed up by the government; that is, people keep their contracts because the government makes sure they do and may punish them if they don't.

We also depend on government to provide security for our lives and property. You won't buy an expensive stereo if you think it will be stolen the next day; you won't send your child to school if there are no traffic laws. Even more important, we expect government to provide for our security as a nation—to protect us from invasion and from international outlaws.

However, the government carries on many activities that have little to do with basic law and order: repaving an interstate highway in Nevada; raising the tax on gasoline; printing a booklet naming the trees along a trail in a national park; sending a check to a blind pensioner in New York. Obviously we must look beyond law and order to answer the question, Why government?

COLLECTIVE GOODS

Government often makes decisions individual citizens can't make by themselves. For example, people want to be sure all cars will be driven on the same side of the road; everyone benefits from the government's power to decide which side.

To understand why this is so, we must know the meaning of collective goods. A *collective good* is a benefit available to every citizen whether or not he has worked for it. If the government opens a new park, I can use it whether or not I helped create it. But if I will benefit anyway, why should I help create the park? I can use it after other people have worked to create it, so I don't need to do anything. Furthermore, even if I try to help create the park, it

A national park is a collective good, paid for through taxes.

probably won't make much difference since my effort—the money or labor I, an average citizen, can contribute—will be small.

For any single individual it makes sense to wait until others have created the collective good. But if everybody felt the same way, collective goods would never be established. Only a binding governmental decision making everyone contribute to a public park through tax payments can create the park.

SUMMARY

We have discussed two different answers to the question, Why government? First, government provides the security that makes it possible for citizens to raise a family, go to school, earn a living, and so on. Second, binding governmental decisions make it possible to turn individual goals into collective goods that benefit all citizens.

Why Politics?

Government would be simple if all governmental decisions were like the decision that everyone must drive on the right. Most drivers don't care whether they drive on the right or on the left, as long as everyone drives on the same side. This type of decision is costless. No one loses by driving on the right instead of on the left.

DIFFERENT PREFERENCES

However, not all citizens favor the same goals. It's not easy to agree on what collective goods government should provide or who should pay for them. Not all citizens benefit equally from any collective good, nor do they pay equally. Thus government involves conflict among individuals and groups trying to get the greatest benefit for the least cost.

A public highway, for example, is a collective good. No single average citizen can afford to build one, and everyone can use it. Yet often there's a struggle over where a highway will be located or whether it will be built at all. Downtown merchants may want a highway to come directly into the city; apartment dwellers may strongly oppose such a plan. Truckers and car makers will favor more highways; conservationists will say the money should be spent on mass transit and public parks instead. Other citizens favor lower taxes; they don't want the highway no matter where it goes, and they oppose mass transit and public parks as well. Still another group, perhaps the largest of all, simply doesn't care.

Thus individuals and groups have different preferences. A large, varied nation such as ours is bound to include groups with different goals: labor and management, whites and blacks, Catholics and Protestants, landlords and tenants, and so on. There are many issues, and on any single issue we're likely to find some citizens on one side, some on the other side, and some who don't care.

DIFFERENT LEVELS OF INVOLVEMENT

Government decisions affect some groups more than others. Any given policy is likely to benefit one group a lot, another a little, and another not at all. It may also hurt some people. The decision to build a highway next to my house benefits the highway builders a lot, benefits commuters a little, has no effect on most citizens, but may hurt me and some of my neighbors. So on any particular issue we will find not only different preferences but different levels of involvement as well. The citizens who are most severely affected will care the most, while those who aren't affected won't care at all.

UNEQUAL POLITICAL RESOURCES

Each citizen has one vote. But citizens differ in the resources they can use to influence the government. For instance, differences in financial resources make some people more powerful than others. Those who contribute heavily to political campaigns have a lot more influence than those who have no money to contribute. And citizens are unequal in the skills they bring to politics, in how well they are organized, in the connections they have, and in the time they can give to political activity.

Government and Politics

We have seen that government provides collective goods, but that collective goods can benefit some groups in society more than others. Even mass-transit systems, schools, and social-security programs don't benefit all citizens

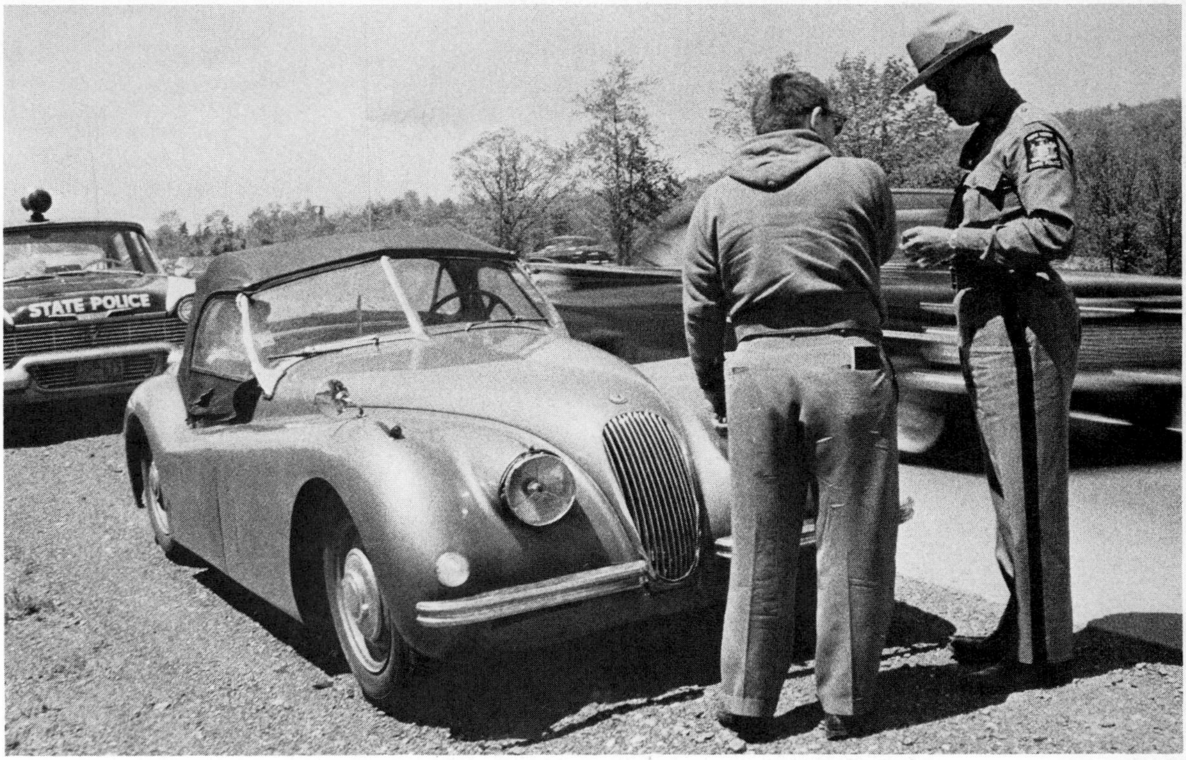

equally, and the cost to each citizen isn't equal either. Thus there is a continuous struggle to influence what collective goods will be provided, who will pay the costs of those goods, and who will benefit from them.

Who wins? You have probably learned that in a democracy the majority should win. But the majority doesn't always win, and maybe it shouldn't. For one thing, there may not be a majority on one side or the other. There may be several groups, each wanting something very different. Rather than a majority and a minority, there may be many minorities.

Besides, as we have seen, not all groups feel equally strongly about any particular issue. Should the views of a citizen who wants to cut five minutes off the time it takes to get from the suburbs to the city count equally with those of a citizen whose home is about to be bulldozed? Simple democracy would ignore differences in levels of involvement.

Even if we believe the majority should always win, we have to admit that it doesn't. Groups bring different resources to the political struggle; very often the resources of a small group outweigh those of a majority. Many governmental programs are provided for well-organized minorities—subsidies for farmers, tax allowances for oil companies, research grants for college professors, and so on.

Government in the United States

Politics is a struggle among individuals and groups with different preferences, different levels of involvement, and different political resources. This is particularly true of American politics, because of some important characteristics of the American people and the American government.

THE AMERICAN PEOPLE

A Large Population. A large population creates big problems: Do we have enough natural resources? Enough space? Schools? Jobs? Problems like these involve governmental action. And big problems mean big government.

A Changing Population. There were 213 million Americans in 1975. A generation earlier there were 133 million. In 1940, 72 million Americans lived in cities; by 1975, nearly twice that many lived in cities. In 1940 there were about 3½ million Americans with college degrees. By 1972 there were 13½ million. We could list changes in the economy, technology, education, and many other areas. The point is that if a large population creates pressures for governmental action, a changing population creates even greater pressures because the government keeps having to deal with new problems.

A Varied Nation. The American public is varied in terms of race, ethnic background, language, occupation, place of residence, and so on. Twenty-three million Americans are black. Twelve million or more are Spanish speaking. In 1971 almost 3 million families earned over $25,000; 7 million families earned under $4,000.

An Iowa farmer has little in common with a black from the south side of Chicago. A Scarsdale stockbroker has little in common with a Houston truck driver. The American public is divided into many subgroups with different interests and preferences. Because of the size of the population and the fact that it's changing fast, there are pressures on the government. And because the population is so varied, these pressures often come into conflict.

THE AMERICAN GOVERNMENT

A Democratic Government. Democracy has many meanings, but most definitions are based on the idea that the decisions of government officials are supposed to be influenced by the public. Because the political system is "open," many different viewpoints can be expressed, and the government is supposed to pay attention to them. (How "open" is the political system, and how responsive is it? Throughout this book we'll be trying to answer those questions.)

A Representative Government. Most government officials are elected, and their decisions are supposed to be based on the preferences of the citizens who voted for them. So to understand how governmental policy is made, we must study how government officials get elected.

A Federal Structure. The American political system divides power between the federal government in Washington and the fifty state governments and, further, among the many local governments. Citizens who want to influence governmental policy can pressure the federal, state, or local government.

A Large and Complex Government. The federal government's budget for 1973 was about $250 billion; if you add up the budgets of the federal, state, and local governments, the total is close to $650 billion. The federal government employs more than 2.5 million civilians; the total number of people employed by the federal, state, and local governments is 14 million. This governmental structure is organized into countless bureaus, agencies, departments, and the like. The result is a complex political system, out of which come policies that affect us in many ways. We will try to show how this happens.

How We Find Out About Politics: I

Politics affects us in many ways: the cleanness of the air we breathe and the water we drink, the quality and costs of the health care and education we get, the safety of the planes and trains we travel in—we could give dozens of examples. Politics matters to us because important issues are involved—issues like security, justice, and equality. For this reason alone it's worthwhile to study politics.

But political issues are complicated and changeable; the language of political debate is confusing; political personalities come and go. It's hard to keep up with politics. A busy student hardly has time to read a daily newspaper, let alone digest the amount of information needed to understand current events. Even when you know what's going on, you may still be puzzled as to why it's happening.

In this book we will be concerned with the "why" of politics. We'll concentrate on the fact that the government provides collective goods and ask why citizens don't benefit equally from those goods or pay for them equally.

We will first look at several characteristics of American society that affect the political struggle: the beliefs of citizens about politics, the many different political groups and the conflicts among them. We'll study the economic system, too, because in our society economics and politics are closely intertwined. Then we'll look at the actors in the political struggle: the political parties, the interest groups, the voting public, and the political leaders. We'll also discuss the framework in which politics takes place—the basic principles of American government such as federalism, separation of powers, and due process of law—as well as the major institutions of the government: the Supreme Court, Congress, the Presidency. We will ask, How do these principles and institutions affect the political struggle? Finally, we'll take a look at how governmental policy is actually made.

This is a lot to cover. There are millions of facts about the politics, principles, institutions, and policies of American government. How do we choose which facts to use?

CHOOSING THE FACTS

To understand politics we need to know both facts and explanations of facts. We can't study politics without knowing something about political parties, interest groups, federalism, due process of law, and so on. It's also useful to have some detailed information about governmental policies. Some facts, however, aren't as useful as others. You may be able to name a member of Congress who is representing you and all the members of the President's Cabinet. But these facts change with each election. Besides, names by themselves don't answer important questions: Why do the President and his Cabinet often favor one kind of legislation while Congress favors another? Why is Congress more likely than the President to consider the particular needs of local areas? Why does a Democratic Congress sometimes

Politics and controversy go together.

support a Republican President? To answer questions like these we need to know about the social backgrounds and careers of Cabinet members and congressmen; we need to know about party identification among voters; we need to know about the organization of Congress and the party ties of congressmen.

We can't present and explain all the facts of American politics. Nor can we keep up with current events as reported in the daily newspapers. Rather, we must choose what to discuss. Our basis is to choose the information that will be most useful in getting a general understanding of American politics.

POLITICS AND CONTROVERSY

Why does political discussion often lead to argument, sometimes very bitter argument? Because people have different political values, and they often believe very strongly in those values.

Those who write about politics—in the press, in magazines and books—are tempted to describe and explain politics from their own particular viewpoint. Thus for any political fact we can usually find many explanations, and often these explanations contradict one another. The study of politics isn't an exact science in which one side is clearly right and the other clearly wrong.

In this book we try to pay attention to the variety of explanations of American politics. We don't present one viewpoint as gospel truth. Rather, we try to focus on some of the major controversies in the study of American politics. Understanding political controversies may be the first step toward understanding politics.

Questions for Review

1. Why do people put up with government?
2. What are collective goods? Give examples.
3. Give examples of collective goods that might not benefit all citizens equally. Explain.
4. What characteristics of the American people and government lead to political conflict?

Chapter 1

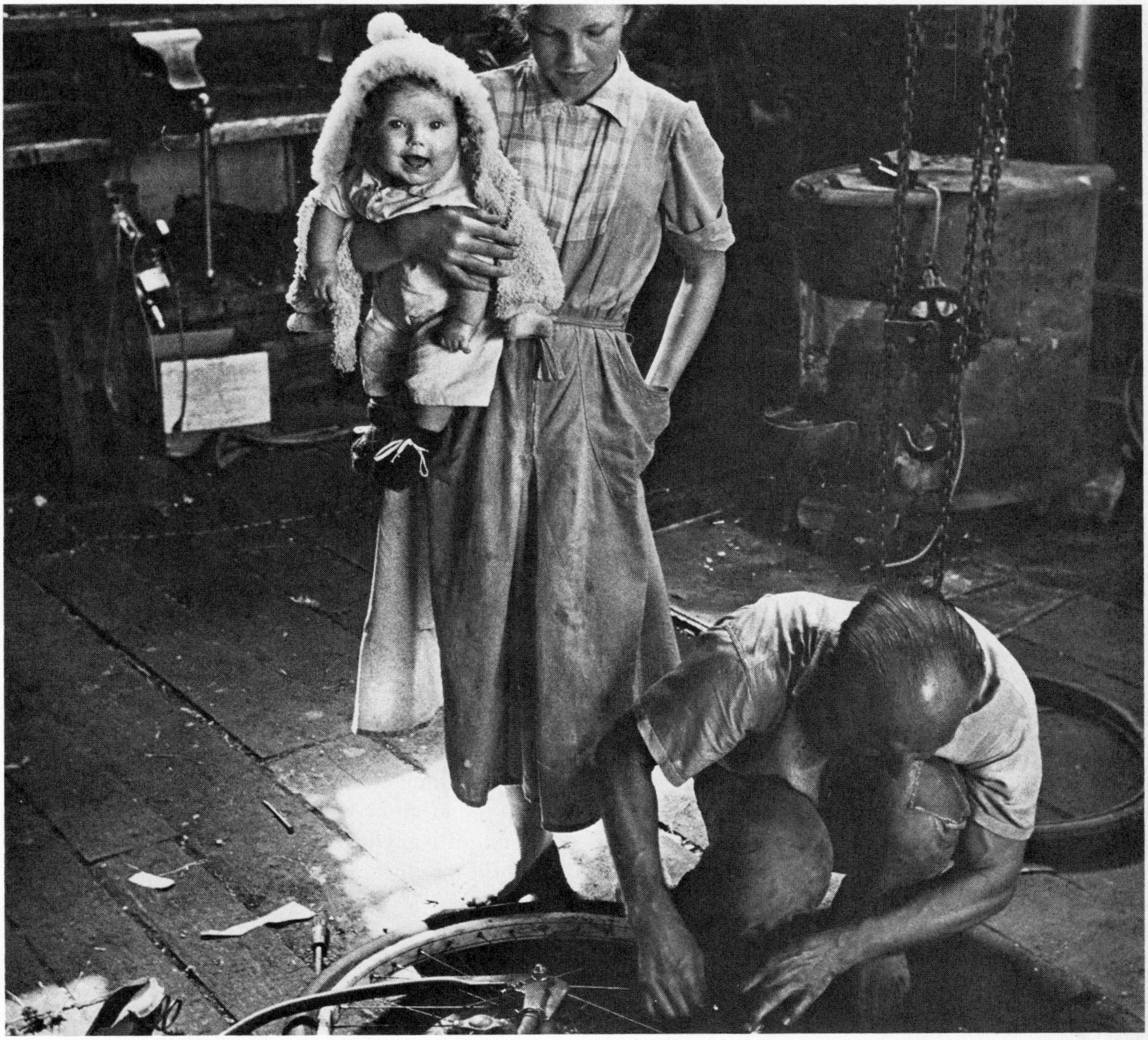

The American Economy and Political Life

Here are some recent news headlines:

Federal Reserve Board Eases Interest Rates
Labor Department Acts to Head Off Coal Strike
White House Acknowledges Recession, Promises to Act
Federal Program for Unemployment Provides City Jobs
Government Investigates Soaring Sugar Prices

What do they have in common? They're talking about an economic issue or problem: interest rates, strikes, recession, unemployment, inflation. And they're talking about a government action or program.

Here are some more headlines. What do they have in common?

Consumer Group Demands Price Controls on Foods
Taxpayer Revolt Predicted If Surcharge Becomes Law
Bank Depositors Threaten Withdrawal Unless Government Increases Protection
Defense Plant Employees Out of Work, Claim Unemployment

Again we see the connection between economics and politics. In these headlines a citizen's economic roles—as consumer, taxpayer, investor, and worker—lead to political actions.

We can't explain American politics without understanding how the government affects the economy and how the economy affects the government. We can't explain citizens' political beliefs and actions without understanding their economic interests.

What Is Economics?

Economics is the study of how society chooses to use scarce resources—labor, minerals, land, water, knowledge—to produce goods and to distribute those goods, now and in the future, among different groups and individuals in society. But such choices aren't easy to make. For what purposes should scarce resources be used? (Should limited oil supplies be used to heat homes, to keep gasoline prices down, or to keep the military at full strength?) Should we satisfy present or future needs? (Should we close a factory in Gary, Indiana, and throw some people out of work, or let the factory continue to pollute Lake Michigan?) And how should the goods in society be distributed among various groups? (Providing free medical care for older citizens may mean less money for research on children's diseases.)

Behind all these questions is the question of *who* will make the decisions. Should they be made by the government?

There was a time when it was unheard-of for the government to make economic decisions. The American economy was a free-enterprise system; the government was expected to keep out. However, throughout American history the government has performed certain economic functions, and its involvement in the economy has increased steadily. We'll discuss the government's economic role in the next three sections of this chapter under the topics of a supported economy, a regulated economy, and a managed economy.

The government's economic activities have not destroyed the free-enterprise system. Many important characteristics of that system remain, though they have been changed by the government's involvement. This will be discussed under the topic of a capitalist economy. The student should remember, however, that while the government plays an important economic role, it doesn't control the economy. This we try to make clear in the final section, a discussion of state capitalism.

A Supported Economy

Economic activities benefit from government support in three important ways. First, the government provides the legal framework needed in a free-enterprise economy. Second, it provides direct subsidies to many economic activities. Third, it is a major, sometimes *the* major, consumer in the economy.

THE LEGAL FRAMEWORK

A free-enterprise economy depends on the right of individuals to enter into valid contracts and have those contracts upheld by law, to sell their products and labor in the marketplace, and to use their abilities to gain material goods. These rights are guaranteed by the U.S. Constitution.

Although capitalism as we know it didn't take hold until after the Civil War, the legal framework existed as early as 1800. Even then a police force protected private property, a court system backed up valid contracts, a monetary system provided the bills and coins used in economic activities, and there was a system of common weights and measures, patents, and copyrights.

SUBSIDIES

Direct support of private enterprise is as old as the nation itself. Alexander Hamilton, first Secretary of the Treasury, insisted that the new government set up a national bank. He got his way, and the government has been supporting private business ever since.

Support for Transportation. Large-scale support of private enterprise began after the Civil War. The period from the 1860s to the end of the century was a time of major economic growth. Government support played an important role in this growth. Canals, harbors, and roads were built and maintained by the government. But the greatest support went to the railroads. By 1870 some 131 million acres—an area larger than Texas—had been granted to private railroad builders; in return the railroads agreed to carry the U.S. mail at a very low cost.

A modern version of the nineteenth-century railroad subsidy is the federal highway program, which benefits the trucking, auto, and oil industries as well as the individual driver. Such subsidies are provided today for the same reason they were in the 1800s: They make possible collective goods that benefit all members of society and that no single individual could afford.

The Protective Tariff. To protect American industry from foreign competition, the government sometimes puts high import taxes on foreign products. A recent example is a special tax on foreign cars, which was intended to make them less competitive with American cars.

Federal Loans. The government not only subsidizes and protects businesses but also lends them money. For example, the Small Business Administration makes loans to businessmen, and a variety of agencies make loans to homeowners and builders. In addition, from time to time the government bails out a huge corporation with a federally guaranteed loan.

Agricultural Subsidy Programs. One of the largest government subsidy programs is intended to keep farm prices stable. Without government supports that guarantee a fair price for his products, the individual farmer would have a very unstable income, often due to causes he can't control.

THE GOVERNMENT AS CONSUMER

The gross national product (GNP) is the dollar amount obtained by adding up all the goods, services, and investments produced by the land, labor, and other resources of society. GNP is a yardstick that tells a society how well it's doing.

When more goods are being produced (apples, TV sets, medicines), more services are available (health care, police protection), and more investments are being made (factories, training programs), a society's GNP is rising. When there's a slowdown in the production of goods, services, and investments, GNP drops.

The importance of the government to the economy can be seen in Figure 1.1. The federal government alone accounts for more than one-fifth of GNP. A large part of this amount is in the form of salaries—for the military, for judges, for clerks in the State Department, for the FBI. But the government is also a consumer of goods produced by private industry—food, typewriters, cars, paper, and so on. This is particularly true of the military. Many of the nation's largest and most powerful corporations hold direct contracts with the government. Not only do these contracts involve huge amounts of money, but some large corporations, such as General Dynamics and Lockheed Aircraft, depend on government contracts for almost all their business. And direct defense contracts are only the tip of the iceberg. The companies that provide the raw materials like aluminum and plastics and parts like airplane tires and gaskets also depend on the government's defense budget.

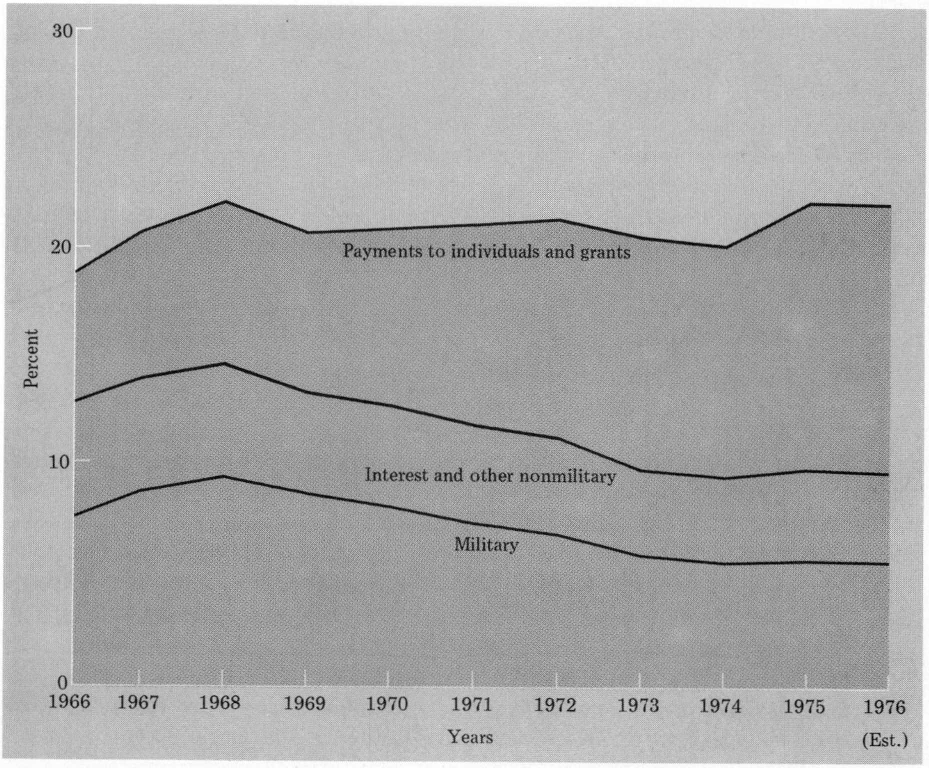

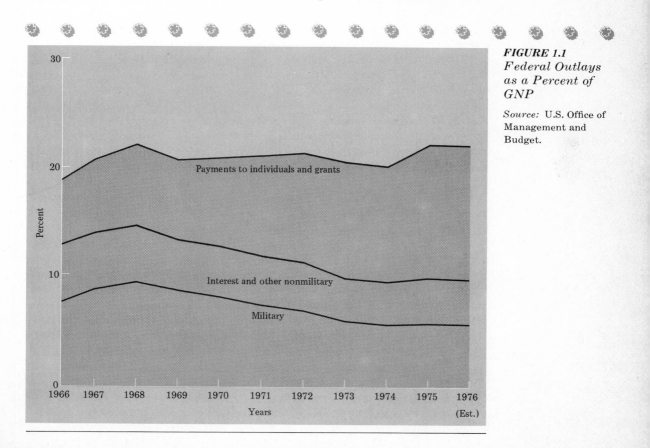

FIGURE 1.1
Federal Outlays as a Percent of GNP

Source: U.S. Office of Management and Budget.

A Regulated Economy

The growth of the economy during the nineteenth century had some harmful effects, but the government paid little attention to them. Government and business leaders felt that a free-enterprise system should benefit from government support but shouldn't be hampered by government regulation. So the government didn't do anything to help citizens who were hurt by an unregulated capitalist economy: small businessmen forced out of the market by monopolies like Standard Oil; farmers gouged by the high prices charged by railroads; workers who toiled long hours in unsafe and unsanitary conditions for very little pay. Judges and politicians often owed their jobs to the groups that opposed regulation the most. They were easily persuaded to accept campaign funds and bribes in return for favors like land grants, tariffs, and freedom from government regulation.

CORRECTING THE FLAWS

In the 1890s dissatisfied groups began calling for government regulation of the economy. Although they weren't very successful, they did create a political climate in which certain flaws of a free-enterprise system—child labor, price fixing, shoddy goods, unsafe working conditions—could be seen and corrected.

Also business leaders themselves began to see the need for regulation. An unregulated economy was hard to manage. Some corporation chiefs saw that the federal government could be very helpful in bringing order to the economy, as long as its role could be limited. And they were largely successful in putting limits on government involvement.

Today the economy is regulated in many ways. There are regulations on the training you need to become a licensed barber; on the number of exits from an airplane, a movie theater, or a day nursery; on the wording of wills and contracts; on the price of electricity and gas. Government regulations affect how a corporation sells stocks, whether it will be allowed to expand, and the way it advertises its products.

"TRUST-BUSTING"

Starting in the nineteenth century and continuing today, industrial corporations put together the money and know-how to build canals and railroads, cut timber, mine coal and oil, and experiment with new products. John D. Rockefeller, the founder of Standard Oil, saw many years ago that the giant corporation would completely change the way business was done all over the world. This new way of doing business, however, sometimes created a *monopoly*, in which a single corporation like Standard Oil had so much power that it could set prices without fear of competition from other companies.

The reformers of the late 1800s felt that monopolies were the root of all economic evil. They wanted to break up the monopolies; "trust-busting" became a popular political slogan. As a result regulatory legislation was passed, such as the Sherman Antitrust Act forbidding monopolistic activities that limit trade and the Federal Trade Commission Act of 1914 banning unfair competition. Laws were also passed regulating working hours and other conditions, particularly for children and women.

FROM MONOPOLY TO OLIGOPOLY

Today, despite government regulation of monopolies, much of the economy is under the control of what economists call oligopolies. In an *oligopoly* a few corporations control a particular part of the economy. A good example is the auto industry, which is dominated by three giant corporations—Ford, Chrysler, and General Motors.

Oligopolies can exist even when there are many companies producing the same service or good. For example, there are 67,000 separate corporations actively involved in the utilities and communication industries. But 33 of these corporations control half of all the assets in electricity, gas, transportation, and communication.

Other areas, however, are free from oligopolistic control. For example, in retail clothing and food distribution the assets are more evenly divided. It is in the most important areas of the economy—transportation, iron and steel, oil, banking and finance—that most oligopolies are found. Government regulation has made it hard for a company to gain monopolistic control but not for huge industrial corporations to pile up large amounts of economic resources.

A Managed Economy

Regulation of the economy shouldn't be confused with management of the economy. Regulatory activities try to correct particular flaws in the economic system such as misleading advertising: The government steps in to protect the consumer from being misinformed about a product or service. But before

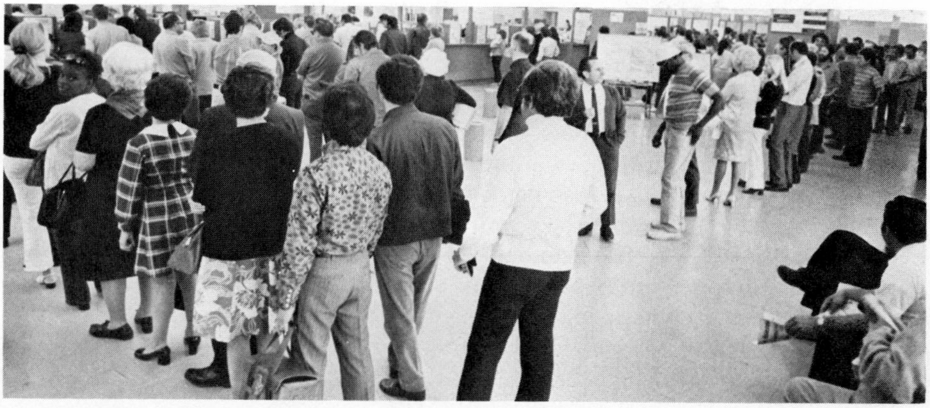

Government policy now provides unemployment compensation when citizens lose jobs.

the Great Depression of the 1930s the government had never tried to manage the economy.

During the period of industrial growth between the Civil War and the Great Depression, most people believed a capitalist economy was self-adjusting. There would be full employment and stable prices if workers freely traded their labor for pay, if production and prices were regulated by supply and demand, and if the rate of growth and investment depended on profits. A few "radical" economists and business leaders, however, claimed that a "boom-bust cycle," in which periods of economic growth are followed by periods of recession and unemployment, is built into an unmanaged capitalist system.

ECONOMIC POLICY IN THE 1930s

During the Depression, as unemployment rose, banks failed, and factories closed, people became less sure that the economy would straighten itself out. Government leaders began listening to a new argument put forward by John Maynard Keynes. Keynes believed government management of the economy—through *fiscal policy*, in which taxes and government spending are adjusted, and *monetary policy*, in which the money supply and interest rates for government loans are controlled—could stop the boom-bust cycle.

These economic tools began to be used in the 1930s. Under President Roosevelt's New Deal the government took on the job of trying to keep unemployment down while at the same time keeping prices from creeping up.

ECONOMIC POLICY TODAY

But the government hasn't been entirely successful in managing the economy. There are still business cycles, although so far they haven't been as severe as in the 1930s. The 1970s have seen particularly hard times. Unemployment has been increasing; by 1975 it had reached levels well above what government economists consider safe. At the same time inflation has become a major problem for many Americans. Prices have been increasing as much as 12 to 15 percent a year—much faster than most people's income. The dollar is buying less. And despite the government's efforts, such as in the area of wage and price controls, so far nothing has worked.

The federal government has been trying to manage the economy with the tools introduced by the New Deal in the 1930s. It hasn't yet tried to *plan* the economy. But in the mid-1970s people started talking about a major economic planning agency. Such an agency would coordinate the many activities of the government that affect the economy. If such an agency is formed, the partnership between the government and the economy will be even stronger. More than ever it will be true that every major economic issue is also a political one and every major political issue also an economic one.

SUMMARY

So far we have learned that the government is actively supporting, regulating, and managing the economy. Later we will see that the government provides economic benefits for individual citizens through such programs as social security, unemployment compensation, medicare, education, and aid to disabled people. It all adds up to major involvement of the government in the economy. And this leads to the question, Is America still a capitalist society?

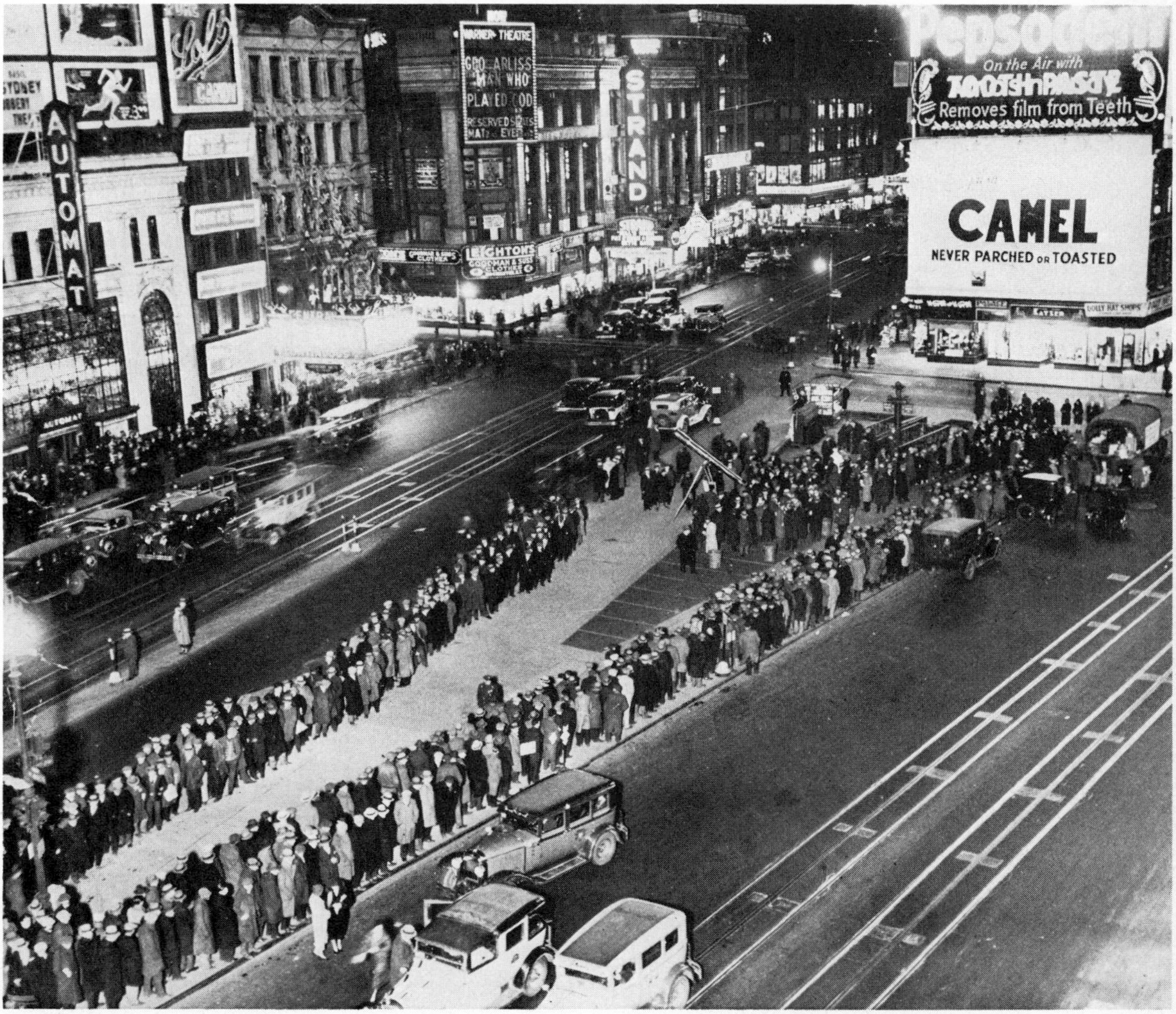

Food lines during the depression led to government involvement in economic matters.

A Capitalist Economy

PRIVATE OWNERSHIP

The United States was founded on the idea that the government's job is to protect life, liberty, and property. But the property itself has changed. To a nation of farmers and tradesmen, land was the most valuable form of property. And though land is still valuable, many other forms of property have become important in today's industrial economy. This is particularly true of natural resources and the production processes that turn them into consumer goods.

Natural resources, production processes, ways of transporting goods, and other elements of an industrial economy are privately owned in the United States. And the economy is run in order to make a profit for the owners. In this way it is still very much a capitalist system. Private individuals and corporations, not the government, own and profit from the economy.

Private ownership of the economy is unusual among industrial nations. Many economic enterprises are publicly owned even in Western democracies like France and Great Britain. The United States is an exception; here there's very little government ownership and operation of natural resources,

Mining in the United States remains a private enterprise.

TABLE 1.1
Public ownership of various industries and services

	Roads	*Postal services*	*Electricity*	*Railways*	*Telephones*	*Airlines*	*Radio, television*	*Gas*	*Coal*	*Oil*	*Steel*	*Banks*
France	S	S	S	S	S	S/p	S	S	S	S	–	S/p
Great Britain	S	S	S	S	S	S/p	S/p	S	S	s	S	–
West Germany	S	S	S	S	S	S	S	S	s	–	–	–
Canada	S	S	S/p	S/p	s	S/p	S/p	–	–	–	–	–
United States	S	S	s	–	–	–	–	–	–	–	–	–

S = mostly state (public) ownership.
s = element of state ownership in mostly private system.
S/p = state and private sectors both large.

Source: Anthony King, "Ideas, Institutions and the Policies of Governments: A Comparative Analysis: Parts I and II," *British Journal of Political Science,* 3 (July 1973), New York: Cambridge University Press, p. 296.

factories, transportation and communication systems, and basic social services.

Table 1.1 makes this very clear. The amount of private ownership in the United States is striking. Note that this table shows facts about ownership, not government regulation or support. The airline industry is as closely regulated in the United States as in the other four nations. But each of the other nations has a major government-owned airline; there is no state-owned airline in the United States.

Americans' strong belief in private ownership of major businesses can be seen in the recent history of the railroads. Railroads, particularly in the Northeast, have been operating at a loss. Under a free-enterprise system a company that couldn't make a profit would simply go out of business. But if its product is a collective good, closing down the business would hurt many citizens. Certainly a transportation system that carries millions of passengers and millions of tons of freight is important to society.

In most countries a bankrupt but important transportation system would be taken over by the government or would have been state owned in the first place. But in the United States a government agency—the U.S. Railway Association—was formed to reorganize the railroads. In early 1975 it announced a major long-term plan that would eventually cost $7 billion. No state ownership is involved. Instead, there will be a private corporation with large-scale federal support.

If an economy is capitalistic when it is privately owned and used for private profit, then the United States economy is capitalistic in spite of major government involvement.

INDIVIDUAL CHOICES

The economy is regulated and managed by the government. And many resources are controlled by large corporations. Yet we live in a society where many economic activities depend on millions of uncoordinated and unregulated individual choices. Take New York City. Eight million people live there, and thousands more pour into the city each day to work. How are these millions of people fed? They don't grow their own crops or livestock. Rather, they depend on a daily supply of food coming into the city from every state and from dozens of foreign countries: Wisconsin cheese, Iowa beef, French wines, Brazilian coffee. If the supply were cut off, the residents and workers of New York would come close to starving in a few days.

What can be said about the process that puts food on the tables of New Yorkers? There's a huge food production, transportation, and marketing network that operates without direction or coordination by any central agency. It depends on millions of individual economic activities.

If an economy is capitalistic when it lets citizens choose what to buy, where to live, what jobs to take, how much of their money to save and how much to spend, then the American economy is capitalistic. We often notice how much the government does to control economic activities. And we often see how much the power of large corporations limits the choices of the individual citizen. But we can't ignore the many ways economic activities are based on individual choices.

MATERIAL REWARDS

There are three facts that lead to social inequality in a democracy:

1. Certain jobs are more important to society than others; some are so important that if they are done poorly, society itself suffers.
2. Certain jobs, often the ones most important to society, require long and difficult training and are not easy to carry out.
3. People will work only if given suitable rewards.

We are interested in item 3: People work for a reward. If they're not rewarded, they work less or not at all. The question is, What should the reward be? In a capitalist society the reward is money. Different wages for different jobs is a basic principle of capitalism. A person's value to society is measured by the income he can get for his labor.

If the shop foreman gets twice as much as the assembly-line worker, it's because the foreman has more experience, skill, and responsibility. If the owner of the factory makes several times as much as the foreman, it's because the owner, after all, took the risk and set up the business. If a line worker's job is done well, the reward is a paycheck and perhaps a promotion. If foremen can't manage their workers, the punishment is the suggestion that they find jobs somewhere else.

The use of unequal wages as a reward for ability and effort is found throughout the economy. In some areas the gap between the highest and lowest wages is very wide. The chairman of the Ford Motor Company, for example, was paid $865,000 in 1973; an assembly-line worker was paid $8,000. The fact that American society accepts differences like these is evidence of the strength of a capitalist system despite the growing involvement of the government in economic affairs.

State Capitalism

Two facts should now be clear. First, the government is heavily involved in economic affairs. This may be seen in the importance of the government's budget. It may also be seen in the structure of the government. The President's Cabinet includes Secretaries of Commerce, Agriculture, Labor, Treasury, Transportation; important executive agencies include the Federal Trade Commission, the Interstate Commerce Commission, the Securities and Exchange Commission; and the most powerful committees in Congress are those dealing with taxation, the budget, and appropriations. The government supports private enterprise, regulates economic activities, and tries to manage general economic conditions.

The second fact, however, balances this picture of government involvement. Most of the economy is privately owned. Private citizens own the mines, the trucks, the chemicals, the factories, the grocery stores, and the land of America. Very often these individuals are organized as corporations, and huge amounts of resources are controlled by the larger corporations. These resources are used to make profits for the owners.

These two facts result in an economic system that can be called *state capitalism*. Large corporations, organized labor, and the government have formed a partnership. This partnership is not without conflict, but it is held together by some important shared goals.

In *The New Industrial State* John Kenneth Galbraith spells out some of those goals: "The state is strongly concerned with the stability of the economy. And with its expansion or growth. And with education. And with technical and scientific advance. And, most notably, with the national defense."[1] These goals are important to the large corporations as well as to the government. Stability is needed for long-term planning; economic growth brings higher profits; trained manpower, scientific research, and technical progress are needed in a modern industrial society; and defense spending directly supports a large part of the economy.

CRITICISM OF STATE CAPITALISM

Critics of state capitalism feel that it's making it harder for citizens to control their own lives. In the words of Milton Friedman, a professor at the Univer-

[1] John Kenneth Galbraith, *The New Industrial State* (Boston: Houghton Mifflin, 1967), p. 304.

sity of Chicago, freedom "is a rare and delicate plant." Great care must be taken to protect it. "Our minds tell us, and history confirms, that the great threat to freedom is the concentration of power." Friedman is particularly worried about concentration of power in the government. Although government is necessary to preserve freedom, it can also threaten freedom. The true free man will ask: "How can we keep the government from becoming a Frankenstein that will destroy the very freedom we establish it to protect?"[2]

Critics like Friedman claim that the government has grown huge *because* it's involved in the economy. If it let the economy take care of itself, there would be less need for large government bureaucracies and budgets. And there would be less danger that the government would limit individual freedom.

Other critics pay more attention to the dangers of great wealth in the hands of a small group. They point out that such wealth can be used to gain political control. If there is unequal control over economic resources, they argue, it's hard to see how there can be equal political influence. The well-known Marxist economists Paul Baran and Paul Sweezy claim that the widely repeated statement that the American political system is a democracy is simply untrue. Citizens don't control the conditions in which they live or the policies of the government. A small group makes all the important decisions.

Whether they express fear of government power or corporate power, the critics of state capitalism share a belief that the political-economic partnership in the United States is a threat to individual freedom and democratic government.

SUPPORTERS OF STATE CAPITALISM

Supporters of state capitalism believe the partnership between the government and the economy is a healthy one. In this view the government, large corporations, and organized labor have joined forces to achieve beneficial goals: steady growth in production; a steady increase in the standard of living; larger world markets for American products; continual improvement in public education to supply trained manpower. Those who argue in favor of the American political economy are aware of the problems of poverty, unemployment, and inflation, but they believe the best way to solve such problems is to strengthen rather than weaken the political-economic partnership.

SUMMARY

Both the critics and the supporters of state capitalism make valid points; these will be discussed in later chapters. We'll look more closely at the conflict between citizenship equality and economic inequality, and we'll see how the distribution of wealth affects political participation and the choice of political

[2] Milton Friedman, *Capitalism and Freedom* (Chicago: University of Chicago Press, 1962), p. 2.

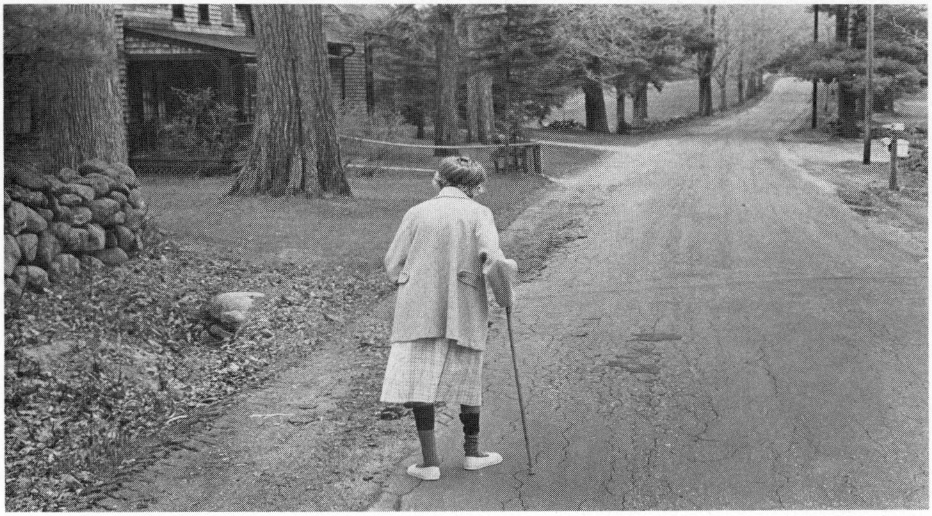

leaders. Many political conflicts take place within the framework of state capitalism. For example, interest groups compete for federal funds: A truckers' association may want more money spent on the federal highway program, while a citizens' action group may want the money spent on mass transit. Public policy making in the legislative, executive, and judicial branches of government is closely linked with the political economy. As we turn to the actual working of the federal, state, and local governments, we will constantly be reminded that state capitalism is a major force in American politics.

Questions for Review

1. What do we mean by a supported economy? A regulated economy? A managed economy?

2. What is gross national product (GNP)?

3. Define monopoly and oligopoly.

4. What important change in the relationship between government and the economy took place in the 1930s? What caused this change?

5. What is state capitalism? Who benefits from it? Is anyone hurt by it?

6. Can you justify the wide gap between the salary of a corporation president and that of an assembly-line worker?

2: Government used this yard stick to tell how well the society is doing

Chapter 2

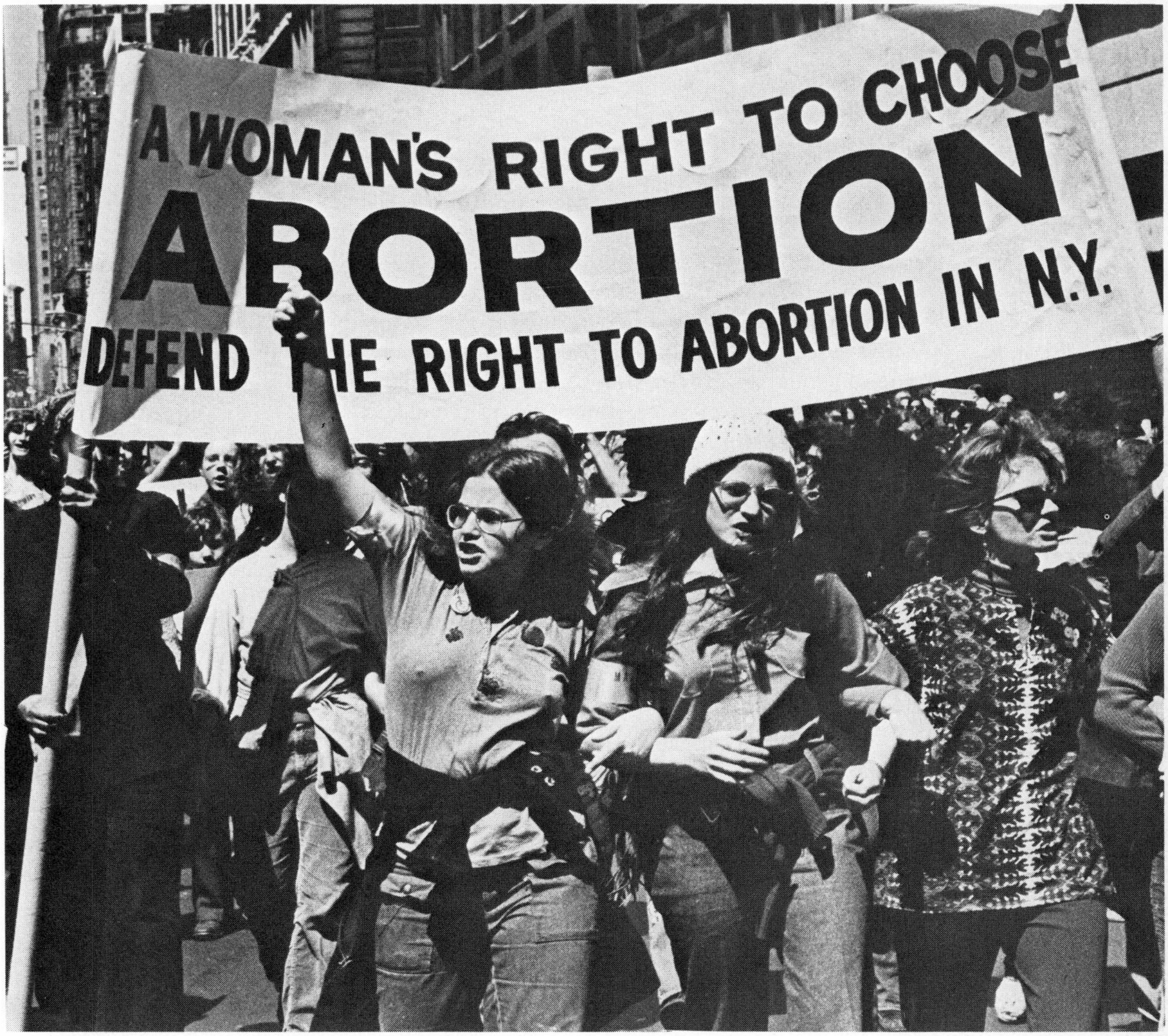

The Constitutional Framework

The Constitution is the "basic law" from which all other laws are derived. The criminal and civil laws that govern everyone living in the United States, as well as U.S. citizens living in foreign countries, are made with an eye to what is constitutional and what isn't.

Understanding the Constitution

In 1790 farmers were free to grow whatever crops they wanted, to pay their help any wages they agreed to, to market their products any way they chose, and to set their own prices. Today, however, dozens of regulations affect how foodstuffs are grown, processed, and marketed.

In 1790 farmers who were rich sent their children to private schools or perhaps hired tutors. If they got sick, their families or neighbors took care of their farms until they could go back to work. When they got too old to run the farms they lived off their savings and the goodwill of their children. Today most farmers send their children to public schools; public-health services and social security protect them against sickness and old age.

The growth of government regulation and services has greatly changed the relationship between the citizen and the government over the past 200 years. But the same basic law—the Constitution—that governed American society in 1790 governs it today. What is this Constitution that could survive so long and adapt itself to a society that has changed so much?

To understand the constitutional basis of our government, we need to look at a bit of American history. As we do so, we'll point out that although a constitution is supposed to "live for the ages," those who wrote it and those who argued for and against passing it were living in their own age. They had an eye on the immediate as well as the future advantages and disadvantages of the new document.

We will next discuss the way our Constitution handles the fundamentals of government. To survive, a nation needs procedures for defending itself against enemies, settling conflicts between its members, making and carrying out laws, and choosing the lawmakers. It's also wise to have some way of limiting the uses of authority. It is often said that the way the U.S. Constitution handles these fundamentals accounts for its surviving so long.

Finally, we'll see how the Constitution has managed to adapt itself to the great political, economic, and social changes that have taken place since 1787.

Creating a Nation

The process of creating a nation during the 1770s and 1780s involved two stages. During the first stage, the Declaration of Independence and the War for Independence, the colonies' ties with Great Britain were broken. A new government, a league of free and independent states, was set up under the Articles of Confederation. The Articles had several weaknesses, however, so there followed a second stage in which conflicting forces threatened to destroy the new confederation. In order to cope with these forces, the U.S. Constitution shifted the center of political power from a loose league of states to a strong federal union.

THE WAR FOR INDEPENDENCE

During the War for Independence the citizens of the thirteen colonies were divided on the wisdom and justice of the war. The Tories, who opposed the war, argued that it was in the interest of the colonies to remain loyal to the authority of Parliament and the legal system of the British Empire. The Patriots, on the other hand, claimed that natural right dictated that a continent shouldn't be governed by an island. But their concerns included economic interests as well as human rights. They were angered by the arbitrary taxes and trade restrictions imposed on the colonies without their consent.

To see the War for Independence simply as a struggle over economic interests is to miss some important results of the conflict. For one thing, many citizens became committed to a view of individual freedom that stressed the right to rebel against central authority when it wasn't based on the consent of the people.

In addition, the small group of leaders who had served in the First Continental Congress, written the Declaration of Independence, and financed the war began to think of themselves as a national political elite. Of course there was no real "nation"—only thirteen independent states loosely linked together by the Articles of Confederation. Still, the people who led the colonies during the war years were aware of their nation-building role.

These national leaders knew that despite the revolutionary talk of individual freedom, effective government demands obedience. Newly formed governments often have trouble taking command after a period of rebellion. During the 1780s the founders of our nation took it upon themselves to make sure authority would be respected.

THE ARTICLES OF CONFEDERATION

The Articles of Confederation, passed in 1781, lasted less than ten years. They were a compromise between a strong central government and complete self-rule by each state. For the most part they reflected the belief that local self-rule was the best way to protect the freedom won in the war. Even to agree on a confederation, however, was to admit that some centralized coordination might benefit all the states. The Articles were unable to provide such coordination.

What kind of government did the Articles provide? First of all, there was no executive power—no king, no president, no one to carry out the laws. Congress was made up of delegates from the thirteen states; they were entirely under the control of their home states. Deadlock was almost inevitable. Regardless of size or resources, each state had only one vote; nine votes—more than a two-thirds majority—were needed to pass legislation; one vote could veto an amendment to the Articles.

Furthermore, there were many limits on the powers of Congress. It had no direct power over individuals; men were citizens only of their home state. No congressional law was binding on an individual unless his state chose to enforce it, and many laws passed by Congress were never enforced by the states.

In addition Congress had no power to impose taxes. The confederation was supposed to be supported by contributions from the states. But Congress couldn't enforce such contributions. Thus the confederation came close to going bankrupt.

Finally, Congress could neither regulate commerce nor impose tariffs. This not only closed off an important source of funds but also led to economic warfare among the states.

CONFLICT BETWEEN DEBTORS AND CREDITORS

Several economic groups were hurt by the weakness of the Articles. Those who had lent money for the war effort would lose everything if the government went bankrupt. Men like Hamilton knew that if the government defaulted on its debts, it would be hard to raise money in the future. Those who wanted to open the vast areas west of the Appalachians to settlement and trade felt that their interests were hurt by the central government's inability to protect settlers from Indians and force the British from their trading posts. In addition, merchant and commercial interests were hampered by Congress' inability to regulate trade.

Some groups—particularly debtors—did benefit from the weakness of the central government under the Articles. Many farmers who were in debt benefited from the cheap paper money issued by state governments. Using their influence in state legislatures, they were able to pass laws delaying the collection of debts.

Debtors also benefited from the central government's lack of effective police power. Open rebellions against creditors, the most famous of which was led by Danial Shays, were common. Although Shays' Rebellion was put down by a mercenary army, the lesson was not lost. Many citizens felt that the central government was too weak.

THE CONSTITUTIONAL CONVENTION

In the mid-1780s Congress asked the thirteen states to send delegates to Philadelphia for the sole purpose of revising the Articles of Confederation. But the fifty-five men who gathered in May 1787 did more than revise the Articles. As soon as they arrived they agreed to keep the meetings secret and to write an entirely new Constitution. Knowing that not all the states would accept the new document, they decided that it would go into effect when nine states had ratified it. It's clear that they went beyond the authority they had been given—but the country was ready for something new, and they provided the leadership.

Writing a constitution isn't easy. Political leaders are often strong willed, and if they differ in their views of what's good for society, in their personal interests, and in the people they represent, they're unlikely to write a document on which all can agree. Yet during a single summer these fifty-five men wrote a constitution that is still perhaps the most effective such document ever written.

Any constitution must balance freedom and authority—the freedom of citizens from arbitrary or unjust government, and the authority of the government to settle conflicts and manage the society. And the politics of the time was as important in the balance between freedom and authority as the beliefs and abilities of the founders themselves. Three political facts go far to explain the success of the Constitutional Convention: (1) The founders agreed on certain basic issues; (2) the convention skipped the hardest issue; and (3) the delegates were willing to compromise.

Agree on Basic Issues. Missing from the convention were conservatives who might have opposed the more liberal parts of the new constitution. Also missing were several forceful Democrats who might have refused to give as much authority to a central government. The men who dominated the convention represented solid, conservative financial interests. Thus they had no trouble agreeing that the Articles of Confederation should be dropped and an entirely new document written. They shared a philosophy that included mistrust of human nature, belief in private property, and concern about the dangers of unlimited democracy. But although they were conservative in these ways, they were also committed to the experiment of self-government.

Skip the Hardest Issue. The strongest political feelings of the time centered on the question, Should there be self-rule for each state, or should authority be given to the central government? *Federalism,* in which power is shared between the states and the central government, was a brilliant compromise. This is probably the main reason the Constitution was finally ratified. But the convention simply skipped the hardest issue of all: whether member states had the right to secede. If that right had been written into the Constitution, it's doubtful that the Union would have lasted more than 50 or 60 years; if it had been denied, it's doubtful that there ever would have been a "united states." This issue was left to later generations, and it took a bitter civil war to settle it.

Compromise. The Constitution was a compromise document in many ways, but the most famous compromise is in the makeup of Congress. The question was whether the individual states would be represented in Congress in proportion to their population, giving an advantage to the larger states, or on an equal basis, giving an advantage to the smaller states. In what's known as the *Connecticut Compromise,* Congress was divided into two houses. Seats in the House of Representatives would depend on the size of the state; in the Senate each state, no matter how small, would have two seats. Because most important legislation must be passed by both the House and the Senate, this compromise prevents the larger states from dominating the smaller ones.

SUMMARY

So far we've briefly discussed the history and politics of the late 1700s. We saw that the Articles of Confederation created a government that was too weak and decentralized to govern effectively. Then we saw that the men who gathered at the Constitutional Convention wanted to create a strong and effective government without repeating the mistakes of the Articles. How were they able to do this? Because they all shared a conservative philosophy and a belief in democracy, they agreed on the basic issues. In addition they were willing to compromise on certain issues, and they simply skipped the hardest issue by not answering the question of whether the states had the right to secede.

Constitutional Principles

The philosophical basis of the Constitution may be seen in these remarks by John Adams to his cousin Samuel Adams:

> Human appetites, passions, prejudices and self-love will never be conquered by benevolence and knowledge alone. . . . 'The love of liberty,' you say, 'is interwoven in the soul of man.' So it is (also) in that of a wolf; and I doubt whether it be much more rational, generous, or social in one than in the other. . . . We must not, then, depend alone upon the love of liberty in the soul of man for its preservation. Some political institutions must be prepared, to assist this love against its enemies.

In other words, without political institutions people couldn't be trusted. They would break their contracts; their desires and ambitions would dominate their reason and self-restraint. Minorities would tyrannize majorities if given a chance; majorities would destroy the rights of minorities.

But if there must be authority, it, too, must be limited. No single group—a minority within the government, the government itself, or the majority outside the government—should have final control. The founders feared the ambitions of leaders just as they feared the excesses of the public. They were as careful to put limits on those in authority as they were to guarantee the authority needed to govern effectively. This was done through three basic principles: (1) a representative form of government; (2) division of governmental powers; and (3) the idea of limited government.

A REPRESENTATIVE FORM OF GOVERNMENT

Titles of Nobility Abolished. One of the first acts of the founders was to abolish inherited titles of nobility and inherited positions of authority. Time and again they stressed their belief in the principle that no arbitrary standard, particularly birth, should give some people the right to rule and deny it to others.

Open Access to Office. The founders *did* feel that the "right" people should rule—that there is a natural elite of wealth, talent, and education. But they argued that no one has a right to rule just because one's parents are already in positions of authority. Public office is open to talented and ambitious people regardless of birth.

Periodic Elections. "Consent of the governed" was to be expressed through periodic elections. However, the right to vote went only so far. Each state could make its own voting laws. Moreover, only members of the House of Representatives were directly elected by citizens. Senators were chosen by the state legislatures until 1913, when the Seventeenth Amendment was ratified.

The President and Vice-President were chosen by an electoral college, which in turn was appointed by the state legislatures. Judicial posts were filled by appointment.

Though limited, the right to vote is firmly stated in the Constitution. Periodic elections mean leaders serve for a definite period and then face the voters that gave them power in the first place. The purpose is to create in political leaders a "habitual recollection of their dependence on the people," as *The Federalist* (No. 57) put it.[1]

Representative Government. Today we think of representative government as a compromise between the principles of "perfect" democracy and the realities of huge, complex nations. Because there's no way for the people to meet, debate, and decide on every issue, we set up a representative government in which a selected group of people meet and decide on the issues but are always aware of the wishes of the people they represent. This way of looking at representative government is shown in Figure 2.1.

What the founders had in mind was something very different. Because they feared arbitrary rule, they believed those with political power must somehow be limited in their use of that power. To them, representative government wasn't a compromise with the commitment to democracy; it was a cautious move away from the tradition of inherited rule. Compare Figure 2.2 with Figure 2.1, and you'll see that the idea of political representation was very different in 1790.

The same point can be viewed from another angle. Today we see political representation as a means by which the population can express itself on political issues; the founders saw it as a way of limiting the influence of the public. The representatives would be wiser and more cautious than the masses.

DIVISION OF POWERS

The Constitution is a search for the means by which a government can rule and yet not rule unfairly. It's a search for the balance between authority, or the ability to rule, and freedom, or protection against unfair rule. We have seen that the writers of the Constitution wanted a strong national government, one strong enough to make a single nation out of thirteen separate states. But they were afraid the national government would have too much power. One limit on this power—periodic elections—has already been discussed. But the founders weren't satisfied with elections alone. As *The Federalist* (No. 51) put it, "a dependence on the people is, no doubt, the primary control on the government, but experience has taught mankind the necessity of

[1] *The Federalist* (sometimes known as *The Federalist Papers*) is a series of essays written by Alexander Hamilton, James Madison, and John Jay. The essays were written to defend the new Constitution and were initially published as political pamphlets.

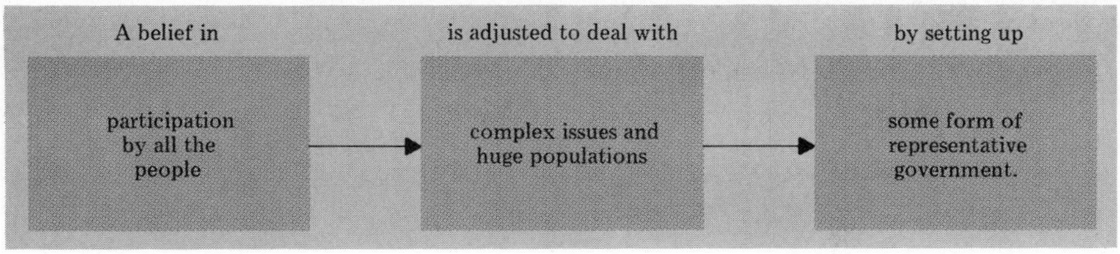
A belief in
participation by all the people
is adjusted to deal with
complex issues and huge populations
by setting up
some form of representative government.

FIGURE 2.1
Concept of Representative Government Today

auxiliary precautions." These extra precautions may be found in the division of powers within the government.

Federalism. First, power was divided between the national government and the states. This served two seemingly contradictory purposes. The first was to set up a strong, effective central government. Nothing else would guarantee law and order, pay the public debt, and make it possible to develop the nation's resources. But it was also necessary to keep the state governments independent, since this would limit the power of the national government. Out of the tension between these two goals grew the federal system.

Separation of Powers. The writers of the Constitution weren't content with federalism. They also gave different powers and resources to the legislative, executive, and judicial branches of government. This distribution would provide protection against political tyranny, defined in *The Federalist* (No. 47) as "the accumulation of all powers, legislative, executive, and judiciary, in the same hands." It wasn't enough to have popular control over government through elections. It wasn't enough to have two layers of government. It was necessary to divide up the powers of government even further—among the three branches of government.

LIMITED GOVERNMENT

The Bill of Rights. There are certain things the government cannot and should not do. It cannot restrict the protections for the individual citizen listed in the

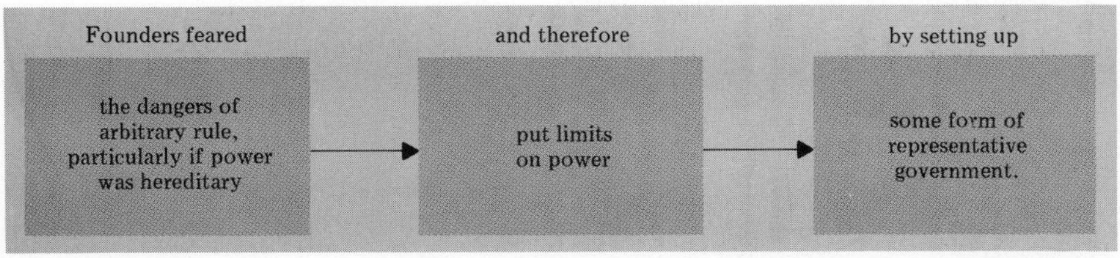
Founders feared
the dangers of arbitrary rule, particularly if power was hereditary
and therefore
put limits on power
by setting up
some form of representative government.

FIGURE 2.2
The Founding Fathers' Concept of Representative Government

first ten amendments, the Bill of Rights. Moreover, the government cannot take life, liberty, or property without due process of law.

Throughout this book there are examples showing that the protections promised by the Bill of Rights have had a checkered political history. At this point, however, we're interested in constitutional principles rather than political realities. The principle of limited government is based on the belief that human rights are derived from "natural law" and should be protected by putting limits on government.

"Government of Laws, Not of Men." The second idea behind the principle of limited government is *constitutionalism.* By this we mean simply the familiar phrase "government of laws, not of men." There is a basic law against which all others should be measured. This law, in our case the written Constitution, is based on the consent of the people. Any laws based on the Constitution, therefore, should also have the consent of the people. Moreover, the basic law as well as the lesser laws derived from it regulate the operation of government and, thus, those who govern. No one should "stand above the law," not even the President of the United States—as was so dramatically shown by Nixon's fall from power in 1974.

Like the Bill of Rights, the idea of a "government of laws" has had a checkered history. Secrecy and dishonesty may be found at the highest levels of government. The law is often bent for those with power and money. Nevertheless the principle of constitutionalism is continually being used to oppose arbitrary government.

"No Man Stands Above the Law"–Nixon was forced to release transcripts of White House tapes during Watergate crisis.

SUMMARY

We've discussed how the Constitution came to be written and the principles on which it is based. We now have some answers to the question we asked at the beginning of the chapter: What is this Constitution that could survive so long and adapt itself to a society that has changed so much? One answer is that the Constitution was and still is a political document. And at least some of the political issues of the 1780s are still with us today, though in different forms. A document based on political realities remains workable because those realities remain important.

Another answer is that the basic principles of the Constitution—popular election of representatives, division of governmental powers, limited government—were supported in 1787. And despite major changes in our society they continue to be supported today. There has been only one major challenge to the U.S. Constitution in 200 years: the attempt by the Confederacy to secede from the Union. As Congress declared in July 1861, the Civil War was fought to "defend and maintain the supremacy of the Constitution and to preserve the union."

But there's another answer to our question: reinterpretation of the Constitution to fit new social conditions.

A Flexible Constitution

"The Constitution belongs to the living and not to the dead," Jefferson wrote. The Constitution has kept pace with the times; if it hadn't, it would have been thrown out long ago. Three things have contributed to its flexibility: (1) its general language; (2) its silence on some points; and (3) a formal amendment process.

GENERAL LANGUAGE

The Constitution seems in some places to be purposely ambiguous. Perhaps this was the only way the founders could get it passed. In any case this ambiguity has allowed later generations to reinterpret the Constitution to deal with changing conditions. For example, the power of the Supreme Court to declare acts of Congress unconstitutional isn't stated in the Constitution; nor is it denied. But the Supreme Court ruled that it did have the power of judicial review. The executive power of the President isn't spelled out in the Constitution either. The change from Washington's staff of half a dozen clerks to today's huge federal bureaucracy has been based on the Constitution's general statement that the President "shall take care that the laws be faithfully executed."

Using general language also allows new meanings to be given to old words. In the case of "unreasonable searches," for example, the Fourth Amendment declares that "the right of the people to be secure in their persons, houses, papers, and effects, against unreasonable searches and seizures, shall not be violated. . . ." Here a clear principle is expressed in such general language that it can still be applied today to challenge the right of the government to use such methods as wiretaps and hidden microphones.

CONSTITUTIONAL SILENCE

A good example of constitutional silence allowing political flexibility is the matter of political parties. Political parties aren't mentioned in the Constitution, yet who could imagine twentieth-century politics in the United States without some form of political parties? Every major elected official and most appointed ones are backed by a political party. And for the most part the parties organize and manage the election process itself, including primaries and nominating conventions. All of this takes place outside the framework of the Constitution.

THE AMENDMENT PROCESS

Since the writers of the Constitution knew that very specific changes would be needed as social conditions changed, they included a formal *amendment* process. This involves two steps: (1) proposing an amendment and (2) ratifying it. It's a complicated process, since there are two separate ways an amendment can be proposed and two separate ways of ratifying it. The standard practice is shown in Figure 2.3.

Most of the amendments to the Constitution have been important in adapting the government to new social conditions. The "Civil War Amendments" (the Thirteenth, Fourteenth, and Fifteenth) outlawed slavery, defined national citizenship, and gave men the right to vote regardless of race, color, or prior servitude. Other amendments have provided for direct election

FIGURE 2.3
Standard Practice of Amending the Constitution

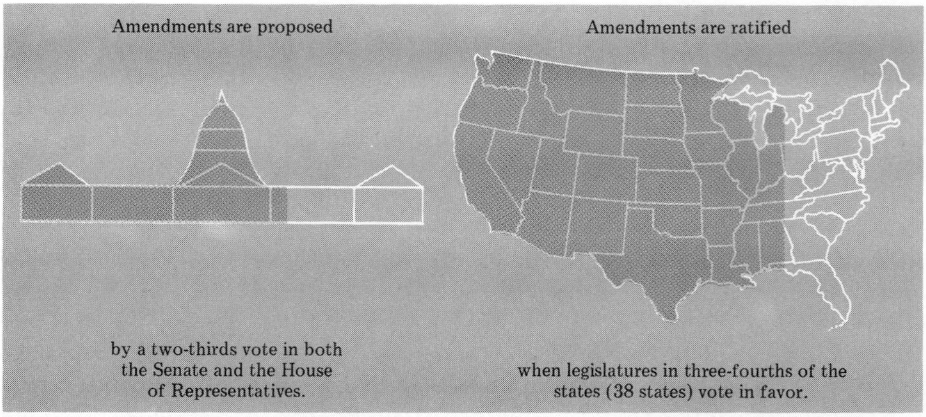
Amendments are proposed
Amendments are ratified
by a two-thirds vote in both the Senate and the House of Representatives.
when legislatures in three-fourths of the states (38 states) vote in favor.

of senators, given the vote to women, repealed the poll tax, and lowered the voting age to 18. One of the most important amendments (the Sixteenth, ratified in 1913) authorized the income tax.

Sources of Constitutional Change

To say the Constitution is flexible is simply to say it doesn't provide ready-made answers to new political and social questions. No general formula can account for each major change in the Constitution, but the following should be kept in mind: The genius of the Constitution is also its weakness. Any document that divides power among different political institutions will sooner or later be caught in a squeeze when the interests of those institutions come into conflict. The conflicts leading to constitutional change have included (1) clashes between the federal and state governments; (2) clashes between different branches of the government; (3) conflicts over the separation-of-powers principle; and (4) conflicts over citizenship rights.

Federalism. We'll see later how easy it is for conflicts to arise over which level of government is responsible for what. The Civil War was fought to uphold the supremacy of the national government, a supremacy backed up by the Thirteenth, Fourteenth, and Fifteenth Amendments. The war didn't put an end to clashes among the branches of government, however; the principle of federalism is continually being tested.

Limits of Authority. Many of the new social conditions the government has had to deal with over the past 200 years have been handled within the framework of the Constitution. But some problems have been so complicated that traditional interpretations of the Constitution have been of little use. New interpretations have been needed to solve these problems. As we will see, sometimes the courts have opposed constitutional change. For example, during the Great Depression the Supreme Court declared important new legislation unconstitutional, claiming that the Presidency was increasing its authority illegally. Under heavy pressure from the Roosevelt administration, the Court reversed itself. At other times, however, the Court has stimulated constitutional change, as in the decisions during the 1950s and 1960s that greatly enlarged citizenship rights and liberties.

Separation of Powers. The separation-of-powers principle has led to many clashes between the Presidency and Congress, between Congress and the courts, or between the courts and the Presidency. Most of these conflicts have been settled without major constitutional changes, but at present we're in the midst of a struggle that could result in such a change. There are signs that one effect of Watergate may be to stimulate Congress to become more active in limiting the authority of the executive branch.

How Institutions Work: I
The Structure of the U. S. Government

WHAT IS THE BASIS OF THE GOVERNMENT'S STRUCTURE?

The structure of the U.S. government is based on the Constitution in general and on two principles in particular: federalism and separation of powers. Under the federal principle the powers and functions of government are divided between the national government and the states. Then, under the separation-of-powers principle, the authority given to the national government is divided among three separate branches: the legislative, the executive, and the judicial. The structure of the government is shown in Figure 2.4.

WHAT ARE THE INSTITUTIONS AND AGENCIES OF THE VARIOUS BRANCHES OF THE GOVERNMENT?

Legislative

All power to make laws rests in a Congress made up of two houses, the Senate and the House of Representatives. Their authority is set forth in the Constitution. The Senate has 100 members (2 from each state) and the House 435 (the number from each state depending on its population). The Constitution doesn't say how Congress should be organized, but both houses have chosen a committee structure.

Executive

The executive power is given to the President alone; however, a huge bureaucracy has grown up around the President. The Executive Office, which serves the President's managerial needs, includes the White House Office, the Office of Management and Budget, and the National Security Council.

The executive branch also includes the eleven executive departments that together make up the Cabinet. All of the executive departments have been created by acts of Congress, the most recent addition (1966) being the Department of Transportation.

In addition, there is a group of indepen-

FIGURE 2.4
The Government of the United States

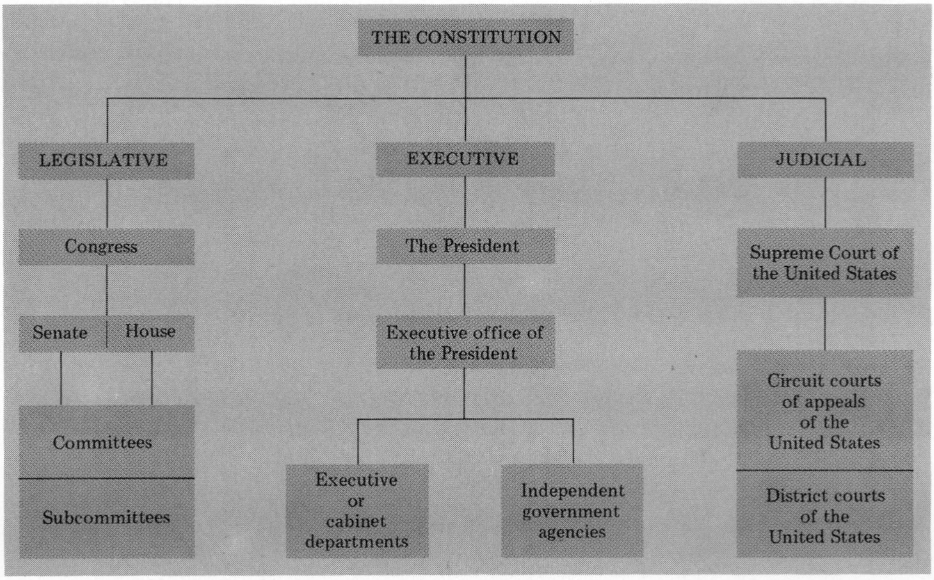

dent government agencies of two general types: executive agencies and regulatory commissions. The former include agencies like the CIA and the Veterans Administration. Also in this group are government corporations such as the U.S. Postal Service and the Tennessee Valley Authority. The regulatory commissions, such as the Interstate Commerce Commission and the Federal Power Commission, though formally part of the executive branch, are independent of the President.

Judicial

The Constitution gives judicial power to the Supreme Court and to any lower courts created by Congress. Even the size of the Supreme Court is left to Congress to decide. Over the years Congress has created a structure of lower courts made up of the U.S. circuit courts of appeals and the U.S. district courts.

Questions for Review

1. What arguments did the Patriots use to justify the War for Independence?
2. What were the weaknesses of the Articles of Confederation? What groups suffered under the Articles?
3. What did the founders have in common that made it possible to write the Constitution?
4. What is the Connecticut Compromise?
5. Name and describe the three basic principles underlying the Constitution.
6. How did the founders' view of political representation differ from the way we see it today?
7. Why is the Bill of Rights important to the limited government set up by the Constitution?
8. What makes the Constitution a flexible document?
9. How does the Constitution itself lead to political conflict? Give examples of such conflicts.

Chapter 3

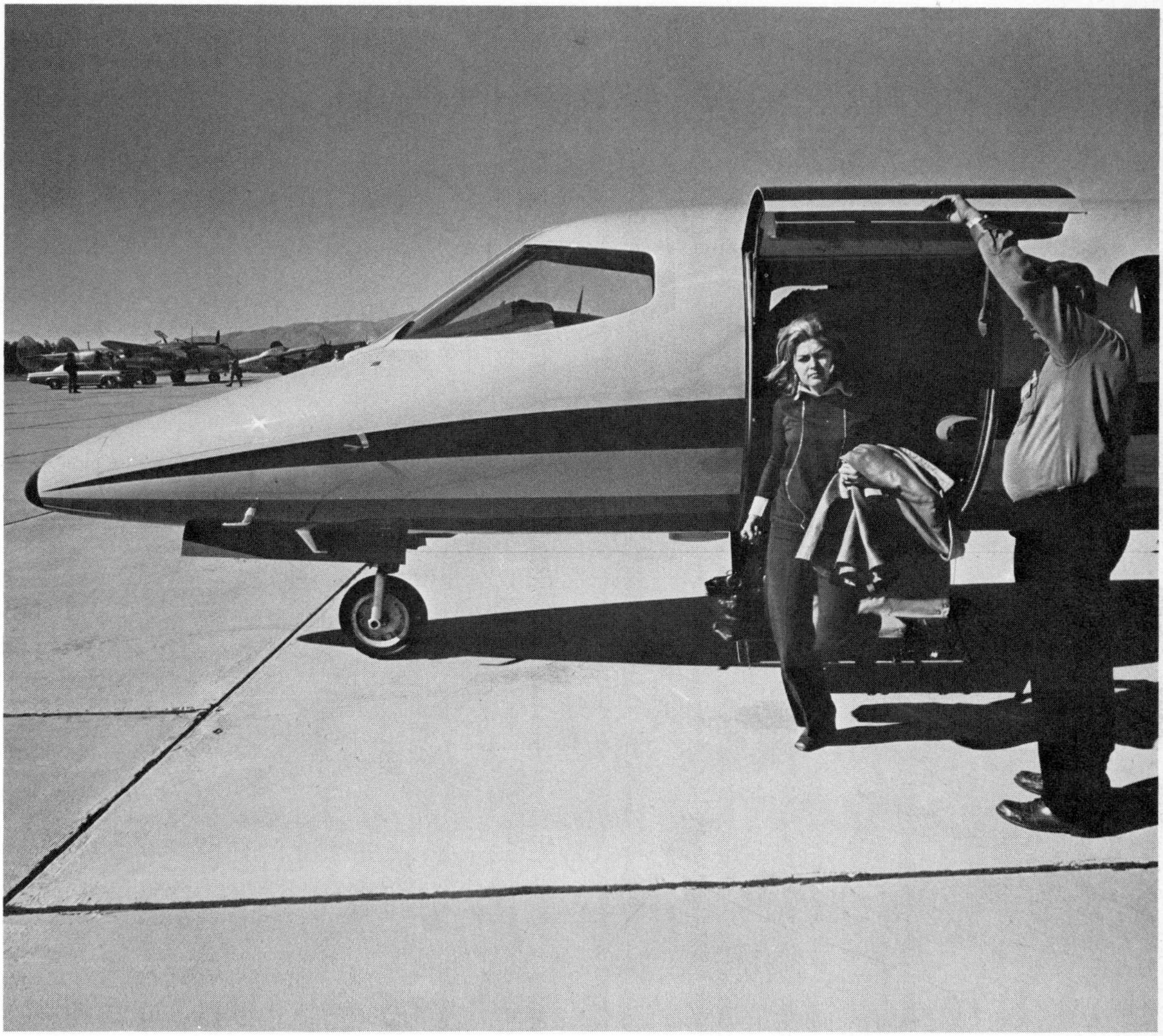

Political Equality, Social Inequality

In medieval times rights and privileges were given to one class of citizens but denied to others. The nobility held positions of authority, but commoners or serfs were subordinate by law. The situation is well summarized by John Stuart Mill in the following passage:

> The lot of the poor, in all things which affect them collectively, should be regulated for them, not by them. They should not be required or encouraged to think for themselves, or give to their own reflection or forecast an influential voice in the determination of the destiny. It is the duty of the higher classes to think for them, and to take responsibility for their lot. . . . The rich should be [like parents] to the poor, guiding and restraining them like children.[1]

Democratic thought rejects the idea that people who are richer, more intelligent, or of nobler birth are somehow "better." The principle of citizenship pushes aside those ancient beliefs, which formed the basis of inherited rule, a class system, and racial prejudice.

"We hold these truths to be self-evident," says the Declaration of Independence, "that all men are created equal." The men who signed the Declaration knew, of course, that all men were not created equal; differences in ability, intelligence, and ambition couldn't be denied. But they wanted to go on record against a political system in which members of society were *legally* unequal.

The Constitution's guarantees of citizenship are supposed to result in the equality promised by the Declaration of Independence. But the Constitution deals with legal citizenship and political citizenship; the idea of social citizenship, to be discussed later in this chapter, is more recent.

Legal Citizenship

Early American political history was dominated by constitutional issues. The problems to be solved included the definition of citizenship rights and the extension of these rights to the entire population. Legal citizenship, or *civil liberties*, includes the basic freedoms of speech, worship, and assembly as stated in the First Amendment. It also includes economic rights, particularly the right to own property, the right to choose one's place and type of work, and the right to enter into contracts that will be backed up by the courts.

The courts are central to legal citizenship. Here the basic citizenship principle is called *due process of law*, which, as stated in the Fifth and Fourteenth Amendments, guarantees that an individual cannot be deprived of life, liberty, or property by an arbitrary act of government. This refers to many things: A citizen is assumed to be innocent until proven guilty. A person has the right to be tried by a jury of fellow citizens. No one can be kept in jail for a

[1] John Stuart Mill, *Principles of Political Economy, II* (Boston: Little, Brown, 1848), pp. 319–320.

crime without evidence of guilt. Due process also includes the right to legal counsel, the right to question witnesses, and protection from unreasonable search and seizure.

Political Citizenship

The second major form of citizenship is political participation. A democratic government is based on the consent of the people. All members of society should have an equal right to choose those who govern them. The principle of equal political citizenship is clearly stated in *The Federalist* (No. 57):

> *Who are to be the electors of the federal representatives?* Not the rich, more than the poor; not the learned, more than the ignorant; not the haughty heirs of distinguished names, more than the humble sons of obscurity and unpropitious fortune. The electors are to be the great body of the people of the United States.
>
> *Who are to be the objects of popular choice?* Every citizen whose merit may recommend him to the esteem and confidence of his country. No qualification of wealth, of birth, religious faith, or of civil profession is permitted to fetter the judgement or disappoint the inclinations of the people.

THE GROWTH OF VOTING RIGHTS

The Constitution didn't really answer the question of who may vote and under what conditions. It has taken four amendments to do this.

At first the Constitution left voting laws to the states; a person who couldn't vote in a state election couldn't vote in a federal election. Generally the states restricted the vote to white male property owners—in some states as few as 10 percent of the white males could vote. However, during the Presidency of Andrew Jackson (1829–1837) most property rules were dropped.

Still, as Figure 3.1 shows, less than 40 percent of the adult population could vote at the time of the Civil War. Blacks were forbidden to vote in the South, and for the most part they were unable to vote in the North. After the Civil War the Fifteenth Amendment stated that "the right of citizens of the United States to vote shall not be denied or abridged by the United States or by any State on account of race, color, or previous condition of servitude." But when white southerners got back in control of their state governments they succeeded in undermining the Fifteenth Amendment through such methods as the poll tax, phony literacy tests, and the all-white primary, as well as fear and violence.

The next major expansion of the voting public was the addition of women. In 1869 Wyoming became the first state to allow women to vote; it was followed by several others, mostly in the West. In 1917 women began marching in front of the White House, only to be arrested and jailed. But in 1920 the Nineteenth Amendment stated that the right to vote cannot be denied because of sex.

In 1964 the Twenty-Fourth Amendment banned the use of the poll tax in federal elections. The Voting Rights Act of 1965 extended the ban to cover state elections, but its real purpose was to put federal authority behind the drive to allow southern blacks to vote. The effect of this legislation was dramatic. Between 1964 and 1968 black registration in eleven southern states went up by over 50 percent. (See Table 3.1.) In 1970 Congress extended the Voting Rights Act to ban the use of literacy and character tests in all states and to set uniform residency requirements (thirty days) for voting in federal elections.

In 1971 the Twenty-Sixth Amendment lowered the voting age to 18. This added about 10.5 million people to the voting public.

Second-Class Citizenship

Citizenship rights are based on the principle that all citizens are to be treated equally. In practice, however, as the history of voting rights shows, black Americans and other minorities, as well as women of all races, have found their legal and political rights to be less than those of white males.

BLACKS

Slavery was protected by law in the United States until after the Civil War, and in the eighteenth century most American blacks were slaves. Slaves couldn't say what they wanted to, be with people they wanted to be with, do

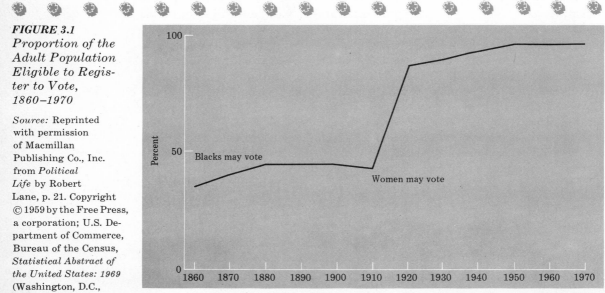

FIGURE 3.1
Proportion of the Adult Population Eligible to Register to Vote, 1860–1970

Source: Reprinted with permission of Macmillan Publishing Co., Inc. from *Political Life* by Robert Lane, p. 21. Copyright © 1959 by the Free Press, a corporation; U.S. Department of Commerce, Bureau of the Census, *Statistical Abstract of the United States: 1969* (Washington, D.C., 1969), p. 369.

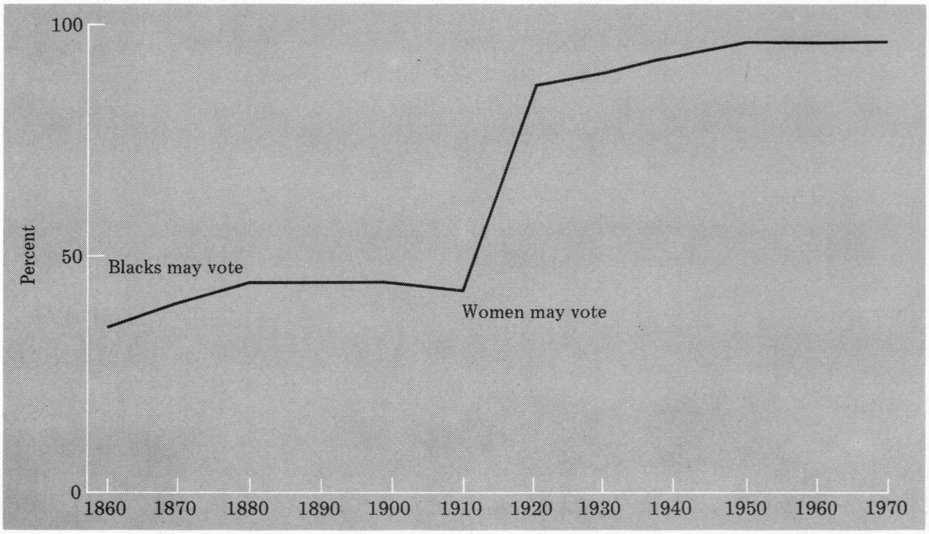

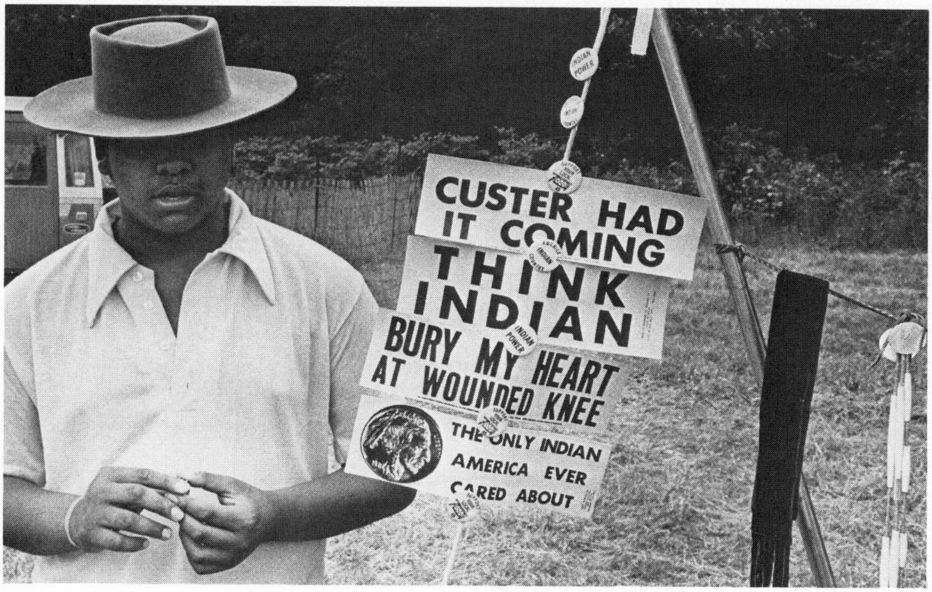

what they wanted with their labor, or enter into contracts. American citizenship gave people the right to the product of their labor; slavery denied this right. Thus despite the promises of the Declaration of Independence, the Constitution gave one class of people rights and privileges and denied them to another class.

Second-class citizenship for blacks continued long after the Civil War had officially ended slavery. The Fourteenth Amendment, which states that "all persons born or naturalized in the United States, and subject to the jurisdiction thereof, are citizens of the United States. . . . No state shall make or enforce any law which shall abridge the privileges or immunities of citizens,"

***TABLE 3.1* Estimated percent of blacks registered to vote in southern states, 1940–1970**

Year	*Percent registered*
1940	5%
1952	21
1960	28
1964	45
1968	62
1970	66

Source: Based on data from *The American Negro Reference Book* by Davis, ed. © 1966 by Prentice-Hall, Inc. Published by Prentice-Hall, Inc., Englewood Cliffs, New Jersey. Harry A. Polshi and Ernest Kaiser, eds., *The Negro Almanac* (New York: Bellwether, 1971).

was blocked by the "Jim Crow" society. *Jim Crow laws* allowed segregation of "waiting rooms, theaters, boardinghouses, water fountains, ticket windows, streetcars, penitentiaries, county jails, convict camps, institutions for the blind and deaf, and hospitals for the insane," according to the Commission on Civil Rights (1963). They also affected schools, businesses, clubs, churches, and the armed forces. The facilities reserved for blacks were always of lower quality than those for whites, though equal prices had to be paid for the unequal services.

Racism was backed up by the Supreme Court. In *Plessy* v. *Ferguson* (1896) Justice Brown wrote: "If one race be inferior to another socially, the Constitution of the United States cannot put them upon the same plane. . . ." This was the "separate but equal doctrine," and it lasted until 1954. So much for the idea that citizenship made everyone equal in the eyes of the law.

WOMEN

"Equality of rights under the law shall not be denied or abridged by the United States or by any state on account of sex." So says the Equal Rights Amendment, which has been passed by Congress and by thirty-four of the thirty-eight states that must ratify it before it becomes the Twenty-Seventh Amendment to the Constitution.

Women have long been second-class citizens. Except in some state and local elections, women weren't allowed to vote until 1920. Certain government jobs, particularly in the military, have until recently been reserved for males. Many states have laws that discriminate against women in the areas of property ownership, employment and salaries, and marriage and divorce. Women find it hard to get loans because credit agencies see women as "bad risks."

In addition there are many informal barriers to full women's rights. Women are paid less than men, even for doing the same work. And it's hard for women to reach high positions. A survey by *Fortune* magazine found only eleven women among the directors and officers of the 1300 largest corporations in America. The number of women in political office is also low. At present there are no women in the Senate, only eighteen in the House of Representatives, and only one women governor.

The Equal Rights Amendment tries to remove the legal barriers that have kept women from enjoying equal rights with men. It states that women are to be absolutely equal to men. For this reason some women's groups have opposed it because it provides "too much equality." For example, it makes women equally liable for child support when a couple gets a divorce, and it makes them equally subject to the military draft.

MINORS

In 1971 nine students were suspended from Columbus, Ohio, high schools after a period of racial unrest. The action took place without any formal hearings. The students challenged the action, claiming that they were deprived of liberty and property (their legal right to an education) without due process of law (no proof of guilt had been provided). The students argued that the action thus violated the Fourteenth Amendment.

In 1975 the case came to the Supreme Court. In a split decision (five to four), the Court ruled in favor of the students.[2] Public school authorities can't suspend students without following certain procedures: giving formal notice of the charges, explaining the evidence against the student, and allowing the student to present his side of the story. Note, however, that the Court didn't give students full rights of due process. A suspended student can't hire a lawyer, cross-examine witnesses, call his own witnesses, or have a jury trial. But the Court left open the possibility that a more formal procedure might be required when students are suspended for a long time or expelled from school.

Citizenship rights for minors is a new area for constitutional lawyers and judges. It's too early to know the results of what is sure to be a long and painful process. But it's clear that the recent changes in the citizenship rights of minority groups and women will stimulate change in the way minors are treated.

Affirmative Action

The definition of citizenship rights took a new turn in the early 1970s. American society is being asked whether it will accept discrimination to make up for past acts of discrimination. In 1971 Marco DeFunis, a white male college graduate, was turned down by the University of Washington Law School. His college grades and test scores were higher than those of some of the thirty-six blacks, Chicanos, and Indians who were admitted to the school. DeFunis claims he was the victim of reverse discrimination—that he was turned down simply because he is white. The University of Washington claims that discrimination in favor of minorities that have long been held back by racism is legal. DeFunis took his case to court, and a local judge ruled that he should be admitted. The University admitted DeFunis but appealed the decision.

The case came to the United States Supreme Court in the spring of 1974.[3] Since by then DeFunis was about to graduate, the Court let the earlier ruling stand. Nevertheless the DeFunis case raised one of the most complicated questions in the history of citizenship rights: Is affirmative action that favors one group over another constitutional? Should law schools or medical schools reserve places for blacks, Chicanos, or women so that in the long run society will have lawyers and doctors from all social groups? Should the government give building contracts only to construction firms that hire workers from all racial and ethnic groups? Where does this leave the principle of equal citizenship rights?

[2] *Goss* v. *Lopez,* 73–898 U.S. (1975).

[3] *DeFunis* v. *Odegaard,* 416 U.S. 312 (1974).

ARGUMENTS AGAINST AFFIRMATIVE ACTION

Those who oppose affirmative action point out that the Constitution doesn't allow for special treatment based on race or sex. A brief written for DeFunis makes this argument: "If the Constitution prohibits exclusion of blacks and other minorities on racial grounds, it cannot permit exclusion of whites on racial grounds. For it must be the exclusion on racial grounds which offends the Constitution, and not the particular skin color of the person excluded."[4] If DeFunis was denied admission to law school *because* he is white, this was racial discrimination and was therefore unconstitutional.

ARGUMENTS FOR AFFIRMATIVE ACTION

Those who support affirmative action argue that equal protection of the law isn't enough to make up for many years of unequal treatment. It's as if there were a race between two people, one of whom has been in training for ten years while the other has been in chains for ten years. If the chains are removed, both runners start at the same place, and the rules of the race apply equally, does each runner have an equal chance to win? Affirmative action is intended to help the chained runner get in condition so the race will be fair.

AFFIRMATIVE ACTION AND CITIZENSHIP

The questions raised by the DeFunis case will be with us for a long time. Affirmative action is a new and troublesome chapter in the history of citizenship. It goes beyond equal protection of the law and even beyond equal opportunity to a new view of citizenship rights: the right to be treated unequally but favorably in order to undo previous unequal and unfavorable treatment. But such treatment can't avoid being called reverse discrimination. Groups that have struggled to succeed under the old rules—white union leaders, for example—will resent any change in the rules that seems to discriminate against them just because they are white or male.

Social Citizenship

The 1944 State of the Union Address contained a surprising change from earlier definitions of citizenship. In it President Roosevelt spoke of America's failure to provide for its citizens and stated the principle behind a whole new area of citizenship rights: "We have come to a clear realization of the fact that true individual freedom cannot exist without economic security and independence." Roosevelt was saying that the legal and political rights set forth in the Constitution aren't enough and that citizenship rights must include social

[4] Philip Kurland and Alexander M. Bickel, quoted in Nina Totenberg, "Discrimination to End Discrimination," *The New York Times Magazine*, April 14, 1974.

well-being and security against economic injustices. He went on to give some specific examples:

- The right to a useful job in the industries or shops or farms or mines of the nation.
- The right to earn enough to provide adequate food and clothing and recreation.

- The right of every businessman, large and small, to be free from unfair competition and domination by monopolies at home or abroad.
- The right of every family to a decent home.
- The right to adequate medical care and the opportunity to achieve and enjoy good health.
- The right to adequate protection from the economic fears of old age, sickness, accident, and unemployment.

This view of citizenship has produced much social legislation by both Republican and Democratic administrations over the past thirty years. A large number of programs—social security, urban renewal and housing, job training, medicare—have been undertaken. These programs have given rise to a lot of controversy, and even today such issues as federal support for education, national health insurance, public housing, and consumer protection are hotly debated. What is interesting about these debates, however, is that even conservatives now accept some form of welfare state.

Social citizenship breaks with tradition in an important way: It separates social services from the price system. People who are strongly committed to a free-enterprise economy don't like this. Medical care, housing, food, insurance, and even education have traditionally been tied to purchasing power: Those who can pay get better medical care, better housing, more nourishing food, more security against sickness and old age, and better education. Social citizenship shifts these services to the public sector of the economy; a decent standard of living thus becomes a right rather than a privilege.

CITIZENSHIP EQUALITY VS. ECONOMIC INEQUALITY

We've discussed three forms of citizenship equality: (1) legal citizenship, which promises equal protection of the law and equal access to the courts; (2) political citizenship, which promises the right to vote and other political rights equally to all citizens; and (3) social citizenship, which promises equal protection from economic disasters beyond the control of individuals.

We have already seen, however, that American society is based on economic inequality. We accept the idea of different wages for different jobs. People who work harder or are more talented or do important jobs should be rewarded more than those who are lazy or untalented or do less important jobs. Anything else is said to be unfair and would be socially harmful because economic growth depends on talent and ambition. So economic inequality is a fact of American life.

Economic inequality means people have different standards of living. Some have big, comfortable houses, work at jobs they enjoy, can take vacations, can send their children to college, and can save enough to protect them against sickness or unemployment. Others live in crowded, low-quality housing; do the dirty, dull jobs; worry more about feeding their children than about what college to send them to; are usually in debt; and are always worried about sickness or unemployment.

Citizenship equality hasn't caused a major change in this pattern. Legal, political, and even social citizenship exist side by side with great inequalities in standards of living. What citizenship equality amounts to is an equal opportunity to compete for the unequal rewards of society. Americans believe everyone should have an equal chance to go after the best jobs and the highest incomes. This may be seen in the government's War on Poverty and other social-service programs.

The War on Poverty. The poor are those who are living below some socially acceptable standard. In a wealthy society, even the very poor should be able to enjoy their political and economic rights. A successful antipoverty program moves every citizen above the acceptable level and thus, in the words of the War on Poverty, eliminates poverty "by opening to everyone the opportunity for education and training, the opportunity to work, and the opportunity to live in decency and dignity."

The purpose of antipoverty programs is to increase the number of people who compete in a free-enterprise economy. The only way the elimination of poverty can affect inequality is by reducing the distance between the rich and the poor, not by making the rich less wealthy but by making the poor better off. The War on Poverty hasn't closed the gap between rich and poor by very much.

Social-Service Programs. Social security, unemployment compensation, public education, and medicare are the major social-service programs in the United States. There's good reason to believe these programs have made citizens more equal. To see how they have done this, we must first describe two different kinds of inequality: inequality of distance and inequality of scope.

Inequality of distance refers to the size of the gap between the richest and poorest citizens. In a society where the richest group earns twenty times as much as the poorest group, the inequality of distance is great. The kinds of social-service programs that protect citizens against sickness, old age, and unemployment don't do much to reduce the distance between rich and poor. The major social-service programs are simply government-managed insurance plans to which citizens contribute during their working years—nine out of ten workers in the United States are now contributing to social security. But these programs don't "level" society by cutting into the wealth of the richest citizens and adding to that of the poorest ones.

Inequality of scope refers to the number of ways the rich are better off than the poor. First imagine that *every* social benefit is available only from private sources and is priced so its owners make the highest profit possible. Education, medical care, insurance, recreation, transportation, and security against personal attack are available in unequal amounts and unequal quality. The less money you have, the less of any of these services you can get. For those without money there's no public education, no free medical care, no public parks, no social security, not even a police force. Under such conditions inequality of scope would be huge. Every social benefit would be more available, and in a better form, to the rich than to the poor.

Social Service Programs aid the old and the alone.

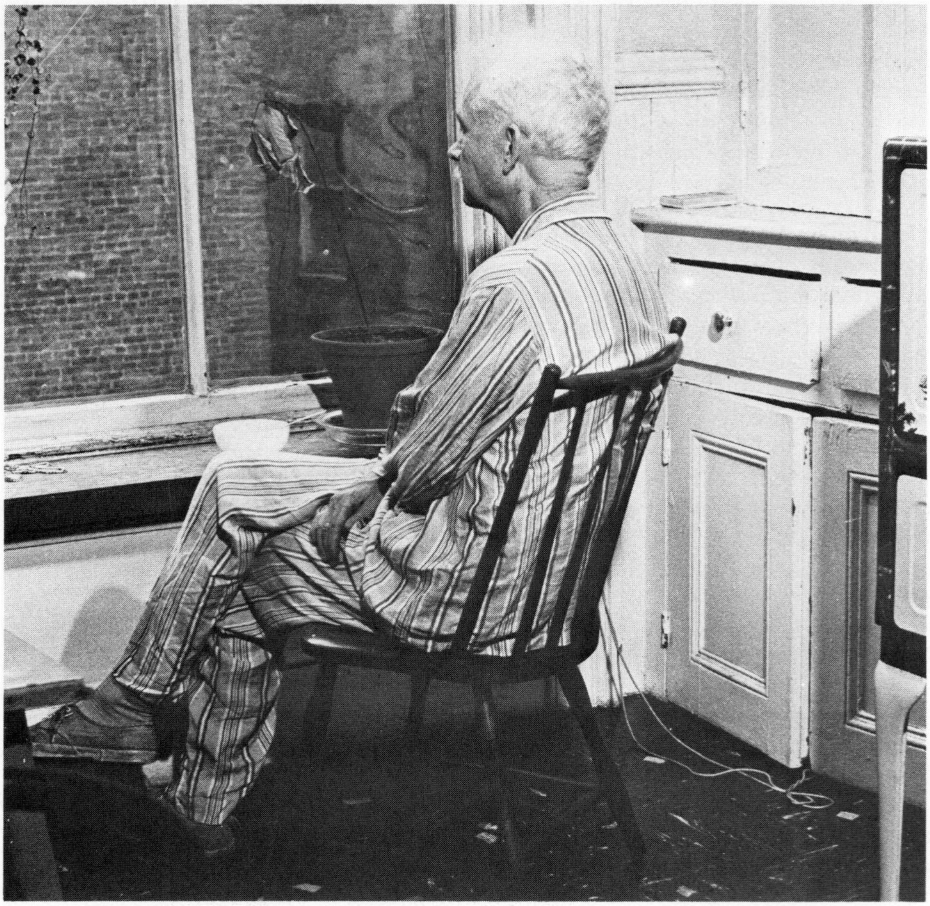

Now imagine the opposite: *No* social benefit has a price; all are equally available to every citizen. Under such conditions inequality of scope is greatly reduced. There are still rich and poor citizens, and the rich can afford luxuries that the poor cannot. But the rich can't buy better social services.

Inequality of distance refers to *how much* better off the rich are; inequality of scope refers to *how many ways* they are better off. The effect of social-welfare programs is to reduce inequality of scope. This point is made by President Julius Nyerere of socialist Tanzania, who argues for

> the provision of social services which are available to all, regardless of income; for a man who suddenly has new medical services available to him and his family, or a new house, or a new school or community center, has

had an improvement in his standard of living, just as much as if he had more money in his pocket.

If social citizenship has reduced inequality of scope, it has made a major contribution to equality. Note, however, that the benefits of social-welfare programs aren't always directed toward the poorer groups in society. Free higher education, for example, has benefited the middle class but hasn't done much for really poor families. Even the programs directed toward the poorest citizens benefit richer citizens as well: A lot of antipoverty money goes to the middle-class professionals who provide social services. The effect of social-welfare programs has also been reduced by the method of paying for them. For the most part the costs of these programs are paid for by taxes, meaning that the poor pay for them through their tax payments.

THE PROGRESSIVE INCOME TAX

When equal political rights were first proposed, many people opposed the idea. They feared that those without money would use their voting power to tax away the profits and savings of talented and hardworking citizens. In other words, they felt that property rights were threatened by "too much democracy." Nearly 100 years later, when the progressive income tax became the federal government's chief method of raising money, the same arguments could be heard.

The principle behind the progressive income tax is simple enough: The more money you earn, the more you pay in taxes. But the progressive income tax isn't as progressive as it's supposed to be. Why?

The Sixteenth Amendment authorized Congress to tax income "from whatever sources derived," but tax legislation has completely undermined this principle. Dollars earned in certain ways—although worth the same amount in consumer goods—aren't taxed at the same rate as dollars earned in other ways. The dollars that are taxed most heavily are earned in wages and salaries; those least heavily taxed are earned on various types of investments: long-term capital gains, real estate, stock options, oil, and state and local bonds. For example, a family of four earning an income of $10,000 would, under present laws, pay the following federal income taxes:

- $905 if the income is all in the form of wages and salaries.
- $98 if the income is all in the form of profits from selling stocks or land.
- $0 if the income is all in the form of interest on state and local bonds.

Thus the person who earns his living by working pays a greater share of it in taxes than the person who earns it without lifting a finger. Moreover, because the income of the wealthy comes chiefly from nonwage sources, it's the wealthy, not the low- and middle-income wage earners, who benefit from the different tax rates.

Every year the government loses billions of dollars through tax deductions and exemptions. If this money could be collected, the official tax rates could be cut nearly in half, or perhaps needed social services such as mass transit or clean air and water could be provided.

The progressive income tax does affect income distribution at lower income levels. For example, it brings the family with an income of $16,000 closer to the family with an income of $8,000. But its effect at higher income levels is much less. In general, under present laws the progressive income tax doesn't reduce the distance between rich and poor. And other types of taxes are even less progressive. The sales tax, for example, takes a much larger share of income from the poor than from the rich. Say a family earns $5,000 and pays a 5-percent sales tax on the $4,000 it spends on consumer goods. This family would pay $200, or 4 percent of its total income, in sales taxes. A family that earns $25,000 and spends $8,000 on consumer goods would pay $400, or 1.6 percent of its total income, in sales taxes. Thus the poorer family is being taxed at a higher rate.

The Political Challenge to Economic Inequality

The War on Poverty, the growth of social-welfare programs, and the progressive income tax have helped make economic conditions more equal. But they

A half-century of progressive income taxes and social-welfare programs have not eliminated poverty.

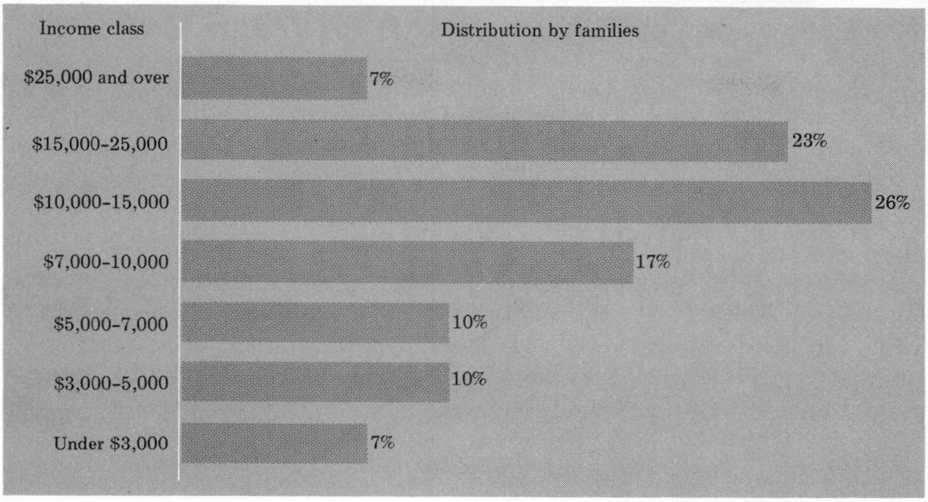

FIGURE 3.2
Income Distribution, 1972

Source: U.S. Department of Commerce, Bureau of the Census, *Statistical Abstract of the United States: 1974* (Washington, D.C., 1974), p. 382.

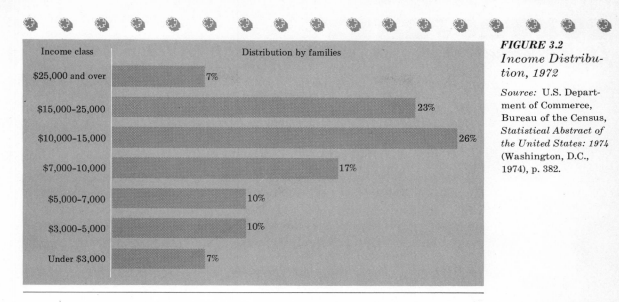

haven't caused a major redistribution of wealth. In fact the income gap between America's richest and poorest families has nearly doubled in the past twenty years. In 1949 the gap between the average income of the poorest fifth of the population and that of the richest fifth was about $10,000; by 1969 this gap had increased to nearly $20,000. Thus great inequalities remain even after nearly half a century of progressive income taxes and social-welfare programs.

Figure 3.2 shows the basic income distribution in the United States today. It's clear that equal legal rights haven't led to a leveling of society. American society accepts economic inequality while extending citizenship equality. Charles A. Beard, in his famous book *The Economic Basis of Politics*, saw this as a major paradox:

> Modern equalitarian democracy, which reckons all heads as equal and alike, cuts sharply athwart the philosophy and practice of the past centuries. Nevertheless, the democratic device of universal suffrage does not destroy economic classes or economic inequalities. It ignores them. Herein lies the paradox, the most astounding political contradiction that the world has ever witnessed.[5]

Yet this "astounding political contradiction" influences many aspects of American politics.

[5] Charles A. Beard, *The Economic Basis of Politics* (New York: Vintage, 1960), p. 69.

CONTROVERSY
Is Reverse Discrimination Defensible?

Continuous discrimination over a long period leads to a social situation that is nearly impossible to correct. If, for example, the black minority has been discriminated against by the white majority in education, housing, and employment, then equal protection of the law won't greatly improve the condition of blacks compared to that of whites. The 1970 census was taken at the end of a period that gave a lot of attention to racial justice. At the end of that period the median income of white families was $9,961, while for black families it was $6,067. And this wasn't just because whites have better jobs. Blacks are paid less than whites for similar jobs. The median income of white male professional and managerial workers was $11,108; for blacks in the same category it was $7,659.

If these are the facts, what should be done?

One Side It is the government's duty to put its authority behind affirmative action. A good way to begin would be to set educational and employment quotas. Colleges should be required to reserve about 10 percent of their places for black applicants. If someday there's to be a fair share of black ownership of the economy, training programs in banks, insurance companies, and the like should also reserve 10 percent of their places for blacks. Similar quotas should apply to construction unions, army offices, college professorships, and so on.

There's a moral case for reverse discrimination. After more than 200 years of slavery and another 100 years of white racism, American society owes something to its black citizens. But perhaps more important than the moral case is the practical argument that equality will result only if we go through a period of reverse discrimination.

The Other Side The government should treat men and women simply as citizens, regardless of race, creed, color, or sex. If there is racial discrimination the government should try to eliminate it, but it shouldn't replace one form of discrimination with another. No matter what moral or practical case can be made, it's going too far to say the government should favor one group over others. This would be just another form of discrimination.

Quota programs, for example, can be fair only if they apply to every group equally. If there's a "black quota" there should also be an "Irish quota," a "southern quota," and a "woman quota." If there's a black studies program there should also be an Italian-American studies program, a Jewish studies program, and a women's studies program. Violating the principles of equality doesn't rid society of discrimination; it only changes its form.

Questions for Review

1. What is legal citizenship? What is political citizenship?
2. How have voting rights expanded since the writing of the Constitution? allowing women the right to vote
3. What groups have been denied citizenship rights in American history? Are there any groups that don't have full citizenship rights today?
4. What is affirmative action? Do you think it's justified? yes
5. How is social citizenship different from other forms of citizenship?
6. Define inequality of distance and inequality of scope.
7. What effect do poverty programs, the progressive income tax, and programs like social security and medicare have on inequalities in American society?
8. What are some of the drawbacks of such programs?

4. the hiring of members of a minority group in order to make up for previous discrimination against that group.

Recruitment in American Politics

How American democracy works depends largely on who participates and how. By participating, citizens tell the government what they want—what goals they want it to set and how they want it to distribute the resources of society. If some citizens participate while others don't, government officials are likely to pay attention to the needs and preferences of the active citizens and ignore the inactive ones. So to understand the role of participation in American politics, we need to know which citizens are active politically.

How Do Citizens Participate?

By participation we mean all the ways citizens try to influence what the government does. And there are many ways they can participate.

VOTING

By voting, citizens help choose their political leaders. The vote of any individual citizen isn't a very powerful political tool. But elected officials are aware of the preferences of *groups* of voters.

CAMPAIGN ACTIVITY

A citizen's vote is only one of thousands or millions and can play only a small role in the results of an election. But a citizen can increase his or her influence by trying to affect how others vote. One of the most common forms of political activity takes place just before an election. Citizens ring doorbells, work at the polls, and talk to their friends and neighbors. Or they give money to a candidate or to a political party. If political leaders pay attention to voters, they may pay even more attention to those who supply the manpower and the money for a campaign.

COMMUNAL ACTIVITY

Citizens have many and varied interests. Sometimes these interests have to do with national issues: American Jews are concerned about Middle East policy; conservationists about nuclear testing; blacks about federal laws on segregation. Sometimes these interests are local. For example, a group of neighbors may want to prevent the building of a road in their part of town or a group of parents may want better school facilities.

An election couldn't possibly offer citizens a choice in all of these areas. Other ways of participating are needed to make it possible for groups of citizens to tell the government how they feel about issues as they arise. *Communal activity* is the activity of groups of people working together to try to influence the government. They may be informal groups, as when neighbors join to protest to the mayor about some city policy. Or they may be more formal organizations such as unions, PTAs, or civic groups. This kind of activity, very

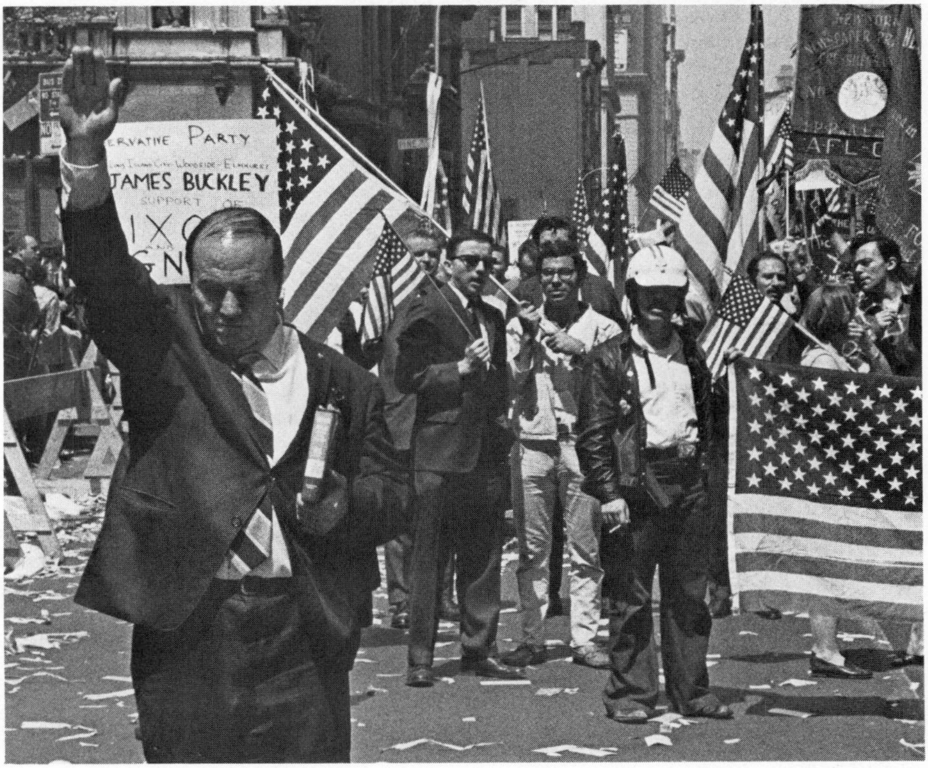

common in the United States, has two important characteristics. First, citizens work together. This is important because the government is influenced more by a group than by an individual acting alone. Second, citizens are active on the problems that concern them most.

ACTION BY INDIVIDUALS

So far we've mentioned ways citizens participate together with other citizens—as part of the voting public, in campaigns, or in communal activities. But some political activity is carried on alone, as when a person writes to a member of Congress or to a newspaper or makes a complaint at a government office. A citizen may ask a member of Congress to help a relative get a discharge from the army or may complain to a local official about the condition of the sidewalk in front of his or her house. We don't often think of this as political participation; here individuals are dealing with specific problems that concern only them. But this is one of the ways citizens influence what the government does.

PROTESTS, MARCHES, DEMONSTRATIONS

People sometimes use more dramatic and direct methods to show how they feel about an issue. They may march to protest American foreign policy or the busing of schoolchildren. Such protests have become more common in recent years. Some of these activities are ways of showing political preferences in a more dramatic way. Some are ways of directly affecting the activities of government—examples are blocking the entrance to an induction center or preventing school buses from running. Such methods are used by citizens who believe "ordinary" methods won't work or think the problem is so urgent that it can't wait for ordinary political processes.

How Active Are Americans?

Some say Americans are very active politically. Others say there's very little political activity in America. If you expect all citizens to be fully active in politics, the fact that only 10 to 20 percent of the population is active will be disappointing. If you expect citizens to be private, home-centered people, you may be surprised to find that as many as two out of ten Americans bother to take part in election campaigns. Table 4.1 shows the percentages of citizens who are active in various ways: voting, campaign activity, communal activity, and individual action.

But what about more dramatic political activities—protest marches, demonstrations, and the like? It's hard to get accurate figures, but it's likely that not many citizens have participated in such activities. During the Vietnam War protests of the late 1960s, one study found that only 8 citizens out of 1500 had taken part in a demonstration about the war—about one-half of 1 percent. A study of a city in upstate New York found that only about 2 to 3 percent of the white citizens had ever been in a street demonstration, and only 4 percent said they had gone to a protest meeting.

Note, however, that although only a small percentage of the population takes part in demonstrations, larger portions of particular groups do so. The same study that found that only 2 to 3 percent of whites had taken part in a street demonstration found that 11 percent of blacks had done so. And over half of the students in college during the Vietnam War years said they had taken part in antiwar demonstrations.

Participation in the United States and Other Nations

Americans are more "participation oriented" than citizens of other nations. They are more likely to believe they can influence the government if they want to, and this makes them more likely to act. Perhaps more important, they are more likely to feel that citizens have a responsibility to be active in their community. When it comes to actual participation, however, the pattern is mixed. Voting turnout is usually lower in the United States than in many European democracies. This doesn't necessarily mean there's a lower level of political involvement in the United States than in other countries. The best explanation of the low voting turnouts is that residency requirements prevent some citizens from voting.

Participation in political activities that take more time and effort may be more important. Only a minority of Americans (28 percent) have ever tried to influence local government policy, and an even smaller number (16 percent) have tried to influence the policies of the federal government. But in both cases the percentages are larger than those found in other nations, as Table 4.2 shows.

In one way participation in the United States seems to be particularly strong compared with other nations. This is in the area of communal activity. Citizens in several countries were asked how they would go about trying to influence the government. In the United States over half of those who believed they could have some influence felt that they could best do so by joining with others. In the other countries studied, citizens would be more likely to work alone or through some formal organization such as a political party.

TABLE 4.1
Political activities of citizens

Type of activity	*Percent active*
A. *Voting*	
Voted in 1972 Presidential election	55%
Voted in 1968 Presidential election	62%
Votes regularly in local elections	47%
B. *Campaign Activity*	
Persuade others how to vote	28%
Ever worked for a party	26%
Gone to political rallies	19%
Contributed money in a political campaign	13%
Member of a political club or organization	8%
C. *Communal Activity*	
Worked through local group	30%
Helped form local group	14%
Active member of organization involved in community activities	32%
D. *Individual Activity*	
Contacted local officials on some problem	20%
Contacted national officials on some problem	18%
Wrote a letter to a public official	17%
Wrote a letter to an editor	3%

Source: All but the first two and last two items based on data from Sidney Verba and Norman H. Nie, *Participation in America: Political Democracy and Social Equality* (New York: Harper & Row, 1972); the last two items in D based on data from 1964 Presidential election study, Center for Political Studies, Institute for Social Research, University of Michigan.

How Equally Do Citizens Participate?

How equal is political participation in America? Are all types of citizens equally active? This question is very important in understanding how participation works in America. Citizens use political activity to communicate their needs and preferences to government leaders. They also use it to pressure leaders to act on those needs and preferences. The citizen who doesn't participate may be ignored.

But the issue isn't whether all citizens participate but whether those who do are representative of the rest. People from all walks of life participate in American politics, but certain kinds of citizens are much more active than others. Studies have come to the following conclusions about which citizens are likely to be active in politics:

1. *Education.* People with a college education are much more likely to be politically active than those with less education.
2. *Income.* People with higher incomes are likely to be active; the poor much less likely.
3. *Race.* Black Americans are on the average somewhat less active than whites. But the difference is not very great for most types of activity.
4. *Sex.* Men are somewhat more active than women, but the difference between the sexes is less in America than in most other nations.
5. *Age.* Both young and old citizens tend to be somewhat less active than those in their middle years.

It's clear that the difference in participation levels among these various groups makes a difference in what the government is told. Those who are inactive—the poor, the less well educated—have different problems than those who are more active. And inactive citizens have different ideas about what the government should do. Suppose we compare the problems of the most ac-

TABLE 4.2
Citizens who say they have tried to influence a governmental decision

	United States	*Great Britain*	*Germany*	*Italy*	*Mexico*
Tried to influence a decision of the local government	28%	15%	14%	8%	6%
Tried to influence a decision of the federal government	16%	6%	3%	2%	3%

Source: Based on data from Gabriel A. Almond and Sidney Verba, *The Civic Culture: Political Attitudes and Democracy in Five Nations.*

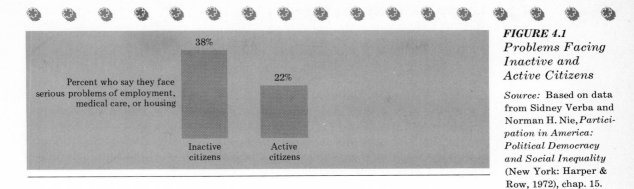

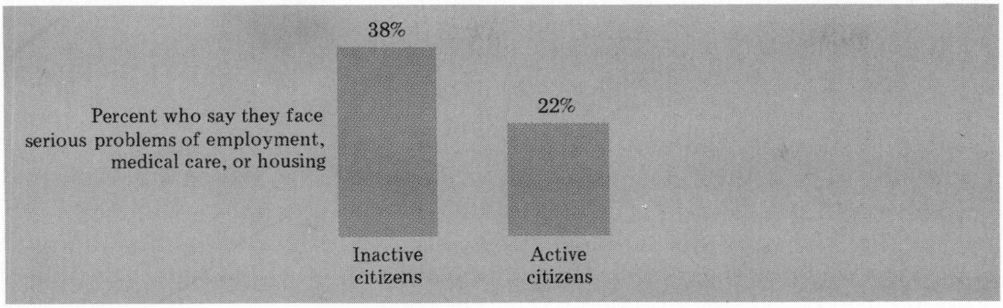

FIGURE 4.1
Problems Facing Inactive and Active Citizens

Source: Based on data from Sidney Verba and Norman H. Nie, *Participation in America: Political Democracy and Social Inequality* (New York: Harper & Row, 1972), chap. 15.

tive citizens with those of the least active ones. (See Figure 4.1.) We find that the inactive citizens are nearly twice as likely as the active ones to say they have recently faced serious problems in paying for medical care, getting a job, or finding adequate housing.

In other words, if participation is the means by which government officials find out about the problems of citizens, these leaders won't be aware of some of the more serious problems citizens face. The ones who have these problems are inactive. Nor do the inactive ones tell the government how they think it should deal with social and economic problems. If they did, the government would get a different picture of citizen preferences than it gets from the activists. Look at Figure 4.2. Active citizens believe the poor must solve their own problems, while those who are inactive are likely to think the government should deal with such problems. But the views of the latter group aren't communicated to the government. The government official who hears from the active citizens will find that a majority believe the economic problems of the poor are their own responsibility and not an area for governmental action.

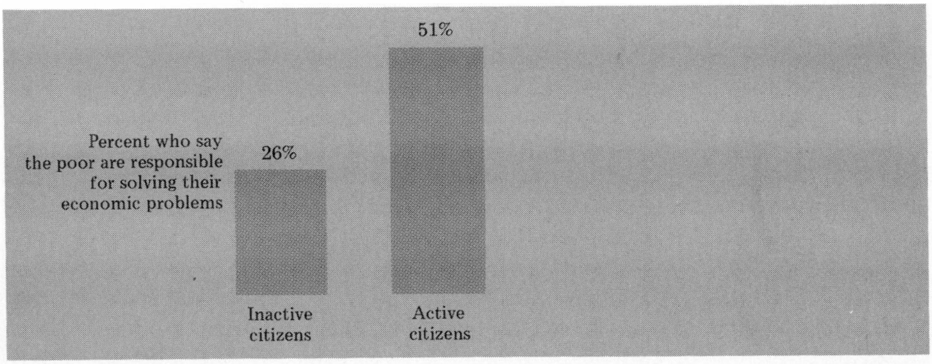

FIGURE 4.2
Differing Opinions of Inactive and Active Citizens on Problem Solving Among the Poor

Source: Based on data from Sidney Verba and Norman H. Nie, *Participation in America: Political Democracy and Social Inequality* (New York: Harper & Row, 1972), chap. 15.

CAMPAIGN CONTRIBUTIONS

Richer, better-educated citizens are more active in many ways. They are more likely to ring doorbells in campaigns, write to members of Congress, and join community organizations. But the difference between wealthy citizens and others was, until recently, greatest in the area of campaign contributions. The 1972 Presidential campaign cost at least $100 million; the average cost of a Senate campaign was about $500,000; major House campaigns cost an average of over $100,000. Where did this money come from? Most of it came from a small number of wealthy contributors. It's estimated tat about 90 percent of campaign funds came from 1 percent of the population. The Public Finance Bill of 1974 is intended to correct this.

PARTICIPATION AND EQUALITY

The importance of large contributions in political campaigns illustrates the fact that the struggle for a voice in governmental policy is an unequal one. Those who would benefit the most from governmental action—the poor, the less well educated, the victims of racial discrimination—are the ones who are least active. Those who need such action the least are the most active politically. Because of the inactivity of the poor and the greater activity of the rich, the government may be unaware of most citizens' preferences.

Why do those who need help the least participate the most? The answer is that what makes them better off in social and economic terms makes them better able to participate. Education and wealth provide the resources needed for participation. Few citizens can give thousands of dollars to political candidates. Those who can are likely to have greater political influence. Skills are another important resource, and these come from education. The educated citizens are more likely to "know the ropes" of politics—know whom to see and what to say.

In addition, studies have shown that better-educated citizens are more motivated to participate in politics. Political motivation is important: It's not enough to have the necessary resources; you must be willing to use them. From education comes the belief that you can be effective politically and that you have a responsibility to be active. We pointed out earlier that half the citizens in the United States think the ordinary person should be active in his community. But among those with no high school education only one-third think the ordinary person should be active politically, while among those with some college education two-thirds feel that way. Educated citizens are also more likely than less-educated ones to believe they can influence the government. These two beliefs—that you have a responsibility to be active and that you can influence the government—lead to political activity.

EQUALIZING POLITICAL PARTICIPATION

Can political participation be made more equal so people who are less well off in terms of income or education aren't the least effective participants? There are several ways participation could be made more equal. One way is to limit individual political activity. The most obvious place this is done is at the polls. Each citizen, no matter how rich or well educated, is limited to one vote. Putting a limit on campaign contributions would also make participation more equal. In 1974 Congress passed the Public Finance Bill, which states that individuals can give no more than $1000 to a candidate in any federal election. This hardly makes campaign contributions as equal as the vote; very few citizens can give $1000. But it should reduce the influence of those who traditionally given contributions well over $1000.

Limits on campaign contributions won't completely equalize political participation. There are many kinds of political activity that can't easily be limited without severely limiting freedom of speech. Since such activities depend on motivation and the better-educated citizens are more likely to be politically motivated, it's still the better-educated and richer citizens who are most likely to participate.

MOTIVATING DISADVANTAGED GROUPS

Another way to equalize participation is to motivate disadvantaged groups to be politically active. Two things are necessary to do this: self-awareness and organization. But the poor in America often lack both.

Self-awareness. It has often been noted that American citizens lack a strong sense of class. This is very noticeable among American workers. Sometimes they think of themselves as workers and make political decisions from that point of view. But other times they think of themselves as Protestants or Catholics, as whites or blacks, and so on. This separates them from other workers—from Protestants if they are Catholics, from blacks if they are white. They have no strong sense of membership in a *working class.*

Organization. Two kinds of organization might help disadvantaged citizens participate more in politics: political parties and voluntary groups. They would provide channels for activity and give the individual a sense of group identity. In many countries political parties are organized in terms of class. Parties that are limited to a particular class tend to do a better job of motivating the members of that class. But political parties in the United States have no clear class basis. Democrats are more likely to get support from workers and Republicans from businesses. But both parties get support from all levels of society. The result is that disadvantaged citizens have no party organizations trying to bring them into politics.

The same can be said for voluntary groups. These organizations can help citizens become more active. But members of such groups tend to be of higher social status. As Table 4.3 shows, citizens who are better educated are more active in organizations. Only about one-half of the citizens who haven't finished high school belong to a voluntary group; over three-fourths of those with some college education do. And only about one-fourth of those without a

TABLE 4.3
Organization membership

	Among those without high school education	*Among those with some high school*	*Among those with some college*
Percent who are members of an organization	49%	67%	78%
Percent who are active in an organization	27%	43%	59%

Source: Based on data from Sidney Verba and Norman H. Nie, *Participation in America: Political Democracy and Social Equality* (New York: Harper & Row, 1972).

high school degree are active in an organization, while over half of the college group is.

BLACK VS. WHITE

Among black Americans—at least in recent years—we can see the beginning of a change in the pattern of participation. This change comes, we believe, through self-awareness and organization. American blacks have a history of effective organization—at least compared to that of white Americans of similar economic and social status. There are many reasons for this, perhaps the most important one being the fact of segregation: Forced to live apart from whites, blacks are better able to organize as a separate group. In addition black organizations ranging from the NAACP to militant groups have played an important role, and so have the black churches. It's clear that blacks have developed an organizational base.

Also, unlike whites they've developed a sense of group identity. The slogans "black power" and "black is beautiful" are examples of this awareness. Again their separation from the mainstream of white society makes this possible.

Studies show that through black self-awareness, citizens who might not otherwise participate can be active in politics. On the average, black Americans participate somewhat less than white Americans. This is what we would expect, given the fact that blacks generally have lower incomes and less education than whites. But if we consider blacks who have a sense of group identity, we find that they are as active in politics as whites. In other words, the sense of black identity is a way of overcoming the disadvantages of lower educational and income levels.[1]

Most participation still comes from the white population, however, partic-

[1] Sidney Verba and Norman H. Nie, *Participation in America: Political Democracy and Social Equality* (New York: Harper & Row, 1972), chap. 10.

ularly those who are richer and better educated. But because blacks have developed a group identity and are well organized, their level of political activity compared to whites has increased. Compare 1952 with the years since 1962 in Figure 4.3.

Another conclusion can be drawn from Figure 4.3. Although direct political activity among blacks has attracted a lot of attention, it's quite clear that along with this has come more ordinary political activity. The past twenty years have seen blacks more and more active in political campaigns.

The Politics of Protest

So far we've given most of our attention to the "ordinary" ways of participating: political campaigns and communal activity. But direct political activities—demonstrations, marches, and violence—have become more important in recent years. Protests have focused on racial matters and the Vietnam War, but they have spread to other issues as well. Though there are no clear data on the subject, it seems likely that groups are more willing to seize a building or march on an office than in the past. Is this something new in America—a new political style that has grown out of the tensions of the 1960s?

PROTEST AND VIOLENCE

To begin with, protest and violence aren't the same thing. A study done for the National Commission on the Causes and Prevention of Violence found that only about one-third of the protests recorded in the news media involved

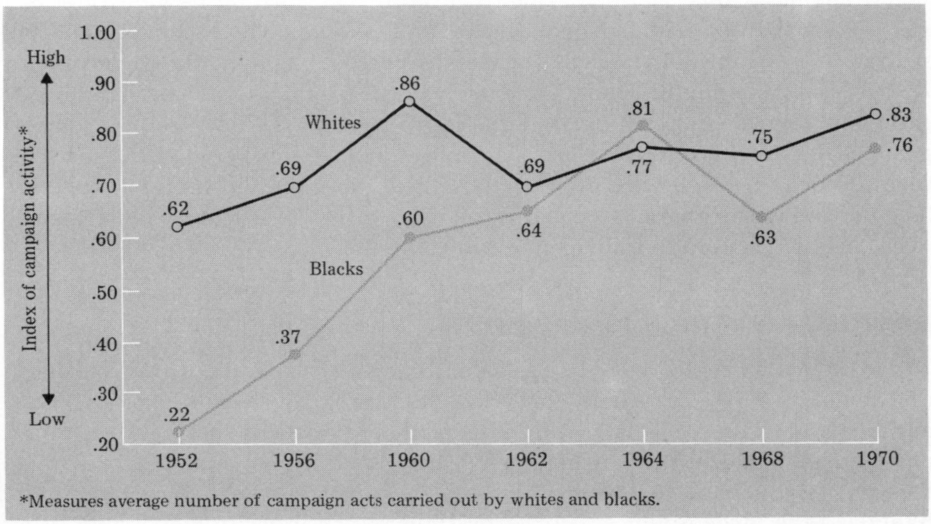

FIGURE 4.3 *Level of Campaign Activity Among Whites and Blacks*

Source: Based on data from Sidney Verba and Norman H. Nie, *Participation in America: Political Democracy and Social Inequality* (New York: Harper & Row, 1972), chap. 14.

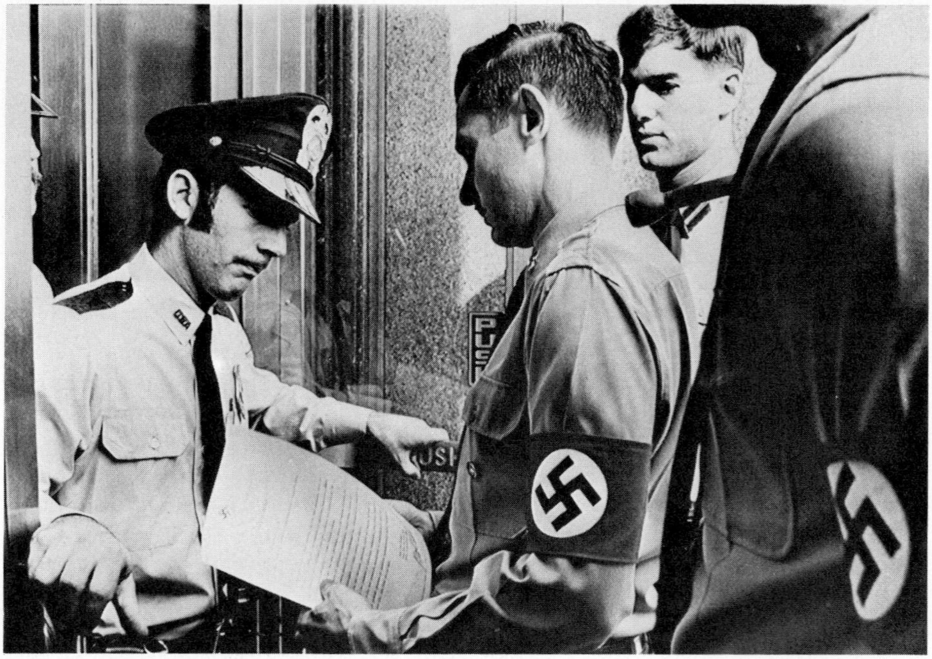

The American Nazi Party focused its protest on racial matters. They opposed the desegregation of Boston schools.

violence; most were nonviolent. In fact the figure of one-third may be high, since newspapers pay more attention to violent protests than to nonviolent ones.

It should also be noted that political protest is nothing new in America; our history is filled with political conflict and violence. The second half of the eighteenth century saw a series of violent protests against the government by poor Appalachian farmers. Violence was used against various immigrant groups in American cities in the nineteenth century. It was used by worker groups to protest economic conditions, and it was used to put down those protests. None of the demonstrations against the Vietnam War matched the violence of the antidraft riots in New York during the Civil War, when draft offices were burned and many people were killed.

MOTIVATION FOR DIRECT ACTION

In recent years protest activity has focused on two issues: the war in Vietnam and racial matters. The busing of schoolchildren is another major issue. But as the historical record shows, there have been protests on many issues. Most protests have in common the belief that ordinary political channels are unresponsive or (perhaps the same thing) too slow. Furthermore, direct action is likely to take place under certain conditions: when a group lives apart from the rest of society, has its own lifestyle, and believes it has little in common with others. If the ordinary political channels are closed, the buildup of tension and frustration may result in the use of more direct methods.

IS DIRECT ACTION APPROPRIATE?

This is a big problem for those who try direct action. Some argue that such activities are never appropriate in a democracy, where there are other, more peaceful channels. Certainly the ordinary channels must be tried first. And even then the switch to direct action may be inappropriate. Using violence to get one's own way would cause the whole structure of society to fall apart.

Others answer that in many cases all channels have been tried. Furthermore, the democratic channels aren't available equally to all; some groups have no choice but direct action. Finally, those who favor direct action argue that some issues—such as stopping a war or preventing the busing of schoolchildren—are so important that citizens must act firmly and directly.

The politics of protest has been directed against busing in Boston.

IS PROTEST EFFECTIVE?

Protests are political acts by citizens who want some response from the government. It's hard to tell whether protests are more effective than the slower processes of ordinary political participation. Many people—particularly government officials—claim that the government pays no attention to direct action. President Nixon made a point of watching a football game on TV while the White House was surrounded by protesters against the Vietnam War. Others—particularly the leaders of demonstrations—claim that direct action is the only effective political activity.

Probably the truth is in between. The most effective political activity is often the slowest and hardest—the doorbell ringing and patient talk that go with campaigning. Protest activities sometimes flash quickly and then fade, leaving no results. But the opposite often happens, too. A demonstration ending in violence, a big march on Washington by angry war protesters, attempts by citizens to block school integration—all such activities may cause government leaders to change their outlook.

Protests are particularly important as "signals." The fact that protests are dramatic and well covered by the news media makes them a powerful tool for communicating dissatisfaction to political leaders. And they may often attract participants as well. It's not an accident that the growth of black participation in voting and campaign activity came when direct protests were becoming more common.

But there's another side to the coin. Most Americans disapprove of direct action—even when they approve of its goals. A great majority (75 to 85 percent) of the American people disapproved of student protests about the Vietnam War. One study showed that this view was shared even by citizens who thought the war was a mistake.[2]

Does direct action do more harm than good? It's hard to tell, partly because the results are mixed and partly because these issues depend on moral values. Some people believe violence is wrong in almost any case. Others feel that it's necessary if social change is to take place. Out of such differences come "ordinary" politics as well as violent politics.

Defining National Leadership

Let's move now from participation to leadership. Who are the leaders and how are they chosen? The most striking fact about national leadership is how few people are directly involved in it. There are 136 million adult citizens in the United States. How many of them are directly involved in planning and directing government programs? There are about 1500 members of Congress, higher officials in the executive branch, governors, top federal and state judges, big-city mayors, and the like. From 136 million candidates come a tiny group of important political leaders.

[2] Milton J. Rosenberg, Sidney Verba, and Philip E. Converse, *Vietnam and the Silent Majority* (New York: Harper & Row, 1970), pp. 44–45.

Defining leadership isn't easy. A person in a leadership position at one level of society—say, a local merchant—may be unimportant in national affairs. Or a person who plays an important role on some issues—say, a general planning military strategy—may count for nothing when economic policy is being planned.

The definition used in this book describes national leaders, that is, people whose positions give them influence that can be felt on a national scale. And leaders in America are people who hold high positions in particular institutions: banks, corporations, universities, law firms, Congress, labor unions, churches, civic groups, and so on.

National leaders have important positions in the major institutions of American society. They are the officers and directors of IBM, the Secretary and Assistant Secretary of Agriculture, the publisher and editors of the *New York Times*, the officers and trustees of the Chase Manhattan Bank, and so on.

Choosing National Leaders

Let's start by asking three questions about these leaders—the "C questions" of leadership in a democratic society:

Choice.
Who is chosen to be a national leader?

Cohesion.
How cohesive is the leadership group?

Change.
In what ways and how fast can the leadership group be changed?

In our discussion we'll focus on political leaders, that is, on top elected and appointed officials in the government.

STANDARDS FOR CHOOSING LEADERS

Look at Figure 4.4 and think of the ancient Chinese box puzzle. In this puzzle different-sized boxes are designed so that the smallest box fits into the next-larger one, which, in turn, fits into the next-larger one, and so on. The largest

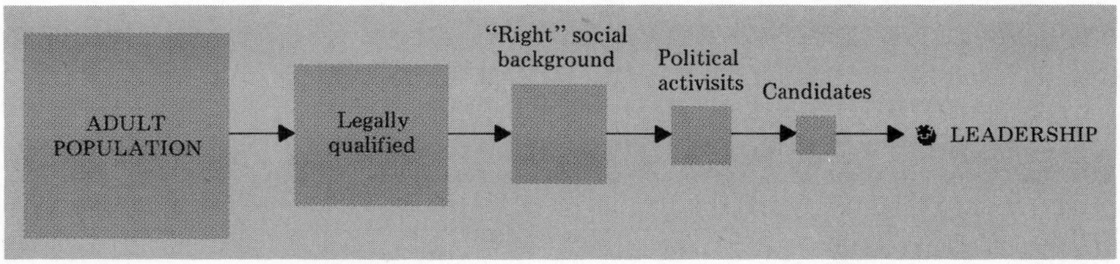

FIGURE 4.4 *Recruitment Criteria for Political Leadership*

box contains all the others. To find the smallest box you have to open all the boxes between it and the largest one.

Now imagine that the largest box represents the entire population and the smallest box represents the leadership group. The other boxes would represent smaller and smaller "recruitment pools" that supply people from the larger groups to the smaller ones. Figure 4.4 is a diagram of that process showing four stages between the population as a whole and the tiny group of leaders chosen from that population.

Legal Qualifications. Within the adult population there is a group of people who meet the legal qualifications for political office. For example, the Constitution sets minimum ages for some positions; residency requirements and professional qualifications (particularly for judicial offices) must also be met by candidates for certain offices. Legal qualifications, however, don't play a very important role in political recruitment. Almost any adult citizen is legally qualified to hold public office.

Social Background. The next standard for choosing political leaders is social background. A large percentage of the leadership group comes from particular social groups within the population. Leaders aren't typical in their social background, in their educational level, and in their occupations before holding office.

Leaders are chosen from a small portion of the general population. If you come from a rich family, if you're white and male, if you go to a well-known college or university, you have a better chance of moving into the group from which leaders are chosen. The son of a corporation lawyer who has just graduated from Princeton and is about to enter Harvard Business School has begun a career that often puts people of his background in line for the highest positions in society. His family, his father's business associates, his Princeton classmates or Harvard professors wouldn't consider it odd if he said his ambition is to be a senator or to head a well-known New York law firm.

But a farmer's son who graduates with honors from Jerseyville High but decides against further education is in a very different social setting. It would be unusual for him to consider himself a future member of the top leadership group. There are few models for him to look up to, no contacts to help him on his way. His idea of success is to own his own farm. Such a self-image is realistic, like the self-image of the Princeton graduate. The point is that people not only select themselves for but also eliminate themselves from the race for the few top positions. Patterns of self-selection and self-elimination can't be separated from social background.

Political Activity. About one out of twenty adult citizens is a political activist, and it's from this group that leaders are finally chosen. Activists pay close attention to political matters, serve on committees and work in campaigns, and know the people who already hold public office. This group is largely, though not entirely, made up of middle-class and upper-middle-class citizens.

There are no universal standards for entry into the group of activists that supplies candidates for the highest positions. However, activists often come from families with a tradition of political involvement. About one-third of those who hold political office in the United States trace their earliest political involvement to the influence of the family.

Candidates. Within the politically active group is an even smaller number of people who become candidates for top leadership positions. How some activists become serious competitors for leadership and others don't is not well understood. One factor, however, is self-assertiveness. President Johnson, for example, once said, "As long as I can remember I've always been the kind of person who takes over in any group, who takes responsibility for calling the gathering together, getting the agenda for the meeting and carrying out the assignments."

Another factor is the help of those who already hold powerful positions. For example, when Johnson was majority leader in the Senate he gave John F. Kennedy's career a boost by helping him get appointed to the Senate Foreign Relations Committee. This gave Kennedy a platform from which to launch his drive for the Democratic party's Presidential nomination.

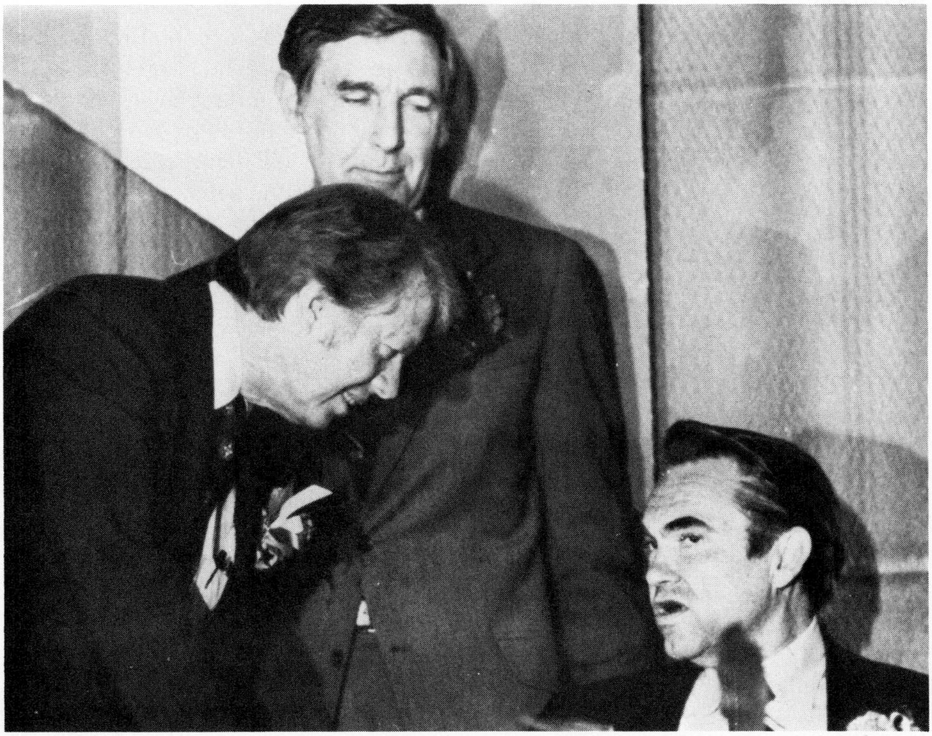

Very few become candidates for the top positions. Carter defeated many who wanted the Democratic nomination in 1976.

THE TEST OF ACHIEVEMENT

The Chinese box puzzle shows how a very large population is gradually narrowed down until a small number of candidates are competing for the even smaller number of top leadership positions. But this doesn't answer the question of ability. Because so many political leaders come from rich families and are white males, some say *who you are* is more important than *what you can do*. But though it's clear that the "right" social background is an advantage, it can neither guarantee a place in the top leadership group nor completely block entry.

Achievement on a Grand Scale. To be in line for national political leadership, you have to show your ability on a grand scale. It's better to succeed at running General Motors than at selling used cars, though selling used cars may take more skill. It's better to be the president of a well-known university than a grade-school teacher, though teaching a roomful of 8-year-olds may take more skill than managing a university. It's better to be the popular mayor of New York City than the popular mayor of Kankakee, though it may take more popularity to get votes in Kankakee than in New York.

Thus it's not just achievements but specific achievements that move a person into the top leadership group. This is one reason why so many of the top leaders come from rich families. They have the education and contacts necessary to reach positions in which ability can be shown on a grand scale. The used-car salesman is a member of the working class, not the upper class; he went to a junior college, not Harvard Business School; he is sometimes active in local politics, but he doesn't give thousands of dollars to Presidential campaigns. On the list of possible appointees to the Cabinet or possible nominees for the governorship, you'll never find the used-car salesman, but you'll often find the head of the company whose cars he sells.

Ability to Win Elections. It's true that American politics often rewards those who have proved that they can direct the nation's large institutions. But it also rewards those who show a very different kind of skill: the ability to win elections.

In a democracy the voting public controls entry into certain key leadership positions. So what matters is the ability to win elections. Nixon built on a series of election victories, starting with his campaign for the House of Representatives in 1946 and ending with his landslide reelection to the Presidency in 1972. Johnson also went from the House to the Senate to the Vice-Presidency to the Presidency. By contrast, Eisenhower turned his popularity as a wartime general into popularity with the voting public and became President without ever having been active in politics. Former California governor Ronald Reagan became governor directly from a career as a movie actor.

Popularity with voters can be used effectively by people from any social background. In American politics it often makes up for the lack of family wealth or a high-status education. As a result, while members of the lower social classes are almost never chosen for high *appointive* office, they sometimes make it to *elective* office.

How Cohesive Is the Leadership Group?

It's often argued that national leaders generally think the same way about public policy. Only small differences are allowed. Leaders are a cohesive group, and it's nearly impossible to introduce new ideas unless the "establishment" approves of them. Others believe leaders are divided into different, competing groups. They have different ambitions. They represent different economic groups, regions, or political viewpoints. The important fact about leadership is not agreement but conflict.

Which view is correct? conflict.

DISAGREEMENT AMONG POLITICAL LEADERS

Leaders have a great variety of opinions on such issues as tax reform, inflation controls, defense spending, and the like. This is because the political-recruitment process brings to top leadership circles some of the basic conflicts and divisions of society. This happens in many ways. For example, Republicans and Democrats have certain differences in outlook. Leaders also speak for the many political and social divisions in society: North vs. South, Protestant vs. Catholic, workers vs. management. And of course there are conflicts between state leaders and government agencies, between Congress and the Presidency, and so on.

The Watergate affair illustrates an important type of disagreement between institutions: conflict between the news media and the government. Political leaders often complain that they're being treated unfairly by the news media; editors, reporters, and announcers often complain that political leaders don't respect the freedom of the press. In the 1960s these complaints took on new force. The press began to see its job as more than reporting the news. It was beginning to argue strongly for or against particular public policies.

The news media and the government have different interests. The media want to stimulate political debate. They "have an interest in exposure, criticism, highlighting and encouraging disagreement . . . within the executive branch." By contrast, national leaders, especially those in the executive branch, want to limit political debate. They "have an interest in secrecy, . . . discipline, and the suppression of criticism."[3]

Conflicts within the leadership group put a great strain on government. It's not easy to decide on a policy when the policy makers can't agree.

[3] Quoted in Samuel P. Huntington, "Post-Industrial Politics: How Benign Will It Be?" *Comparative Politics*, January 1974, 184.

Bargains and compromises are common as a result. In addition such conflicts allow the public to play off one set of leaders against another. Democrats can be replaced by Republicans, or those who favor a larger military budget can be replaced by those who want it reduced. Thus competing viewpoints within the leadership group give the public some control over public policy.

AGREEMENT AMONG POLITICAL LEADERS

Leaders share many experiences. They often have similar backgrounds. They know how hard it is to get and use power. They worry about how to keep the economy and the government working effectively. Out of these shared experiences comes a form of agreement among leaders. This is because most leaders are recruited from the political mainstream.

Agreement on Policy. The political mainstream includes the policies that most Americans support or at least tolerate. Take military policy, for example. Americans agree that the nation should be prepared to defend its national interests with military force. Most, but not all, take this view. There are some who oppose the whole idea of military preparedness. Their attitude is considered "outside the mainstream of American thinking."

The recruitment process tends to choose leaders from the political mainstream. One reason is that voters aren't likely to support candidates whose viewpoints conflict with their own. This doesn't mean every political leader is equally acceptable to every voter. A member of Congress elected by white Mississippi farmers probably has opinions about racial matters that are offensive to northern black voters. But the leadership group as a whole has policy views that go along with those of the majority.

Within the mainstream, and thus within the leadership group, many different viewpoints are represented. Again consider military policy. To say there's general agreement that the United States should be prepared to defend its national interests is not to agree on what those interests are. But the recruitment process bars from the top leadership circles those whose views strike most Americans as "extreme" or "going too far."

Agreement on Procedure. Much that is important about American politics may be found in the phrase "working within the system." There is an acceptable way of doing things and an unacceptable way. Political hostility toward peaceniks, ecology freaks, and black militants stems from the belief that without "the system" there's no hope for such goals as lasting peace, clean air, or racial justice. You can "vote the rascals out," but you won't be allowed to destroy the system that allows a later group of rascals to be voted out. You can petition and demonstrate, but you can't destroy the system that allows petitions and demonstrations.

Leaders agree on the importance of working within the system, and in this way they reflect the political mainstream. Agreement on *how* to bring about change cuts across sharp disagreement on *what* changes, if any, are needed. The long climb to high office generally results in commitment to the rules of the game despite different points of view.

Leadership and Change

Membership in the national leadership group isn't permanent. New social forces—black power, women's liberation, consumer protest—enter the picture, and very often they push aside more established groups. In this way new viewpoints, new groups, and new skills find a place in leadership circles.

NEW SKILLS

The main job of leadership is to be prepared for the problems of society and to solve them. This job is done unevenly, however. Consider today's social problems: pollution of air and water, crowded cities, high costs of social services, racial tension. Would these problems be less severe today if previous leaders had been aware of them earlier? To put the question another way: Today are there signs of future problems that aren't noticed by present leaders but that will be on the political agenda when today's college students are trying to raise their families?

During the Great Depression of the 1930s, none of the traditional economic solutions seemed to work. Then in 1932 the Roosevelt administration took over. Dozens of new methods and programs were tried. The people in leadership positions had very different skills from previous administrations. Out of this "skill revolution" came the New Deal, a collection of government programs and social services unheard of ten years earlier.

This shows the link between a skill revolution and the political agenda. The agenda contains a number of serious problems. When the right skills are lacking, the problems get worse. When the right skills are provided, appropriate programs are undertaken. What are often called "national crises" occur while people with the skills to deal with those problems have not yet been recruited to leadership.

NEW SOCIAL GROUPS

Earlier we pointed out that certain social groups provide most of our political leaders. National leadership has long been a white male club. But within this club some important changes have taken place over the years. The ministers, lawyers, and rich landowners who led the nation to independence didn't expect that a century later the United States would be governed by men who had made millions by building up huge industrial corporations. And the industrialists and bankers of the late nineteenth and early twentieth centuries didn't expect that a half-century later they would be sharing power

Shirley Chisholm has become an important black female leader.

with the leaders of labor unions. White males continue to dominate leadership positions, but the groups they represent have changed dramatically.

Today new social groups are getting into the club. Each year more blacks and women are found among the national leaders. Table 4.4 shows the number who have entered Congress over the past twenty-five years. Connecticut has a woman governor, and several large cities have black mayors. Changes are taking place in business, universities, newspapers, and law firms as well. It's a slow process, but once started it continues to put pressure on the leadership group.

SUMMARY

A small group of people govern the nation. These are the people who have important positions in the dominant institutions of society: banks, universities, government agencies, businesses, legislatures. These leaders decide how the resources of society will be used. The level of military spending is such a decision; so are the interest rate on the money borrowed by a homeowner, the tuition at state universities, and the types of scientific research funded by the government.

We've said that leaders are recruited in a way that gives an advantage to particular social groups. They share common experiences, though they don't agree about the kinds of policies the nation should support. We've also said that the leadership group is under constant pressure to change—pressure to allow new social groups a voice in the government and pressure to recruit new skills as the political agenda changes.

TABLE 4.4
Number of black and women members in Congress, 1947–1974

	BLACK MEMBERS IN THE		WOMEN MEMBERS IN THE	
Congress[a]	*Senate*	*House*	*Senate*	*House*
80th		2	1	7
81st		2	1	9
82nd		2	1	10
83rd		2	3	12
84th		3	1	16
85th		4	1	15
86th		4	1	16
87th		4	2	17
88th		5	2	11
89th		6	2	10
90th	1	5	1	11
91st	1	9	1	10
92nd	1	12	2	13
93rd	1	15	0	14
94th[b]	2	16	0	18

[a] Each congressional session lasts two years. There are a total of 435 members of the House and a total of 100 members of the Senate.

[b] As of November 1974 election.

Source: Based on data from *Current American Government* (Washington, D.C.: *Congressional Quarterly*, Spring 1973), pp. 25–26; and *Current American Government*, Spring 1975, p. 17.

But, for democracy to work the leaders must be responsive to the nonleaders. In this chapter we learned that the leaders are a very small group. Throughout the book we'll ask how well the democratic promise of government by, for, and of the people is protected.

CONTROVERSY

Should Leaders Be Chosen Only According to Ability?

Citizens have different amounts of political influence and involvement. At the bottom are the inactive citizens who care little about political matters and don't even bother to vote. Next come the large number of Americans who vote and get involved in political activity now and then. Then come the real activists, who are very involved in the political life of their community or of the nation. Next come those who try for public office: the candidates. Then come those who succeed: the officeholders. And these range from minor local officials up through the ranks to the top national leaders.

At each of these levels the population is more and more elite in social and economic terms: At each step upward we find a greater number of people with high levels of income and education. Some say this is the way American democracy is supposed to work. Others say it's a major flaw.

One Side The fact that richer and better-educated citizens find their way to the top of American politics says nothing bad about American democracy. Lower-status citizens are less interested. And if as a result they have less influence than richer citizens, it is they who are to blame, not the system. As long as citizens are free to participate and free to run for office, democracy is working.

Furthermore, the higher you go, the more qualified the group you find. Skilled people are hard to find. Choosing successful lawyers and business leaders to hold public office means making fewer mistakes. These people have shown that they can succeed where the competition is toughest. They are the people we need as leaders. A corporation executive is likely to have the background needed to deal with the complicated problems of American society.

The black longshoreman active in trade-union affairs will know how to develop a race-relations program that makes sense for the docks of San Francisco. It's not clear, however, that he will have the experience to set up a national program to deal with the same problem. A good national program will have to take into account race relations on Alabama farms, on army bases in Europe, in the sales forces of Boston insurance companies. It will also have to be coordinated with other government programs. Perhaps our Princeton graduate—now an IBM executive who has served on the Civil Rights Commission, is a member of the board of trustees of several colleges, and recently advised the Ford Foundation on its grants to inner-city schools—is the best person to direct a federal race-relations program.

The color or sex or social background of leaders isn't the issue. But the skills and outlook are. American society will suffer if it chooses people of low achievement as its leaders.

The Other Side

Democracy works only when all citizens have an equal voice in the government. The fact that richer and better-educated citizens are more active in politics and more successful in climbing the political ladder is therefore a major flaw in American democracy. It's not fair to say poorer citizens don't go far politically because they choose not to. The opportunities to participate aren't equal. If lower-status citizens participate less than others, it's not because they don't care but because they don't have the resources. If election campaigns cost millions, those who can't give large amounts of money aren't "equally free" to participate effectively. And they're even less likely to be able to run for office themselves.

Besides, those who make it to the top leadership circles may have more education, but there are important skills they may not have. The skills that might lead to racial harmony, decent education and health care, and well-planned communities aren't necessarily found in white upper-class males. Leaders should be chosen from the groups that have direct experience with the problems of American life.

The white corporation executive may have more organizational ability and more education than the black union leader. But whose career is likely to develop the skills necessary to reduce racial tension within the American working class? And whose career will provide the experience that could bring a fresh outlook to the Department of Health, Education and Welfare?

American society may be short-changing itself by always choosing leaders from the successful business and professional classes.

Questions for Review

1. How do citizens participate in American politics?
2. Which citizens are likely to be active in politics? Why?
3. How could political participation be made more equal?
4. What factors have made blacks more active politically?
5. Why do people participate in "direct" political activities? Under what conditions is such action likely? Do you think it's effective?
6. How does the Chinese box puzzle illustrate how leaders are chosen in American society?
7. What is the role of ability in the choice of political leaders?
8. Do you think it's all right for national leaders to come from the economic and educational elite of society?

Chapter 5

Political Beliefs in America

To understand American politics we must understand what the American people believe about politics and government, and how they act in relation to those beliefs. Some people think you can understand politics by studying the formal structure of government—the fact that we have a presidential rather than a parliamentary system; a division of power between the national and state governments; a constitution with formal guarantees of freedom. These things are important, of course, but here we're dealing with something more basic. It isn't enough to know the formal structure of government because the political beliefs of the people affect how that structure works.

Political Beliefs and Democracy

What political beliefs are basic to democracy? Many agree that they include the following:

1. Citizens must believe the government is legitimate, that is, that it deserves their support.
2. They must support the "rules of the game," such as free speech and fair elections. If citizens don't believe the government is legitimate and don't support the rules of the game, democracy won't survive long.
3. But if democracy is to *work*, citizens must make it responsive to their needs by electing candidates who support the policies they prefer. Therefore, they must make rational choices—decide what policies they prefer and vote for candidates who support those policies.

Does the American public really hold this set of beliefs? In recent years methods like the sample survey have been developed to find out about public

Most Americans consider the government to be legitimate.

TABLE 5.1
How many citizens are proud of political aspects of society?

	United States	Great Britain	Germany	Italy	Mexico
Percent proud of "nothing"	4%	10%	15%	27%	16%
Percent proud of political aspects of society	85%	46%	7%	3%	30%

Source: Based on data from Gabriel A. Almond and Sidney Verba, *The Civic Culture: Political Attitudes and Democracy in Five Nations.* Copyright © 1963 by Princeton University Press. Reprinted by permission of Princeton University Press.

attitudes. We now have detailed information about the political beliefs of the American people.

BELIEF IN THE LEGITIMACY OF THE GOVERNMENT

Legitimacy of government refers to the belief that public officials deserve support and the law must be obeyed. Legitimacy is basic to democracy because democracy depends on voluntary consent. If citizens don't give their consent to the policies of the government, it is likely to rely more and more on force, and political movements that oppose democratic government will get more support.

In 1959 a major study compared what Americans were proud of in America with the views expressed by citizens in four other countries. (See Table 5.1.) Two results are important. For one thing, few Americans—only 4 percent—said there was nothing they were proud of. (In the other four countries, 10 to 27 percent responded this way.) And 85 percent showed pride in political aspects of American society—the Constitution, political freedom, democracy. In the next-highest country only half as many citizens felt this way.

American politics has changed a lot since 1959, but the basic attitude of the American people hasn't changed that much. In 1972 citizens were asked to choose between two statements: "I am proud of many things about our form of government" and "I can't find much about our form of government to be proud of." Eighty-six percent chose the first statement. And when asked whether our form of government needs major change, only 15 percent said a "big change" is needed.[1]

Although surveys show that the public still respects the American form of government, there has been a large increase in the number of people who are dissatisfied with the way the government is actually being run. Over the years citizens have been asked questions like "Do you think the government is run for all the people or for a few special interests?" and "Do you trust the government to do what is right?" In 1958, 18 percent of the public thought the

[1] Jack Citrin, "The Political Relevance of Trust in Government," *American Political Science Review,* 68 (September 1974), 975.

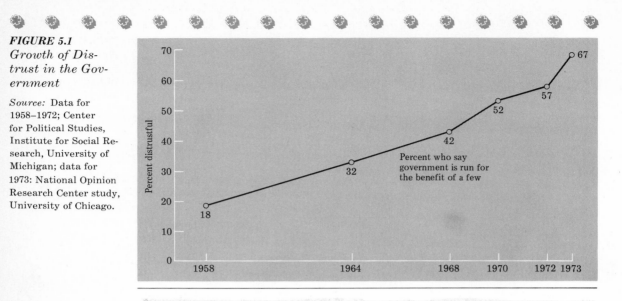

FIGURE 5.1
Growth of Distrust in the Government

Source: Data for 1958–1972; Center for Political Studies, Institute for Social Research, University of Michigan; data for 1973: National Opinion Research Center study, University of Chicago.

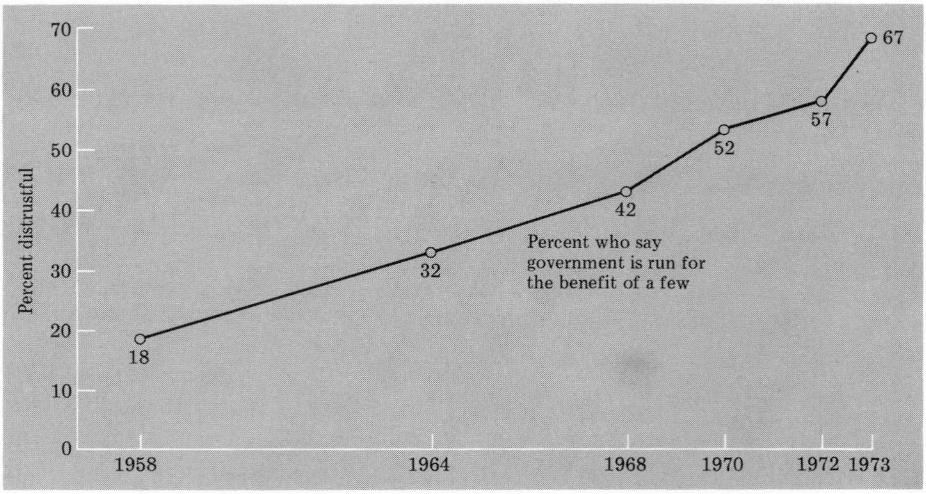

government was run for the benefit of a few; by 1973, 67 percent felt this way.[2] (See Figure 5.1.)

This decline began well before the Watergate affair, though Watergate had a strong impact on public trust in the government. The dissatisfaction with government seems to have its roots in a feeling that it couldn't cope with the big problems of the late 1960s and early 1970s: racial tension, Vietnam, pollution, inflation, and so on.

Some think this decline won't last long, while others argue that there's a growing feeling of alienation among the American people. So far the evidence shows that the public is unhappy with the way the government is being run but not with the democratic form of government itself. They seem to be saying "The system is all right—it's just not working well." Such dissatisfaction could lead to a general decline in support for the political system as a whole. The evidence doesn't show that this is happening, but it does show that the American people no longer support their government as firmly as they once did.

Political Efficacy. The term *political efficacy* refers to one's belief that he or she has a voice in the government. If people don't think they can influence the government, they are less likely to feel that it deserves their support.

Do Americans believe in their political efficacy? In general, yes; but the number of people who feel this way has declined recently. Most Americans believe government officials can be controlled through the vote and that they

[2] Data for 1958: Survey Research Center election study, Institute for Social Research, University of Michigan; data for 1973: National Opinion Research Center study, University of Chicago.

are responsive to the people. Compared with citizens of other nations, Americans are more likely to think they can do something about a law they consider unjust.

Studies of "citizen efficacy" during the 1950s and 1960s show that feelings of efficacy rose in the 1950s and fell in the 1960s and early 1970s. In 1952, 69 percent of a sample agreed that "people have some say about what the government does"; by 1960, the figure had risen to 72 percent—but by 1973 it had fallen to 49 percent. The percentage is still high, but the decline is significant.[3]

SUPPORT FOR THE RULES OF THE GAME

The "rules of the game" are the basic procedures of democracy, such as fair elections and free speech. If a democracy is to work, groups must be able to get together and express their views; there must be public control over government officials through the vote; those officials must be willing to step down when the voters choose other leaders. These procedures are law, but they survive only because the American people believe in them. For example, even supporters of the losing candidate agree that it's right for the winner of a Presidential election to take office.

Free speech is perhaps the most important rule of the game. It is guaranteed in the Bill of Rights, but without public support the Bill of Rights would be meaningless. If Americans agree on this basic rule, they can disagree on other issues such as national health insurance or the Equal Rights Amendment. But as long as everyone agrees on the right of opponents to express their views, democracy can survive.

Do Americans Really Support the Rules of the Game? Several studies have shown that the American people generally agree with the principles of democratic government.[4] In the early 1970s, for example, the Harris poll found that 91 percent agreed that "every citizen has the right to express any opinion he wants to" and only 5 percent disagreed.[5]

Is Their Support Consistent? Other research shows that commitment to the rules of democratic procedure seems weak in certain areas. The same people who say free speech is a good thing aren't sure certain unpopular groups should have that freedom. A large number are against letting such groups make speeches in their community; about two-thirds would oppose freedom of

[3] Data from Survey Research Center studies, Institute for Social Research, University of Michigan.

[4] James W. Prothro and Charles M. Grigg, "Fundamental Principles of Democracy: Bases of Agreement and Disagreement," *Journal of Politics*, 22 (Spring 1960), 276–294; Herbert McClosky, "Consensus and Ideology in American Politics," *American Political Science Review*, 58 (June 1964), 361–382.

[5] Louis Harris, *The Anguish of Change* (New York: Norton, 1973), p. 278.

TABLE 5.2
Citizens favor free speech more when they approve of the views of the speakers

Should a group be allowed to petition the government . . .	*Percent who say yes*
To stop a factory from polluting the air?	93%
To crack down on crime in their community?	95%
To legalize marijuana?	52%
To make sure blacks can buy and rent homes in white neighborhoods? (*asked of whites only*)	70%
To prevent blacks from buying or renting in white neighborhoods? (*asked of blacks only*)	51%

Source: National Opinion Research Center study, University of Chicago, 1971.

speech for communists or atheists.[6] A study in Tallahassee, Florida, found general agreement that minority groups have a right to full participation in politics. But among the same people 42 percent thought a black shouldn't be allowed to run for mayor.[7]

If you agree on the rules of the game, you should favor free speech no matter how you feel about the speaker or what he has to say. But in 1971 the National Opinion Research Center found that citizens would allow free speech about the policies they favor (such as pollution control) but not about those they oppose (such as legalization of marijuana). (See Table 5.2.)

Do They Act on Their Political Beliefs? The attitude of Americans toward the rules of the game is unclear. If citizens support democratic procedures in general but not when it comes to specific cases, democracy won't last long. Fortunately, however, people don't act the way some of their attitudes would lead us to expect. In Tallahassee, for example, a black ran for mayor and no one tried to stop him. And in communities where citizens said certain unpopular groups shouldn't be allowed to make speeches, such speeches were permitted.

So Americans support the rules in general, but when you ask about specific cases their support seems to weaken. When you go further and ask what they actually do, however, you find that they don't act on their undemocratic views.

It's possible that the Tallahassee citizens who said a black shouldn't be allowed to run for mayor were simply expressing negative feelings toward blacks. There's another explanation, however. Studies have shown that much of what people say in an interview represents opinions they believe in but not very strongly, or at least not strongly enough to act on.

This is not true of all Americans. Those who are politically active form, as we have seen, a minority of the population. They are more likely to have a col-

[6] Samuel Stouffer, *Communism, Conformity and Civil Liberties* (New York: Wiley, 1955).

[7] Prothro and Grigg, 294.

lege education, and they are more likely to support the general principles of democracy when applied to specific cases.

Thus although up to two-thirds of all Americans oppose freedom of speech for certain unpopular groups, most government officials and leaders of organizations favor free speech for all. (See Table 5.3.) These data suggest that most Americans don't support democratic principles as firmly as is generally believed, but that people who have a greater voice in how the government is run—those active in politics—have a stronger commitment to the rules of the game.

In short, the political system works, but not exactly the way it's supposed to. Americans are committed to the political system, but not as strongly as is generally believed.

THE CITIZEN AS RATIONAL VOTER

Politics is about the competition among citizens for a larger share of the benefits distributed by the government. How can citizens make the government responsive to their interests? They are supposed to act as rational voters—to know their own interests, find out which candidate is most likely to favor those interests, and vote for that candidate.

Are Citizens Rational Voters? A University of Michigan study in the 1950s found that Americans were far from rational voters. For one thing, they often didn't know which policies each candidate supported. More important, they might answer questions on a large number of public issues, but their answers usually weren't well-formed opinions.

Furthermore, studies found that the average American didn't have clear political views. Journalists, scholars, and politicians themselves are likely to have consistent views on many issues, you can call them liberal, conservative, or radical. In each case their opinion on a specific issue—such as school desegregation or U.S. policy toward communist countries—is part of a consistent general outlook.

TABLE 5.3
Community leaders are more tolerant than ordinary citizens

	Among ordinary citizens	*Among community leaders*
Percent who say they would allow a communist to make a speech	27%	51%
Percent who say they would allow a socialist to make a speech	58%	84%
Percent who are "more tolerant" of minorities	31%	66%

Source: Based on data from Samuel Stouffer, *Communism, Conformity and Civil Liberties.*

But surveys made in the 1950s and early 1960s showed that Americans didn't usually think in liberal or conservative terms when deciding how to vote. And there was no way to predict a citizen's views on one issue from what he or she said about other issues. One might be conservative on racial issues and liberal on foreign policy.

This meant election results didn't depend on the issues, since the public was uninformed about what policies the candidates supported and, in any case, didn't have consistent opinions on those issues. It also meant there wasn't a sharp division of the American people into conservative and liberal groups.

Why Did Citizens Vote the Way They Did? Studies found that one of the major influences on a person's vote was *party identification:* 77 percent of the public called themselves either Democrats or Republicans. Most citizens got their party identification, like their religion, from their parents, and most kept that identification throughout their lives.

In 1956, 91 percent of the voters voted for their party's congressional candidate. They might leave their party to vote for a popular Presidential candidate; millions of Democrats voted for Eisenhower in 1952 and 1956. But they did so because of his personal popularity, not because they agreed with his views on the issues. And they still called themselves Democrats.

Are Political Parties as Important as They Used To Be? The 1950s were an unusual time in American history. Eisenhower, a World War II hero, was President; the government didn't face any big problems; and there was little political conflict. Studies made since then have shown some important changes. For one thing, Americans seem to have become more aware of political issues. An increasing number of citizens have fairly consistent political opinions. Furthermore, they more often judge candidates by their views on the issues.

In each Presidential election since 1952, researchers from the University of Michigan have asked people what they liked and disliked about the candidates. Some mention candidates' personalities and some mention their parties; others talk about the issues. (See Figure 5.2.) Although people still pay a lot of attention to a candidate's personality, note the fall in the percentage of citizens who like or dislike a candidate because of party identification, coupled with the rise in the percentage who judge a candidate by views on the issues.

There is evidence that political parties are no longer as important as they used to be. In 1956, 77 percent of the American people called themselves Democrats or Republicans; by 1974, this figure had fallen to about 60 percent. Young voters in the late 1960s and early 1970s often called themselves independents—a big change from the 1950s. More and more citizens were voting for the other party's candidate, and the importance of the issues had gone up.

Yet studies continue to show that the public is often uninformed on basic political issues. In 1972 a study found that only about half of the citizens know the name and party of *one* of their senators; about one-third could name both

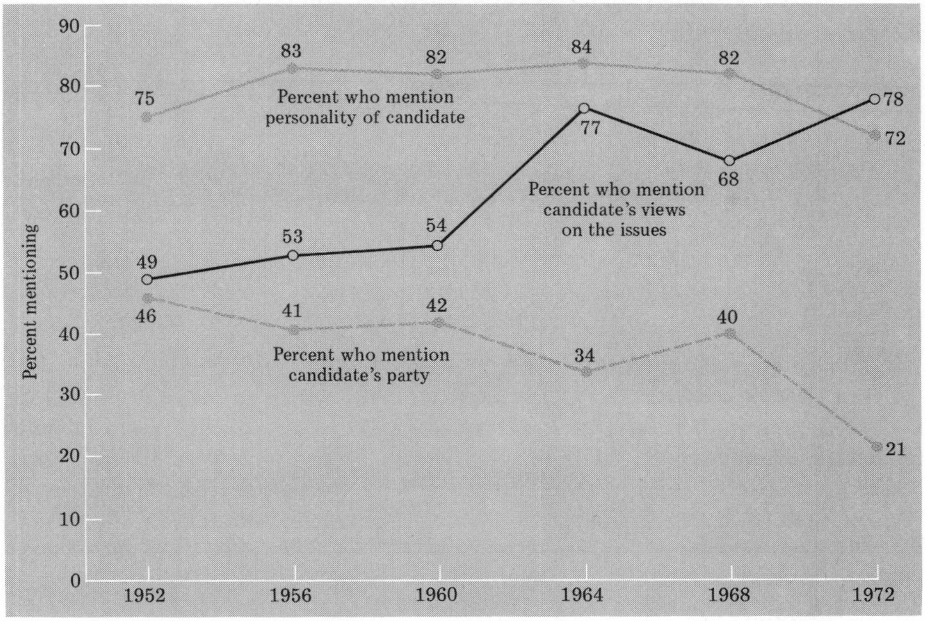

FIGURE 5.2
Candidate Evaluation in Terms of Personality, Issues, and Party Ties

Source: Based on data from the Center for Political Studies, Institute for Social Research, University of Michigan.

senators and their parties.[8] And even when issues become more important, party identification remains strong. In short, citizens are thinking about political issues and are less closely tied to their parties. But this doesn't mean they have become fully rational voters.

Where Do Political Attitudes Come From?

Citizens usually have no direct information about a political issue: "What's really going on in Portugal?" "Who is to blame for unemployment?" When people can't test their opinions against reality, they test them against other people's opinions. If they have already formed opinions but find that others feel differently, they will likely change their views, especially if those others are people they respect.

Who are those "others"? They include the following:

1. Peers. Studies have shown that people who spend a lot of time together are likely to have similar opinions. Primary groups—friends, families, neighbors—have similar views because they face similar political and social problems.

[8] U.S. Senate Subcommittee on Intergovernmental Relations of the Committee on Government Operations, *Confidence and Concern: Citizens View Their Government,* December 3, 1973.

People will change their opinions to win greater acceptance in the groups they belong to. This also makes it easier to get along with friends and relatives and gives people the feeling that their views are right—after all, others agree with them.

2. Political authorities. People respect the views of the leading political authorities. For example, if the Supreme Court has expressed an opinion, many Americans believe it must be the right one. The President, too, is important in the public mind. And since he is well covered by the news media, his views are widely known and usually respected.

The Watergate scandal and Nixon's resignation temporarily made the President less important as a political authority. But since no one else gets as much attention from the public, he is likely to remain a major source of political opinion.

3. Political parties. For a long time party identification was an important source of political attitudes. Political parties are less important now, but issues are often complicated, and they change all the time; also, a candidate's views on a specific issue may be unclear. So it is understandable that many citizens use their party as a guide in forming political opinions.

Currents and Crosscurrents

We seem to be saying here that all Americans are the same, but that isn't what we mean. When we look more closely at public opinion, we find a great variety of viewpoints. Most Americans agree on the general principles of democracy, but when it comes to specific cases the number falls to one-third, one-half, or two-thirds, depending on the groups we're talking about. This means there's quite a bit of disagreement.

SOCIAL BASES OF POLITICAL CONFLICT

This disagreement among opposing groups—and the question of which groups are important—is what American politics is all about. What groups of the population are opposed to one another? In other words, what are the social bases of political conflict? In the United States there are many such bases: people who live in different parts of the country; people who have different kinds of jobs; people of different race, age, religion, or ethnic background. The population could be divided up in many ways, and each group would show interesting differences in political attitude. Yet we would still find general agreement on basic democratic principles.

The most meaningful division of the population in terms of basic political beliefs is between the better-educated citizens and those who are less well educated. We have seen that commitment to democratic principles is strongest among political leaders. This is probably because such commitment is most often found among people with higher education, and these people are most likely to be politically active. Among citizens with a primary education, only one-third believe you have an obligation to be active in your community, but among those with a college education two-thirds feel that way.[9]

Black Americans and White Americans

Suppose we turn from the average American to the minority groups: the blacks, the Chicanos, the poor people of Appalachia. What are their political attitudes? We might expect such groups to show less support for "the system" and demand faster and bigger changes. It's hard to get information about some of these groups, but we know quite a bit about the political attitudes of blacks.

Blacks and whites seem to have similar views on the political system in general. But when asked about specific issues that affect them blacks respond much more negatively than whites. For example, a 1963 study found that almost 90 percent of white Americans expect equal treatment from the government, while a little less than half of the blacks expect such treatment. (See Table 5.4.)

Similar differences in political viewpoint have been found in more recent studies. Most dramatic are the differences between the races in their attitude toward the police. Blacks have less trust in the police and are less likely to expect fair treatment from them. In addition blacks are less satisfied with public services in their neighborhoods and complain more about high prices and low-quality goods in neighborhood stores.

So the different outlooks of black and white Americans mean the general agreement we see in the average American covers up basic differences between majority and minority groups? Let's look at some of the evidence.

RACIAL ATTITUDES

Have blacks and whites become more hostile toward each other since the 1950s? Certainly someone reading the daily paper would say so. But this simply means racial conflict has come out into the open. It doesn't mean racial hostility has increased.

In 1971 the National Opinion Research Center asked Americans how they felt about various groups. Both whites and blacks rated the opposite group favorably. On the average blacks don't say they dislike whites and whites don't say they dislike blacks. The two groups differ somewhat in their views toward black militants. Whites on the average say they dislike black militants, while blacks aren't hostile toward the militant group. But still the average black has a more favorable attitude toward whites than toward black militants. Thus there is evidence for a difference in viewpoint, but not for racial hatred.

[9] Gabriel A. Almond and Sidney Verba, *The Civic Culture* (Princeton: Princeton University Press, 1963), p. 176.

TABLE 5.4
Blacks are less likely than whites to expect equal treatment

	White Americans	*Black Americans*
Percent who say they expect equal treatment in a government office	87%	49%

Source: Based on data from Gabriel A. Almond and Sidney Verba. *The Civic Culture: Political Attitudes and Democracy in Five Nations.* Copyright © 1963 by Princeton University Press. Reprinted by permission of Princeton University Press.

White attitudes toward blacks have changed dramatically since the 1950s. In general whites have become more responsive to blacks and to their demands for change. In 1949 the National Opinion Research Center found that only 42 percent of white Americans thought blacks were as intelligent as whites. By 1956 this figure had risen to 78 percent. In 1942 only 30 percent of whites said white and black children should go to the same schools. By 1956 this figure had risen to 48 percent, and in 1972 the Harris poll found that 71 percent of white Americans thought schools should be desegregated.

But many whites still oppose desegregation, especially if it involves busing. In addition, along with white support for black demands has come

FIGURE 5.3
Differing Positions of Whites and Blacks

Source: National Opinion Research Center study, University of Chicago, 1971.

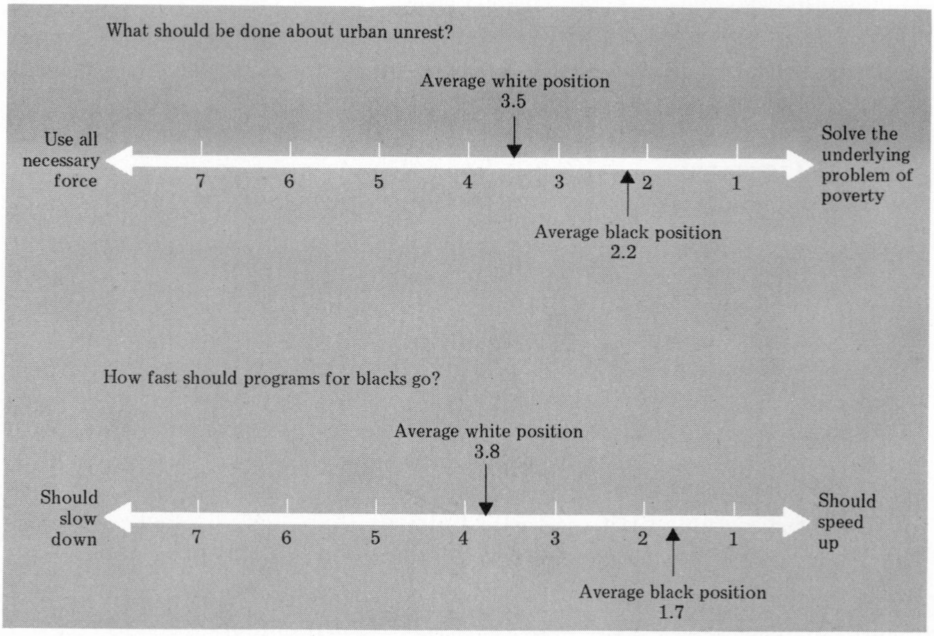

growing rejection of black militant tactics. In fact whites have generally rejected direct action by black groups, even when it is peaceful and legal. In 1968 the Harris poll found that 80 percent of black Americans supported the Poor People's March on Washington, compared to 29 percent of whites. Many whites feel that although black demands should be supported, things are moving too fast. (See Figure 5.3.)

The danger of continuing conflict lies in the greater differences between the races when you get down to specific issues, such as what the government should do about segregated housing, a subject both whites and blacks feel very strongly about. Blacks may trust the system in general, but they often distrust government officials. Whites may support black goals, but they aren't sure about specific aspects of those goals and are opposed to black demands for fast results.

Radical Politics in America

In the 1960s and early 1970s there was a great increase in radical politics in America. We can't discuss basic political beliefs without asking why some radical groups have challenged the democratic system in recent years.

We're not talking here about groups who are radical on a specific issue but about those who have radical attitudes toward the democratic system itself, who think the game should be played by other rules. Such an attitude can come from either the left or the right. Democratic procedures may be rejected by people who think they stand in the way of social change or by those who see such procedures as a cause of violence and social decay.

In fact, however, few groups feel that way. The young show greater distrust of the system than the population as a whole. According to a 1972 poll, about six out of ten think the country is democratic in name only and is run by special interests. But only 18 percent think the system is too rigid and needs radical change. Sixty-two percent are dissatisfied with political parties, but only 12 percent think the Constitution needs radical change.[10]

Many of the more radical attitudes toward American politics are found not among those who think the rules of the game should be changed but among those who see the rules working poorly. These would include people who want a greater voice in how governmental policy is made.

SUMMARY

Perhaps the most striking thing about the basic political beliefs of Americans is the fact that there have been important changes in the past ten years. Americans are much less satisfied with the political system than they used to

[10] Daniel Yankelovich, *The New Morality: A Profile of American Youth in the 1970s* (New York: McGraw-Hill, 1973), p. 116.

In the 1960s and early 1970s there was an increase in the numbers challenging the legitimacy of American government.

be. At the same time, people have become more aware of political issues and seem to be developing more consistent political viewpoints.

These changes in attitude, combined with major political issues such as race or Vietnam, can lead to a situation in which groups of citizens are in conflict on a large number of issues. The evidence on the political beliefs of blacks and whites suggests that this may be happening, but not as much as we might think if we talked to only the most radical members of each group.

Does Public Opinion Make a Difference?

Does public opinion influence governmental policy, or do officials largely ignore it? Most government officials—especially elected ones—pay a lot of attention to public opinion. Not only do political leaders follow the Gallup and Harris polls, they also have special *public opinion polls* taken for them to find out what people think about a specific issue. They believe public opinion is important and should be used as a guide—up to a point. Yet governmental policy isn't usually made in direct response to public opinion. Why?

AN ACTIVE MINORITY HAS MORE INFLUENCE

In 1972 the Harris poll asked citizens whether there should be a strict federal law requiring that hand guns be registered. Seventy percent said yes. But no such law has been passed. You might say these things take time; if the public still feels that way, a law will be passed sooner or later. But in *1940* the Gallup poll had asked a similar question, and 79 percent favored a gun-control law.

How can the majority of the population favor a specific policy for thirty-two years and still get no response from Congress? The answer is that the large majority favoring gun control doesn't feel very strongly about it, but some members of the group opposing gun control feel so strongly about it that they are politically active on this issue.

The example of gun control teaches two important lessons. One is that a small active minority has more influence than a large majority that doesn't care much. The other is that public-opinion polls, as we have seen, can sometimes give misleading information. Seven out of ten citizens favor gun control. But if the people who say yes don't care much while those who say no are strongly committed, it would be misleading to say these answers show great support for gun control.

PUBLIC OPINION REACTS TO PUBLIC POLICY

On many issues the public is uninformed and doesn't have clear preferences. However, people will often *react* strongly to governmental policy.

The history of public attitudes toward the Vietnam War is a good example. From the time the war first became a major public issue—around 1964–1965—the number of Americans satisfied with governmental policy declined. Yet public opinion was a poor guide for specific policy. When citizens were asked what they thought we should do about the war—escalate to win, deescalate and get out, or continue our present policy—their answers usually were divided among all three policies. How could the President use that as a guide? Furthermore, the public seemed to be pleased whenever the President did *anything*, as long as he did something.

It's clear that the public was unhappy and wanted results. Political leaders had to pay attention or they would lose in the next election, as the Demo-

Small groups of citizens, by being active, can have a bigger impact than their numbers would allow.

crats did in 1968. But what the public wanted was unclear. Johnson and Nixon were under pressure to do something, but public opinion couldn't tell them what that something should be.

LIMITS TO PUBLIC TOLERANCE

It's often said that public opinion sets limits: There are some things the public simply won't tolerate. This may be true, but there's a problem. You can't tell in advance what those limits are; you have to test the public to find out.

An example is public attitudes toward foreign policy. For many years it was believed that Americans wouldn't tolerate U.S. recognition of Communist China. Polls showed that a large majority of the American public was against such a policy. But when Nixon went to China in 1972 the Harris poll found that 73 percent of the people approved. The belief that the public wouldn't tolerate better relations with China was based on misleading information.

This example also shows the importance of political authorities as a guide to public opinion. Governmental policy toward China didn't reflect public attitudes; public attitudes reflected governmental policy. Change the policy, and the attitudes change.

On issues closer to home the limits set by public opinion may be more rigid. Attitudes on racial issues are harder to change, and the threat of punishment by voters who are unhappy about racial issues may be more real to an elected official than the threat of public dissatisfaction with foreign policy. On such issues public attitudes may be a strong influence on political leaders. Yet even here you can't be sure. As we have seen, public support for desegregation showed a large increase after 1956, when the Supreme Court declared segregated schools unconstitutional.

A NATION OF MANY PUBLICS

Usually you can't think of "the public" without dividing it up. There are many publics: the citizens who are politically active and those who aren't; the people who don't care much about a specific issue and those who care a lot. Above all there are differences in the things citizens care about. Different citizens become politically active on different issues. This is important in understanding how public attitudes affect governmental policies. Political leaders are likely to be responsive to the groups that care about an issue and are active in support of their views.

How We Find Out About Politics: II
Finding Out About Public Opinion

When you are given information about politics you should ask, Where did that information come from? How was it gathered? Could it be biased? In this book we present a lot of information about the attitudes and behavior of the American public. How do we get this information?

We all think we know how the American public feels about things, but we are often wrong. For one thing we sometimes look at our own views and assume that other people feel the same way. But people have very different attitudes toward political issues and react to governmental policies in different ways.

Sometimes we think we can learn more about public opinion by talking to our friends, neighbors, or fellow workers. This, too, can give us a distorted view of public opinion, since most of us meet only certain kinds of people. For example, during the late 1960s students at some colleges, seeing a lot of political activity against the Vietnam War, began to think everybody under 30 was against the war. But if you looked at the whole under-30 age group—including all college students plus those who didn't go to college—you found a wide variety of opinions and a great deal of support for the war. Thus by talking only to people like themselves some students got a distorted view of public opinion.

Even reading newspapers or watching TV can be misleading. For example, it's hard to tell whether people who write letters to newspapers represent the general public. Furthermore, the mass media usually look for the most dramatic news: a demonstration by a small minority or a speech by a well-known celebrity. Again, it's hard to say whether this represents public opinion.

THE SAMPLE SURVEY

The sample survey, or public-opinion poll, was developed to get around these weaknesses. Such surveys—the Gallup and Harris polls, studies by university groups, surveys done for political candidates—can give a very good picture of public opinion. They must be used with care, however, or the results may be misleading. Whom the pollster talks to and the questions that are asked are very important.

The Sample

The best way to find out about public opinion would be to talk to all Americans. But obviously that would take too much time and money. You can talk to only a small part of the population. The important thing is to choose people who represent the public as a whole—in other words, a sample.

Imagine a government inspector who wants to find out whether the jam made by a certain company meets government standards of purity. To find out if the jam is pure, the jars must be opened and tested. Since all the thousands of jars the company puts out cannot be opened, only a sample of the jars are tested. But what is a good sample?

1. *An adequate number.* Like the inspector who tests many different jars of jam, the good public-opinion pollster interviews a large number of people. Talking to one, two, or a few dozen citizens is not satisfactory. Even if they are chosen at random, they will be too few to tell us much about the general population. There's too great a chance that they will be very different from the rest of the public.

2. *A Wide Geographic Spread.* Just as a careful inspector tests jars from all of the company's jam factories, public-opinion surveys interview people from all over the country.

3. *A Variety of Types.* A jam inspector shouldn't limit the testing to one kind of jam; whatever is determined about strawberry jam has little to do with the raspberry jam. The most important thing about a sample is that it should try to include all types of citizens; otherwise it won't represent the population as a whole.

4. *A Random Selection.* The choice of jars to be tested is made by the jam inspector—oth-

erwise company officials might select a few jars from the most sanitary part of the factory for sampling. Similarly a good pollster chooses—on the basis of statistics—the people to be interviewed and doesn't wait for volunteers.

This aspect of randomness is important, it's what makes the sample survey more accurate than other ways of finding out about public opinion. The congressman or congresswoman who judges public attitudes by letters received is assuming that the opinions of "volunteers" represent public opinion in general. The great strength of the poll is that it finds out how *all* citizens feel, not just those who volunteer to express their views. But this can be a source of weakness as well, since many citizens don't have strong political opinions. They will usually answer a question even if they haven't thought about it before—and they might give a different answer the next day. This can produce misleading results.

The Questions

Sometimes two different polls come up with what seem to be contradictory results. When this happens it's usually because they have asked different questions. This, then, is another general rule of poll taking: The answers you get depend on the questions you ask.

People who have worked with sample surveys know how even small changes in wording can change the results. If you ask a question about "Russia," people will answer one way. If you ask about "Communist Russia," they'll respond more negatively, simply because you've included the word communist. Similarly if you ask about "aid to families with dependent children" you'll get different answers than if you ask about "welfare" or "government giveaway programs."

Thus polls are quite accurate in telling us how Americans respond to a specific question; however, the response depends on the wording of the question. Public-opinion polls give us useful information about the American public, but this information must be used carefully.

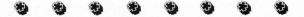

Questions for Review

1. Why do we need to find out about the political beliefs of Americans?
2. How strongly do Americans support the "rules of the game"? In what areas is their support weak?
3. How have the political beliefs and attitudes of Americans changed in recent years?
4. Are citizens rational voters? Do they have clear political views?
5. Discuss the role of party identification in Presidential elections since the 1950s.
6. Where do political attitudes come from?
7. Name an issue on which you would expect each of the following pairs of groups to differ: (*a*) blacks and whites; (*b*) old and young; (*c*) rich and poor; (*d*) northerners and southerners; (*e*) short people and tall people; (*f*) college-educated people and those who didn't finish high school.
8. Why have some groups developed radical attitudes toward the democratic system?
9. Why hasn't Congress passed a gun-control law even though most people would favor the law?
10. How do government officials respond to public opinion? Does public opinion have any effect on governmental policy?

Chapter 6

Social Bases of Conflict

Politics in America is about conflict and competition. The reason is clear: The government distributes benefits to citizens. Its major decisions involve the questions of who gets the benefits and who pays the costs. Even if everyone agreed on what kinds of policies the government should favor, there would still be conflict simply because the benefits to be distributed are limited. For example, even if everyone thought the most important thing for the government to do was to build more roads, there would still be conflict over what kind of roads to build and where.

But not everyone wants roads. Some people think more should be spent on mass transit and less on roads. Some think spending on transportation is less important than spending on education or housing. And some think what's most important is cutting spending in order to cut taxes.

Thus conflict arises not only about who should benefit from a particular policy but also about which policy to favor. Conflict also arises because a policy that benefits one group is seen by others as unfair or harmful to them. For example, a decision to build public-housing projects in suburban communities may be favored by blacks but opposed by white suburban residents.

This chapter is about the various groups that compete for benefits. Note that we're talking about groups, not individuals. Look at the following headlines:

Auto Workers Question Wage Guidelines
Legislature Seat for Chicanos Demanded
Pilots Call for Hijack Protection
Women's Group Challenges All-Male Court Nominations
Fishermen Protest Shortened Season

In each case we see a group of citizens demanding, challenging, protesting. Groups like these are called *interest groups* or *pressure groups*. Their members have interests in common; this is the basis for their political activity. And they pressure the government to favor those interests. But not all groups have common interests, and those that have common interests don't always put pressure on the government. This brings us to the question, Which groups are politically relevant and why?

What Makes a Group Politically Relevant?

Anything people have in common can be the basis of a political group. In the headlines we see groups based on sex (women), occupation (auto workers, pilots), recreational interests (fishermen), and ethnic background (Chicanos). Almost any interest or common characteristic can be the basis of a group: What about citizens of Japanese descent, red-haired citizens, tea drinkers, sausage makers, people who live in odd-numbered houses? Obviously not all groups are politically relevant. Chicanos and blacks are. A few years ago women were not; now they are. Suburban residents may or may not be politically relevant, depending on the suburb. But people who live in odd-numbered houses are unlikely ever to be a politically relevant group. Why is this so?

Three things make a group politically relevant: a common interest, awareness of that interest, and organization. In addition, groups are likely to be more successful if they can get their members to give time and money to the group.

COMMON INTERESTS

A group can be politically relevant if the characteristic that defines it—sex, occupation, place of residence—is something that creates a common interest, particularly an interest that can benefit from favorable governmental policy. Blacks clearly have such common interests in governmental policy on housing, school desegregation, and the like. Tea drinkers have a common interest in government tariff policy on tea. But people who live in odd-numbered houses don't, and it's hard to believe they ever will.

However, not all common interests lead to the creation of politically relevant groups. Some interests are more important than others. In the case of tea drinkers, the change in the price of tea that might result from a change in tariff policy doesn't affect them enough to make a difference. On the other hand, it would make a difference to tea importers. The price of tea has a large impact on those who earn their living by importing and selling tea; it has a small impact on those for whom it's just one item in a shopping basket.

This illustrates an important principle of American political life: Different groups of citizens are interested in different areas of governmental policy. Tea drinkers may be interested in tea tariffs; coffee drinkers probably couldn't care less. Chicanos will be interested in Spanish-language teaching in the public schools; citizens in states with no Spanish-speaking minority won't be interested. Furthermore, the level of interest may be very high for some groups but fairly low for others. Chicanos will be interested in Spanish-language teaching in the schools, and so will non-Spanish-speaking residents of the community. But for the Chicanos this is an important issue having to do with their culture, while for the other residents it may be a less-important issue having to do with the cost of public education. What this means is that on any issue some citizens may be very concerned and others only mildly concerned; many won't care at all.

What kinds of interests can be the basis of a politically relevant group?

Economic Interests. Economic interests are the most common basis for political activity. Workers want higher wages. Businessmen are concerned about price controls, tariffs, and other governmental policies that affect their income. And all citizens are interested in the government's tax policies.

Power Interests. Citizens want political control over their own lives and over the government of their community. So there are conflicts over who gets elected or appointed to office, how districts are zoned for elections, and so on.

Political power can be used to get favorable action on economic matters. But people also want political power for its own sake. Many of the most bitter conflicts in America are about who will control the government.

Way-of-Life-Interests. It's hard to give a precise name to this broad set of interests. They aren't clearly economic or political but, rather, are based on the desire to live a particular kind of life. Citizens may want to keep their community the way it is—residential, not industrial; white, not integrated. Or they may want to change it. These interests, too, can be the basis of a political group.

SELF-AWARENESS

It's not enough for a group of citizens to have interests in common; they have to be aware of those interests. Groups become politically relevant only when their members are aware of their common interests. In recent years women's groups have been active in trying to get equal pay for equal work. The problem is not a recent one; unequal pay is traditional. But because women have become *concerned* about unequal treatment, they have become a politically relevant group.

ORGANIZATION AND LEADERSHIP

Groups that are organized can pressure the government more effectively, and groups that have leadership have people who can speak for them to the government. Also, good leadership can get greater effort and commitment from group members. One of the most important jobs of a leader is to increase the self-awareness of followers. This may be seen in the case of the migrant farm workers, who until recently had common interests and some self-awareness but little organization. Under the leadership of Cesar Chavez this group has become politically relevant.

MOTIVATING GROUP MEMBERS

Why do citizens with similar interests join with others to participate in political activity? At first the answer seems obvious: Citizens work together to pressure the government to respond to their needs. Women work with other women to influence governmental policy on sex discrimination; blacks join other blacks to get the government to build more low-cost housing; businessmen form groups to lobby for favorable economic policies.

Goals like these are the policy goals of political groups; they're what the group wants the government to do. However, as we saw in the Introduction, it's not "rational" for a citizen to join a group to work for these goals. Why should a woman work with other women to get the state government to pass the Equal Rights Amendment? One more person won't make much difference, so it won't make much difference if she does nothing. Besides, she'll benefit from the amendment even if she doesn't work to get it passed.

The government offers the citizen no choice about contributing to the common goal. Citizens must pay taxes and obey the law. Groups of citizens with common interests, by contrast, can't force their members to work for the policy goals of the group. For example, the women's movement can't force other women to join.

Why do people contribute time and money to political groups even though it isn't "rational" to do so? One answer is that people don't always do things because they're rational. But the groups that succeed in getting people to work for them usually offer something more than a chance to work for the group's policy goal. Successful groups offer their members other rewards. One such reward is the feeling of group identity. Social movements like the women's movement give their members a sense of belonging, and this plays a big role in keeping members active and committed.

There are other rewards for members of groups. Some political groups can provide economic benefits or recreational opportunities. For some, joining a political group is a way of meeting people. We're not saying that members of political groups claim to be committed to the group's policy goals but really participate only in order to make friends or get a feeling of group identity. Participants may be strongly committed, but the other rewards the group offers may stimulate them to greater activity. Political groups that can offer these rewards are likely to be more successful.

Groups in America: Many and Varied

In recent years there's been a growing tendency for citizens to become aware of their common interests and to organize themselves into politically relevant groups. The women's movement is a good example, but many other types of groups have recently become more relevant—groups of consumers, commuters, tenants, homosexuals, and so on. These groups have had interests in common for a long time, but they have only recently added to those interests the self-awareness and organization that make them politically relevant.

Let's look now at some of the different types of political groups in America.

ETHNIC AND RACIAL GROUPS

When we talk about ethnics or ethnic politics, we tend to think of Irish Americans, Polish Americans, Jewish Americans, or perhaps black Americans. There's no absolute definition of ethnicity, but what we're talking about is fairly clear. Within an *ethnic group*, *ethnicity* is a fundamental sense of group identity based on national origin. This sense of identity is passed down through the family. It has to do with where you live or where you come from. It's what you say when someone asks, "What are you?"

Ethnicity is often based on specific things like language. People who speak the same language have something very fundamental in common: the ability to communicate. Groups of people who have lived together for a long time also develop an ethnic identity. Or—and this is particularly true in the United States—ethnic identity may be based on country of origin. Other ties such as race or customs hold such groups together.

America has always been called a melting pot. Here people from Europe, Asia, and Africa melted together to become the American people. This is what the history books say, and it's partly true. For one thing, most immigrants have become American citizens. For another, the people who poured into the

United States in the late nineteenth and early twentieth centuries wound up speaking the same language. The earlier language sometimes survived, but English became the dominant language. Teachers and government officials believed being an American meant speaking English, and for the most part the immigrants accepted this situation.

Thus, say the history books, out of the immigrants from Europe, Asia, and Africa the melting pot made one nation. Not quite. Some groups didn't "melt" easily. Blacks were denied freedom and citizenship until the Civil War. Even then they didn't get all the benefits of citizenship. Similarly—though not as openly—immigrants from Asia were denied full citizenship. And the only Americans who weren't immigrants—the American Indians—were also denied full citizenship. Even white ethnics refused to melt completely. Ethnic identity remains strong, ethnic organizations are active, and ethnic interests come into conflict. Ethnic patterns are found throughout American politics.

Ethnic politics has to do with the interests, direct and indirect, of the various ethnic groups. The direct interests involve the desire of a group—despite the melting pot—to keep its ethnic identity. But the indirect interests may be more important politically. The groups that today form the various ethnic communities came to this country as immigrants. Each group in turn found itself the most deprived. The Irish, when they came in the nineteenth century, found themselves with the worst jobs, living in poor neighborhoods, and dealing with local governments controlled by the Yankee residents. They had to struggle with better-established groups for better jobs and housing and for political power. A generation later when the Italian immigrants came, history repeated itself, now with the Irish in a somewhat more stable economic position and in control of the local governments.

Black immigration from the South to northern cities again repeated this pattern, at least in part. Like the previous immigrants, the blacks often find themselves in the lowest positions in terms of housing, jobs, and political power. And they often face a city government controlled by other ethnic groups.

The "White Ethnics." The waves of immigrants who came to America in the late nineteenth and early twentieth centuries often gathered in the cities. And because they came in groups, joining family members or looking for familiar faces or a familiar language, large numbers of people from the same "old country" would gather in particular cities. These groups—the Irish, the Poles and Slavs, the Italians—found themselves at the lowest economic levels. But they had one basis of power: the vote. The big political machines in New York, Boston, and Chicago depended on the ethnic vote.

The white ethnics illustrate the three factors that make a group of citizens politically relevant. They had common interests because they were newcomers in a strange country; they were aware of those interests because they lived in ethnic neighborhoods; and they were organized by the political parties that wanted their votes. These groups also gave their members a strong sense of group identity.

As generations pass, the interests that hold ethnic groups together fade.

They are no longer new residents holding low-level jobs. Many move out of the ethnic neighborhoods into areas that are ethnically mixed. This makes for fewer interests in common and less self-awareness. Besides, the political machine has lost much of its power. In short, the basis for ethnic politics seems to be fading.

Yet many third-generation ethnics are developing a sense of ethnic self-awareness. Ethnic voting is still common in many cities: The candidate with the right name can count on support from many people with a similar ethnic background. Studies show that ethnicity also plays a role in Presidential elections. In part this renewal of ethnic politics is a reaction to the challenge from other groups such as black Americans. Many of the white ethnic groups have "made it"—have skilled work, a decent income, a house and car. Challenged by the blacks—a group with a firm sense of identity—white ethnics have begun to renew their ethnic ties.

Blacks. From the beginning black Americans have been important in American politics—but as the subjects of governmental policy, not as participants. Before the Civil War blacks were barred from political life. Even in states where there was no slavery, free blacks were usually denied the right to vote. As mentioned earlier, there's some similarity between the position of blacks as the newest immigrants to northern cities and the position of the earlier white immigrants. But it would be unrealistic to ignore the great differences, which can be summed up in two words: slavery and race.

The white immigrants were poor and often uneducated. They were discriminated against, and they were crowded into ghettos. Still, they came to a nation dominated by the principle of equality, and they entered a society where the laws supported this principle. By the 1840s almost all men could vote. But the principle of equality and the right to vote were clearly limited to whites.

The Civil War and the Thirteenth, Fourteenth, and Fifteenth Amendments to the Constitution tried to change this situation. Black Americans couldn't be denied citizenship, the vote, or the protection of the laws. But the meaning of these amendments was watered down. The vote was taken away from blacks in the South; segregated facilities were legally accepted; and in many ways the gains of blacks were seriously reduced.

The continuing conflict between black Americans and white Americans is a result of two factors: interdependence and conflicting goals. When the conflict is severe and there seems to be little chance of agreement, one solution is to reduce the interdependence—to separate. In the early days of the Republic, many white leaders thought the solution to the issue of slavery would be to send the blacks back to Africa. Black leaders often supported that position. More recently the various black separatist groups have called for separation within the United States: separate communities, separate schools, sometimes separate parts of the country.

Separatist movements have never been successful, but they have led to increased black self-awareness. Blacks have become a strong political force in recent years because they have developed self-awareness and organization. The growth of black self-awareness has many sources. The role of the civil-rights movement of the 1950s and 1960s is important, and so is that of the news media—particularly TV—in communicating the new movement to blacks in every part of the country.

As for organization, the history of the civil-rights movement has been a history of organization as well. The NAACP, the Urban League, the Southern Christian Leadership Council, CORE, the Black Panthers, Operation Breadbasket—the list could be made much longer—show how many and how varied are the bases of black political organization. Blacks aren't organized in one common group, nor are they all organized. But a variety of organizations are making blacks a relevant political force.

OTHER TYPES OF GROUPS

In the following sections we'll describe some of the other types of groups in America. We can then turn to the more interesting question of how they relate to one another.

Occupational Groups. Everyone is concerned about his occupational group—how well teachers, farmers, doctors, or plumbers are doing. But not

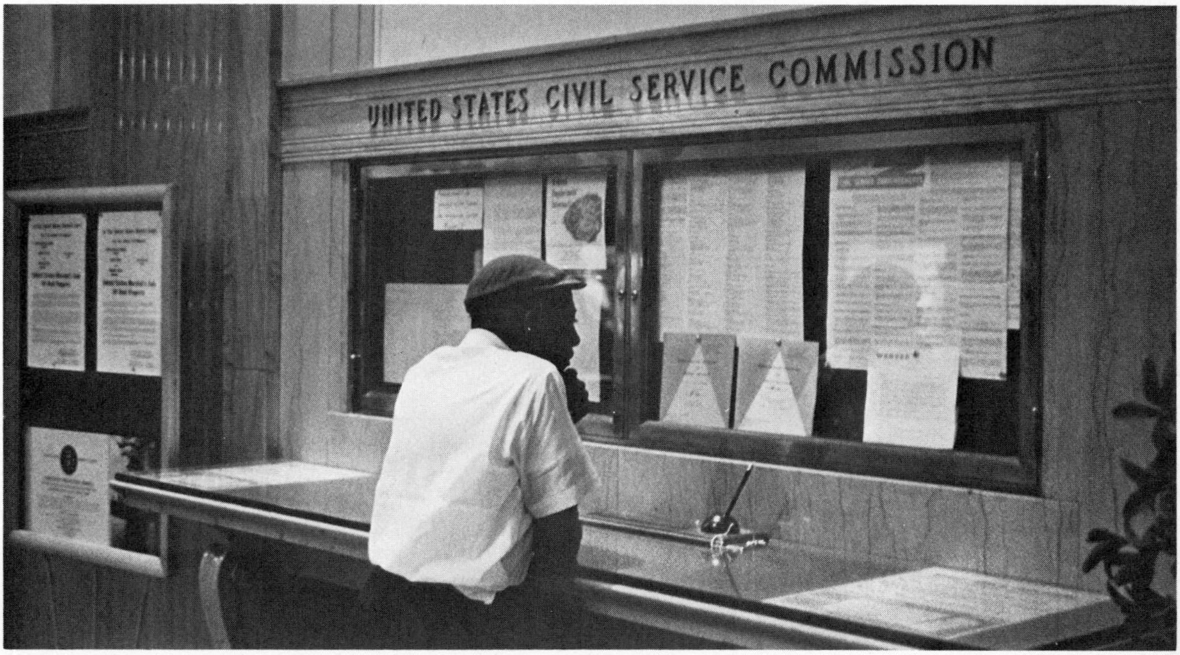

Government policies affect the economic interests of black Americans.

all occupational groups are politically relevant in terms of common interests, self-awareness, and organization.

Take common interests. Small shopkeepers are an important occupational group, but the members of the group don't have a "common fate"; one shopkeeper may do well while another goes bankrupt. Of course all shopkeepers may be hurt by inflation or recession, but then they're affected as members of the general economy, not as shopkeepers.

Compared with shopkeepers or lawyers, such groups as teachers or auto workers are much more likely to have a common fate and common interests. Teachers have interests in common because their salaries and working conditions depend on the governments they work for; auto workers have common interests because they depend on a single industry.

The more the government's activities affect a particular occupation, the more likely it is that the occupational group will be politically active. Look at the difference between doctors and lawyers. Governmental policies affect the practice of medicine much more than the practice of law. And doctors are active as an occupational group through the American Medical Association (AMA). Lawyers are more likely to run for office, but in so doing they aren't representing the legal profession.

This difference is related to a simple but important political fact: Where the government is active, citizens are likely to be active as well. When governmental programs touch the lives of particular groups, they're likely to become politically involved.

Occupation becomes the basis for group action when government policy affects a group. Here truckers protest speed restrictions.

Occupational groups also differ in self-awareness and organization. These two characteristics are linked: The better a group is organized, the more likely it is that its members are aware of their common interests. Take, for example, the difference between organized and unorganized labor. Workers who aren't unionized are politically weak, both because they have no leaders to speak for them and because they are likely to have less self-awareness. For a long time teachers were unorganized because they believed unionization wasn't appropriate for a professional group; migrant farm workers were unorganized because their working conditions made it hard to form groups. In recent years, as both groups have become better organized, they have become more active politically.

Income Groups. Income and occupation go together to create what is often called social class. So why don't the poor form a relevant political group to pressure the government to redistribute the resources of society?

Efforts have been made in the past to form such groups, and recently there have been poor people's groups cutting across occupation and race. But there are problems with political groups based on income. It's true that the poor have interests in common, but there are many factors that keep them from becoming politically active in relation to those interests. For one thing, political action depends on resources like time and money, which the poor can't afford. And the poor are divided by occupation, race, and ethnicity. The poor could become important as a political group, but income isn't yet a strong basis for organized political action.

Regional Groups. The place where people live and work is also a basis for common interests. Regional politics has played an important role in U.S. history. The South, for example, is a distinct region in terms of culture, history, and political behavior. Southern voters have traditionally identified with the Democratic party. And its representatives in Congress have tended to vote as a group, often joining northern Republicans to form a strong conservative force. However, the "solid South" has become less solid since the Eisenhower years. Industrialization and population shifts, as well as the political awakening of the southern black, have changed the social and political life of the region.

Regional politics is important in America because it's always well organized. By this we simply mean elections have a regional structure: We elect representatives to Congress from particular districts or states. This point is so obvious that it's easy to overlook its importance. Why don't we elect representatives from occupational groups—some to represent plumbers, some to represent lawyers or farmers? Or by race—the blacks elect their representatives, the whites theirs, the Chicanos theirs? The argument for regional representation is that citizens living in the same region have similar interests, but this is only partly true. In some ways we have interests in common with people living in the same state or district, but in some ways we may have more in common with people of the same race, religion, or occupation living in other parts of the nation.

But the fact is that the American system of representation is organized on the basis of place of residence, and this is unlikely to change. This automatically makes regional politics important.

Sex and Age Groups. Can either sex or age be the basis for a politically relevant group? Ten years ago we might have said "maybe" for age but "no" for sex. Today we would say "yes" to both. The special needs of older citizens, together with the youth culture, have made age more relevant as a political force, and sex discrimination has become a major issue.

Women aren't a minority; they account for 51 percent of the population. But the history of the women's movement is similar in many ways to that of minority groups in American politics. As pointed out earlier in the chapter, the case of women illustrates the importance of self-awareness as well as common interests in creating a politically relevant group.

Special-Interest Groups. We've been describing groups of American citizens in terms of ethnic background, occupation, sex, and place of residence. Political groups are often based on social characteristics like these, but they become politically relevant only if their members are aware of their common interests.

However, some groups are based more directly on shared interests and less on social characteristics. These interests also show great variety. Groups form around common recreational interests such as skiing or bird watching; around social concerns such as mental health or pollution; around cultural interests such as books or theater. Like other groups these special-interest groups become politically relevant when their interests are affected by governmental policy. For example, a recreational group may begin simply as a group of citizens with a common interest in skiing or bird watching. But when these nonpolitical activities begin to depend on governmental policies such as preservation of wilderness areas, the group may become politically active.

Overlapping Memberships

To understand how group identifications affect political life, we must first look at the relationships among groups in America. Two points are important here: (1) There is a great variety of groups in America. There is no set of dominant groups. (2) These groups can overlap. Each citizen belongs to many groups at once. Citizens have at the same time ethnic identity, occupational status, regional location, religion, and so on.

Which of these group identifications will be important politically? It varies. At some times and on some issues, one group identification will be important; at other times others will matter more. Catholic steelworkers living in a suburb of Cleveland will sometimes think of themselves strictly as steelworkers, supporting policies or candidates that seem favorable to workers. At other times they'll think of themselves as Catholics, looking at an issue like abortion law or aid to parochial schools from that point of view. And at still other times they'll think of themselves as suburban residents, perhaps opposing a plan to tax people from the suburbs who work in the city.

For some Americans, however, one group identification is stronger than any other. Black militants respond to all issues in terms of racial identity; militant members of the women's movement respond in terms of sexual identity. The results for political life are important. Citizens having a variety of group identifications are unlikely to feel very strongly about any of them; they are more willing to compromise, less firm in their beliefs than "single-identity" citizens. The single-identity citizen is likely to be more militant, firmer, less compromising.

An important characteristic of group identifications in America is that they tend to crosscut rather than reinforce one another. To understand these concepts, imagine a society where people are divided by religion (into Catholics and Protestants), occupation (into workers and managers), and place of residence (into city and suburban residents). If these three divisions of society were reinforcing rather than crosscutting, citizens who were similar in one of these ways would be similar in the other two ways as well. The society might be divided into Catholic workers living in the city and Protestant managers living in the suburbs. This division would affect all areas of politics. Catholics want aid to parochial schools; Protestants don't. Workers want controls on profits; managers want controls on wages. Those who live in the city want suburban residents to share the costs of city services; suburban residents don't want to share these costs.

Such a situation could produce a lot of political tension. The two groups have nothing in common; they're divided on every issue. If one group gets control of the government, the other will have little reason to believe its interests will be protected, since the group in power differs from it in every way.

But suppose these group identifications are crosscutting rather than reinforcing. In this case some workers will be Protestant and others Catholic; some will live in the suburbs and some in the city. Citizens who are divided on one issue will be united on others. The Protestant worker will disagree with the Catholic worker on aid to parochial schools, but they'll agree on profit controls. Protestant workers who live in suburbs will have interests in common with other citizens who live there—Catholic or Protestant, workers or managers.

In general American politics is characterized by crosscutting patterns of group identification. Catholic workers join with Protestant workers on some issues (economic ones) and with Catholic businessmen on others (parochial schools, perhaps). These patterns have an important impact on American politics.

Patterns of Division and Competition

We've described the politically relevant groups in American society because it's between these groups that the political struggle takes place. These groups have different interests and therefore put different pressures on the government. Each tries to get the government to support policies that benefit it and, in so doing, often comes into conflict with other groups.

It will be useful to look now at the variety of patterns of competition and conflict among groups. You'll find it easier to understand any particular issue if you can fit it into one of these patterns.

Political conflict begins with conflicting interests. One group of citizens prefers one policy (call it A); another prefers a different policy (call it B). In addition some citizens feel strongly about the issue, others feel less strongly, and some don't care. In Example 1 the space under the curved line stands for the number of people who take various positions. In this example the largest group of Americans are indifferent between A or B, and those who do have an opinion believe in it rather mildly. Furthermore, the number of citizens on each side of the issue is about the same. Many issues take this form, and on these issues there's little conflict, little excitement, and perhaps no governmental activity at all. It makes little difference what the government does, because there's little concern on either side. Government officials are fairly free to do anything they want about the issue.

Example 2 shows a different pattern. Like Example 1, it's a situation where you'd expect little conflict or competition, simply because all citizens seem to agree in strongly supporting position A. An example of such a situation might be the hostile attitude of Americans toward the enemy in most wars before Vietnam. Such a pattern doesn't lead to conflict between groups. It can be a strong political force; government leaders can use it to get public support for an all-out war effort. Or it can greatly limit freedom of actions, for example, if the government favors a milder policy toward the enemy.

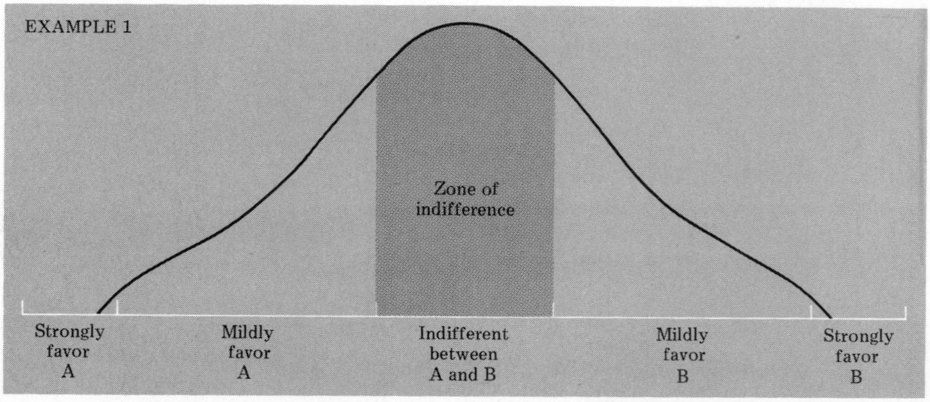

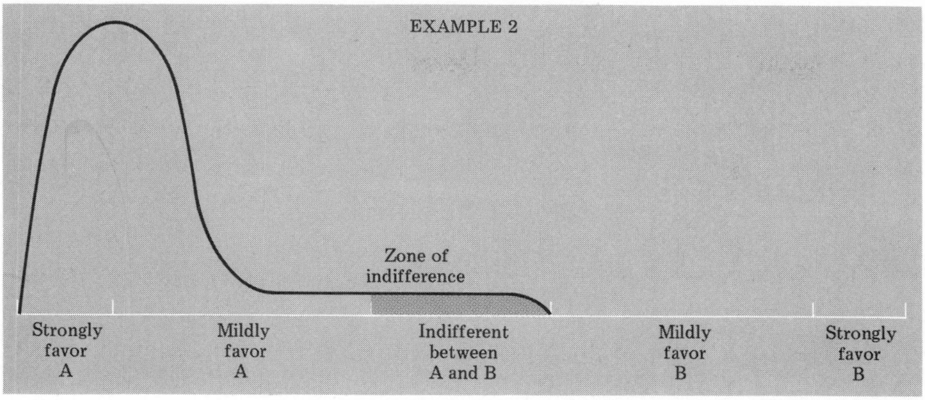

A pattern of this type, however, can have dangerous results for democracy: Woe to the few citizens who support position B! Even those who don't care may be in trouble. In wartime the freedoms guaranteed by the First Amendment have often been suspended or limited.

Example 3 is very different from the first two. It shows a major division of the population: About half the citizens strongly prefer A and about half strongly prefer B. Very few are in between. It's obvious that a population divided in this way—particularly if the choice between A and B is an important one—is in a situation that can lead to severe conflict. This may describe the United States just before the Civil War.

This pattern is rare, however (though a similar pattern, discussed later, is becoming more common). Issues that split the population down the middle don't arise very often. For example, during the Vietnam War citizens were asked their policy preferences in relation to the war. They could place them-

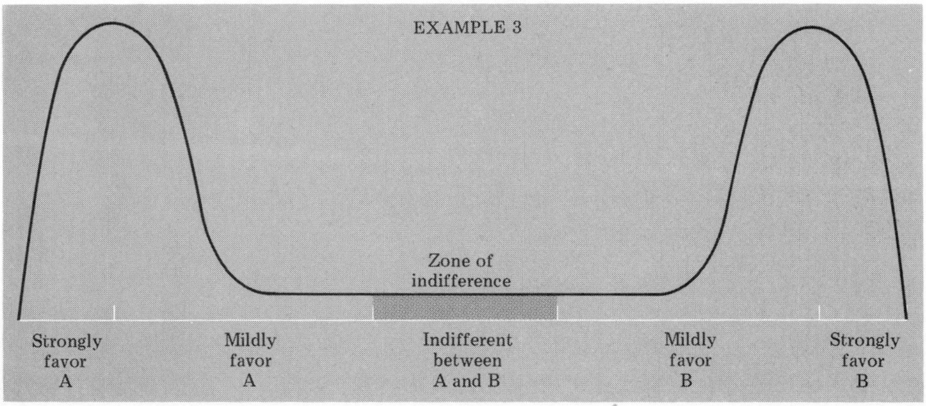

FIGURE 6.1
Positions on Vietnam

Source: Based on data from an unpublished study on Vietnam and the urban crisis by Richard Brody, Benjamin Page, and Sidney Verba, 1968.

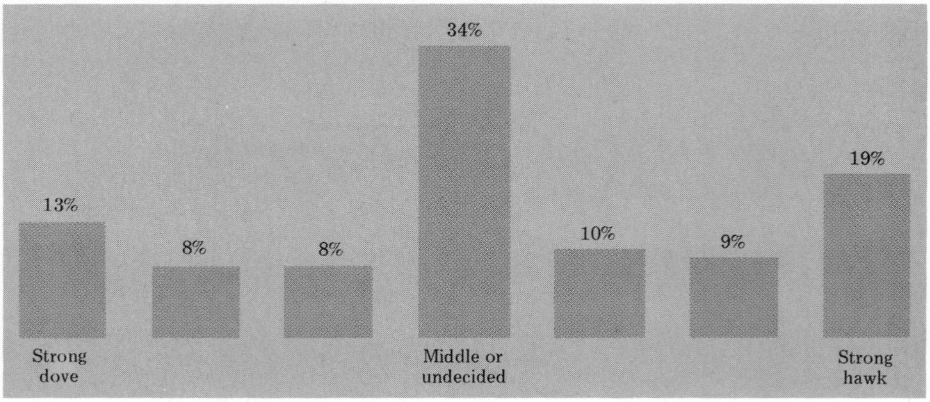

selves in a "strong dove" position (withdraw immediately from Vietnam); they could place themselves in a "strong hawk" position (use all possible force to win). Figure 6.1 shows where they placed themselves. Some citizens took a strong position at one extreme or the other. But the largest group is found in the middle, and many others took a mild position on one side or the other.

This tendency toward the center is seen in the results of a 1970 Gallup poll, which asked people whether they considered themselves liberal or conservative in politics. (See Figure 6.2.) These results differ slightly from what the poll found in previous years: The conservative group has become somewhat larger than the liberal group. But the important point is that opinions tend to lie near the center. In fact the pattern of citizen preferences across a number of issues often takes this form. It can be seen in Example 4.

FIGURE 6.2
Positions on Liberalism and Conservatism

Source: National Opinion Research Center study, University of Chicago, 1973.

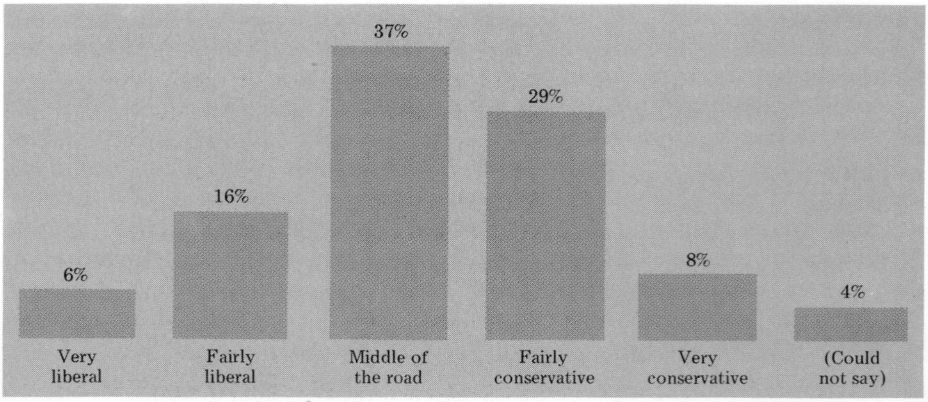

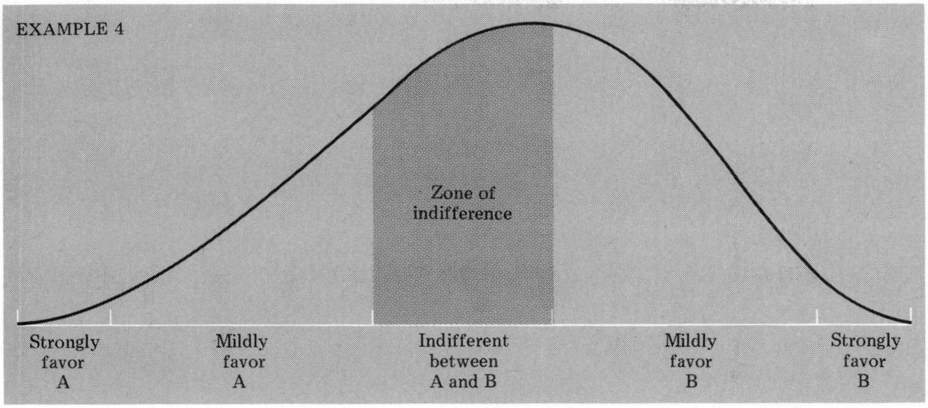

This situation is similar to what we saw in Example 1. There's no strong political opinion, but what there is seems to favor position B. Many ordinary political issues take this form: A fairly large part of the population mildly favors one position; another group, not quite as large, favors the other. And in between there's a large group that doesn't care. Policy B stands a good chance of getting favorable action from the government, though this is by no means certain. Those who favor position B may have no organization or leadership. Or they may need support from some of those who don't care, and because they feel mildly about the issue they may not try hard enough. Even if they succeed there won't be much conflict.

This pattern is a fairly good illustration of the division of the American population into Democrats and Republicans. Most Americans identify with one party or the other; some are independent. But few would be strongly opposed to having members of the other party in leadership positions. Over the years more citizens have identified with the Democrats than with the Republicans. But this doesn't mean a Democrat is always elected President. Since these party identifications aren't very strong, citizens often switch from one side to the other.

In general the pattern of division in the United States tends to be like that shown in Example 4. Such a situation is often praised because it makes for stability. Granted, a society divided as in Example 3 is more likely to fly apart. But the pattern shown in Example 4 means stability in another sense: Nothing happens. Such a pattern can stand in the way of needed social change.

Two other patterns are relevant in American politics—one a traditional pattern that has applied to many issues, the other a pattern that has developed in recent years. Look at Example 5. Here a small part of the population, strongly in favor of a particular position, faces the bulk of the population, which either doesn't care or mildly favors the other position. The fact that such a pattern is common should come as no surprise; as we saw earlier, dif-

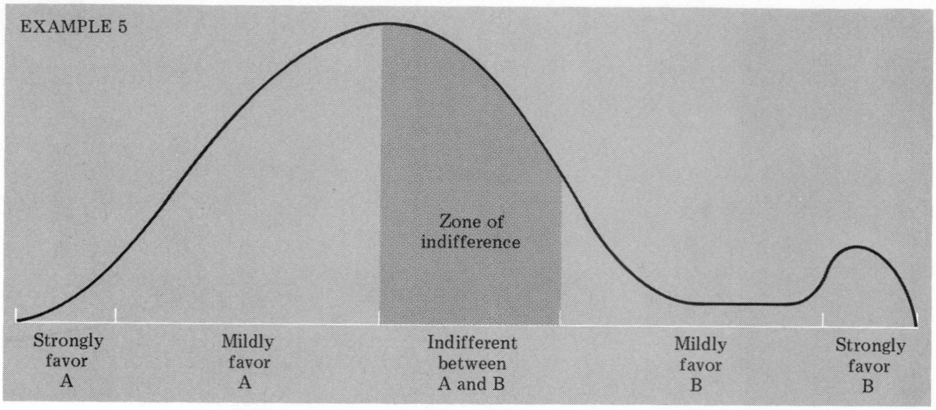

ferent groups of citizens have different levels of concern about various problems. Drug manufacturers care a lot about government regulation of the manufacture or sale of their products, since it might cut into their profits. Citizens who don't use many drug products don't care. Citizens who use a lot of drug products would prefer such regulation, but they still are unlikely to care as much as the manufacturers.

The pattern seen in Example 5 can lead to pressure-group politics. An example is the issue of gun control. About 70 percent of the American public favors gun control. The opposing group is small, but it cares very strongly about the matter. This intense minority is more likely to be organized and to express its views to the government; therefore it's more likely to get its way.

In Example 6 we see an intense minority facing an equally intense majority. Such a situation would exist if a social group was severely deprived and was cut off from the rest of the population by a series of reinforcing divisions.

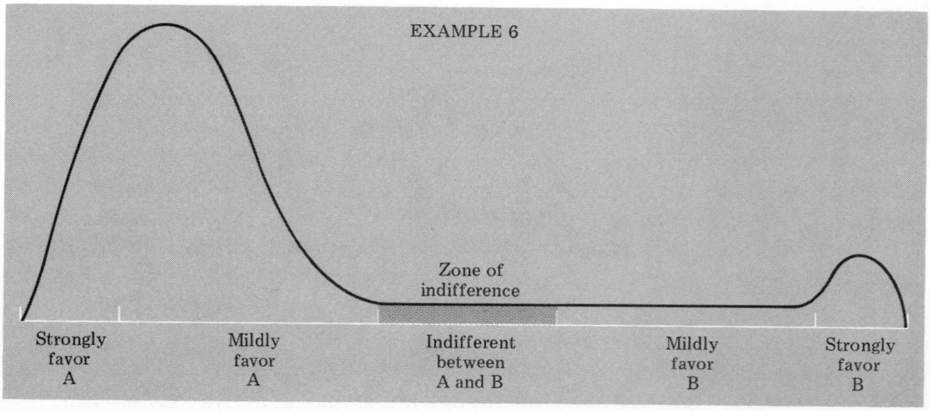

Consider the situation in many American cities. In the decaying central city lives a group that is poor and black; in the surrounding suburbs lives a group that is white and better off. They are divided by race, income, and place of residence, and therefore they have few interests in common. The central-city residents want more social services, and they want the suburban residents to share the costs of those services; they want integrated schools and housing. The people who live in the suburbs are opposed to them in every way.

In 1973 citizens were asked their policy preferences on integrated housing: Should the government make sure blacks can buy houses in white neighborhoods or should it not get involved? The answers showed that most Americans hold one view or the other and feel strongly about it. Those who believe the government shouldn't get involved outnumber the others by two to one. Such an issue is said to "polarize" the society. If we consider white and black opinions separately, we find that while there are some whites who strongly favor integrated housing, the bulk of the white population is opposed. The majority of the blacks, on the other hand, want the government to support a policy of integration. Such a pattern leads to conflict.

CONCLUSION

There are many patterns of division and competition in America. On some issues there's general agreement among almost all Americans, on others the public may be divided into two hostile groups, and on still others an intense minority may face a less-intense majority. We can't predict the particular issues that will arise. But the patterns just described should be helpful in understanding new issues and the impact they're likely to have on the political process.

CONTROVERSY
Can There Be a Poor People's Political Movement?

The bulk of the income in America is earned by a minority of the population. About 75 percent of the income is earned by the richest 49 percent of the population. Why doesn't the other 51 percent organize and become active politically in order to change that situation? After all, they account for a majority of the citizens.

Political struggle between the haves and the have-nots has been rare in America; political conflict has never involved all the rich vs. all the poor. Most people agree that this is the case, but there is controversy over why this is so and whether politics should be organized in this way.

One Side What is needed in America is a poor people's movement, a union of all those who don't get the full benefits of American society. Such a union of poorer citizens—blacks, Chicanos, and other minority groups; factory workers; low-paid clerks; old people living on pensions—could elect a government that would equalize the wealth in America. And such a movement would be "natural"; everyone is concerned about his or her income. Such an important issue could overcome all the differences among the various groups of poorer citizens. If this part of the population isn't aware of its common interests, it's because it lacks political leadership.

The Other Side The reasons why America won't be divided into the haves and the have-nots in the future are the same ones that have prevented such a division in the past. The only thing the poor have in common is low income. They don't think of themselves as members of a single group—a white unskilled worker doesn't identify with a black unskilled worker or with a white farmer. They have a common interest in higher income; who doesn't? But there's so much else that divides them—race, region, sex, age, and so on—that the poor are unlikely ever to put together a political movement. And it's a good thing, too. If the nation were divided politically between the haves and the have-nots, that is, if there were no other bases of political division, the possibility of severe conflict would be very great.

Questions for Review

1. What is an interest group?

2. What three factors make a group politically relevant?

3. Which of the following groups is likely to be politically relevant? Why? (*a*) teachers; (*b*) left-handed people; (*c*) doctors; (*d*) people opposed to abortion; (*e*) women; (*f*) southerners; (*g*) suburban residents; (*h*) skiers; (*i*) Jews; (*j*) college presidents; (*k*) blacks; (*l*) vegetarians

4. What motivates people to give their time and money to political groups?

5. Why did the immigrants who came to America in the nineteenth century develop into politically relevant ethnic groups?

6. What effect does governmental activity have on the activity of political groups?

7. Why don't poor people organize as a political group?

8. Define reinforcing and crosscutting identifications. Which type is more common in America?

9. Describe some of the patterns of conflict in American society. Give examples.

Treat.

Chapter 7

Interest Groups in America

As we saw in the preceding chapter, the American public is divided into many different interest groups. We discussed the reasons why some groups become politically relevant while others don't. Groups that are organized are likely to have a greater effect on governmental policy than groups that are not organized.

In this chapter we'll look more closely at political organizations, organizations that try to influence governmental policy. How many interest groups are there in the United States? How powerful are they? What makes some more powerful than others?

The Role of Interest Groups

Students of politics disagree about the power of interest groups. Some argue that all you need to know about American politics can be learned by studying the role of interest groups. Policy doesn't start with Congress and the President; rather, it starts with the demands of lobbies and organized interest groups. The government acts as a "broker," seeing that each group gets a little something in response to its demands. Thus the conflicting pressures from organized groups determine governmental policy.

Most writers on politics think this is an exaggeration. Governmental policy isn't just a response to interest-group pressures. Organized groups aren't all-powerful. But organized groups are better able to pressure the government than unorganized groups. And this is important in determining who will benefit from governmental policy.

People also disagree on the question, Do the activities of interest groups hurt society as a whole? Pressure groups speak for the "selfish" interests of particular groups of citizens: doctors, farmers, teachers, veterans. These aren't just groups of rich citizens trying to get an even bigger slice of the economic pie. Organizations also represent the interests of blacks, welfare mothers, labor, and so on. These groups are "selfish" not because their demands aren't reasonable but because they represent only the interests of particular groups of citizens. They don't take into account the needs and problems of other groups. Each is out to "take care of its own."

Critics of pressure groups argue that this system is harmful to society as a whole. Pressure groups compete for the attention of government officials in order to get some benefit for their group. The general public interest is ignored; no one plans for the problems of society as a whole. In fact interest groups often develop close ties with the government, in which case the result is a governmental policy that benefits a particular group and may hurt the rest of society.

Critics further point out that the pressure-group system also limits the range of citizen interests communicated to the government. In general the interests of the richer and better-educated members of society are more likely to be communicated in this way.

On the other hand, it's often argued that there's no conflict between the selfish interests of particular groups and the general public good. The public good doesn't exist outside of the selfish interests of groups of citizens. Rather, it is the sum of the needs and preferences of these various groups, and out of the competition among these groups comes the most effective governmental policy.

Those who defend the pressure-group system admit that not all groups are represented equally, but they argue that the answer is *more* group activity. If some interests are well represented and others aren't, then the others should organize as well.

Who Are the Members of Organizations?

America has often been called a society of joiners; Americans are known for their tendency to form organizations and for the great number and variety of those organizations. It's estimated that about six out of ten adult Americans belong to organizations. Does this mean most Americans have some organization that takes care of their political interests? The answer is unclear. Although a majority of Americans belong to organizations, there's a large minority—four out of ten—who don't. More important, perhaps, is the fact that not all social groups are equally likely to join organizations. As we saw earlier, higher-status citizens are more likely to be members of organizations than lower-status citizens. If you're rich, if you have a college education, if you're white rather than black, then you're more likely to join an organization.

POLITICAL AND NONPOLITICAL GROUPS

Not all organizations are formed around political interests. As can be seen in Table 7.1, only 8 percent of the citizens belong to political groups—political party clubs, the League of Women Voters, the NAACP. Most organizations are formed for other purposes.

But it would be a mistake to think only groups with a political purpose communicate citizen interests to the government. All kinds of groups can become politically active, and some are active all the time. Any group may be affected by governmental activity or need some response from the government. An example is the National Rifle Association. Organized as a recreational group for hunters and sportsmen, it became a major political force when its interests were challenged by supporters of gun-control legislation. The same can be said for other types of groups. Church groups don't have political goals, but they get involved in conflicts over issues like abortion law or school prayers. And groups representing economic interests are constantly involved in political activity.

LOBBIES

Some organizations are more active than others in trying to influence the government. They have offices in Washington or in state capitals, and they

In recent years, however, consumer groups and "citizens' lobbies" have become important politically. The largest such group is Common Cause, which has 323,000 members and is active in areas ranging from consumer protection to reform of campaign financing. With their professional attitude and willingness to do battle in Congress and in the courts, such organizations have been quite successful.

Are these new organizations unlike other pressure groups in that they work not for selfish interests but for the general public good? Or are they simply lobbying for a different set of selfish interests—consumer interests instead of producer interests, conservationist interests instead of mining or lumber interests? Here's how one American business leader describes environmental and consumer groups:

> The political system is out of balance. . . . We find our fate increasingly in the hands of a few relatively small but highly vocal, selfish, interest groups . . . . These groups . . . pursue their own interests with complete disregard for the impact of their wants on the rest of the economy . . . . And while they shout about the environmental impact of almost everything, they have no concern whatever for the economic impact of their corrective legislation.[1]

Citizens' groups describe business lobbies in the same words. But whether the new citizens' groups represent the public interest or a new kind of selfish interest, they are an important addition to the system of organized groups in America.

Beneficiary Groups. Whenever the government helps an interest group, it creates "beneficiaries." Members of such groups have an interest in seeing that government support is continued and perhaps increased. Farmers lobby for price supports or import controls; veterans lobby for veterans' benefits; people on welfare lobby for continued or increased welfare benefits. In this way these groups act like business lobbies; in fact we could have listed farmers with the business groups.

Organizations as Pressure Groups

It's clear that there's a lot of organized political activity in America. But how does this activity affect governmental policy? Does it have any effect? If so, who benefits?

Putting pressure on the government is the best-known role of organized interest groups; they act as lobbies in Washington, in state capitals, and in local governments. Some say the government is dominated by lobbies. They describe governmental policy as the automatic result of the pressures put on the government by organized groups. According to this description, the public

[1] *Consumer Reports*, January 1975, 53.

as a whole plays no part, nor does the government itself. The government simply reacts to pressure groups or, at most, acts as a broker among them.

This description greatly exaggerates the power of organized groups and plays down other factors influencing governmental policy. These other factors include public opinion and the opinions and feelings of congressmen. Above all the executive branch of the government plays a dominant role.

In short, organized interests aren't all-powerful. But they are far from weak. Therefore it's useful to consider what kind of group is likely to be effective, on what issues, and where.

ORGANIZATIONAL RESOURCES

Financial Resources. Lobbying is expensive. The major lobbies have large, full-time staffs. They sometimes carry on expensive campaigns to influence Congress or the public; for example, during its campaign against medicare the AMA spent over $1 million in three months. Lobbies also contribute large amounts to political campaigns. The milk producers' lobby was severely criticized for contributing heavily to President Nixon's 1972 campaign, supposedly in return for an agreement to raise price supports for milk. But this didn't stop it from giving $2.2 million to various congressional campaigns in 1974. Recent laws have curbed such spending.

People. Organizations that can get their members involved in political activity are also likely to be effective. The number of members isn't as important as their willingness to give time and effort to the organization. When a group has many members who can put pressure on government officials, it can be very effective.

One of the strongest lobbies is the National Rifle Association (NRA). It has 1,050,000 members (including at least 35 congressmen) in 12,000 state and local gun clubs across the country. This is a large membership, but not all that large. Public-opinion polls show that about seven out of ten Americans favor some kind of gun control; this means the NRA members are outnumbered by over 100 to 1. The effectiveness of the NRA comes from the fact that its members really care about the issue, while the majority that favors gun control is less intense.

Technical Knowledge. Lobbies have another important resource: They have experts working for them. Therefore they often have much greater technical knowledge than members of Congress, who have many other problems and issues to think about. The National Education Association has a lot of information about research on new teaching methods. Representatives of the textile industry know the number of yards of goods imported from Hong Kong each month. The National Association of Retail Druggists can tell you how many drugstores fail each year. These groups are given a voice in policy making because they know what policies they want to influence and what changes are important to them. In addition they often have more information than the government officials involved.

A good example is recent activity on environmental issues. Most citizens are interested in preserving wilderness areas or keeping down the pollution of rivers. But when it comes to decisions on the use of public land, the groups that have experts working for them usually get their way. And these are usually business interests that want to use the land for mining, private development, or cattle grazing. These groups know how to use government agencies and the courts for their purposes, and they put in the time and effort needed to be effective. An unorganized public is ineffective against them. However, organizations like the Sierra Club put professional skills and energy on the other side by hiring a full-time legal staff whose job is to fight private development of public land.

Access. Access to government officials can make organizations particularly effective. Full-time professional lobbyists often develop close ties with government officials. Their knowledge helps in this, and they work at it very hard. The job of lobbyists is made easier by the fact that they may have to work with only a small number of officials. In Congress most business is done in committees. The good lobbyist develops a close relationship with the chairperson and a few key members of the committee, as well as with the government agencies active in his area.

MOBILIZING MEMBERS

The effective pressure group must be able to depend on its members. For one thing it must keep up its membership. Not all the doctors in American belong to the AMA; in fact only about half of them do. And only about half of the lawyers belong to the American Bar Association. An organization that claims to speak for a group will try to have a large portion of that group as members. In addition it needs membership dues to carry on its activities. And if it can get its members to be active, it can increase its influence.

As we saw in the preceding chapter, one of the ways groups get their members to be active is by offering them certain benefits. For example, the following benefits are available to members of the American Bar Association:

- Lawyer placement service.
- Retirement income plans.
- Group life insurance program.
- Group disability insurance program.
- In-hospital insurance program.
- Specialized information on all sections of the law.
- Legal publications and reports.

Services of this sort are important in keeping members active. And members who join for these reasons provide the basis for a politically powerful organization.

On What Issues Are Pressure Groups Effective?

The policy-making process—a subject we'll deal with more fully later—goes on at two different levels. Congress sets general policy guidelines, but the actual policy depends on the detailed legislation worked out in the committees and subcommittees of Congress, the way the law is administered by government officials, and the way the courts interpret the law. The rules set down by Congress are so general that they have little impact until the details of the law have been settled.

Pressure groups are active in the struggle for major legislation, but this isn't where they have their greatest effect. Congress must keep an eye on the public, and the news media are keeping an eye on Congress. Pressure groups have much more influence on the details of legislation worked out in committee or in executive agencies. Here they can use their professional knowledge and access to government officials.

TAX LEGISLATION

A good example of the two levels of policy making—the general statement of principle and the detailed working out of practice—is tax legislation. The principle of a progressive income tax is found in the Sixteenth Amendment. The idea is to tax those who can pay more at higher rates. This could have a major effect on income distribution in America.

Few argue with the general principle of a progressive tax. And there's no need to argue, because the principle is hardly ever applied.

Although there have been many attempts to reform income-tax laws, the results are almost always the same. Congress sets some general guidelines, and then the House Ways and Means Committee or the Senate Finance Committee approves a number of exemptions. At the hearings on the major tax bills you'll find hundreds of groups making statements on what seem to be very small issues, but these issues are important to them. On each issue there's no one to oppose them.

The result is that while there's never any direct challenge to the principle of a progressive tax, actual policy doesn't come out that way. As has often been noted, the law allows for a maximum tax rate of 70 percent, but few pay as much as 50 percent.[2] This isn't the result of a decision by the government that a rate of 70 percent is too high. Rather, the principle of a progressive tax holds, but the practice is to allow so many exceptions—tax-free municipal bonds, depletion allowances, lower rates for capital gains, and the like—that the principle never takes full effect.

[2] See William L. Cary, "Pressure Groups and the Revenue Code," *Harvard Law Review*, 68 (1955), 745–780.

BUSINESS REGULATION

This pattern of principle vs. practice can be found in many areas. In the area of business regulation, for example, Congress will pass general legislation to regulate things like the quality of food products, the amount of pollutants that may be dumped in rivers, and the flameproofing of fabrics. The general principle is clear: Sell pure food, don't pollute, manufacture only flameproof fabrics. But the details of the regulation—How pure? Is a little pollution all right? What about slow-burning fabrics?—are usually worked out with representatives of the businesses to be regulated. This isn't necessarily a bad thing, since the businesses involved have the necessary information. But it does give businesses a special voice in policy making.

It's at this level that interest groups are most effective. If, for example, representatives of large corporations tried—through the NAM or the U.S. Chamber of Commerce—to have Congress pass a law greatly reducing the rate at which they are taxed, they would face strong opposition and would probably lose. If, on the other hand, the House Ways and Means Committee approves a stock-option plan in which profits from sales of stock received under such a plan can be treated as capital gains if sold at least two years after the grant of the option and six months after the transfer of the stock, the public is unlikely to be aroused.

On such a technical issue the pattern of division is likely to be as shown in Figure 7.1. A deeply interested and technically skilled group favors position B. It looks like a technical issue about which the public has little knowledge or concern, so there's no opposition. Under such conditions an interest group can be quite effective.

Citizens' lobbies try to change the situation shown in Figure 7.1 into the one shown in Figure 7.2. One lobby opposes another. The knowledge and activity of, say, the lumber interests are balanced by the professional staff of an organization like the Sierra Club. It's hard to say how many situations in the United States are like the one in Figure 7.1 and how many like the one in Fig-

FIGURE 7.1
Specific Interest Group with No Opposition Due to Technicality of Issue

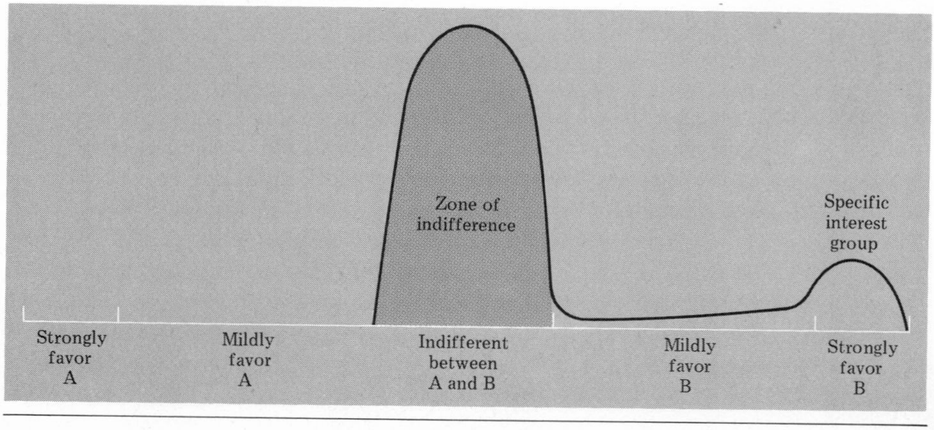

Citizen lobbies often challenge business lobbies now.

ure 7.2. Despite the activity of the new citizens' lobbies, it's likely that the situation in Figure 7.1, where an interest group isn't opposed by any other group, is still a dominant pattern.

Where Are Pressure Groups Active?

CONGRESSIONAL COMMITTEES

Pressure groups are active in trying to arouse the public through campaigns in the news media or by supporting candidates for public office. But they're probably much more effective in dealing with the various congressional committees. Here they can develop close ties with members of Congress, who

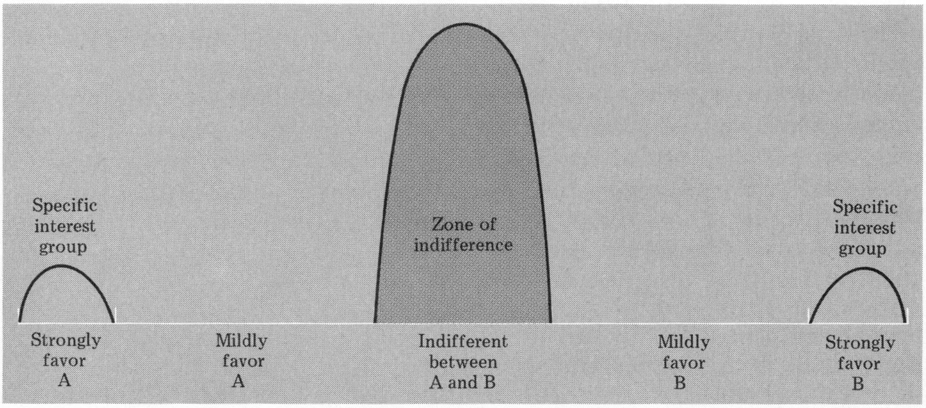

FIGURE 7.2
Specific Interest Group Opposed by Another Group

often come from districts where that particular interest is well represented. They often provide the information needed to write legislation affecting that interest.

THE EXECUTIVE BRANCH

Organizations may also develop ties with the agencies of the executive branch that regulate their interests: farm groups with the Department of Agriculture; business groups with the Department of Commerce; labor unions with the Department of Labor. In particular a close relationship may be formed between independent regulatory commissions and the businesses they're supposed to regulate: trucking interests with the Interstate Commerce Commission; radio and television interests with the Federal Communications Commission; airlines with the Civil Aeronautics Board.

THE COURT SYSTEM

The real impact of governmental policy often comes through the courts' interpretation of the law or the Constitution. Interest groups have been active in this area as well. Organizations provide the professional skills to prepare cases; they choose the test cases and file *amicus curiae* briefs (briefs filed by someone not a party to the case defending one side or another). Perhaps the most dramatic example is the long series of cases prepared and carried through by the NAACP. Of these, the school segregation cases, such as *Brown* v. *Board of Education of Topeka*, are the best known (see Chapter 11).

Groups that are interested in such issues as civil rights or separation of church and state are particularly active in the federal courts. Such groups as the American Civil Liberties Union and the Congress of Racial Equality (CORE) are active in this way.[3]

ELECTION CAMPAIGNS

Organized groups are also very active in election campaigns, supporting candidates they believe will favor them. We've mentioned the large-scale campaign contributions of the milk producers. As the president of the Mid-American Dairymen put it, "I have become increasingly aware that the soft and sincere voice of the dairy farmer is no match for the jingle of hard currency put in the campaign funds of the politician."[4]

Many interest groups have special committees for campaign activity—the AFL-CIO has COPE (Committee on Political Education); the AMA has AMPAC (American Medical Political Action Committee); the milk produc-

[3] See Clement E. Vose, "Interest Groups, Judicial Review and Local Government," *Western Political Quarterly*, 19 (March 1966), 85–100.

[4] Quoted in "Dollar Politics," *Congressional Quarterly*, 2, p. 13.

ers have C-TAPE (Committee for Thorough Agricultural Political Education). Each gives large amounts of money to the candidates it favors. Recent laws limit such activity.

Interest Groups as Quasi-Governments

Interest groups are politically important in another way: They sometimes function as quasi-governments. Government, as we said in the Introduction, exists whenever binding decisions are made for a group of citizens, that is, decisions that have the force of law and about which citizens have no choice. Private organizations are often given the power to make such decisions.

CONTROLLING ENTRY INTO AN OCCUPATION

Many groups control entry into the occupations they represent. Medical, legal, educational, and craft associations have control over examinations, apprentice programs, and accreditation. In addition these groups may control access to important facilities such as hospitals or labor exchanges.

This activity is a form of government because it's binding on citizens. You can't practice law or medicine without accreditation; you can't get work as a plumber without union membership (and for that you have to complete an apprentice program). In this way private organizations act as governments.

Everyone would like a way to judge doctors or lawyers as professionals so that people who need medical care or legal advice can trust them. And who but members of the profession itself can judge? But control can be used for

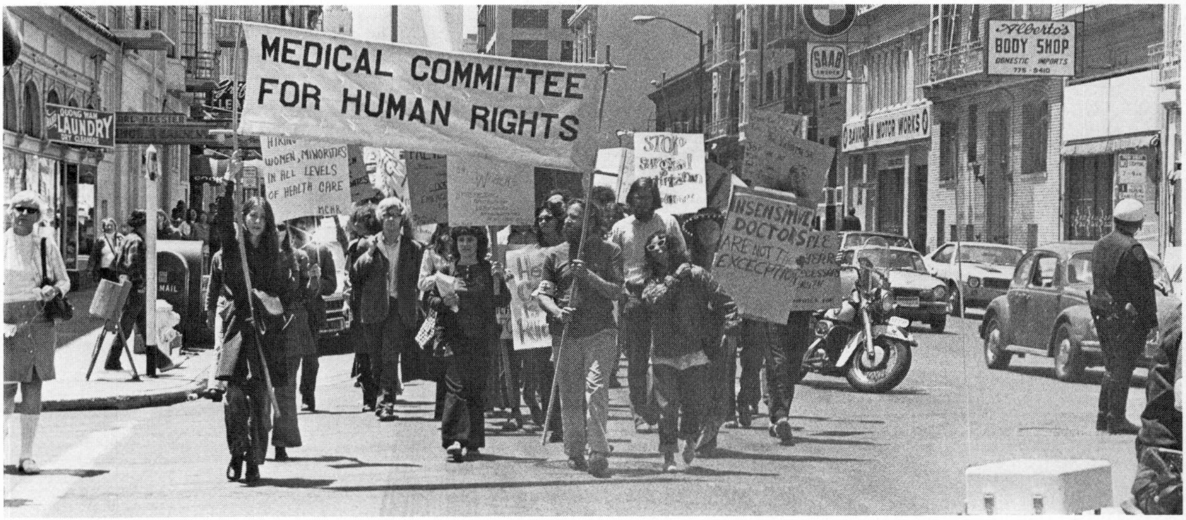

The leadership of the AMA has recently been receiving more opposition.

other purposes as well. The fact that the AMA controls entry into the medical profession and, often, access to hospitals means it could control the activities of doctors. And the AMA has used its power to keep doctors in line behind its policy on medical care.

Citizens who oppose such controls can challenge them in the courts or appeal to Congress for a change. But this doesn't alter the fact that these controls have the force of law.

CONTROLLING THE DISTRIBUTION OF PUBLIC FUNDS

Many public programs are carried out by private groups that distribute government funds. Of course the government sets guidelines for this activity, but the control is in the hands of the private group.

There are many examples of this kind of setup. Urban-renewal funds are often controlled by private developers; funds for hospitals and other welfare activities are often controlled by private charities; and funds for poverty programs are often distributed by local groups.

This kind of activity involves the participation of citizens who are familiar with local conditions. But it also gives local groups day-to-day power over government resources. These groups aren't as accountable to the public as government officials and may not really represent the people they claim to represent.

For Whom Do Interest Groups Speak?

Organized groups can be most effective in getting action on particular interests. Sometimes, however, it's not clear whose interests these are. When an interest group expresses an opinion, the opinion is supposed to be that of its members—the AMA claims to speak for doctors and the National Education Association for teachers. But *do* such organizations speak for their members?

We often don't know. There's a tendency for organizations to be run by a small group of members who give their time and effort to the group's activities. These members tend to become a special group of professional leaders unresponsive to the demands of other members. The AMA is a classic case of an organization closely controlled by a leadership group. Its members meet rarely, if ever, and control over the group's activities is in the hands of a few elected officers and, above all, a professional staff.

The fact that organizations are generally controlled by a small group of leaders makes you wonder whether they represent the interests of their members. But there's another side to the coin. Central control makes it possible for organizations to plan careful campaigns, so that when they do speak for their members they can speak more effectively. Moreover, central control often develops because the members aren't interested enough. When some of the members want to challenge the leaders, they often have quite an impact.

In recent years, for example, the conservative leaders of the AMA have been challenged by younger, more liberal doctors. This group hasn't taken over control of the organization, but it has had an impact.

How Powerful Are Interest Groups?

Interest groups are most effective when they work quietly on issues that don't arouse public concern. When it comes to major conflicts over governmental policy, they're just one voice among many. Members of Congress don't respond only to particular interests, and the news media often arouse Congress and the public when interest groups get too much power.

Consider the AMA and medicare. If the AMA was all-powerful, we wouldn't have a medicare program, because the AMA was strongly opposed to it. Yet today we do have a medicare program. But that does not mean the AMA is powerless. It succeeded in delaying medicare for many years. In addition the AMA played a major role in shaping the program when it finally came into being.

Later we'll look more closely at the way policy on medical care, as well as other policies, are made. When we consider all the factors that go into policy making, we'll find that interest groups are just one of many—an important force, perhaps, but not always the dominant one.

CONTROVERSY

Does Pressure-Group Politics Contribute to the Public Good?

One Side

Pressure groups communicate to the government the needs and preferences of various groups of citizens. Without such groups policy makers wouldn't have the information they need. Interest-group activity, particularly at the level of detailed policy making, allows governmental policy to be "fine-tuned" to each situation as it comes up. In a society as complex as ours, this is necessary if governmental policy is to respond to the great variety of citizen interests.

Pressure groups don't discriminate against any particular group of citizens. It's true that they're not all equally organized or equally active, but they all have a right to organize and to petition the government. The fact that a group is organized and active shows that it cares about its interests.

If other groups don't pressure the government, it means they don't care enough.

The close ties between interest groups and the government are a way of using the skills and energy of professionals in making governmental policy. Moreover, when citizens voluntarily work with the government in the policy-making process they are more willing to go along with the policies that result. This is all to the good—the less force that is used, the better off everyone is.

Finally, the policy that results from conflict between interest groups can't hurt the public good, because the public good is the sum of those interests.

The Other Side

Pressure groups don't always represent the most important interests of citizens. Many groups with serious needs are unorganized. It's not necessarily lack of interest that keeps some groups from becoming active; they may lack the resources to organize. As a result the interests that are represented are those of higher-status groups, particularly the well-organized business groups. And the interests of other groups aren't represented equally—unionized workers do better than nonunionized ones, though the nonunionized ones may need governmental action more. The result is that governmental policy tends to benefit those who need it least. This situation is made worse when power is given to the groups the government should be regulating.

Pressure-group politics may be voluntary, but social change may require force—at least it may require that citizens be forced to accept changes they don't want. A major change in American society requires stronger action by the government. And it's in this area that pressure-group politics is weakest: No one is planning for the general public good, which isn't just the sum of the interests of various groups. To solve the serious problems facing American society, the government will have to listen to other voices besides those of interest groups.

Questions for Review

1. What are the arguments for and against pressure-group activity?
2. Give examples of various types of lobbies. On what issues are these groups likely to be politically active?
3. What is the political significance of the new "citizens' lobbies"?
4. Why are groups like the AMA and the NRA effective in influencing legislation?
5. Why might a group like the Disabled American Veterans put most of its effort into pressuring congressional committees rather than trying to influence public opinion?
6. Why are groups that are interested in issues like civil rights active in the federal courts?
7. In what ways do interest groups act as quasi-governments?
8. Why is it hard to tell whether the leaders of an organization like the National Education Association actually speak for its members?

Chapter 8

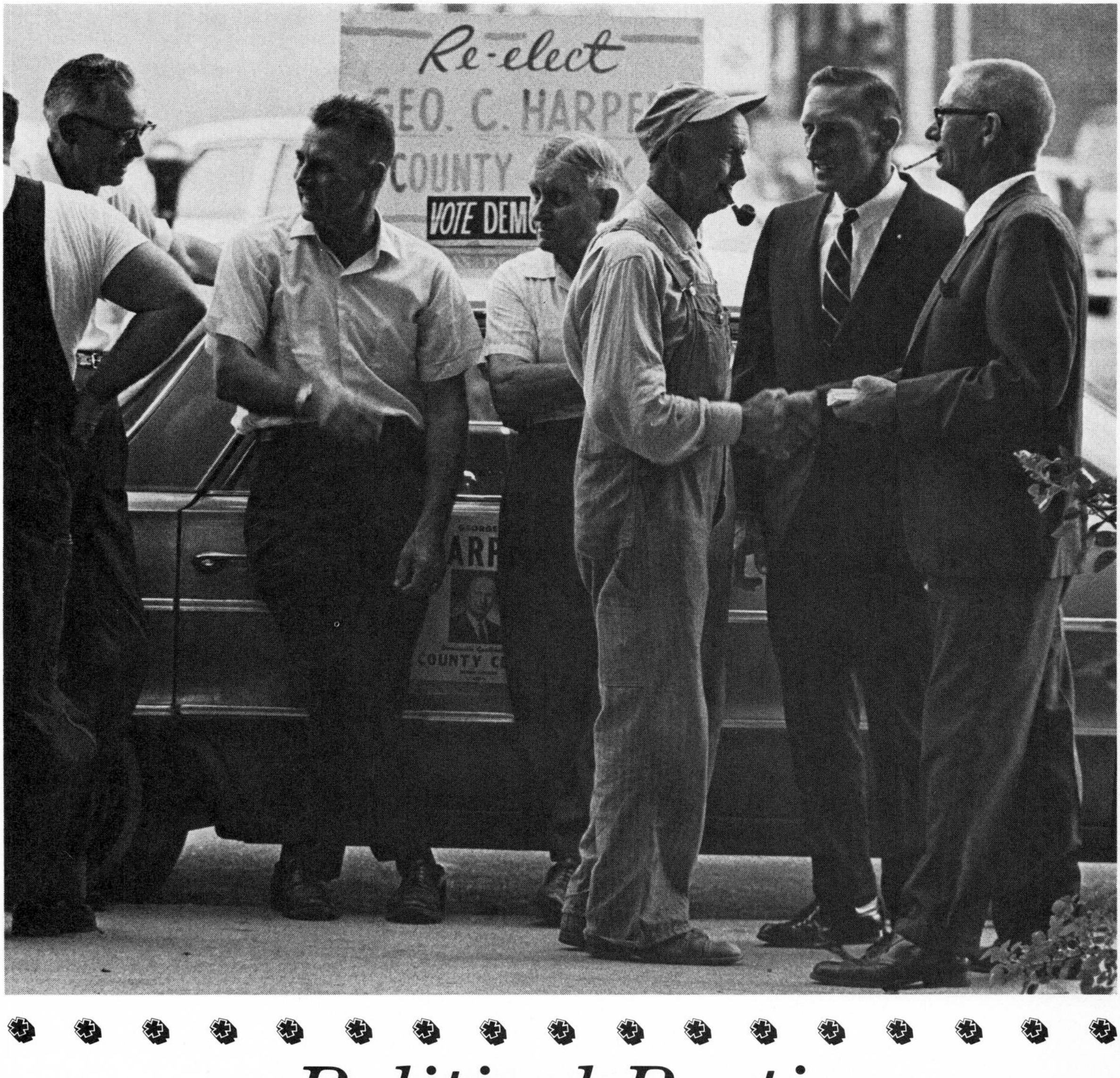

Political Parties and Elections

Every four years there is a Presidential election. A "typical" Presidential election year begins in the spring, when either or both major political parties hold primary elections (special elections to see who the party members think should be nominated). In the summer the parties hold conventions to choose a "ticket"—a person to run for President and another to run for Vice-President. After two or three months of campaigning, one of the tickets wins in the November election. The winning President and Vice-President hold office for four years. At the same time the voters choose all the members of the House of Representatives and one-third of the senators.

In addition to the Presidential election every four years, there is a *midterm election* (also called an off-year election) that takes place midway through the Presidential term of office. Thus there was a Presidential election in 1976 and there will be a midterm election in 1978. In a midterm election all members of the House of Representatives and a different one-third of the senators are either reelected or replaced by newcomers (a senator's term of office is six years). Certain state and local elections also take place at the same time as Presidential and midterm elections.

In this chapter we'll focus on the role of political parties in the election process—the process by which power changes hands in a democracy. Managing the transfer of power is one of the really tough issues for any political system. From Kennedy to Johnson, from Johnson to Nixon, from Nixon to Ford: How is power passed from one to another? In the United States the political parties do this job. First, however, let's look at some of the important characteristics of American political parties.

American Political Parties

In some societies political parties involve the general public in the political life of the nation. For example, some parties organize lectures and programs to educate the public about political issues; they print booklets that explain policy questions and ask the public to express their views on these questions. Parties in many societies have youth groups and similar organizations. They have a chain of command that links local groups with district and national offices.

None of these activities is common in the United States. In fact the major parties don't even have members in any formal sense. It's rare for a citizen to actually "join" a political party, and few pay dues regularly.

Our political parties hardly ever meet, and when they do the meetings involve very small groups. Almost all party meetings—local, state, or national—take place around election time to nominate candidates and plan campaign strategy. We would be very surprised to hear that the Santa Clara Democratic party is meeting to discuss tariff policy or school busing and intends to give its opinion to government officials in Sacramento. And we don't expect the Republican party of Illinois to organize a series of public meetings so citizens can express their opinions on issues facing the Illinois legislature.

VARIETY OF VIEWPOINTS

There are a variety of political viewpoints within each of the major parties. The Democrats and the Republicans each have a "liberal wing" and a "conservative wing." The Democratic party, for example, has long been the party of the conservative South (conservative on civil-rights and social-welfare issues). But during the Great Depression the Democrats attracted the support of some very different social groups: ethnic workers, blacks, the urban poor. The result is a coalition of a liberal, northern, urban group with a conservative, southern, rural group.

This variety of viewpoints has put a barrier in the way of cohesive party programs. The issue that most unites Republicans is the desire to defeat Democrats, and vice versa. Yet the nomination of liberal George McGovern in 1972 caused many Democratic leaders to sit out the election or support Nixon. And between elections there's even less party unity.

DECENTRALIZED ORGANIZATION

When we call the United States a two-party system, we don't mean there are only two major party organizations. Rather, we mean there are only two major party labels. Elections are contests between one group of candidates using the Republican party label and another group of candidates using the Democratic party label; they aren't contests between two unified organizations.

One reason for this is the federal structure of American government, which has had a lasting effect on party structure. There are in fact fifty separate Republican parties and fifty separate Democratic parties—more if we include some of the stronger city and county organizations. The state and local organizations are loosely linked together by a national committee, but this committee has little control over them. In short, party control is decentralized. The active units of the party (where there *are* active units) are at the local level. This contributes to the variety of viewpoints just mentioned. The Democratic party of Biloxi, Mississippi, is very different from the Democratic party of Palo Alto, California.

Within the party a process of bargaining and compromise goes on whenever a decision must be made that affects the party as a whole, such as the nomination of a Presidential candidate. On other types of decisions each unit goes its own way, not worrying about what another county or state organization may be doing. For example, nomination of congressional candidates is entirely under the control of local activists, or perhaps local voters if there's a primary. Even fund raising is mostly a local matter; national headquarters pays for the Presidential campaign, but state and local organizations raise funds for their candidates.

PARTIES WITHOUT PROGRAMS

Neither the Republicans nor the Democrats have a general program that most of the party officials agree on. From time to time one of the parties tries to develop a program, but these efforts usually come from a group that is bothered by what another group is doing in the party's name. For example, Republican mayors might meet to put together a program for loans from the federal government to the cities because they think Republican members of Congress are acting too slowly on this issue.

There are two documents that are sometimes thought of as party programs. The first is the party *platform* put together at the convention for the benefit of the Presidential nominee. However, it isn't binding on party leaders, not even the nominee himself. The second is the package of legislation proposed by the President in his State of the Union Address, Budget Message to Congress, and other speeches. But these proposals are made by the President, not his party.

SUMMARY

American political parties lack many things—mass membership, a regular source of funds, an effective central organization. They lack a cohesive program that voters can respond to; they can't control what their candidates do once they're in office. And yet the major political parties are powerful. They've been around a long time. Their position in American politics is based on the simple fact that they manage the transfer of power; they control the routes to public office.

Political Parties and Election Campaigns

In November 1976 the American voters elected 435 people to the House of Representatives and 33 to the Senate; they also chose 14 governors. In these elections several hundred independent and minor-party candidates tried to defeat candidates from the two major parties. Only one succeeded.

Was the 1976 election unusual? Not at all. Recruitment to public office is "reserved" for those nominated by a political party. This isn't a matter of law. The Constitution doesn't say public office may be held only by members of certain political parties. But what is not a matter of law is very much a matter of tradition and practical politics. Almost from the beginning the struggle for control over the government of the United States has been a party struggle.

Two factors explain why political parties control the routes to public office: (1) party loyalty, and (2) the problems and costs of organizing a campaign.

PARTY LOYALTY

As we saw earlier, most citizens identify with one of the major parties the way they identify with a particular religion. Listen to a Republican with a strong party identification: "I'm a born Republican. We're all Republicans from start to finish, clear back on the family tree. I won't weaken my party by voting for a Democrat."

People support their party by always voting for that party's candidates. If candidates didn't have party labels, the typical American voter would be confused. Voters expect a candidate to be backed by one of the major parties. A "major candidate" is one who has won the Democratic or Republican nomination. The typical voter may know nothing about how the party is organized, how it nominates its candidates, or how it raises money. But he does know one thing: One candidate is a Democrat and the other a Republican. In the typical American election the party identifications of voters are translated into winning and losing candidates.

POLITICAL CAMPAIGNS

Party loyalty is one reason why political parties control recruitment to public office. A second reason is that political parties make sure the voters know who the candidates are. This is important. No matter how qualified a political candidate may be, the voters have to know who he is.

Campaign Organization. The political candidate must somehow convince thousands or even millions of voters that he's the best person for the job. To do this, he or his staff must see that speeches are planned, leaflets distributed, advertisements put in newspapers, announcements made on radio and TV. Political campaigning is very complicated; it can also be very expensive.

The political parties provide a campaign organization that comes to life around election time. Party officials open temporary campaign headquarters; volunteers come in and lick stamps; contributors are asked to write checks. The 1972 *Democratic Party Manual* lists some of the major campaign activities: Methods of Raising Money, Coffee Hours, Polling, Voter Registration, Buttons, Bumper Stickers. And here are some of the people involved: Campaign Director, Director of Communications, Telephone Volunteers, "Bell-ringers."

An independent candidate has to build up this campaign organization himself. This will cost him money and time that could otherwise be used in trying to defeat his opponents.

Campaign Costs. "Money is the mother's milk of politics," says California Democrat Jesse Unruh. Buttons and bumper stickers cost money, to say nothing of TV time, newspaper ads, and airline tickets. And campaign costs keep going up. In 1952 campaign costs at all levels totaled less than $150 million; in 1964 the total was estimated at $200 million; by 1972 the costs of political campaigns had risen to over $400 million.

Most of the money used in election campaigns is collected by the political parties. This is another reason why the parties play such an important role in determining who is elected to public office. A person running for office independently of the major parties would have to be rich or be backed by others who are rich. He would have to convince contributors that he can win despite the lack of party support. This is hard to do; many independents and third-party candidates have tried to get elected, but few have succeeded.

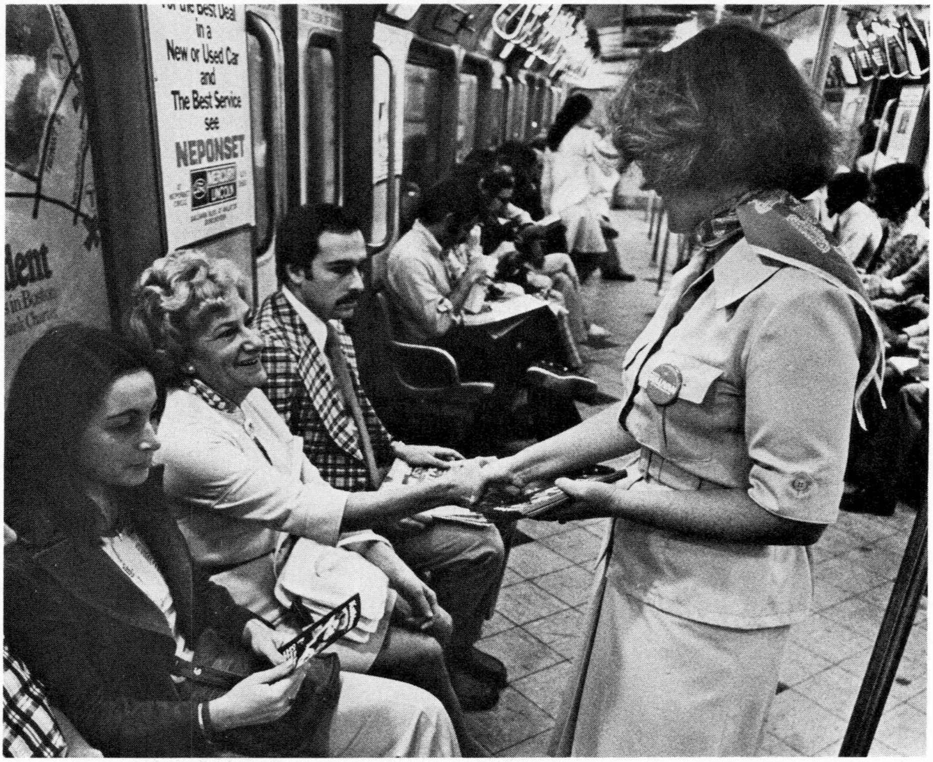

A subway has a captive audience for a campaigner.

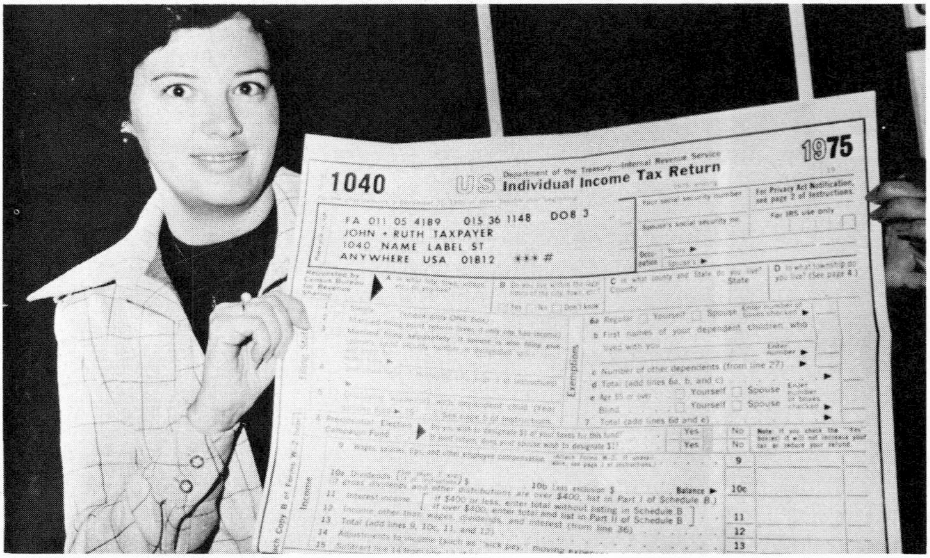

To help cover the cost of campaigning, taxpayers can donate money on their income tax form.

Political Parties and Election Results

The different branches (executive, legislative, judicial) and levels (national, state, local) of the government are rarely controlled by the same party. Voters do not have to vote a *straight ticket;* they do not have to vote for all Democrats or Republicans. Instead they can vote a *split ticket.* A voter may choose the Republican candidate for President, switch to the Democratic candidate for governor, and then switch back to the Republican candidate for senator or representative. For example, after the Carter-Mondale victory in the 1976 Presidential election the Democrats still controlled Congress. Even when voters don't split tickets, different parties can control different levels of government. Illinois voted Republican in 1976, voting for Gerald Ford for President and electing a Republican governor, James Thompson. Ford lost. Thus while the Democrats controlled the White House there were Republican governors in Illinois and 13 other states.

No matter which party is in control, the different branches and levels of government must cooperate. A Republican President can't ignore congressional leaders just because they happen to be Democrats, and Congress can't ignore the executive branch just because it happens to be controlled by Republicans. Under these conditions a loosely organized, decentralized party system works well. Parties with strong, inflexible programs would make cooperation among the various branches and levels of government nearly impossible.

ELECTIONS AND SOCIAL CHANGE

No society stands still. Citizens become concerned about new social problems and make new demands on the government. Many of the problems we face today—pollution, street crime, drug abuse—weren't public issues twenty years ago. The social groups that are politically active also change. No one thought of "youth" as a separate political group twenty years ago, but today the youth movement is something to be taken seriously.

Is the political-party system responsive to such changes? Do the major parties give people a way of expressing new social concerns? Do they make room for new social groups? Let's look at some of the evidence.

Protest Movements. From time to time political-protest movements arise among groups that see a need for social change. There have been five serious protest movements in the past ten years: (1) the civil-rights movement; (2) the youth movement, centering on political protests against the Vietnam War; (3) "Nader populism," a middle-class movement concerned with environmental issues and consumer protection; (4) the women's liberation movement; and (5) a protest led by Alabama Governor George Wallace, which opposes the national leaders who have "given in" to black demands.

At first none of these movements depended on either of the two major parties. Take the antiwar movement. Those who disapproved of American policy in Vietnam didn't turn to the political parties to express their views. Rather, they communicated through the news media, in universities and churches, and in the streets. The other protest movements have also operated independently of the two major parties. In 1968 Wallace ran for President on the American Independent ticket and got 10 million votes. Among the major protest movements of the 1960s, only the civil-rights movement got any party support: Throughout the 1960s and early 1970s the Democratic party tried to respond to some of the demands made by blacks.

People involved in protest movements often say the two-party system is too inflexible to be used for political protest. However, there is evidence that this isn't quite true. Again take the antiwar movement as an example. Its leaders were ignored at the 1968 Democratic convention in Chicago. Despite the fact that the antiwar movement had led to President Johnson's decision not to run for reelection, the Democratic party nominated his Vice-President, Humphrey. Yet only four years later the Democratic party invited to the convention in Miami the same groups that had demonstrated in the streets of Chicago. The convention nominated McGovern, a strong antiwar candidate. Thus in only four years the antiwar groups won a chance to take their case to the American voter.

Minor Parties. Third parties are often formed to challenge one or both of the dominant parties. Although after a while these minor parties fade from the political scene, they usually have some impact. One type of minor party is the protest group, such as the Populist party of the 1880s, which was formed to express dissatisfaction with monopolies and trusts. It also successfully pressured for direct election of senators, the primary system, and other political reforms.

Another type of minor party breaks away from one of the major parties when compromise fails to hold it together. Theodore Roosevelt's Progressive party was formed as a result of a split in the national leadership of the Republican party. More recent examples are the regional parties of the South, often led by "states' righters" within the Democratic party. In 1948 Strom Thurmond (now a Republican) broke away from the Democratic party to lead the Dixiecrats after the Democrats nominated Harry Truman.

Not all minor parties have resulted from splits within a major party. The Socialist party is generally outside the American political mainstream. Such a party may last longer than the breakaway parties just described, but it usually won't have as much influence on governmental policy.

Minor parties bring new issues, or new ways of looking at old issues, to the political agenda. As they succeed in forcing the major parties to support new policies, they tend to disappear. What we see in the 1970s is a repeat of earlier history. As the Democrats and Republicans absorb the protest groups of the 1960s, they're doing what major parties have always done. This is one way the party system stays responsive to changing conditions and issues.

Three Types of Elections

We're about to discuss elections in a way that is probably unfamiliar to you. Usually we focus on whether our candidate won, by a landslide or just squeaked by, or if there were dirty tricks in the campaign. Here we're going to discuss three types of elections: maintaining, deviating, and realigning.[1]

We've mentioned the fact that the majority of American voters tend to identify with one of the major political parties. They become part of a coalition that may last through a series of elections. For example, in most elections between 1932 and 1976 the Democratic party could depend on urban, working-class voters and the Republican party could depend on small-town, middle-class voters. Such an election maintains the existing balance of forces and is called a *maintaining election;* the Carter-Mondale victory in 1976 was an example.

From time to time, however, particular issues upset this balance. Voters leave their party to vote for a popular candidate of the other party or to vote against an unpopular candidate of their own party. People cross party lines for many reasons. Eisenhower won in 1952 and 1956 because many Democratic voters simply "liked Ike." In the 1960 election John F. Kennedy, a Roman Catholic, attracted a few Catholic voters who normally supported the Republicans, but many Protestants who traditionally voted Democratic switched their support to Nixon, the Republican candidate.

Sometimes a large enough number of voters who normally identify with the majority party vote for the candidate of the other party so that the majority party loses. Such an election is called a *deviating election.* The elections of 1952 and 1956 were deviating elections: There were fewer Republican Party identifyers than Democratic ones, but enough Democrats voted for Eisenhower so that he won. Such deviations are temporary, however; the usual balance of forces is regained in the following election.

A third type of election is the *realigning election,* in which new party loyalties are formed. Some people who have been loyal Democrats become Republicans, and vice versa. Other people who have not voted in the past give their loyalties and votes to what had been the minority party. This is different from a deviating election because the change in party identification is more or less permanent. Thus the makeup of one or both parties is greatly changed. Between 1932 and 1936, for example, the Democrats put together the coalition that has dominated American politics almost up to the present day. They did this by attracting new kinds of voters—particularly immigrant groups—and some traditionally Republican voters.

[1] The discussion draws upon studies conducted by the Survey Research Center, Institute for Social Research, University of Michigan. See especially Angus Campbell, Philip E. Converse, Warren E. Miller, and Donald E. Stokes, *The American Voter* (New York: Wiley, 1960), and by the same authors, *Elections and the Political Order* (New York: Wiley, 1966).

Realigning elections bring new groups and issues to the political scene. Groups that have been in power fade into the background; other groups become politically relevant. New issues arise and old ones fade. In the 1930s, for example, programs like social security, unemployment compensation, and public welfare were passed as a result of the political realignment that took place during the Great Depression. These issues simply weren't on the political agenda during the 1920s.

How Different Are the Two Major Parties?

Does it make any difference who wins an election? When conservative Barry Goldwater won the Republican Presidential nomination in 1964, he claimed that the voters finally had "a choice, not an echo." Goldwater argued that the two parties had become so alike in their political outlook that the voters had no real choice. Many people agree with this argument; they say a two-party system actually reduces choice because each party tries to get the support of a wide variety of groups. As a result each party tends toward the middle of the road, where most of the voters are supposed to be. (See Figure 8.1.)

Others disagree. In a competitive party system, they say, the parties reflect the basic conflict between haves and have-nots, between rich and poor, businessmen and workers, producers and consumers.

Early American history showed this view to be correct. The first political parties were formed around conflicting economic interests. Under Hamilton's leadership the Federalist party protected the interests of business and trade, while the Jeffersonians were more favorable to the small farmer and the debtor class. Class differences between the parties may be found throughout American history and, some say, may be seen today in the Republicans and Democrats.

Such a pattern is illustrated in Figure 8.2. Here the parties oppose each

FIGURE 8.1
The American Electorate

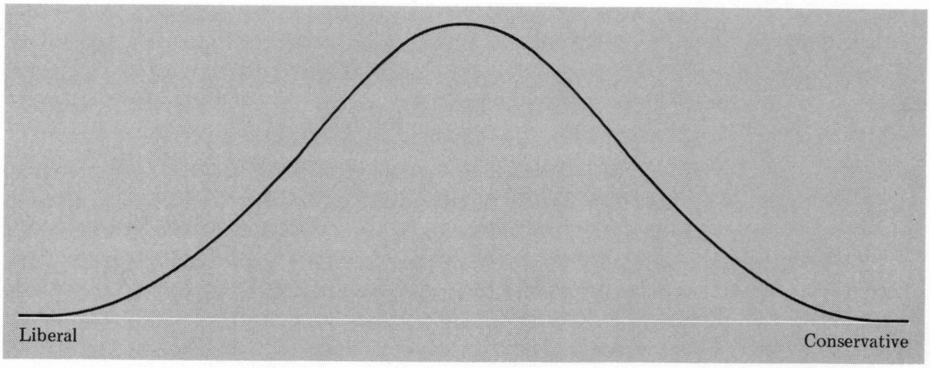

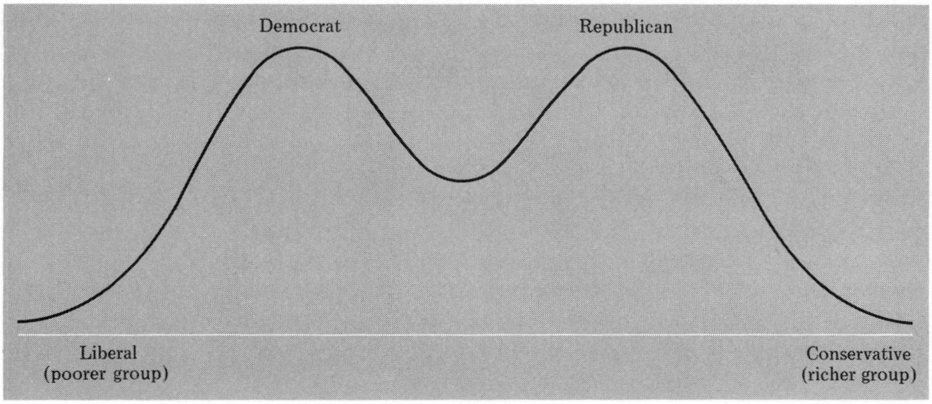

FIGURE 8.2 *Party Support Based on Social Class*

other; the Democrats get support from the poorer social classes and the Republicans get support from the richer social classes.

Which view is correct? Are the parties more or less the same in their political outlook, or do they reflect conflicting interests? Let's look at four kinds of evidence:

1. Whether the parties get their support from different social groups.
2. Whether the parties depend on different sources for campaign funds.
3. Whether the party leaders differ in their policy views.
4. Whether support for legislation differs between the parties.

THE PARTIES GET THEIR SUPPORT FROM DIFFERENT SOCIAL GROUPS

Different social groups support the two major parties. The differences go back to the coalition formed by President Roosevelt during the Great Depression. During this period the Republican party continued to favor conservative policies and thus kept the support of business interests and white Protestant voters. Meanwhile the Democrats introduced social-welfare programs such as social security and unemployment compensation and thus attracted the support of blacks, immigrant workers, and the poor.

The difference between the social groups supporting the Republicans and Democrats can still be seen today. In general Republicans tend to be of higher social status than Democrats. They tend to have better jobs, higher incomes, and more education than Democrats. However, the coalitions of the 1930s aren't as strong as they used to be. Important changes are taking place. Workers still tend to identify with the Democratic party, but they're more willing to listen to Republican candidates. And at all social levels party ties are loosening. This is particularly true among younger voters.

Note, however, that other factors besides social class affect party identification. Regional, ethnic, and religious divisions cut across class lines. For example, a Catholic business executive is more likely than is a Protestant business executive to be a Democrat.

VOTERS SEE DIFFERENCES BETWEEN THE PARTIES

Voters see differences between the Republicans and the Democrats. They're likely to think of the Republicans as the party that favors business interests. Some voters like the Republicans for this reason: "I like to string along with big business and big money. Under the Republicans the country has prospered." Others vote against Republican candidates for the same reason: "Republican leaders are controlled by people with money—the Republican party is run by large corporations."

People have a very different picture of the Democratic party; they think of it as more likely to take care of the working class: "They try to improve working conditions—shorter hours—a higher wage rate—and are more interested in benefits for working people." Voters who are worried about inflation and welfare costs feel differently, however: "The Democrats are a giveaway party. Democrats always want to spend more than the government has. Business suffers when the Democrats are in power."

DIFFERENCES IN CAMPAIGN SUPPORT

Party differences may also be seen in the groups that give money to the major parties. A lot of Republican party money comes from wealthy individuals and businesses. On the other hand, a lot of Democratic party money comes from organized labor and liberal interest groups. For example, in 1968 national labor committees gave $7.1 million to political campaigns, an average of five or six cents per union member; nearly all of this went to Democratic candidates. The National Committee for an Effective Congress spent $400,000 in 1972 on House and Senate candidates; all but five were Democrats or independents.

DIFFERENCES IN POLITICAL OUTLOOK

Studies show that Democratic party leaders usually have a more liberal outlook than Republican party leaders. Democratic leaders favor social-welfare programs and are more willing to expand government social services. They are critical of big business and usually favor a more progressive income tax. By contrast, Republican leaders oppose many social-welfare programs and believe the government's role in this area should be limited. Republicans tend to fear the influence of labor unions and oppose increased business regulation.

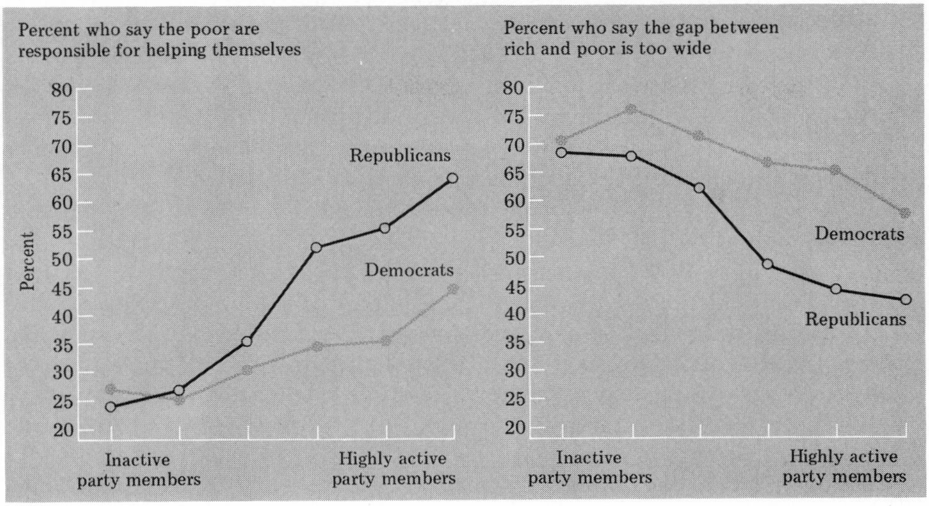

FIGURE 8.3
Welfare Attitudes of Democrats and Republicans at Various Activity Levels

Source: Based on data from Sidney Verba and Norman H. Nie, *Participation in America: Political Democracy and Social Inequality* (New York: Harper & Row, 1972).

A study of the political opinions of delegates to the Presidential nominating conventions in 1956 found that the Democratic party "is marked by a strong belief in the power of collective action to promote social justice, equality, humanitarianism, and economic planning, while preserving freedom." The Republican party "is distinguished by faith in the wisdom of the natural competitive process and in the supreme virtue of individuals, 'character,' self-reliance, frugality, and independence from government."[2]

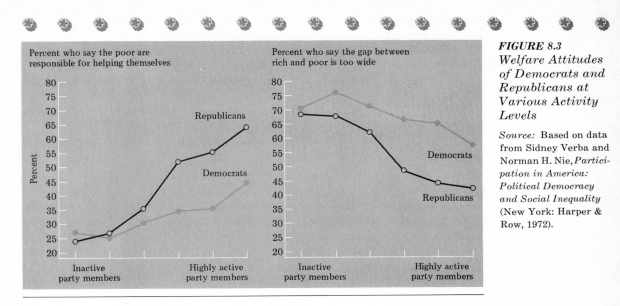

A survey ten years later had similar results. (See Figure 8.3.) Politically active Democrats were less willing than active Republicans to say the poor are responsible for helping themselves, and Democrats were more likely than Republicans to think the income gap between rich and poor is too wide.

PARTY LEADERS SUPPORT DIFFERENT LEGISLATION

Neither party can force its representatives in Congress to stay loyal to the party or to support the policies the party favors. As we have seen, the parties are loose, regionally based coalitions, not centrally directed organizations with cohesive programs. Although the President and congressional leaders can put pressure on party members, they can go only so far. Members of Congress are influenced less by their parties than by their financial backers and the interest groups that helped get them elected. So if we find that Demo-

[2] These findings are taken from a study of the delegates to the 1956 Presidential nominating conventions of both parties. These delegates come from every part of the country and from every level of party and government. For a full report see Herbert McClosky, Paul J. Hoffmann, and Rosemary O'Hara, "Issue Conflict and Consensus Among Party Leaders and Followers," *American Political Science Review,* June 1960, 420.

crats and Republicans vote differently in Congress, this must reflect differences in political outlook between the two parties.

Political scientists have studied how Democrats and Republicans vote in Congress and have reached these conclusions: (1) Party members tend to vote the same way, and there are major policy differences between the two parties; (2) when members of Congress vote differently from other members of their parties, it's usually because of pressure from the voters back home or, more likely, from important interest groups in their home districts.

Differences between the two parties may be seen in *roll-call votes* or votes on various policies in the House of Representatives. Table 8.1 lists votes on a number of bills over the past twenty-five years; it shows a striking contrast between Republicans and Democrats. On balance, the Republican party has opposed social-welfare programs and government regulation of the economy and has favored policies that stimulate free enterprise. The Democrats have tended to favor greater government involvement in the economy; they have tried to reduce income differences through tax reform; and they have favored social-welfare programs.

However, this description is not entirely accurate. Each party has sometimes protected conservative principles and sometimes called for reform. The first major attempt to regulate trusts was made by a Republican President, Theodore Roosevelt. And conservative southern Democrats have often blocked social-welfare legislation, particularly in the area of civil rights.

Still, various types of evidence show meaningful differences between the two major parties, differences based at least partly on conflicting class inter-

TABLE 8.1
Party differences in the House of Representatives, 1945–1975

Year	*Selected legislation*	*Democrats in favor*	*Republicans in favor*
1945	Full Employment Act	90%	36%
1947	Maintain Individual Income Tax Rates	62	1
1954	Increase Unemployment Compensation	54	9
1961	Emergency Educational Act	67	4
1964	Antipoverty Program	84	13
1969	Tax Reform	86	22
1971	Hospital Construction	99	41
1973	Increase Minimum Wage	88	27
1974	Federal Aid to City Transit Systems	81	23
1975	Emergency Jobs for Unemployed	92	13

Source: Compiled from Robert A. Dahl, "Key Votes, 1945–1964," *Pluralist Democracy in the United States*, © 1967 by Rand McNally College Publishing Company, Chicago, pp. 238–242; *Labor Looks at the 91st Congress*, adapted from an AFL-CIO Legislative Report, 1971; *Labor Looks at Congress 1973*, adapted from an AFL-CIO Legislative Report, 1974; *Labor Looks at the 93rd Congress*, adapted from an AFL-CIO Legislative Report, 1975.

ests. The argument that Republicans and Democrats don't give the voter a choice doesn't hold up, nor does the argument that it makes no difference which party controls Congress.

POLITICAL PARTIES AND FOREIGN POLICY

In many foreign-policy issues political parties play a minor role. These are the nonpartisan issues of war and peace and national defense. Here both parties follow the lead of the President and his advisers. Since World War II foreign policy has been the responsibility of a small group of experts independent of serious party politics. This may be seen in a number of major foreign-policy decisions on issues like the Vietnam War, involvement in military alliances such as NATO, and the stationing of American military forces around the world. These policies aren't made by party leaders meeting to plan a bipartisan role for the United States in world affairs. They are made by the President, acting as leader of the nation rather than as head of his party, with the help of advisers from universities, major corporations, law firms, the State Department, and the Pentagon.

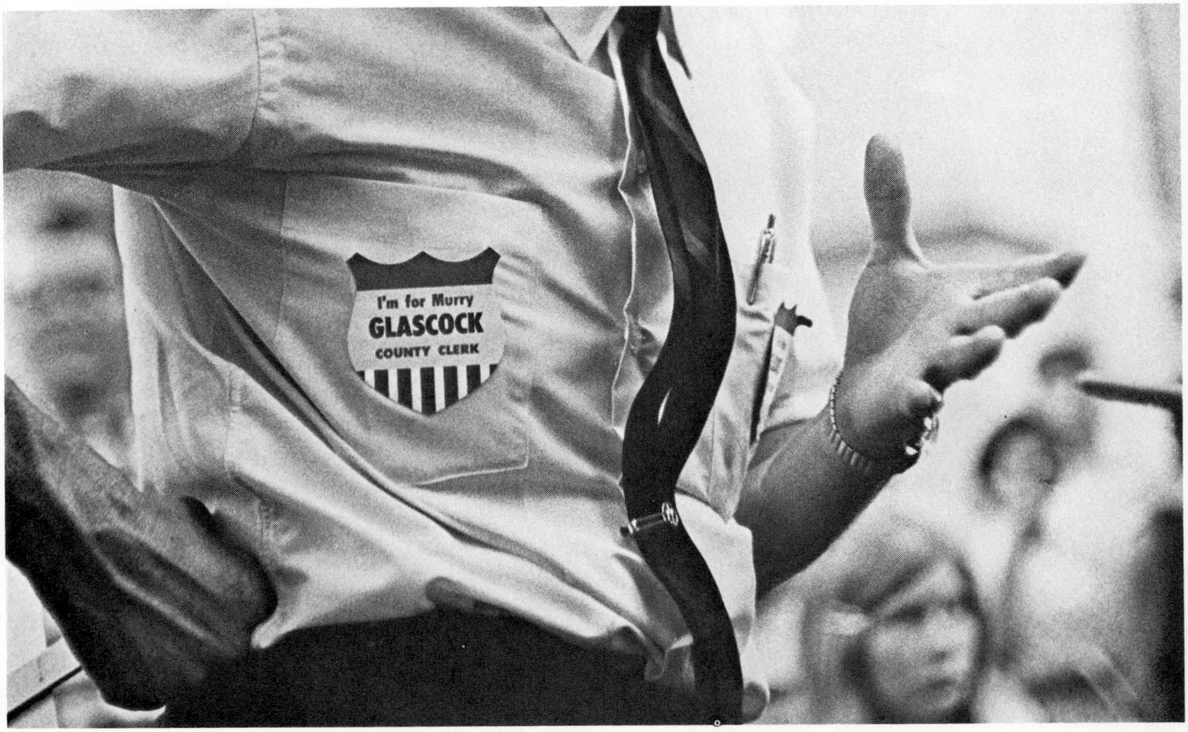

SUMMARY

Our discussion of American political parties has touched on several important points. First, the political parties manage the transfer of power in American politics. They do this even though they aren't organized and don't have a cohesive program. In fact the decentralization of the political parties makes it possible for them to manage the election of political leaders ranging from the President of the United States to the mayor of a small town.

Second, the parties' control over the routes to political office is a matter of tradition rather than law. There's nothing to stop people from winning elections completely outside the party system. But this isn't easy; millions of voters identify with the major parties, and the parties provide campaign funds and organization for the candidates they nominate.

Third, the relationship between political parties and election results is a complex one. The parties are continually challenged to make room for new ideas and new social groups. Sometimes these new ideas or groups can't find a place in the Democratic or Republican party and turn instead to a third party. When voters give their support to a minor party, the leaders of the major parties worry. A major party will often change its policies and programs to attract those voters back, or perhaps to attract voters from the other major party. On the other hand, it's possible for a party to lose so much support that it simply disappears; this happened to the Whig party before the Civil War. Some people think the Republican party is threatened in the same way; we'll discuss this question in the next section.

The fourth major point we've discussed is the difference between the two parties. There are various kinds of evidence showing that it makes a difference who wins elections. Governmental policies and programs differ depending on which party is in control.

The Future of the Two-Party System

It's almost impossible to imagine American politics without the Democratic and Republican parties as we know them. But the party system, along with other American political institutions, is going through some major changes. And it's very hard to tell what effect these changes will have.

The variety of protest movements in the past few years is a signal that "politics as usual" won't work any longer. This has put the party system under some strain. New groups—blacks, women, ethnics—are demanding a greater role in the nation's political life. One of their demands is for more open politics. Already this is changing the kinds of candidates who run for public office. In 1974, for example, six of the winning congressional candidates were under 30.

Along with these pressures for change has come a decline in party loyalty. This may be seen in the growing number of people who call themselves independents and in the increase in ticket splitting.

But the strongest evidence that major changes are taking place is the actual voting behavior of citizens. In the 1972 Presidential election large numbers of Catholic and ethnic voters switched from the Democratic to the Republican ticket in the traditionally Democratic northern states; the Jewish vote remained Democratic, but just barely (it has traditionally supported the Democratic party by a 9-to-1 ratio); southern support for the Democratic party continued to weaken; and the youth vote, which had been expected to strengthen the Democratic party, actually favored Nixon.

However, in all but the Presidential race the results of the 1972 election were fairly typical. The Democratic party didn't lose its majority in Congress; it still won more governorships than the Republicans, and it stayed in control of the stage legislatures it usually controls. Perhaps the 1972 election was a deviating election rather than a realigning one. In 1976 the blacks, the Catholics, the ethnics, the Jews, the southerners, and other traditionally Democratic voters supported the Democratic ticket of Carter-Mondale.

The major parties will continue to try to find room for the new groups on the political scene. They will try to deal with today's political agenda of inflation, recession, consumer protection, tax reform, and social welfare. They won't remain unchanged. But if they can't absorb the new groups and deal with the issues, the two-party system as we have known it will fade.

Additional analysis of the Democratic Party victory in 1976 can be found at the end of the book in the section dealing with the 1976 election.

CONTROVERSY

Should Political Parties Present a Clearer Choice to the Electorate?

In choosing its Presidential ticket, should a political party simply try to pick winners or should it stress the differences between the two parties? Most of the time the two major parties nominate middle-of-the-road candidates. In doing so they smooth over important differences in political outlook between the Republicans and the Democrats.

One Side Americans tend to vote for Presidential candidates who stand midway between a conservative and a liberal outlook. Because it's the job of political parties to win elections, they should give the voters what they want. Nominations of "extreme" candidates have resulted in serious defeats. In 1964 the Republican convention nominated Goldwater, who led the party's conservative wing. The Democratic nominee, Johnson, won more than 60 percent of the vote. In 1972 the Democratic party chose McGovern, who represented the party's liberal wing. McGovern's defeat by Nixon was similar to Goldwater's defeat eight years earlier—and for many of the same reasons.

In 1976 the Republican Party selected Ford, the choice of the moderates, over the more conservative challenger, Reagan.

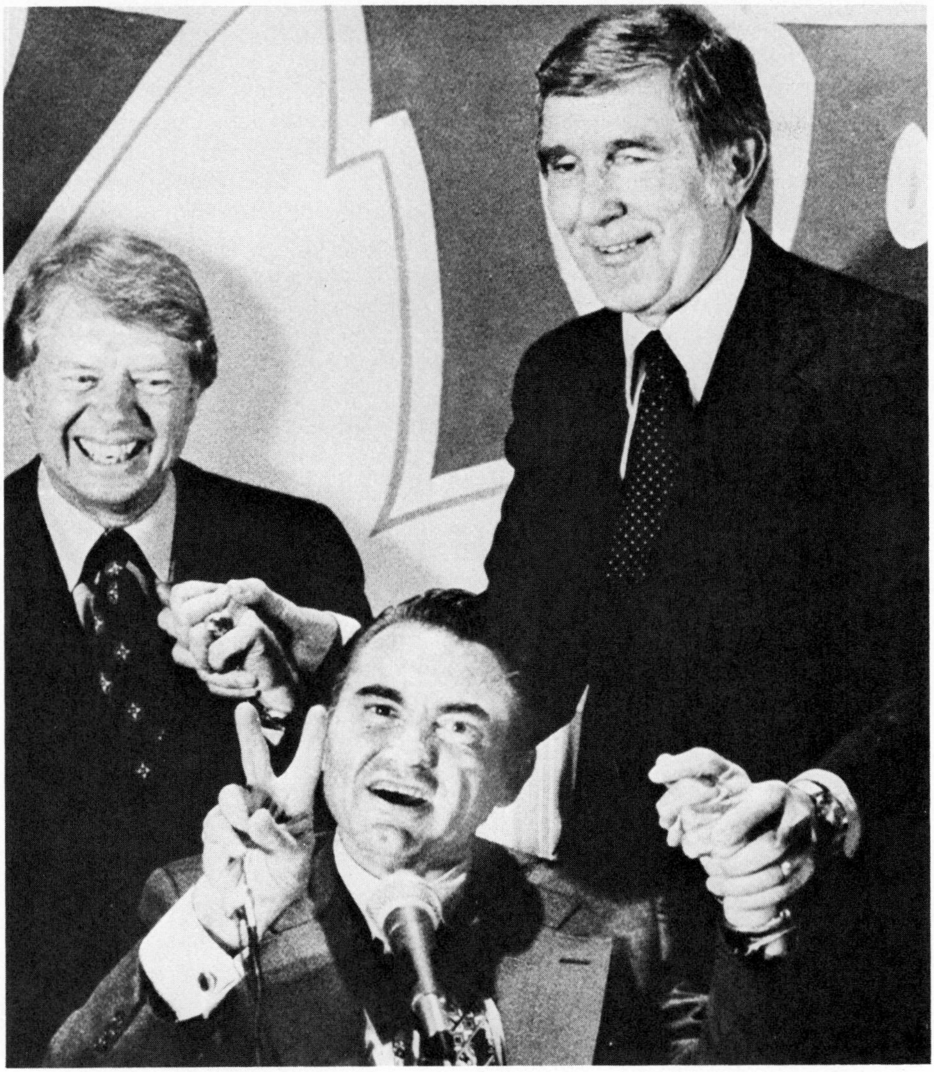

The Democrats in their most recent primaries selected a moderate, Carter, for the party's nomination.

If a Presidential candidate is very conservative or very liberal, many voters will switch to the other party.

The Other Side

While it's true that voters seem to prefer middle-of-the-road candidates, the major parties should think about other things besides winning. They should use the election as a chance to express different goals and policies for the nation.

Such a choice is particularly important in a Presidential campaign.

Most citizens pay attention to politics only at this time. If the typical citizen is going to think seriously about the choices facing society, these issues will have to be debated in a Presidential campaign. When the Presidential campaign smooths over major differences about how to handle the nation's problems, the democratic process isn't working.

Candidates who clearly differ from their opponents play an important educating role, even if they lose. They remind the nation that different policies are possible. This is part of the responsibility of leadership. In 1972, for example, McGovern's strong antiwar stand probably contributed to his defeat, but it might also have spurred the Nixon administration's efforts to make peace. McGovern, the loser, saw it this way: "There can be no question at all that we have pushed this country in the direction of peace," he said. "I think each one of us loves the title of peacemaker more than any office in the land."

When the political parties fail to give the voters a choice, they fail to provide leadership, and in this way they fail the American public.

How Institutions Work: II
How the Political Parties Are Organized

WHAT IS THE ORGANIZATIONAL BASIS OF AMERICAN POLITICAL PARTIES?

The parties have several layers of organization. Each layer—city or county, state, and national—puts most of its effort into elections in its own area. But the ties that link one layer to the next are more formal than real. Party organization is decentralized, which means the parties are less organized at the state level than at the local level and least organized at the national level.

HOW ARE THE PARTIES ORGANIZED AT THE NATIONAL LEVEL?

Each party has a national committee made up of one man and one woman from each state. The Republican national committee also includes state chairpersons from states that voted Republican in the last election. Committee members are chosen in various ways in different states.

The national committee rarely meets; in reality it amounts to little more than the national chairperson (elected at the convention) and the party staff in Washington.

ARE THERE ANY OTHER PARTY STRUCTURES AT THE NATIONAL LEVEL?

Both the Republicans and the Democrats have campaign committees chosen by the party members in each house of Congress. They are independent of the national committee; their purpose is to raise money and provide campaign organization for House and Senate candidates.

HOW ARE THE PARTIES ORGANIZED AT THE STATE LEVEL?

At the top of the state structure is each party's state committee. Its members are chosen by each county or district. They organize state party conventions, manage campaigns, and raise money. Like the national committees, state organizations tend to be weak except when a dominant leader—the governor or a big-city mayor—can attract a lot of support.

Patterns of political strength at the state level vary widely. It's estimated that there is serious competition between the parties in about half the states. And even in these states the pattern may be very uneven. In Michigan, for example, the Democratic party organization is centered in Detroit and Wayne County, and the Republicans dominate the rest of the state.

WHAT MAKES SOME PARTY ORGANIZATIONS OPERATE SUCCESSFULLY?

In the United States parties operate mostly at the local level. The basic unit is the precinct or election district, which contains from 300 to 1000 voters. The precinct captain is responsible for getting out the vote. The captain and the ward leaders may be volunteers or may be chosen in the primaries. They are the building blocks of the district, city, and county organizations that make up the local layer of party structure. Such political "machines" are rare today, though the Cook County Democratic organization of Chicago continues to operate in this way.

In general, areas where local political units are well organized are dominated by one party—and for good reason. Party strength depends on money, organization, and many hours of work. These are scarce resources that usually can't support two well-organized parties in the same area.

Questions for Review

1. How are American political parties different from those of other nations?
2. What do we mean when we refer to the two-party system?
3. Why do political parties control the routes to public office?
4. How do political parties respond to social change?
5. What is the role of minor or third parties?
6. Define maintaining, deviating, and realigning elections. Give examples.
7. From which social groups do the Democrats and the Republicans get most of their support?
8. Do party leaders differ in political outlook?
9. What kinds of changes are occurring in the party system?

Chapter 9

Congress

Separation of powers in the federal government means that three separate branches share among themselves control of public policy and government resources. Of these three branches—executive, judicial, legislative—it is the legislative branch that is formally given the task of representation. The writers of the Constitution intended to establish a democratic government and immediately faced the difficult problem of how public preferences could be taken into account in making governmental policy. This problem they tried to solve by creating Congress, a group of representatives who owe their political careers to the voters back home. Members of Congress, aware that they are elected representatives, legislate on behalf of the people and groups who send them to Washington.

In some respects the hopes of the founders have been realized. Of the three branches of government, Congress is the most responsive, or at least the most visible. Congress is made up of 535 men and women who come from every part of the nation, bringing with them to Washington the hopes and fears of a very complicated society. Congress is at the center of the hustle and bustle of everyday politics; it is the meeting place of journalists, lobbyists, protesters, and average citizens.

Congress Under Attack

Not all observers of American politics believe that Congress is doing an effective job of legislating and representing, and it has received more than its share of criticism in recent years. Many critics believe Congress hasn't caught up with the twentieth century.

NATIONAL ISSUES AND LOCAL TIES

The issues the federal government must deal with are national in character, yet Congress is basically local.

American society has become a national society. Transportation, housing, legal justice, national security, and education affect the whole society. And the important groups in our society are also national in character: the National Council of Churches, the National Baseball League, the National Education Association, the National Association of Manufacturers. We still have the Main St. Methodist Church, the community baseball team, the Horace Mann PTA, and the local shoe factory, but they are nowhere near as important politically as the huge national organizations that have grown up during the twentieth century.

The agencies and activities of the government—the Federal Aviation Administration, the National Institutes of Health, the National Science Foundation—have also grown in response to social problems that are national in character. There are federal agencies and programs in every important area of national life: employment, civil rights, highway safety, consumer protection, and many more.

Congress represents and legislates for the American public. When you're bothered by high prices, racial injustice, polluted rivers, street crime, war spending, and so on, you're bothered about things Congress is supposed to deal with. But the members of Congress represent the voters back home. Can they deal with national issues?

CONGRESSIONAL CAREERS

Members of Congress are closely tied to one particular part of the country. Typically they have lived all their lives in the district or state they represent. They went to local colleges, state universities, or law schools. In contrast to the leaders of the executive branch, members of Congress have usually come up through the ranks of local offices and perhaps state legislatures.

Congressional careers also depend on local ties. Members of the House of Representatives must try to get reelected every two years. This helps them remember campaign promises and also keeps them in close touch with local groups.

Some people claim that this pattern isolates Congress from the changing issues of society. As long as members of Congress continue to satisfy the narrow interests of the important groups back home, they are reelected. And the longer they stay, the easier it is to take care of their supporters, since the old-timers in Congress control the distribution of defense contracts, federal loans, highway construction funds, and other programs which can benefit their *constituents*, that is, the people who provide important support and who expect their interests to be represented in government policies.

A MIDDLE-CLASS GROUP

Bella Abzug, Democratic representative from New York, says that a truly representative Congress would include 51 percent women, 11 percent blacks, more young and working-class people, and more people representing occupational groups such as teachers and artists. She's right in claiming that Congress is dominated by college-educated white males representing the professions (mostly law) and business. Why are only 3 percent of the members of Congress women when women make up 51 percent of the population? Why are there so few black or Chicano members when minority groups make up 11 percent of the population?

The reformer believes that changing the makeup of Congress will change its social outlook. When civil-rights groups campaign for black candidates, it's because they think blacks can best represent racial minorities; when the Women's Caucus calls for more women in Congress, it's because they assume that feminist demands can be presented more strongly by women than by men. But a man doesn't care about the interests of the working class just because he works in a factory; not all women support the demands of the feminist movement; and a black skin can cover an Uncle Tom as well as a Black Panther.

It's true that Congress, with its local ties, has trouble dealing with national issues. And it's true that certain groups in society are not well represented. But these criticisms overlook some of the important ways Congress acts as a representative assembly.

Members of Congress as Representatives

Are members of Congress supposed to represent the wishes of those who voted for them, or are they supposed to use their own judgment? Some say that representatives who don't follow the instructions of their constituencies aren't representative at all, while others ask, If all representatives are tied to their constituencies, why bother to have a legislature? Most members of Congress take the middle road. They either mix the two viewpoints, depending on the issue, or use their own judgment except in cases that clearly affect their district or state.

REPRESENTING THE INDIVIDUAL CITIZEN

The federal bureaucracy touches the life of the individual citizen in many ways: social-security payments, income-tax laws, small-business loans, medicare, consumer protection, and so on. When citizens get poor treatment from

Congressional staff spend much time answering requests from voters back home.

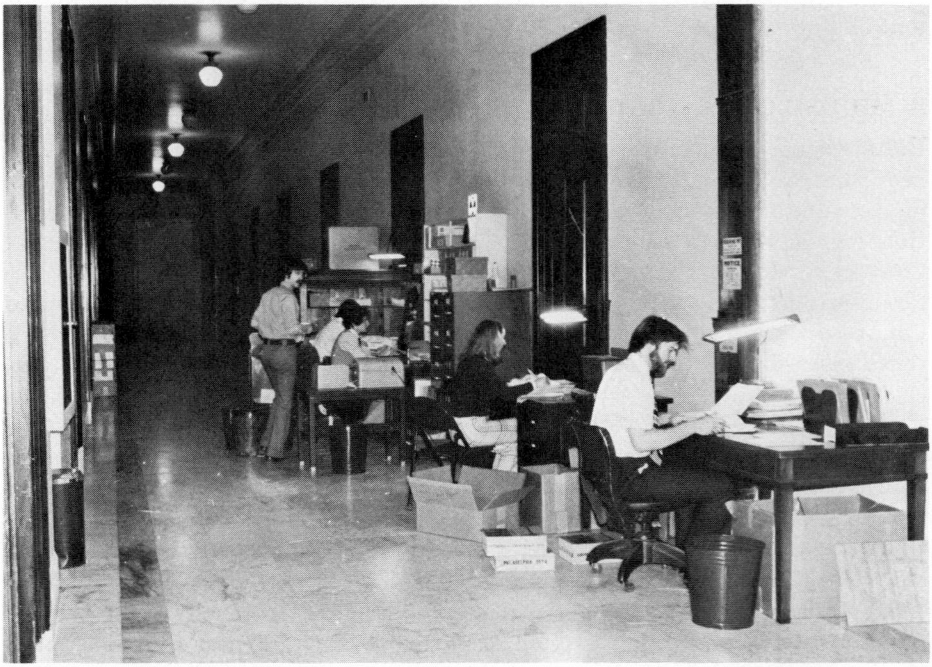

an executive agency or need some government service, they ask their congressman or congresswoman for help. So the work of congressional members includes running errands for citizens or helping them get better treatment from the government. It's hard to tell how much time they spend in this way, but some estimates go as high as 50 percent. And their staffs spend a lot of time on individual problems.

Some say errand running takes up too much time. Representative Henry S. Reuss describes a congressman as a harried man and says "the days are hardly long enough for him to think and act soundly on all the great issues of war and peace, national prosperity and civil rights," let alone the problems of individual voters.

Yet they do pay attention to those problems. Reelection can depend on being helpful to your constituents, no matter how you vote on matters of governmental policy. Thus while members of Congress are paying close attention to citizens' *problems*, they're not paying as much attention to citizens' viewpoints.

REPRESENTING THE VOTERS

As a senator, John F. Kennedy wrote:

> In Washington I frequently find myself believing that forty or fifty letters, six visits from professional politicians and lobbyists, and three editorials in Massachusetts newspapers constitute public opinion of a given issue. Yet in truth I rarely know how the great majority of the voters feel, or even how much they know of the issues that seem so burning in Washington.

It's often hard for members of Congress to represent voters accurately. Voters aren't very well informed, and not many people participate in politics. How can the winning candidate tell what all the voters want, having the support of only less than one-fourth of the eligible voters in the district? In addition, average voters know very little about their representatives. And in any campaign candidates have to talk about a lot of different issues. Did they win because they supported price controls or because they opposed busing? Maybe they won not because of what they said but because their opponents lost votes by supporting different policies.

Furthermore, Congress has to deal with a great variety of issues: civil rights, foreign treaties, funds for space exploration, welfare programs, tax reform, energy programs, and so on. Representatives do not check with their constituencies before every vote. Only a few voters are informed about the bills being studied and debated in Congress, let alone what their representatives are doing about them.

Still, it would be wrong to assume that the opinions of voters have no influence on how a member of Congress votes. The civil-rights voting record of Shirley Chisholm, liberal black congresswoman from New York, is very different from the voting record of William Poage, conservative congressman from Texas. But a person with Chisholm's views wouldn't be elected in Poage's district, and someone with Poage's views wouldn't stand a chance in Chisholm's district.

There appears to be a high correlation between how members of Congress vote and how their constituents feel about governmental policy on civil rights and race relations.[1] This can be explained in two different ways. A congressman or congresswoman may feel the same way as the voters, or may not see eye to eye with them but may fear to oppose them on such a major issue. The evidence shows that the second explanation may be closer to the truth: Members of Congress change their own views on racial issues according to how their constituents feel.

But note that this pattern was found only in the area of civil rights. On foreign-policy issues, for example, they don't seem to be affected by their constituents' opinions. Perhaps voters aren't sure how they feel and are willing to give Congress and the President more leeway in this area.

REPRESENTING INTEREST GROUPS

Members of Congress may be unsure of the views of individual voters, but they know what the important groups back home want, particularly when proposed legislation affects their interests. These groups represent a lot of votes, and they let their representatives know how they feel about an issue. Some of these interest groups have lobbies in Washington. Their job is to inform, persuade, and sometimes threaten in order to get favorable treatment from Congress.

The leaders of interest groups can't easily control the votes of their members. But they do control campaign funds, and they keep their members informed about their representatives in Congress. Nearly all the political pressure on congressmen and congresswomen comes from interest groups. This kind of activity is especially important if one or two major interests dominate the district or state, such as auto manufacturing in Michigan and citrus growing in Florida.

Two Forms of Group Politics. Interest groups are active in two ways. First, they try to persuade members of Congress to support legislation that will benefit their areas. For example, a group of local businessmen trying to affect the route of a federal highway may use political pressure. Usually they have no trouble getting the help of their representatives. The struggle takes place *within* Congress: More than one part of the country wants to influence the route of the highway. The same can be said for defense contracts, research centers, favorable treatment from the Department of Agriculture, and so on. Congressmen and congresswomen are often judged by how well they compete for such benefits.

[1] The study cited here and in the next paragraph is from Warren E. Miller and Donald E. Stokes, "Constituency Influence in Congress," *American Political Science Review,* 57 (1963), 45–57.

Interest groups can also compete with other national groups trying to influence legislative policy. Members of Congress often hear from such powerful groups as the AFL-CIO, the AMA, the American Legion, and the NAM. These groups claim to speak for members across the nation. When they try to influence legislation, the results are very different from what happens when a local interest group puts pressure on its senator or representative. The issues are much more important: Congress becomes the battlefield for a conflict between business and labor or between farmers and consumers, and congressmen and congresswomen are under pressure from both sides.

GROUP POLITICS AND GEOGRAPHIC REPRESENTATION

The Constitution makes place of residence the basis for electing members of Congress. But doesn't a doctor in St. Louis have more in common with a doctor in Dallas than with the grocer who lives next door? It depends on the issue. Look at the following table:

	Citizen A	*Citizen B*	*Citizen C*
Place of residence	Chicago suburb	Chicago suburb	Small town in Kansas
Occupation	Retired military	Public-school teacher	Shop owner
Race	White	Black	White

On an issue directly related to place of residence, we would find Citizens A and B opposed to Citizen C, but on other issues the lineup might look like this:

Federal support for mass transit	A and B vs. C
Higher veterans' benefits	B and C vs. A
Hiring of minority groups	A and C vs. B

Election of representatives on a geographic basis is a permanent part of our political system. This is what makes national organizations so important in the legislative process. On many issues they cross geographic boundaries and support citizens' viewpoints on issues that affect them because of their job, sex, age, or race. Thus the AMA "represents" doctors from Honolulu to Huzzah; the National Council of Senior Citizens "represents" older citizens from Mississippi to Maine. So if Congress is responsive to national organizations when it's dealing with national issues, it's much less local in its outlook than some critics claim.

Congress: The Legislative Branch

Richard Bolling, Democrat from Missouri, is among a group of reformers who believe Congress is an organizational mess and that this keeps it from doing its job as well as it should. There are two questions here. First, what are the organizational problems? Second, would a reorganized Congress really be able to do its job better?

The Constitution divides Congress into two houses, the Senate and the House of Representatives. But it doesn't say how the two houses should organize themselves. How Congress chooses its leaders, divides up its work, and debates and votes on issues are decisions to be made by its members.

DIFFERENCES BETWEEN HOUSE AND SENATE

The Senate is the smaller group. It is made up of only 100 people, two elected from each state. It has a more informal way of working than the House. By contrast, the House has 435 members; the number from each state depends on its population. Legislation in the House is carefully regulated, and it is controlled by 10 to 15 percent of its members. Many members, especially newcomers, have no real power at all.

The Senate is more nearly a club of equals. The senator stays in office for six years, the representative only two. So even a new senator will be in Washington long enough to be noticed. Many are as well known as state governors or even the President; in fact four of the recent Presidents (Truman, Johnson, Kennedy, and Nixon) were once senators.

However, the fact that the average senator has more power than the average representative doesn't mean the Senate is stronger than the House. Bills must be passed by both houses. Only the Senate can confirm Presidential appointments such as Supreme Court justices and ambassadors, but only the House can introduce revenue bills. Such bills must pass the Senate as well as the House, but the power to introduce these bills is the power to set the agenda, and this means the House has a lot of influence over legislation.

LEADERSHIP IN THE HOUSE

The member of the House with the greatest power is the *Speaker of the House*, currently Carl Albert. He controls the debate and can often influence legislation in this way. He also appoints members of special committees, though not those of standing committees. The Speaker is always a member of the majority party; in fact he is the recognized leader of the majority party.

Working closely with the Speaker is the majority party *floor leader*. The floor leader deals with committee chairmen and with the House Rules Committee, which controls what bills come before the House. The majority party *whip*, along with deputy whips, is responsible for knowing how many party members are likely to support a particular bill. They also try to round up members in time for an important vote.

LEADERSHIP IN THE SENATE

According to the Constitution, the Vice-President presides over the Senate; because he is rarely present, the *president protempore* takes his place. But the recognized leader of the Senate is the *Senate majority leader.* He is elected by the majority party, and his power comes from his position as head of the party and his personal leadership skills. The personality and drive of the Senate majority leader are especially important in such a small group.

MINORITY PARTY LEADERS

In both the House and the Senate, the minority party chooses its own leaders and whips. An important job of the minority party leader is to act as a link with the White House when the President is a member of the same party. For example, the *Senate minority leader* met often with President Ford to plan party strategy in a Congress dominated by Democrats.

Legislation by Committee

It's impossible for 535 people working together to make decisions on dozens of complicated issues. Even dividing them into two groups doesn't solve the problem. And even if they had nothing else to do and could meet and debate

Mike Mansfield, recently retired Senate majority leader, spent 24 years in the Senate.

each bill, no senator or representative could be reasonably well informed about the great variety of things Congress has to deal with.

STANDING COMMITTEES

Complicated issues require complicated legislation, and this should be done by a small group of experts—a committee. That's why Congress has set up *standing committees* in both houses. These committees are responsible for reviewing all bills referred to them, consulting executive agencies about the possible effects of a bill, writing and rewriting the actual legislation, holding public hearings if necessary, and sending the bill to the House or Senate with the committee's recommendations. The committees are where legislation really happens. Table 9.1 lists the standing committees of Congress in order of importance.

SUBCOMMITTEES

Because any committee may have to deal with many issues and because some committees are so large (the House Appropriations Committee has 50 members), subcommittees are necessary. There are now nearly 250 subcommittees in Congress.

COMMITTEE ASSIGNMENTS

Committee assignments are made by the party leaders of the Senate and the House and depend on the strength of each party. Thus if two-thirds of the senators are Democrats and one-third are Republicans, each committee will include about two-thirds Democrats and one-third Republicans. Seats on the more powerful committees are highly prized, and this gives party leaders a lot

Members of the Senate Rules Committee preparing to vote.

of power. Assigning new congressmen and congresswomen to committees gives party leaders a chance to reward the ones they approve of and punish those who don't play by the rules.

Reelection to Congress often depends on committee assignment. Senators and representatives from farm districts try to get seats on the Agriculture Committee so they can serve their areas better and keep an eye on the Department of Agriculture. Party leaders can hurt members' careers by assigning them to a committee where they can't serve their constituents. When Representative Herman Badillo first came to Congress, he was assigned to the Agriculture Committee, where he felt unable to do much for his constituents in the Bronx. As he told Speaker Albert, "there isn't any crop in my district except marijuana."

TABLE 9.1* *Standing committees of congress (ranked in groups, by order of importance)

	Senate (18)	*House (21)*
I	Appropriations Finance Foreign Relations	Appropriations Rules Ways and Means
II	Agriculture and Forestry Armed Services Budget[a] Commerce Judiciary	Agriculture Armed Services Budget[a] Government Operations International Relations Interstate and Foreign Commerce Judiciary
III	Aeronautical and Space Science Banking, Housing and Urban Affairs Interior and Insular Affairs Labor and Public Welfare Public Works	Banking, Currency, and Housing Education and Labor Interior and Insular Affairs Public Works and Transportation Science and Technology
IV	Government Operations Post Office and Civil Service Veterans Affairs	Merchant Marine and Fisheries Post Office and Civil Service Standards of Official Conduct Veterans Affairs
V	District of Columbia Rules and Administration	District of Columbia House Administration

[a] New committees with important formal powers but not as yet clearly established policy influence.

Source: Rankings based on data from several sources, including Donald H. Matthews, *U.S. Senators and Their World* (Chapel Hill: The University of North Carolina Press, 1960); H. Douglas Price, as cited in Stephen K. Bailey, *The New Congress* (New York: St. Martin's Press, Inc., 1966); and the 1975 *Congressional Quarterly Almanac.*

It's reasonable for senators or representatives to want seats on a committee where they think they can serve their constituents, but it's also true that this contributes to a local outlook. Committees become dominated by special interests, and policy is made in a series of compromises among small groups more interested in satisfying their constituencies than in dealing with national issues. The House Agriculture Committee, for example, has long been dominated by representatives from the farm belt. But it is responsible for legislation that affects other people besides farmers. In recent years it has had a strong influence on school-lunch and good-stamp programs. It finally became clear to representatives from the cities, where hot school lunches and food stamps are needed most, that the Agriculture Committee must be made to serve consumers as well as producers.

SOURCES OF COMMITTEE POWERS

Committees get their power from four sources: (1) control over the flow of legislation; (2) the knowledge of their members; (3) ties with executive agencies and interest groups; and (4) public hearings.

Control Over the Flow of Legislation. This is a result of congressional rules as well as custom and is often attacked by reformers. Although the legislative agenda is largely set by the executive branch, the committees control what happens to that agenda after it gets to Congress.

Knowledge. This is a natural result of the committee structure. Because all members of Congress can't be equally informed on all the issues, this is reasonable. If the committees are permanent, as they are in Congress, and the same people stay on them for a long time, then it's no surprise to find that each committee has a lot of knowledge in its area. In many policy areas a division of labor among committees develops. In most cases the recommendation of a subcommittee is accepted ("They're the experts; they know what they're doing"), and the recommendation of the full committee is accepted by the House or Senate. It's *within* the committee or subcommittee that you find sharp debate, lobbying, and the careful writing of legislation.

Ties with Interest Groups and Executive Agencies. The fact that a committee is responsible for a certain policy area and some members (the more powerful ones) stay on it for a long time makes it easy for the committee to form close ties with the groups that are most interested in that policy area. The two Agriculture Committees, for example, will be led not only by senators and representatives from the farm belt but also by those who get campaign support from the American Farm Bureau Federation. These committees also have close ties with the Department of Agriculture. Each of these three partners supports the other two and protects them against "enemies." Similar partnerships are found in the areas of labor, commerce, finance, welfare, education, and defense, as well as many others.

Public hearings. Committees and subcommittees can hold public hearings if necessary to get information and opinions from interested groups. This helps Congress decide on policy, and it gives groups and individuals a way to try to influence policy. Witnesses before congressional committees often represent an executive agency. They may also speak for major interest groups that would be affected by the legislation being discussed. Sometimes a committee wants testimony from a person who doesn't want to appear. In such cases it can issue a subpoena.

COMMITTEE CHAIRS

The committee chair is the person with the most power within the committee. The chair can appoint subcommittee members, hire and fire committee staff members, call committee meetings, set the agenda, decide whether to hold public hearings, control the debate, and consult with members of the executive branch and chairs of other committees, and so on.

THE SENIORITY RULE

The standard way of becoming chair of a committee is simple. You get re-elected, continue to serve on the same committee, and wait for your party to become the majority party. Until very recently committee chairs were chosen on the basis of the *seniority rule.* The majority party member who has served on the committee longest is the chair. The minority party member who has

An anonymous witness prepares to testify before a House committee investigating the use of confidential funds by the Internal Revenue Service.

served longest is the "shadow chair," who has some control over the committee staff and the assignment of the minority party's members to subcommittees, but this power is always much less than the chair's.

There are many criticisms of the seniority rule. For one thing, it ignores ability and rewards a person simply for staying on the same committee for a long time. Thus seniority rewards age as well as long service, and people in their sixties and seventies get control over Congress. Sometimes these people change with the times, but sometimes they don't. Reelected from safe, one-party districts, they can easily ignore today's political agenda.

But a major reform is under way. The first step was taken in 1970, when Republicans in the House decided to use secret ballots to decide who was the highest-ranking Republican on each House committee. But because the Republican party doesn't control the House, this didn't affect how chairs were chosen. However, the 1974 election brought 92 new representatives to Washington, 75 of them Democrats. They provided the votes that broke the seniority rule. Powerful committee chairs like William Poage of the House Agriculture Committee, F. Edward Herbert of the Armed Services Committee, and 82-year-old Wright Patman of the Banking and Currency Committee were removed.

REFORMING THE COMMITTEE SYSTEM

A major problem of the committee system is the question of which committee has control over what issues. Which House committee, for example, should be responsible for energy policy? A good energy policy would include new international trade agreements, revised tax laws, regulations affecting mining and nuclear plants, and research on new sources of energy. Half a dozen different House committees claim energy policy is in their area, and the same is true in the Senate.

As a result there is now a committee to study committees, led by reformer Bolling. If Bolling can persuade Congress to accept a new committee system, it will affect much more than the seniority rule. It could do a lot to help Congress match the executive branch in deciding on national policy.

How Legislation Is Passed

How is a bill passed? As shown in Figure 9.1, a bill must be introduced in both houses of Congress; it is then referred to committee. The committees hold hearings and then write and rewrite the legislation. If a committee "reports out" a bill, it is placed on the legislative calendar. It is then debated, perhaps amended, and voted on. If the House and the Senate pass different bills, a *conference committee* representing both houses of Congress works out a compromise bill. If this bill is passed by both the House and the Senate, it goes to the President, and if he signs it, it becomes law. If the President vetoes the bill, it can still become law if it is passed again by a two-thirds majority of both houses of Congress. (See the special section at the end of the chapter for a more detailed description of congressional procedures.)

Thus it's often hard for a bill to get through Congress. It might be referred to an unfriendly committee where it will be watered down or simply left to die; it might get bottled up in the House Rules Committee, which must put it on the calendar before it can be debated in the House; or it might be killed by a Senate *filibuster*, unlimited debate in which a small group can hold up Senate business for as long as it can talk—sometimes several days or even weeks. But the moment of truth is when the bill is put to a vote.

FACTORS AFFECTING CONGRESSIONAL VOTING

Many things affect congressional voting: the influence of an executive agency or the President himself; congressional career hopes as well as political beliefs; instructions from party leaders; campaign promises; committee recommendations; friendships, bargains, compromises. But there are times when the issue itself is so important that other factors have little influence on the vote. An example is the 1969 Senate vote on Nixon's plan to deploy the Safeguard antiballistic missile. A marathon debate lasting nearly five months involved dozens of witnesses, heavy media coverage, serious study by many senators, and lobbying on both sides. The vote was a 50–50 tie, allowing Spiro Agnew, then Vice-President, to vote for the President's plan. A few days before the vote Senator James B. Pearson, a Kansas Republican, said: "You know, this issue will come as close as any to turning on the quiet conscience of

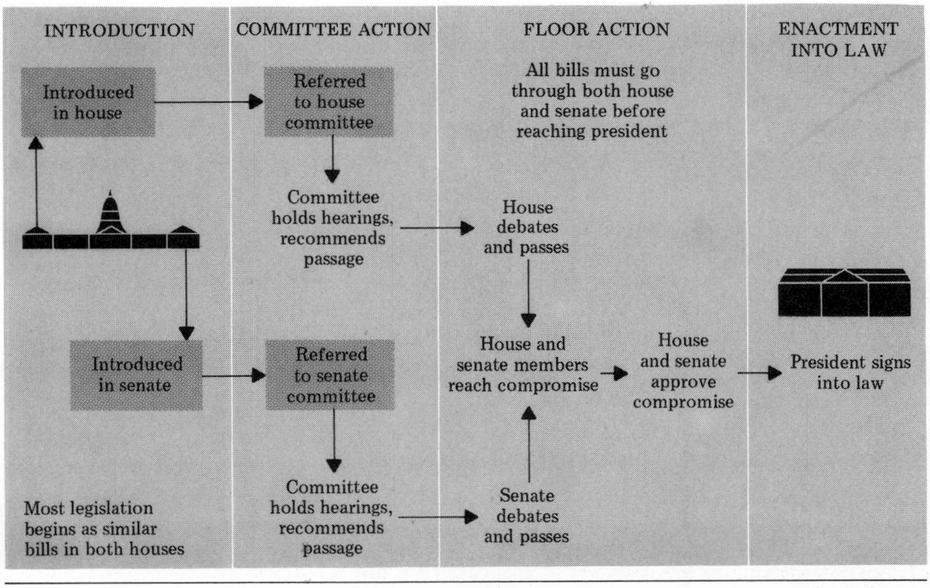
INTRODUCTION
COMMITTEE ACTION
FLOOR ACTION
ENACTMENT INTO LAW
Introduced in house
Referred to house committee
All bills must go through both house and senate before reaching president
Committee holds hearings, recommends passage
House debates and passes
Introduced in senate
Referred to senate committee
House and senate members reach compromise
House and senate approve compromise
President signs into law
Committee holds hearings, recommends passage
Senate debates and passes
Most legislation begins as similar bills in both houses

FIGURE 9.1 *How a Bill Becomes a Law*

the individual senators. The Senate would be a powerful instrument if all the issues were debated in this manner."[2]

Bargaining. Such issues are rare, however; usually there are many other factors affecting the vote. Often there is outright bargaining between congressional members. Here's an example from a 1956 debate on support for burley tobacco:

> *Mr. Langer (North Dakota):* We do not raise any tobacco in North Dakota, but we are interested in the tobacco situation in Kentucky, and I hope the Senator will support us in securing assistance for the wheat growers in our state.
>
> *Mr. Clements (Kentucky):* I think the Senator will find that my support will be 100 percent.
>
> *Mr. Barkley (Kentucky):* Mr. President, will my colleague from Kentucky yield?
>
> *Mr. Clements:* I yield.
>
> *Mr. Barkley:* The colloquy just had confirms and justifies the Woodrow Wilsonian doctrine of open covenants openly arrived at. (Laughter.)[3]

Friendship. In August 1971 the Senate voted on a bill to bail out Lockheed Aircraft by giving federal guarantees to a huge loan. Lee Metcalf, a Montana Democrat, was opposed to "big-business slush funds" and planned to vote against the bill. But his friend Alan Cranston of California, where many voters worked for Lockheed, begged him not to throw 30,000 people out of work. Metcalf was persuaded to vote for the Lockheed loan, which passed by a vote of 49 to 48.[4]

Economic Interests. Some members of Congress are personally interested in the legislation itself. Mississippi Democrat James Eastland, a member of the Agriculture Committee, always votes against ceilings on farm subsidies. In 1971 his wife was paid $159,000 in subsidies for farmland held in her name. Russell Long of Louisiana, chairman of the Senate Finance Committee, opposes any changes in tax laws which benefit oil companies. Between 1964 and 1969 his income from oil was $1,196,915, of which more than $300,000 was tax free. In 1969 the *Congressional Quarterly* estimated that 183 members of Congress held stock or other interests in companies doing business with the federal government or affected by federal legislation.[5]

[2] Cited in Nathan Miller, "The Making of a Majority: Safeguard and the Senate," in Charles Peters and Timothy J. Adams, eds., *Inside the System* (New York: Praeger, 1970), p. 158.

[3] *Congressional Record*, February 16, 1956, pp. 2300–2301.

[4] Mark J. Green, James M. Fallows, and David R. Zwick, *Who Runs Congress?* A Ralph Nader Congress Project Report (New York: Bantam, 1972), p. 211.

[5] Evidence for this paragraph comes from ibid., p. 140.

Committee Recommendations. In the long run the most important factors affecting congressional votes are committee recommendations, party identification, and the needs of the constituencies. A study of the 84th Congress found that if a bill is supported by a large majority of the committee in charge of it, its chances of being passed by the Senate are nearly perfect. But a recommendation from a divided committee passes only about half the time.[6]

Party Identification. Our political parties are different from those of Great Britain in that party members are free to vote against the wishes of party leaders. But this doesn't mean there's no connection between party identification and congressional voting. Members prefer to vote with their party rather than against it. Usually this means those belonging to the President's party try to support his programs, while the "opposition" party tries to block them. Some students of Congress feel that party pressure, whether direct or indirect, is the strongest influence on congressional voting.

Voters Back Home. When members of Congress vote against their party, it's usually because of what they think the voters back home want. Citizens know very little about their senators and representatives, let alone how they might vote on a complicated issue. But there are times when constituents become very interested in what a congressman or congresswoman is doing about a particular issue. A representative from Seattle, where many people work for Boeing Aircraft, wouldn't have voted against federal funding for the Boeing SST. No senator who depends on the state's labor unions for campaign support would vote for a bill outlawing the right to strike. Thus voter opinion *does* matter some of the time, and it seems to matter most on the issues that matter most to the people back home.

CONTROVERSY

Should Constituency Interests or the National Interest be Represented in Congress?

There's been a lot of debate over whether Congress represents the American people, but this question misses the point. When members of Congress try to get a federal program for their districts, they are representing. When they vote for a bill that gives tax advantages to wealthy constitu-

[6] Donald R. Matthewes, *U.S. Senators and Their World* (New York: Vintage, 1960), p. 170.

ents, they are representing. The real question is: Should members of Congress represent the interests of the voters who send them to Washington, or should they have the national interest in mind?

One Side Members of Congress should support their constituents' interests, and they should try to represent the groups and organizations that give them campaign funds. If funds for the SST mean jobs for the voters in your state, you should fight for those funds. No one expects a black congresswoman from a northern city to prefer subsidies for Montana wheat growers over an educational head-start program, and no one should expect a representative from Montana to support the head-start program over wheat subsidies. A senator who gets campaign funds from the AMA should oppose medicare, while a representative who gets help from the Senior Citizens should support it.

Take Jamie Whitten, Democratic representative from Mississippi. As chairman of the House Appropriations Subcommittee on Agriculture, he forced the Department of Health, Education and Welfare to leave Mississippi out of the National Nutrition Survey. He has blocked programs that would provide food for schoolchildren or other hungry citizens. He opposes any program aimed at social reform. And he has been reelected sixteen times.

Reelection is the true test of democracy. When members of Congress want to get reelected, they support policies that will benefit their constituents, as well as the interest groups that give them campaign funds. And this is what elected representatives should do.

The Other Side Some congressional members believe there is more to political representation than satisfying the needs of their supporters. Someone has to look at the whole picture and decide which policies are best for the nation as a whole. And the best place for this to happen is in Congress.

Let's look again at Representative Whitten. During World War II some people in the government wanted to plan a study that would help the nation prepare for the social and economic problems black veterans would face when they came home. Whitten killed the plan. He felt that the Department of Agriculture's job was to help the cotton planter, not the poor black. And this seemed to be the opinion of his supporters.

But by killing the proposed study and blocking similar ideas Whitten may have helped cause the huge migration of southern blacks to northern cities that has changed American society so much since the war. Creative government programs might have prepared the cities for the migration and reduced the suffering it caused. A Congress full of representatives who pay attention mainly to narrow constituent interests isn't likely to think up and fund such programs. But this is what a truly representative legislature would do.

How Institutions Work: III
How a Bill Becomes a Law

WHERE ARE BILLS INITIATED?

Any member of the House or Senate may introduce a bill, except that all revenue bills must be introduced in the House. Because no bill can become law unless it is passed by both House and Senate, similar bills are usually introduced at about the same time in both houses of Congress.

WHAT'S THE NEXT STEP AFTER A BILL IS INTRODUCED?

The bill is referred to a committee, depending on the issue involved.

WHY IS THE COMMITTEE IMPORTANT IN THE LIFE OF A BILL?

As the figures in Table 9.2 show, each session of Congress faces far more bills than it can possibly handle. So do most committees. It's the committee chairs who decide which bills their committee will put on its agenda. And it's at this point that 80 to 90 percent of all bills introduced in Congress die. Committees kill far more bills by ignoring them than by voting them down.

WHAT HAPPENS TO A BILL IN COMMITTEE?

The bill is first put on the committee's agenda or sent to a subcommittee. It is then studied, and if it is important enough, hearings are held. These may be either public or private. The subcommittee then amends, rewrites, or "marks up" a bill and sends it back to the full committee. The committee then votes on whether or not to "report out" the bill to the House or Senate. At this stage the committee can kill a bill by voting against it or by simply not acting at all.

IF A BILL IS REPORTED OUT BY A HOUSE COMMITTEE, HOW IS IT BROUGHT TO THE FLOOR FOR A VOTE?

A bill coming out of committee is placed on one of several legislative calendars. Bills from certain committees, such as Ways and Means, can be reported to the full House any any time for action. All other important public bills are assigned to the House Calendar. They need a "special rule" from the House Rules Committee before they can be sent to the floor for debate.

WHY IS THE RULES COMITTEE SO IMPORTANT?

The House Rules Committee has been compared to a traffic cop. It decides not only the order in which bills get to the House floor but also how they will be debated. Normally when a bill is reported out of a House committee and

TABLE 9.2 Legislation by the 90th congress, both sessions

	House of Representatives	*Senate*
Bills introduced and referred to committee	20,587	4,199 (total, 24,786)
Bills reported by committee	1,319	1,403
Bills enacted into law	1,133	1,286 (total, 2,419)

Source: Adapted from Nelson W. Polsby, *Congress and the Presidency*, 2nd ed., © 1971, p. 90. Reprinted by permission of Prentice-Hall, Inc., Englewood Cliffs, New Jersey.

put on the calendar, the next step is for the committee chair to ask for a special rule taking the bill off the calendar and putting it before the House. The Rules Committee usually holds hearings at which both the managers and the opponents of the bill argue for or against the granting of a special rule.

Any bill that doesn't get through the Rules Committee has probably been derailed for good. But although the Rules Committee sometimes blocks important legislation, the majority of the bills killed by the Rules Committee aren't of major importance. Besides, the Rules Committee doesn't control all bills reported out of House committees. Most of the bills brought to the floor each session are put on the "consent" and "private" calendars. Here the Rules Committee plays no part. During each session of Congress there are perhaps only 100 bills that need to be debated on the House floor. It's for these bills that the Rules Committee is important.

IF A BILL IS REPORTED OUT BY A SENATE COMMITTEE, HOW IS IT BROUGHT TO THE FLOOR FOR A VOTE?

There is only one legislative calendar in the Senate, so bills reported out of Senate committees are all placed on the calendar. In the Senate the majority party's Policy Committee has the power to schedule floor debate.

WHAT ARE THE RULES FOR FLOOR DEBATE?

The rules for House debate are usually contained in the special rule that comes from the Rules Committee. This states how long a bill may be debated and whether it may be amended on the floor. If floor amendment isn't allowed, this is a "closed rule"; only members of the committee in charge of the bill can make any changes in wording. When amendments are allowed from anyone on the floor, this is an "open rule."

Debate in the Senate is unlimited and can run far off the legislative track. When senators opposed to a bill go on debating for days or weeks to prevent action, it is a filibuster. Filibusters can be broken only if two-thirds of the senators present vote to do so. Thus although filibusters are rare, successful attempts to end them are even rarer.

WHAT HAPPENS IF THE HOUSE AND SENATE PASS DIFFERENT VERSIONS OF A BILL?

If the differences are small, one house may simply agree to the other's version. But if the differences are great, it's necessary to appoint a conference committee made up of senior members from both the House and Senate committees that managed the bill. They work together to write a version acceptable to both sides, but a majority vote of each group is needed for approval. If the conference is successful, the final wording of the bill must still be passed by each house of Congress.

WHEN A BILL HAS BEEN PASSED BY CONGRESS AND SENT TO THE WHITE HOUSE, WHAT CHOICES DOES THE PRESIDENT HAVE?

The President has four choices. (1) He can simply sign the bill. (2) If he fails to sign it within ten days and Congress is still in session, the bill becomes law automatically. (3) If Congress has adjourned, the President's failure to sign it is a *pocket veto* and the bill does not become law. (4) The President can veto the bill by refusing to sign it and returning it to Congress. If Congress passes it again with a two-thirds majority in both houses, it becomes law. Otherwise it dies.

WHAT DOES THE SERIES OF STEPS A BILL GOES THROUGH TO BECOME LAW TELL US ABOUT POWER IN CONGRESS?

Power in Congress is basically negative. Any bill introduced must get over a series of hurdles. If it stumbles along the way, it's probably out of the running. The result is that interest groups and political opponents can tie up, rewrite, or defeat a bill at any point along the way. So the kind of power needed to get a bill through Congress is the power to satisfy majorities in subcommittee and full committee, on the floor, and in conference. This power is largely in the hands of the President and his congressional supporters, the leaders of the House and Senate, and the managers of bills in committee.

Questions for Review

1. Why did the founders create a Congress of elected representatives?
2. Why do people sometimes call Congress a local institution dealing with national problems?
3. What difference does it make if most members of Congress are white, middle-class males?
4. How is Congress organized? What are the main differences between the House and the Senate?
5. What difference would it make if members of Congress were assigned to committees by lot? If persons who chaired committees were chosen by lot?
6. What are the sources of committee power?
7. What happens to a bill after it is introduced in Congress?
8. Name some of the factors affecting congressional voting.

Chapter 10

The Presidency

More than any other person, the President of the United States can affect—but not control—history. Here's what John F. Kennedy had to say about the President's job:

> He must above all be the Chief Executive in every sense of that word. He must be prepared to exercise the fullest powers of his office—all that are specified and some that are not. He must master complex problems. . . . He must originate action. . . . It is the President alone who must make the major decisions of our foreign policy. That is what the Constitution wisely commands. And even domestically, the President must initiate policies and devise laws to meet the needs of the nation. And he must be prepared to use all the resources of his office to insure the enactment of that legislation. . . .
>
> No President, it seems to me, can escape politics. He has not only been chosen by the nation—he has been chosen by his party. And if he insists that he is "President of all the people" and should, therefore, offend none of them—if he blurs the issues and differences between the parties—if he neglects the party machinery and avoids his party's leadership—then he has not only weakened the political party as an instrument of the democratic process—he has dealt a blow to the democratic process itself.
>
> But the White House is not only the center of political leadership. It must be the center of moral leadership. . . . For only the President represents the national interest. And upon him alone converge all the needs and aspirations of all parts of the country, all departments of the Government, all nations of the world.

Kennedy, a strong President, probably claimed more powers for the Presidency than the Constitution intended. But in doing so he was following in the footsteps of Presidents like Jefferson, Lincoln, and the Roosevelts, and this tradition was carried on by Johnson and Nixon. These men poured a lot of meaning into Article 2 of the Constitution: "The executive power shall be vested in a President of the United States of America."

The Growth of the President's Powers

The Constitution has more to say about the Presidency, but not much more. Article 2, Section 2 states that the President is Commander-in-Chief; in Section 3 the President is instructed to inform Congress about the state of the union and to propose legislation. These duties have been the basis for the huge growth of the executive branch of the government.

THE PRESIDENT AS COMMANDER-IN-CHIEF

In 1957 a federal court ordered Little Rock, Arkansas, to desegregate its public schools. The white citizens of Little Rock, the school officials, and even the governor of Arkansas refused to obey. When citizens won't obey a federal court order, what can the President do? In this case President Eisenhower acted as Commander-in-Chief. He sent federal troops to Little Rock. Eisenhower explained his action in these words:

> I have today issued an Executive Order directing the use of troops under Federal authority to aid in the execution of Federal law at Little Rock, Arkansas. This became necessary when my Proclamation of yesterday was not observed, and the obstruction of justice still continues.

If the President didn't act, Eisenhower argued,

> Anarchy would result. There would be no security for any except that which each one of us could provide for himself. The interest of the nation in the proper fulfillment of the law's requirements cannot yield to opposition and demonstrations by some few persons. Mob rule cannot be allowed to override the decisions of our courts.

Five years later President Kennedy called on the same powers to deal with a threat from outside the nation. In October 1972 the CIA discovered that the Soviet Union was arming Cuba with missiles that could destroy nearly any city in the United States. A week of secret meetings between the President and his advisers resulted in the Cuban blockade, a military act that prevented Soviet ships from delivering the missiles.

WAR POWERS

We might question the wisdom of sending troops to Little Rock or blockading Cuba, but we can't question the authority of Eisenhower and Kennedy to act as they did. The Constitution clearly states that the President is Commander-in-Chief of the armed forces.

But there's a paradox here. The Constitution gives Congress the right to declare war. Does this mean the President is Commander-in-Chief only when a war has been declared? No, he can use these powers whether there's a declared war or not. There was no war in Little Rock in 1957, and we weren't at war with either Cuba or the Soviet Union in 1962. In fact Congress has declared war only five times since 1789, but during this time U.S. forces have been involved in overseas military action more than 150 times.

This situation has been challenged by some members of Congress. Recent congressional resolutions have limited the kinds of military action the President can order in Vietnam and Cambodia. But these resolutions haven't changed the fact that war and military action have separate Constitutional status. The history of the twentieth century makes it clear that the President's power as Commander-in-Chief is actually the power to make war. And this power has greatly expanded the role of the President in national and world affairs.

THE PRESIDENT AS CHIEF DIPLOMAT

Tradition as well as the Constitution have made the President the nation's chief diplomat. Early in our history, however, this was a matter of debate. Daniel Webster argued that the state legislatures could make separate agreements with foreign nations: "Every state is an independent, sovereign political community." On the other hand, Chief Justice Taney claimed that the writers of the Constitution intended "to make us, so far as regarded our foreign relations, one people and one nation; and to cut off all communications between foreign governments and the several state authorities."

Taney wasn't entirely correct; a close reading of the Constitution doesn't prove beyond a doubt that the states have no role in foreign affairs. But Taney's argument was accepted, and as a result all foreign relations are handled by the federal government.

This sets the stage for the President to become chief diplomat. But that didn't happen automatically. Whether Congress or the President should make foreign policy has long been debated. In the 1960s and 1970s this issue came up again in the struggle over who would control the direction of the Vietnam War.

THE PRESIDENT'S FOREIGN-POLICY POWERS

If it's hard to tell what the Constitution intended, it's easy to see what has happened in practice. Most American foreign policy has been handled by the President, particularly in the past fifty years. Only the President is in "continuous session," and this gives him an advantage. Things happen quickly, and what happens in one part of the world affects what happens in other parts. American business, military, and diplomatic interests are scattered around the world. The United States has over 2000 military bases in foreign countries; there are U.S. aid programs in more than 80 different countries; and private investments in foreign countries total more than $110 billion. A language riot in India, a border clash in South America, a monetary crisis in Europe—these and thousands of other events affect American programs and people. They demand quick attention and action.

The President is in a position to act. He's in charge of the network of U.S. embassies and agencies around the world; he's in command of the military forces; he has access to information from the CIA. Acting as Commander-in-Chief and chief diplomat, the President can't help making foreign policy.

Nixon's dramatic visit to China in 1972 is a good example. Plans for the visit were kept secret. The approval of Congress wasn't necessary, and the public wasn't told about the trip until final arrangements had been made. Yet this visit was the most significant foreign-policy action of Nixon's first term. It had an immediate impact on China's entry into the United Nations, and U.S. aid policy toward India, on relations with Japan, and on summit talks with the Soviet Union. It had longer-term effects on our trade and tariff policies, nuclear strategy, and balance of payments.

But the President doesn't have unlimited control over foreign policy. From time to time Congress tries to use its influence. It can cut off funds for foreign programs it doesn't like, and it can refuse to agree to treaties. However, the President can get around this congressional power by making an *executive agreement*. Such an agreement doesn't need congressional approval, and it can include major arrangements such as location of military bases and types of aid programs.

THE PRESIDENT'S LEGISLATIVE PROGRAM

Under the separation-of-powers system, Congress is supposed to make the laws and the executive branch is supposed to carry them out. In practice, however, separation of powers means struggle for power. And in this struggle both the legislative and executive branches have come up with strategies not mentioned in the Constitution.

One of these strategies is the President's legislative program. The Constitution says the President "shall from time to time give to the Congress information of the State of the Union, and recommend to their consideration such measures as he shall judge necessary and expedient." The annual *State of the Union Address* is most often used to announce a Presidential program. An example is Nixon's 1972 State of the Union Address, in which he made legislative proposals in eighteen different areas, including items such as trade and monetary affairs, welfare reform, environment, health care, hunger and nutrition, women's rights, consumer protection, and so on. In the area of technology, for example, Nixon said:

> I shall soon send to the Congress a special message proposing a new program of federal partnership in technological research and development with federal incentives to increase private research, federally supported research and projects designed to improve our everyday lives in ways that will range from improving mass transit to developing new systems of emergency health care that could save thousands of lives annually.

These Presidential proposals become the legislative agenda. About 80 percent of all major laws passed in the last twenty years have started in the executive branch. Roosevelt's New Deal, Kennedy's New Frontier, and Johnson's Great Society were legislative programs proposed by the President and acted on by Congress.

THE PRESIDENT AND HIS ADVISERS

Where do the President's proposals come from? Not entirely from one person. A group of advisers and assistants largely plans and carries out the President's program and tries to organize a strategy for dealing with the other important groups—Congress, the federal bureaucracy, the public—that will determine the program's success or failure.

In the early 1900s the President carried out his duties with the help of a secretary and few clerks. The modern Presidency dates from the Roosevelt administration of the 1930s. But even then there were only a few dozen people on the President's staff. The past thirty years have seen a major expansion. The total payroll for the executive office in 1973 was more than $60 million, and the Presidential staff numbered over 2000.

The quality of leadership provided by the White House depends largely on the quality of the President's staff. This is what we mean when we speak of "Ford's administration" or "Kennedy's team." An important job of any President is to find the right people and to make the most of their skills.

There are some problems in the relationship between the President and his staff. To get information and advice on a variety of subjects, the President looks for experienced advisers. While these people have strong ideas of their own, there's a great temptation to say what the "Chief" wants to hear, since although the President expects independent ideas from his staff he also expects loyalty to himself and his program. Ford fired Secretary of Defense James Schlesinger because Schlesinger publicly opposed the policy of conciliation toward the Soviet Union that the State Department, under Henry Kissinger, was following. In Ford's view Schlesinger had ceased to be a team player and had to go. Ford and Vice-President Nelson Rockefeller also differed over federal support for New York City; as a result Rockefeller declared himself unavailable for the Vice-Presidency in 1976.

WHERE DO PROPOSALS COME FROM?

A Presidential proposal can come from a number of sources within the executive branch—and can be greatly changed or even blocked before it reaches the President and his closest advisers. This can happen in several ways; here we'll describe one fairly common method.

An executive agency or department plans a new program or proposes changes in an old one. It may consult with a congressional committee at this stage; it might also check with the interest groups affected by the program. For example, if the Department of Health, Education and Welfare is working on a scholarship program it will probably get in touch with the congressional committees that handle education bills. It will also get in touch with organizations such as the American Association for the Advancement of Science. The program will begin to take shape, adding some proposals and dropping others in response to advice or opposition from these groups. It will then be sent to the Office of Management and Budget (OMB).

The OMB's job is to coordinate the hundreds of programs proposed each year by various executive agencies. It has the power to tell the President or his advisers that a program can't be fitted into the budget. A proposal that doesn't get through the OMB has very little chance of reaching the President, let alone becoming law. The OMB also keeps in touch with congressional leaders so it knows what legislation various committees are working on. Sometimes the OMB will tell an executive agency to shelve its program because a group in Congress is already working along the same lines.

Even when a proposal gets through the OMB it won't necessarily become part of the President's program. But many such proposals do become part of that program. The President doesn't have the time to think through all the details of legislative proposals. He depends on his staff, advisers, and executive agencies to do this job. Most of the President's proposals to Congress come from these sources.

This again shows the importance of the people a new administration brings to Washington. A President wants to leave his mark on history. To do so he depends heavily on a staff that can come up with legislative proposals likely to get support in Congress.

GETTING THE PROGRAM THROUGH CONGRESS

What the President wants and what he gets aren't always the same thing. But the President and his staff have many resources—executive agreements, party leadership and control over appointments, a huge bureaucracy to give them information and proposals. In addition the President can put pressure on important members of Congress. Johnson and Kennedy, who had both been congressmen themselves, often used this strategy. Here's how one powerful member of the House Rules Committee reacted to a phone call from President Johnson:

> What do you say to the President of the United States? I told him I'd sleep on it. Then the next day I said to myself, "I've always been a party man, and if he really wanted me of course I'd go along even if the bill wasn't set up exactly the way I wanted it." Probably I took half a dozen guys with me. We won in the crunch by six votes. Now, I wouldn't have voted for it except for this telephone call.[1]

Sometimes the President goes on national radio or TV to speak directly to the public and to ask the public to put pressure on Congress. Franklin Roosevelt did this in his famous fireside chats. Here is Roosevelt in 1942 asking for price controls:

> Today I sent a message to the Congress, pointing out the overwhelming urgency of the serious domestic economic crisis with which we are threatened. . . . I have asked the Congress to pass legislation under which the President would be specifically authorized to stabilize the cost of living, including the price of all farm commodities.

Roosevelt expected action within three weeks. If Congress didn't act, he promised to act himself:

> In the event that the Congress should fail to act, and act adequately, I shall accept the responsibility, and I will act. The President has the

[1] *Newsweek,* August 2, 1965, p. 22.

> powers, under the Constitution and under Congressional Acts, to take measures necessary to avert a disaster which would interfere with the winning of the war.

Whether or not Roosevelt actually had these powers was never tested, however, because Congress decided to act.

RESTRAINTS ON THE PRESIDENT

As we'll see later, the separation-of-powers system works, but not the way the founders expected it to work. The President is restrained because he shares powers with Congress. In addition he is restrained by the difficulty of starting new programs and stopping old ones.

Starting New Programs. When Gerald Ford became President he inherited serious economic problems: unemployment, recession, and steep inflation. A major cause of these problems was the rapidly increasing cost of energy, which was linked to large increases in the price of imported oil.

It was a tough time to become President. As Ford said in a speech to a World Energy Conference, "Exorbitant prices can only distort the world economy, run the risk of worldwide depression and threaten the breakdown of world order and safety."

With such big problems we might expect a wide range of new economic policies and energy programs. Nothing of the sort came out of Ford's administration. Why not? Because new policies and programs aren't easy to think up, and when they are thought up they aren't easy to carry out. Even the powers and prestige of the Presidency can't always attract people with the right skills and the ability to cooperate. And even if a new policy is planned, it's not easy to put the plan into operation. A program that would solve the nation's energy problems would affect the habits and well-being of millions of people, thousands of businesses, and dozens of existing government programs.

Stopping Old Programs. If things are hard to start, they're often even harder to stop. When a new President comes to town there's no guarantee that existing programs will be changed. Interests and careers are at stake. The President must adjust to the personalities, quarrels, and commitments involved in existing programs.

Most policy is made by adding to or subtracting from existing programs. Eisenhower, a Republican, didn't end the New Deal programs begun by Democratic administrations. Nor did eight years of Democratic control of the White House lead to a sharp break in public policy, though many new programs were added. Nixon tried to cut spending for programs started in administrations before his, but the job was nearly impossible. Here is his 1972 campaign promise:

> We would like to operate the Federal Government at less cost, and we think we know how to do it. . . . We are for lower costs, for less function

in the Federal Government. . . . My goal is not only no tax increase in 1973, but no tax increase in the next four years.

But as one writer remarked,

Where can the Administration cut enough to make its next budget consistent with this pledge? Roughly 40 percent of the projected budgets are allocated to defense, space and related activities—and it is clear the Administration does not want to cut here.

Of the domestic budget, well more than half goes directly to people, either in cash benefits (Social Security, unemployment insurance, veterans' pensions, welfare, civil-service retirement, etc.) or in kind (Medicare, Medicaid, public housing). These people have real needs, real votes and real representatives on Capitol Hill. It is inconceivable that the President would propose legislation to cut these benefits back or that the Congress would pass it.

Contractual obligations of the Government, such as interest on the debt, cannot be tampered with, and no one really wants to cut out such services as national parks or fish and wildlife preservation.

This leaves grants to state and local governments as the prime candidates for cuts. . . . In practice, however, it has so far proved . . . impossible to cut the total funds. . . . Each program brings identifiable benefits to a particular group which is aware that the program exists and resists its elimination. Moreover, and perhaps more important, most of these programs support the services of particular professional groups—librarians, vocational-education teachers, veterinarians, psychiatric social workers, sanitary engineers. Each of these groups believes it is doing something important and useful—and it doubtless is—and fights to preserve and expand the programs it knows will support its activities.[2]

Nixon did reduce federal spending on some social-welfare programs, but the federal budget continued to grow. Whether the President is a Republican or a Democrat, it's very hard to stop federal programs once they are started.

The President as a Symbol

The government is a collection of institutions, organizations, laws, and policies. The nation is more than this. It includes the idea of a political community: "We are all Americans." This sense of community cuts across differences of opinion about particular policies or personalities.

The President is a major symbol of the political community and the main actor in many public ceremonies. It's the President who announces National Codfish Day, who dedicates a national arts center, who is the central figure in

[2] Alice M. Rivlin, "Dear Voter: Your Taxes Are Going Up," *New York Times Magazine*, November 5, 1972, pp. 113–114.

bicentennial celebrations, who entertains emperors and kings in the name of the United States. When he does these things the President speaks for the entire political community.

The President is also expected to provide moral leadership. In the early 1970s, for example, newspaper columnist James Reston described the United States as "a divided and selfish nation, dominated by powerful special interest groups that have no common concern for the national interest." He went on to say:

> In such a situation, the role of the Federal Government, and particularly of the President, is critical, for in a secular society that is full of doubt about the church, the university and the press, the White House is still the pinnacle of our civil life and the hope of some moral order and presiding national purpose. . . . More than anybody else, the President has the power to establish the standard and set the model, to direct or manipulate the powerful forces of the nation, to encourage the best in us. . . .

The Watergate affair was a dramatic illustration of the role of the President as the nation's moral leader. The President had clearly let the country down, not because his policies were failures but because he had failed as a moral leader. Figure 10.1 shows how sharply Nixon's popularity dropped as the cover-up was revealed. The Watergate affair showed that for better or worse the President is at the center of the nation's political hopes and fears.

FIGURE 10.1
Nixon's Popularity

Source: Based on data from the Gallup poll.

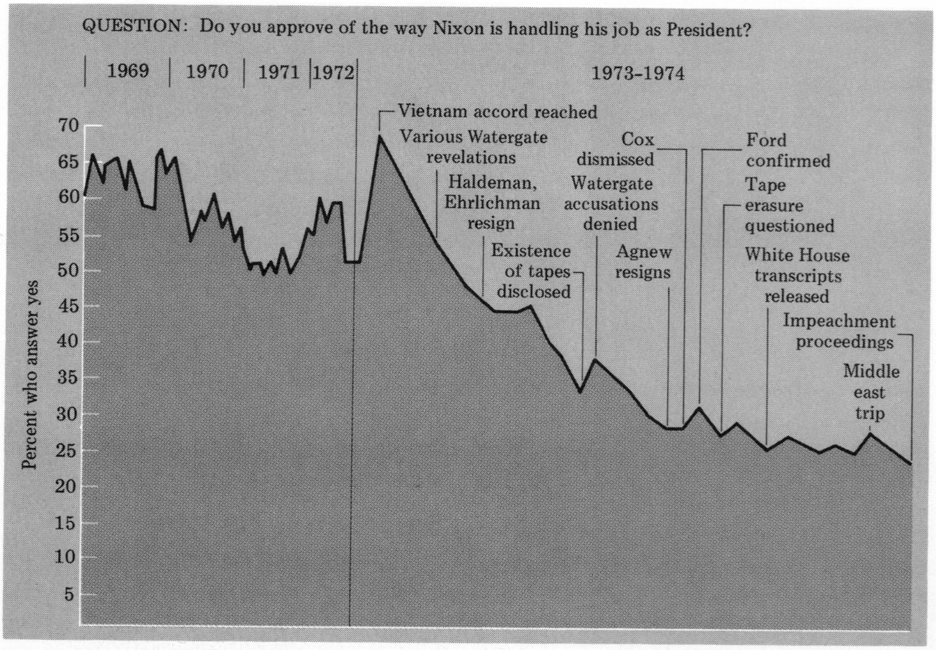

The Road to the White House

In 1976 a former Governor from Georgia who had no national political experience and who before his campaign was virtually unknown to the American people engineered a stunning political victory by winning 17 of 30 statewide presidential primaries through the winter and spring, capturing his party's nomination on the first ballot at its convention in July, and defeating the incumbent President in the November election. In a few short years Jimmy Carter had come a long way from the peanut farm in Plains, Georgia. His success seemed to many nothing less than a "phenomenon," and for good reason. With the exception of popular military leaders like Dwight Eisenhower, Presidential politics had long been the preserve of nationally known party leaders. Carter was neither military hero nor party leader. Why, then, was the election of a Jimmy Carter possible in 1976? Have the rules of the electoral process really changed, or was Carter's success a fluke caused by the anti-Washington mood in the immediate post-Watergate period of American politics? To answer these questions we must trace the road to the White House.

PRESIDENTIAL HOPEFULS

Parents and teachers are fond of stories with a "log cabin to White House" theme: stories that contribute to the democratic myth that anyone can grow up to be President. Yet it is the son, not the father, who has the political insight in the following exchange:

> *Father to Son Watching TV:* Why aren't you studying? When Abe Lincoln was your age he was reading law by the flickering light of the log cabin fire.
> *Son:* And when he was your age, he was President.

Truly it is said, "Many are called but few are chosen." Only 38 people have made it to the White House so far.

If every 10-year-old hopes someday to become President, this is not true of every 50-year-old. Only a very small number in the suitable age bracket seriously hope to become President. Carter's success notwithstanding, most serious Presidential aspirants are likely to come from a small set of already powerful, visible people in national political life. Governors of large states, especially New York, Pennsylvania, Illinois, and California, fall into this small group. So do forceful, articulate senators. Members of the House of Representatives have usually not been in this group, but Morris Udall's respectable showing in the race for the Democratic party nomination in 1976 indicates that this may be changing. Popular war heroes, if the war was a popular one, might count. A widely known college president might be mentioned but is not likely to be nominated unless there also was an important government position somewhere in his career. And of course Vice-Presidents are in the pool, a special group about which we will have more to say.

The Presidential selection process starts with a group of "eligibles," eligible because they are of the right age group, the right sex, the right race. But more important, eligible because of their positions and accomplishments in national political life.

How many from this group really hope to become President? The answer will vary depending on important conditions, mainly, who is currently in the White House.

Members of the In-Party. It's convenient to call the political party of the current President the in-party. Going into the 1976 election Ford was a Republican, so the Republican party was the in-party. The number of Presidential hopefuls in the in-party depends on whether the current President can be reelected. Presidents are limited to two terms by the Twenty-Second Amendment (passed after Franklin Roosevelt had been elected President four times). If the President can't be reelected, then the field is open, unless a particular person, such as the Vice-President, is clearly the front runner. In 1960, for example, Eisenhower was in the last months of his second term. And in that year Eisenhower's Vice-President, Nixon, faced almost no serious challenge for the Republican party nomination.

Traditionally the current President has been renominated by his party without serious opposition. But one of the most interesting things about recent American politics is the way this tradition is changing. In 1968 Johnson was President; legally he could serve another term. But he was challenged within his own party. First Eugene McCarthy and then Robert Kennedy declared themselves candidates for the Democratic party nomination. They won

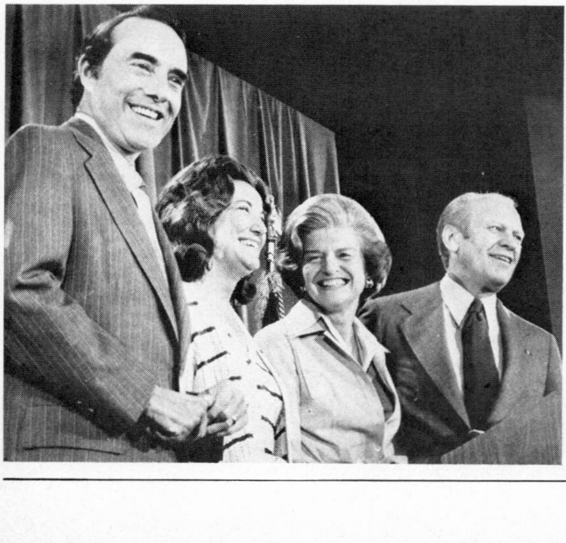

so much support that Johnson decided not to run again. Thus a President was forced out of office by a serious challenge from within his own party. In 1976 the conservative ex-Governor of California, Ronald Reagan, aggressively challenged Republican President Gerald Ford in primary elections. Though Reagan failed to win the nomination, his near success confirms that the importance of incumbency is no longer as great as it once was.

Members of the Out-Party. In the party that has no current President, the number of people who will seriously hope to become President can grow to a dozen or two. In both 1972 and 1976 the Democrats fielded a large number of candidates. The number tends to be largest in the fall and winter preceding the first Presidential primaries. By January of 1976, for example, twelve Democrats had entered the race: five senators and one former senator, one member of the House of Representatives, two governors and two former governors, and a previous Vice-Presidential nominee. The "winnowing process," as one unsuccessful candidate described it, began shortly after the first state primaries. Within a few months only a handful of the original twelve remained serious contenders. There was the possibility, of course, that no one would win the nomination on the first ballot at the convention and someone who had not even entered the primaries would be selected as the nominee. But in the end Jimmy Carter prevailed.

Public Financing. One factor that partly accounts for the decreased importance of incumbency in the "in-party" and the proliferation of candidates in the "out-party" is the campaign finance legislation passed in 1974 (see Chapter 9). The new law gives Presidential aspirants valuable additional funds for launching their campaigns. Thus it makes it possible for more candidates to take their case to the American people. But because the amount of public money allotted is based on the amount raised from private sources, once the private contributions dry up, as usually happens after poor performances in the early primaries, candidates tend as before to drop out of the race very quickly. On the side of the "in-party" the new law has the further effect of decreasing the President's control over campaign funds, a control that resulted in the past from his position as head of the party and his influence over potential political contributors. Now the challenger has access to public moneys to augment his own grass roots fund raising effort.

STRATEGY

Whether Republican or Democrat, the Presidential hopeful must develop a plan of action. He has to get past a series of barriers. First he has to get his party's nomination. This involves a strategy aimed at the nominating convention and perhaps the primaries leading up to it. Winning the election is the next goal. The Presidential campaign involves a lot of major decisions: where to campaign, on what issues, with what resources, and so on.

NOMINATING A PRESIDENTIAL CANDIDATE

We mentioned earlier that the road to public office in the United States includes some sort of nomination process. This has been the case for nearly 200 years, though the way the process worked in 1800 was very different from the way it works today.

King Caucus. The earliest political parties were small groups of men gathered in party "caucuses" controlling who could become a candidate for office. King Caucus, as this system was called, didn't last long, but it was the first step toward party control over recruitment to public office. The second step was replacement of the caucus system with the convention system. Conventions were made up of delegates chosen by state and local party organizations and thus were supposed to be more representative than caucuses.

Primary Elections. Throughout the nineteenth century nomination of candidates for nearly all public offices was done by party conventions. Today, however, conventions are important mainly for Presidential candidates. Candidates for most governorships, state and national legislatures, and many local offices are nominated in primaries.

Primary elections were introduced to reform "nondemocratic" politics. At the turn of the century various reform groups claimed that party conventions had come under the control of political bosses and that candidates were controlled by interest groups. Primaries are a way of involving party members in the nomination process. From among several candidates of the same party the party members choose the one they want to run for office. Various kinds of primaries may now be found in every state.

As a means of nominating candidates the primary has many flaws. Voter turnout is always low, and often the choices aren't clear. At the same time, the costs can be very high, using up resources the party needs for the general election. But while primaries haven't resulted in widespread participation in the nomination process, they have reduced the control of a small group of people over who gets nominated. They give an opposing group a way of putting forward its own candidate.

Presidential Primaries. One of the biggest changes to have occurred in recent years in the process of electing a President has been the increasing importance of the primaries. As recently as 1968 Hubert Humphrey received his party's nomination without even entering the primaries. But in 1976 it was clear that the long primary route had become *the* way to the nomination. Thirty states held primary elections over a three-and-a-half-month period, beginning with New Hampshire in February and ending with California, New Jersey, and Ohio in June. This was up from 23 in 1972 and 17 in 1968. On the Democratic side Jimmy Carter won 17 of the 26 primaries that had Presidential preference votes, and finished second in eight others. He collected 39% of the total vote, with his nearest rival, Governor Brown of California, at 15%. Carter was so successful in the primaries that his victories there alone gave him nearly enough convention votes for the nomination. In any case he was so far ahead of his competitors that the party unified around him in the weeks before the convention in New York City. On the Republican side the expanded 1976 primaries gave Ronald Reagan the opportunity to mount a serious, sustained challenge to the incumbent Gerald Ford. In this case, however, the primaries did not settle the nomination, for they ended in a virtual dead heat. What they did was to allow the challenger to take his case directly to the party rank and file.

Of course, 1976 was not the first year that the primaries played a decisive role in the nomination process. In 1960, for example, John Kennedy's victory in the West Virginia primary was a major boost to his candidacy, proving that a Catholic could win in a heavily Protestant state. Eight years later Senator Eugene McCarthy's strong showing in the New Hampshire primary helped to convince President Johnson not to run for reelection. Presidential primaries were even more significant in the 1972 contest. Senator George McGovern, a strong anti-war candidate, was an insurgent within the Democratic party. The party professionals, especially labor leaders, made it clear that they preferred Hubert Humphrey. McGovern took his case to the voters in a series of primary campaigns, starting with New Hampshire in March and ending in California in June. His primary victories helped immensely in gathering the delegate strength needed to win the Democratic party nomination in 1972.

No longer are the Presidential primaries just so many test cases for the benefit of the party regulars to measure the appeal the various candidates have to different kinds of electorates. Instead the primaries have come to replace the nominating convention and the party regulars as the effective selector of the party nominee. Without consciously deciding to do so, we have been moving steadily toward a kind of national presidential primary, though administered in numerous distinct parts over a three-and-a-half-month period. This has opened up the electoral process to outsiders, like Jimmy Carter, who strike a responsive cord with the American people. It also puts increased emphasis on the role of the media, especially television, as the candidates try to make a favorable impression on the electorate in state after state.

PRESIDENTIAL NOMINATING CONVENTIONS

Every four years the major and minor political parties meet in convention to nominate a Presidential ticket. Party conventions provide many hours of TV viewing for the American public. Several thousand party members meet to debate the issues and put together a party platform as well as to choose a Presidential nominee. When the two major conventions are over, two people out of 100 million adult Americans are serious candidates for the Presidency. Only these two nominees have a realistic chance.

How Delegates Are Selected. Delegates to the Presidential nominating convention are selected in a variety of ways. Some states have Presidential primaries that bind the delegates to the candidate winning the primary election; other states have primaries that allow the voters to show their preferences but still leave the delegates some independence. In yet other states the primary election chooses unbound delegates. In some states the voters choose some delegates, but other delegates from that state are chosen by district or state party committees. All told, the use of some form of Presidential primary accounts for the selection of three-quarters of the delegates to the nominating conventions. But a sizeable fraction of states rely on party caucuses or conventions to select convention delegates.

Although the primaries now account for the selection of a substantial majority of the convention delegates, delegate selection in the caucus states is not unimportant. In a close race like the Ford-Reagan contest in 1976 every vote counts. Reagen saw that he could offset some of Ford's success in the early primaries by concentrating on delegate selection in the caucus states. For a different reason Jimmy Carter campaigned vigorously for support in the Iowa caucus that preceded the primaries. This was not so much to garner the few votes at stake as it was to generate favorable national publicity from an early victory.

Who Are the Delegates? Convention delegates are a cross-section of the party membership. They may include members of Congress, governors, mayors, party activists, and important contributors. Delegates have tended to be white, male, and richer than the general population.

In recent years both parties have reformed their methods of choosing delegates. In 1970 the Democratic party reform commission reported that too many delegates were chosen in closed meetings. It also reported that minorities like blacks and women were discriminated against and suggested guidelines for correcting this flaw. Table 10.1 shows the results: The number of minority group delegates to the Democratic convention in 1972 showed a large increase from 1968 figures. In 1976, however, the percentage of minority delegates was down from the 1972 peaks, though still quite a bit higher than in 1968. Many women and blacks were not content to let the gains achieved in 1972 slip away. Blacks managed to get the party's Rules Committee to adopt a resolution calling for affirmative action to increase minority representation at future conventions, and women got acceptance of a resolution calling on the state parties to move toward equal division between the sexes on future state delegations.

TABLE 10.1 *Delegates to the democratic national convention: 1968 and 1972*

	Blacks	Youth[a]	Women	Chicanos and others
1968	5%	4%	13%	–
1972	15%	21%	38%	5%

[a] Under 30.

Source: The Party Reformed, Final Report of the Commission on Part Structure and Delegate Selection (Washington, D.C.: Democratic National Committee, 1972), pp. 7–8.

The Republican convention was attended by delegates who looked more "Republican" in their social background. Only three percent of the Republican delegates in 1976 were black, and only one percent had Spanish surnames. About one-third were women. The delegates were generally from business and the professions, especially lawyers. And they were generally well-off. Two-thirds had incomes of $25,000 or more. And whereas only 14 percent of the general public have a college degree, 65 percent of the Republican delegates at Kansas City were this well educated.

The Convention Chooses. In 1976 the Democratic party held its convention in New York City in July, followed by the Republican party in Kansas City in August. When the conventions were over there were two national tickets. But did the delegates who poured into New York and Kansas City in the summer of 1976 actually decide anything? Or were they only there to confirm what had already been decided? Although the Democratic and Republican conventions displayed the striking contrast between an easy victory and a close-fought contest, in both cases it is clear that all but a handful of delegates made up their minds, or were obligated to vote in a certain way, before the convention began. Especially on the Democratic side, the convention functioned less to choose a party leader than to confirm a choice already made.

It hasn't always been so. Past conventions have seen bargaining and compromise resulting in an unexpected nomination. At other conventions there have been intense battles between opposing groups, with the outcome depending on how the uncommitted delegates finally voted. Today, however, much of the struggle that used to take place at the conventions has shifted to the preconvention period—the Presidential primaries and the state and local meetings in which delegates are chosen. This is the conclusion of a study by the Brookings Institution, which goes on to say, "with . . . access to information about delegate commitments and intentions, most of the losers in recent times have probably known that they were beaten before the convention opened."[3]

[3] Paul T. David, Ralph M. Goldman, and Richard C. Bain, *The Politics of National Party Conventions*, ed. by Kathleen Sproul (New York: Vintage, 1964), p. 324.

Still, if the party is very divided and there are strong candidates fighting it out in the primaries, it's likely that by convention time no single candidate will dominate. In such a case the party will choose its nominee at the convention itself.

THE PRESIDENTIAL CAMPAIGN

If anything political attracts the attention of the American public, it's the Presidential campaign. The faces and views of the candidates bombard the citizen from billboards, bumper stickers, newspaper ads, and most of all, TV. The citizen may not care about the results, but it isn't easy to avoid the campaign itself. Walk past a newstand and the candidates smile at you from magazine covers. Turn on the TV and sooner or later you'll hear an ad saying how much this election means and how a particular candidate can solve the nation's problems. More than national holidays, more than public ceremonies, more than patriotic songs and speeches, the Presidential campaign brings home to the citizen what democracy is all about.

The Electoral College. A candidate for the Presidency must decide where to put his time and effort. Should he campaign mostly in the larger states or in those where the election is going to be close? These are important questions because of the *Electoral College*.

Each state has a number of electoral votes (see Figure 10.2); the number

FIGURE 10.2
Electoral Votes for Each State

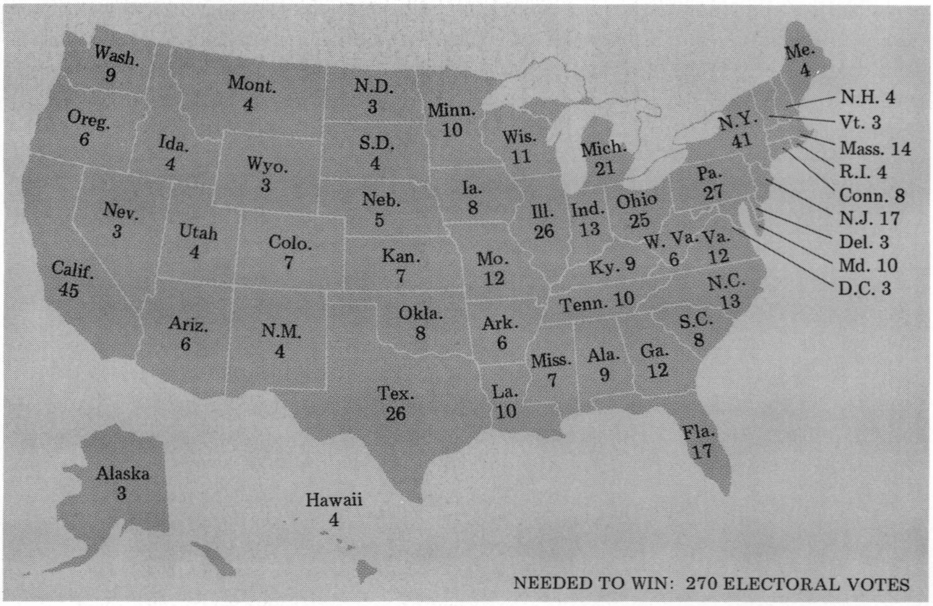

varies from 3 to 45. Electoral votes are under the *unit rule;* that is, all of a state's electoral votes go to the candidate who wins most of the votes in that state. This makes the largest states most important politically. For example, a candidate who wins in the two largest states California and New York) has almost one-third of the electoral votes he needs to win the Presidency (86 out of 270). This situation has had a major impact on twentieth-century politics. Because large states can be so much more important than small ones, the large states tend to dominate the nomination process and both parties put much of their effort into winning in those states. (Additional discussion of the electoral college appears in the special section at the end of this chapter.)

Campaign Costs. Campaigns involve many activities—travel and speeches, TV and radio spots, phone calls and mailings. These activities cost a lot of money. Traditionally campaign funds have come from individual gifts and interest groups. For example, at least half a dozen individuals each gave more than a quarter of a million dollars to Nixon's 1972 campaign. Such gifts stand out, but they don't completely dominate campaign giving. A lot of campaign money has come in the form of gifts of $100 or less. Also important are interest groups, like the Associated Milk Producers, that collect money from their members and give it to political candidates.

The Presidential Election Campaign Fund. The Watergate affair, along with the huge increase in the costs of campaigning, led to major reform legislation. Now there are limits on campaign contributions and spending. In addition, a federal fund was set up, to be paid for through taxes. Each taxpayer can contribute $1.00 of his tax money to the Presidential Election Campaign Fund. The money raised in this way is given to Presidential candidates in order to make them less dependent on wealthy contributors and interest groups.

A candidate can choose to take advantage of public financing or to depend on private financing. If he chooses public financing he's limited to spending no more than 15¢ for each voting-age person in the United States. A candidate using the public fund could ask for private contributions only if the public fund didn't cover campaign costs under this rule, and he could ask for only enough to make up the difference.

It's too early to tell how public funding will work out. But the huge amounts spent in 1972 should be reduced, and this, in turn, should reduce the role of wealthy contributors and interest groups in Presidential elections. (A special essay on the 1976 election begins on page 330.)

Vacancies in the White House

Nine times in American history the Vice-President has become President because of a vacancy in the White House. Three of these cases are crowded into the period since World War II. Franklin Roosevelt was reelected in 1944, only to die in the spring of 1945; Truman then became President. In 1963 Kennedy was assassinated in Dallas, Texas, and Johnson became President. But the most recent case was different in two ways. Before 1974 all vacancies in the White House were caused by the death of the President; Nixon was the first President ever to resign. And before 1974 all Vice-Presidents who stepped into a vacated Presidency had been elected to the Vice-Presidency. But in October 1973 Vice-President Spiro Agnew had resigned in the face of charges of bribery, tax evasion, and conspiracy. He was replaced by Ford under the conditions set forth in the Twenty-Fifth Amendment. Ford took over when Nixon resigned and nominated Rockefeller to be Vice-President. Thus in 1975 the American people had a President and Vice-President who had not been elected to those positions.

Presidential Personality

When the noise and politics of nominations and campaigns are over, one person is suddenly on top. How he handles pressure, how he works with advisers, how he speaks to the public, and how clearly he thinks about national problems have a large impact on this and other societies. Nixon had the creativity to reduce tensions with China and the Soviet Union, but he had the arrogance to think he could fool most of the people most of the time about Watergate. Johnson had the energy and forcefulness to introduce new civil-rights, welfare, and medical-care programs, but the same energy and forcefulness led him into the huge problems of the Vietnam War.

Throughout American history only 37 people have had the chance to make—or avoid—mistakes like these. And those 37 people have brought to the Presidency different political habits and different outlooks toward their own life. One student of Presidential personality uses the word *style* to describe the political habits and the word *character* to describe the attitude toward self.[4]

Presidential style may be active or passive. For example, William Howard Taft, President from 1908 to 1912, had a very limited view of the Presidency. "The President," he said, "can exercise no power which cannot be fairly and reasonably traced to some specific grant of authority." This is the passive Presidential style, a style in many ways repeated by Eisenhower. Eisenhower disliked the nitty-gritty of politics. He was uninterested in using the huge powers of the Presidency; he refused to meddle in congressional politics; he didn't like making speeches; he ignored the news media as much as possible; and he avoided summit meetings.

Other Presidents have favored an active role. Kennedy, for example, viewed the Presidency as the "vital center of action in our whole scheme of government." Rejecting the passive role, he argued that the President should "place himself in the very thick of the fight."

The idea of character refers to whether the President seems generally

[4] James David Barber, *The Presidential Character: Predicting Performance in the White House* (Englewood Cliffs, N.J.: Prentice-Hall, 1972).

happy and optimistic toward himself and his duties or moody and irritable, weighed down by his job. This concept is useful if it can uncover something about the personality of the President. Johnson, for example, became more and more unhappy as opposition to his Vietnam policies increased; toward the end of his term he was complaining that "everybody is trying to cut me down" and asking "why don't people like me?" Nixon, too, became moody and irritable as it became clear that he would be impeached for his role in the Watergate affair.

Does the President's personality make a difference? Many students of American politics think not. Decisions are based on demanding situations and conditions; no matter who is in the White House, the same decision will be made. They point out, for example, that Johnson was under so much pressure to win a military victory in Vietnam that he really had no choice. When Johnson became President there was an already existing framework in which foreign policy toward Southeast Asia was made. It was generally believed that saving South Vietnam from communist domination was important to America's national security. Given this framework, how could Johnson have acted differently?

This argument leaves little room for personality but leads to a different question. Couldn't Johnson's way of handling the war—his choice of bombing targets, his dealings with congressional critics, his response to the antiwar movement—have been different? Even small differences can have great political significance. And this is where the personality of the President becomes important.

Watergate brought this lesson home with a force unimagined even during the Vietnam War years. Nixon's secrecy and moodiness made him a target for those who wanted to get to the bottom of Watergate. If early in the cover-up he had simply confessed his poor judgment, he would probably have been forgiven. But Nixon saw himself as a fighter against many "enemies." He chose to fight, not confess. He paid a high price, and so did the American people.

Questions for Review

1. What are the powers of the President?
2. Why does the President handle most matters of foreign policy?
3. What resources does the President bring to the battle with Congress over legislation?
4. What is the President's legislative program? Where does it come from?
5. What is the role of the OMB?
6. Why does the President have limited control over the executive bureaucracy?
7. What social groups do Presidential hopefuls come from?
8. Describe the nomination and election process.
9. What are some of the advantages and disadvantages of primary elections?
10. What is the unit rule?
11. What is the significance of the Electoral College?

Chapter 11

The Supreme Court

Separation of powers is a central idea in our form of government. As set forth in the Constitution, the legislative branch makes the laws, the executive branch carries them out, and the judicial branch passes judgment when conflicts arise over their meaning or application. In practice, however, separation of powers is actually a sharing of powers and, therefore, a struggle for power.

We've discussed the legislative and executive branches of government; we turn now to the judicial branch, or the court system—particularly the United States Supreme Court. But first we need to describe the job of the court system.

What Is Adjudication?

Adjudication is the process by which a judgment or decision is made by law. Courts differ from legislatures and executive agencies in the way they arrive at new policies. Courts don't take action; rather, they wait until a case comes to them. A case becomes a chance for a court to state a general rule.

To understand this it's necessary to be clear about the roles of the participants. American courts will hear only cases in which there's a real conflict between two parties—a *plaintiff* and a *defendant.* They refuse to supervise nonadversary proceedings whose purpose is to get a statement of policy on a general social issue. Nor will they hear cases in which the injury is a future possibility. American courts exist to cope with the legal issues involved in the suffering, or supposed suffering, of one party at the hands of another. Unless the courts can determine the actual injury one party has already suffered—or will suffer if the court doesn't issue an order requiring or preventing a particular act, called an *injunction*—they can't determine how to remedy the injustice.

The court supervises an adversary proceeding between two parties. If the case involves a challenge to an act of the government, one of the adversaries is the challenger. Examples might be convicted criminals claiming they weren't given a fair trial; businessmen or businesswomen claiming the government has gone beyond its authority to regulate their businesses; schoolchildren claiming they aren't getting equal protection of the law because they're being sent to a segregated school. The other adversary is the government—federal, state, or local.

All court proceedings are contests between adversaries. In a divorce case one adversary sues the other for divorce; in a civil suit one party accuses the other of doing it some injury; in a criminal prosecution the government prosecutor faces the lawyer of the accused party.

THE ROLE OF THE LAWYER

The role of the lawyer is often misunderstood. Lawyers don't always believe their clients are right. They may even strongly dislike the people—or views—they defend. But lawyers believe their client's case should be presented as strongly as possible. Even an accused criminal whom the lawyer himself believes to be guilty has a right to the best defense possible. In other words, lawyers aren't looking for "justice" or "the truth." These will result, they believe, if the lawyers on each side of the case present the strongest arguments they can.

THE ROLE OF THE JUDGE

The role of the judge, too, is often misunderstood. In the United States judges aren't expected to make their own investigations—to decide which accusations are true, which false, and which facts are being hidden or overlooked by both parties. Rather, they're expected to base their decisions on the arguments and evidence presented in court. Their job is to make sure a proper adversary proceeding is carried out—that legally correct claims and charges are made; that each party has a chance to present his or her case; that evidence obtained by illegal methods isn't used; and so on.

It's true that many court proceedings are somewhat different from what we have described here. Poor clients sometimes get less than full support from their lawyers, and some judges go well beyond the needs of the case to make general statements on public policy. But in general this is an accurate description of adversary proceedings, and this helps explain the moral force of court judgments in the United States.

ADVANTAGES OF ADJUDICATION

Adversary proceedings have the advantage of showing what citizen interests are actually affected by public policy. Even the most careful lawmaker can't foresee all the possible effects of a law. Adjudication lets those who are actually affected by a law state their case and ask for a reasonable interpretation of the law in the light of those problems. Moreover, the adjudication process makes use of self-interest. Legislatures may casually pass laws they half understand; adversaries in a court proceeding can't afford to be casual.

Another advantage of adjudication is that it provides legal channels through which minorities can protect their rights against majorities. Minorities can include unpopular citizens accused of crimes, very rich citizens, blacks, Jehovah's Witnesses, birdwatchers, corporations, and communists. None of these groups would fare very well in a democracy wholly controlled by majority rule.

In trying to protect such minorities the courts have sometimes blocked social reform. In the late 1800s and early 1900s, for example, they protected the giant corporations from government regulation. Here it's easy to see the courts as defending special interests against the will of the people. But the courts have also defended the rights of less-powerful minorities. Blacks were long ignored by the legislative branch of government. Recently, however, a series of important judicial decisions has begun to right the wrongs of racial discrimination.

DISADVANTAGES OF ADJUDICATION

A disadvantage of adjudication is that the case-by-case method of arriving at public policy may be slow and cumbersome. Judges in court face a dilemma: If they limit their decisions to the case before them, they risk adding a partial solution to a complex problem; but if they go beyond these limits they may reduce the moral force of their decisions. Moreover, the adversary process itself has the disadvantage of implying that only two possible points of view exist and that only one of these is right.

We have seen that adjudication protects the rights of individuals and minorities, but we must add that often these minorities are those who can't pay for such protection. The adjudication process—particularly the cost of a lawyer—is expensive. Courtroom procedures are complex and often cumbersome, and without a skilled lawyer you risk losing simply because you lack technical knowledge. But a trial involves other costs as well: courtroom fees, the cost of a delayed settlement, the cost of a transcript if you want to appeal the decision. If you lose the case, you also face whatever damages and court costs the judge may require. It's not surprising that many people who are sure they are right are still afraid to go to court.

There are other barriers for disadvantaged citizens. The poor, the less well educated, and certain minorities feel out of place in court. They usually appear in court to meet charges of breaking a contract or as defendants in criminal cases. Civil law is rarely written for their benefit, and they are less likely to know how to use the law to their own advantage. They know that most lawyers and judges look down on them and that (at least until recently) the members of the jury will come largely from the white middle class.

ADJUDICATION AND SOCIAL REFORM

How effective is adjudication in social reform? It's sometimes argued that a single ruling by the courts may bring about reform more effectively than years of lobbying. Abortion lobbies, for example, are putting much of their effort into bringing test cases to the courts. Environmental-protection groups, discouraged by the slow progress of the bills they support, have tried to short-circuit the legislative process by getting favorable court rulings.

But this strategy is open to question. Democratic government depends on persuasion and on agreement in the political community. Judicial rulings offer a tempting shortcut, particularly because they often have greater moral force than political solutions. However, this strategy is easily strained by overuse.

The Supreme Court

The tension between courts and legislatures may be seen in the central processes of American democracy. Its focal point is the United States Supreme Court. No other court in the world has stayed as dramatically in the public eye; none has as repeatedly blocked the elected branches of government and yet remained as firmly a part of a democratic political system. Public-opinion polls show that the Supreme Court is the most respected of the three branches of the federal government. For most Americans it's a symbol of the principle that no government official—not even the President—may act above the law. Two famous cases illustrate how this principle became established.

THE CASE OF THE CHEROKEE NATION

At the beginning of the nineteenth century the Cherokee Nation was the largest and most important Indian tribe in the southeastern United States. Although it had sided with Great Britain in the War for Independence and had continued to struggle against the colonies until 1794, it signed a peace treaty at that time that it observed for the next thirty years.

Then in 1828 the Cherokee Nation suffered two disasters at once. Gold was discovered on Cherokee land by a white prospector. And Andrew Jackson, a famous Indian fighter, was elected President of the United States. One of Jackson's first acts was to push through Congress the Indian Removal Act, which gave him authority to drive all Indian tribes west of the Mississippi. The Georgia legislature then declared all treaties with the Cherokee Nation null and void, and the Cherokee lands were given to interested whites in a lottery.

John Ross, the tribal chief, appealed to President Jackson and other officials to stop the seizure, but with no success. However, the Cherokees had one last defense. Georgia's action was an outright violation of the Cherokees' treaty with the federal government. It also violated the Fifth Amendment's prohibition against deprivation of property without due process of law. On these grounds the Cherokee Nation took its case to the United States Supreme Court. The Court tried to duck the issue but was finally persuaded to hear the case. Referring to the "original natural rights of the Cherokees . . . and the settled doctrine of the law of nations," the Court made the actions of the Georgia legislature legally void.

President Jackson was furious. "John Marshall [the Chief Justice] has rendered his decision; now let him enforce it," he said. As Jackson knew very well, this was impossible. The Court and the Constitution couldn't stop a determined legislature and a determined executive. Soon a new federal treaty was signed with a small group of Cherokees who did not represent the Nation; gold prospectors and other settlers poured in, and General Winfield Scott was sent to drive the Cherokees off their lands.

TRUMAN AND THE STEEL MILL CASE

About 100 years later, in 1952, President Truman found himself in an awkward position. American troops were in South Korea trying to hold the line at the 38th parallel. In this effort they depended on steel. Yet the United Steel Workers of America had announced a strike to begin April 9, 1952.

Allowing the strike to occur was politically and morally unthinkable in time of war. Further attempts at mediation clearly would do no good. The Taft-Hartley Act had given the President the authority to order striking workers back to work for an eight-day "cooling-off" period, but Truman, who had made this "antilabor" act a campaign issue in 1948, couldn't bring himself to do that. Instead, claiming it was his constitutional duty to protect the security and welfare of the nation, he ordered the Secretary of Commerce to take over the steel mills until the dispute could be settled.

The mills tried to get a federal district court injunction preventing the Secretary of Commerce from acting. Because the dispute raised such major issues, the Supreme Court accepted an appeal from the district court with unusual speed. On June 2 it ordered President Truman to return the mills to their owners. The President obeyed.

As we have seen, President Jackson's violation of the Constitution was far worse than President Truman's, but Jackson was strongly supported by public opinion. In the early nineteenth century the President could argue that his interpretation of the Constitution was as good as the Court's. By the middle of the twentieth century this argument was unthinkable. Not only was the President bound by the Constitution; the Supreme Court alone could interpret that Constitution. This was the most significant aspect of the case: that a group of nine men, without control over public funds or military forces and without having been elected to office, could become the final authority on the interpretation of the Constitution.

The Supreme Court and the Constitution

THE RIGHT OF JUDICIAL REVIEW

The Constitution states that it is the supreme law, the law that takes precedence over laws passed in Congress or in state legislatures. But the Constitution is unclear about who should decide if a particular law is in conflict with the Constitution. This may have been done on purpose. The writers of the Constitution knew they couldn't settle everything at a single convention. If they had given a group of nine judges appointed for life the authority to veto all legislation they thought was unconstitutional, the convention would probably have broken up. However, if they had failed to provide for a federal Supreme Court responsible for guarding the Constitution, many delegates would not have been satisfied.

HAMILTON'S SUPPORT OF JUDICIAL REVIEW

Alexander Hamilton used *The Federalist Papers* to describe the role of the Supreme Court. He argued that the idea of judicial review by judges appointed for life had a place in a democracy. According to Hamilton, a constitutional government can't depend on legislators' judgments. Self-interest will keep them from seeing any difference between what they want and what the Constitution permits. A judicial body outside the legislature—such as the Supreme Court—is needed. Hamilton admitted that Supreme Court judges are no different from legislators and executives, but he claimed that they are less to be feared. Lacking "influence over either the sword or the purse," the Court has "no direction over either the strength or the wealth of the community," he stated. It must judge "in accordance with rules that other agencies have prescribed," and must "depend upon the aid of the executive arm even for the efficacy of its judgments."

The "least dangerous" branch of government offers no serious threat to the other two branches or to the general public. The dangers are quite different—that the judicial branch will lose its independence and become absorbed into one of the other two branches, or that it will be ineffective in protecting the rights of citizens under the Constitution. Hence the justices are appointed for life; the Court would be unable to protect minority rights and basic freedoms if its members could be changed with every election.

Hamilton's view was accepted, but two issues had to be settled first. Opposed to Hamilton's position were, first, those who felt that Congress was the institution best suited to interpret the Constitution, and second, those who believed the state supreme courts had the power to interpret the Constitution in relation to the laws of the various states.

THE MARBURY CASE[1]

The success of the Jeffersonian party in the 1800 election threatened the Supreme Court as an independent institution. Before he left office President Adams, who had appointed Federalist John Marshall as Chief Justice, rushed through a series of "midnight appointments" of new federal judges. It was clear that there would be a contest between the Presidency, controlled by the Jeffersonians, and the courts, controlled by the Federalists.

An issue soon came up. In its hurry to pack the judicial branch with Federalists, the Adams administration had neglected to deliver to William Marbury his commission as justice of the peace for the District of Columbia. President Jefferson's Secretary of State, James Madison, refused to deliver the commission, and Marbury sued for a *writ of mandamus* ordering him to do so. This put the Supreme Court in an awkward position. The justices knew Madison had no intention of delivering the commission to Marbury, and the Court didn't want an open struggle with the executive branch. Such a struggle could only weaken the Court. But to admit that Madison had the right to deny Marbury his commission would be a humiliating surrender.

Chief Justice Marshall met the challenge. Madison's refusal to deliver the commission to Marbury, he wrote, was illegal. However, the Supreme Court didn't have jurisdiction in this case. For although the Judiciary Act of 1789 allowed the Court to issue writs of mandamus, that section of the law was unconstitutional and thus was not valid.

Marbury v. *Madison* was a masterpiece of judicial strategy. Marshall succeeded in diverting the attention of both parties to what was clearly the most significant element in the decision—the bold statement that the Supreme Court, on the basis of *its* interpretation of the Constitution, could set limits on Congress.

The Marbury decision firmly established the Supreme Court's right to set limits to governmental activity. This power has been used sparingly, however. Only 85 acts or parts of acts have been declared unconstitutional in the 173 years since the Marbury case. Some of these acts have been important ones, but most students of the Constitution believe the significance of judicial review is not as much in the acts declared unconstitutional as in the threat of a Supreme Court veto.

THE McCULLOCH CASE[2]

This case arose from the efforts of the Maryland state legislature to protect the banks it had chartered by taxing all other banks in the state. Among the competing banks was the Bank of the United States, set up by an act of Congress in 1816. McCulloch, cashier of the Baltimore branch of the Bank of the United States, refused to pay a $15,000 annual fee to the State of Mary-

[1] *Marbury* v. *Madison* 1 Cranch 137 (1803).

[2] *McCulloch* v. *Maryland* 4 Wheaton 316 (1819).

land or to put Maryland tax stamps on the bank notes he issued. Maryland won a judgment against McCulloch in one of its county courts, arguing that within its own borders it could tax as it pleased. The Bank's lawyers replied that Maryland's claim would hopelessly restrict the federal government's economic powers. The Maryland State Court of Appeals rejected their argument, so the Bank appealed to the United States Supreme Court. It was a clear clash of federal vs. state power.

Chief Justice Marshall, who fully agreed with the Bank, wrote that all levels of government derived their authority from the Constitution and therefore no level of government could claim natural supremacy over the others. However, we're wrong if we think that because a particular power isn't listed in the Constitution the federal government doesn't have the constitutional authority to take necessary action. The Constitution gives Congress implied powers, the right "to make all Laws which shall be necessary and proper to carrying into Execution the . . . Powers vested by this Constitution in the Government of the United States." This clause, Marshall argued, gives the federal government broad powers:

> Let the end be legitimate, let it be within the scope of the constitution, and all means which are appropriate, which are plainly adapted to that end, which are not prohibited, but consistent with the letter and spirit of the constitution, are constitutional. . . .

The Maryland tax, which had "the power to destroy," stood in the way of a policy related to the goals of the federal government; therefore it was unconstitutional.

The McCulloch decision is an important landmark in the establishment of the Supreme Court as the interpreter of the fundamental law of the nation. In it the Court justified both the growth of federal power and the role of the Court in settling disputes between the states and the federal government.

The Struggle for Judicial Supremacy

Throughout its history the Supreme Court has been a center of controversy. But the most serious challenge to the power of the Court occurred in 1937, at the beginning of President Roosevelt's second term.

After the Civil War the Supreme Court turned its attention to the relationship between the government and the economy. For the next seventy years the Court felt itself responsible for maintaining legal conditions favorable to the rapid growth of industrial capitalism. Both the federal and state legislatures were blocked if their actions threatened free enterprise.

DUE PROCESS

The Court held that the U.S. Constitution prohibited both the federal and state governments from interfering with competition. This argument was based mainly on the due process clause of the Fourteenth Amendment: "No State shall . . . deprive any person of life, liberty, or property, without due process of law." This clause was intended to protect freed slaves, but it was almost immediately taken over by powerful business interests to prevent the government from setting limits on profits. The due process clause became a constitutional guarantee that owners of private property could successfully bring suit against all forms of state regulation beyond those protecting the health and safety of the citizen.

FDR AND THE SUPREME COURT

In normal times the Court might have gone unchallenged. But in October 1929 the stock market collapsed. Ruined speculators, bankrupt merchants, unemployed workers, and farmers facing foreclosure joined in the demand for sweeping governmental action. From this point on the Supreme Court was defending business interests against a major coalition calling for economic reform.

As the economic crisis deepened, a governmental crisis grew. The Roosevelt administration introduced laws to deal with the economic situation. But these laws were often blocked by the Supreme Court. By 1935 the Court was rejecting most of the major programs of the New Deal. Between 1935 and 1937 the Court vetoed a total of twelve congressional acts—acts designed to bring relief to the nation's farmers, the oil industry, the coal industry, and other groups.

The Court said it had no choice; the laws were clearly unconstitutional. And the Court believed it could ignore the rising tide of public disapproval, congressional anger, and Presidential frustration. In other words the Court believed it was above politics; it was merely comparing laws to the Constitution and rejecting those that didn't fit. But the Court couldn't ignore political currents; nor were its decisions automatic. Other justices would see things differently.

The battle was lost by the conservatives when Roosevelt was reelected. The "swing men" on the Court, Justice Roberts and Chief Justice Hughes, began to accept the legislation passed under Roosevelt's leadership. Laws hardly different from those that had been found unconstitutional by 6-to-3 majorities were now upheld by a majority of five justices. On March 29, 1937 the Court found that the Fourteenth Amendment's due process clause no longer stood in the way of a minimum-wage law in the state of Washington. Two weeks later Chief Justice Hughes stated that Congress had the right to set up a National Labor Relations Board to deal with conflicts over union organization and collective bargaining. Earlier the Court had ruled such a grant of power unconstitutional, but the Chief Justice simply said, "These cases are not controlling here."

The change in the Supreme Court opened the way for government regulation of the economy. In a clash with the other branches of the government, the Supreme Court had backed down. But this doesn't mean the Court is the weakest branch of the government. It had dominated economic policy making for almost fifty years despite the pressures from the other branches of the government. It is a powerful institution but, as the events of the 1930s showed, not all-powerful.

The Supreme Court and Racial Discrimination

In the years after the Civil War the Supreme Court did little to end racial discrimination. The most famous case of this period is *Plessy* v. *Ferguson*, which involved a Louisiana law requiring segregated railroad facilities.[3] The Court's decision replaced the principle of equal protection of the law with the "separate but equal" doctrine. The Court stated that

> in the nature of things [the Fourteenth Amendment] could not have intended to abolish distinctions based on color, or to enforce social, as distinct from political equality, or a commingling of the races on terms unsatisfactory to either. . . . Legislation is powerless to eradicate racial instincts or to abolish distinctions based upon physical differences, and the attempt to do so can only result in accentuating the difficulties of the present situation. . . . If one race be inferior to the other socially, the Constitution of the United States cannot put them on the same plane.

For the next fifty years the Supreme Court turned its back on America's black minority. The only exception was in the area of voting rights. Voting had a special stutus under the Fifteenth Amendment, and the Court did deal with the worst attempts to deny blacks this right. As early as 1915 the Court ruled against Oklahoma's *grandfather clause* according to which one's voting rights depended upon whether one's grandfather had voted; ten years later it struck down efforts by Texas to bar blacks from voting in Democratic party primaries. By the end of World War II there was no longer any question that laws denying racial minorities the right to vote were unconstitutional.

CIVIL RIGHTS AFTER WORLD WAR II

World War II greatly changed the status of black Americans, though this change was not seen right away. Blacks moved north in large numbers to get better-paying jobs in the defense industries, and most of them stayed on afterwards to become "swing" constituencies in close elections in the northern cities.

THE NAACP'S FIGHT AGAINST RACIAL DISCRIMINATION

The National Association for the Advancement of Colored People, convinced that Congress would not respond to its demands, decided to expand its fight in

[3] *Plessy* v. *Ferguson* 163 U.S. 537 (1896).

the courts. A lot of planning was needed, since court action rarely brought about basic social reform. The plaintiff might run out of money or lose interest in the case; he might compromise before the constitutional issues had been settled; or the courts, as they usually did, might find other issues on which to settle the case. Even if the case was won, the courts might define the constitutional issue so narrowly that the decision would have little effect on the status of 15 million people. Despite these problems, the NAACP was strikingly successful in a number of cases involving discrimination in public transportation and housing.

THE FIGHT FOR EQUAL EDUCATION

But the NAACP's biggest battle still lay ahead. In the middle of the twentieth century the schools of all the southern and border states were still segregated by law, and in the northern states racially segregated housing resulted in *de facto segregation* in many schools. The question of racial segregation in the public schools was the most explosive civil-rights issue that could be put on the Supreme Court's agenda. Before this could be done, the principle of integration had to be firmly established in other areas.

At first the question seemed to be one of equality of facilities. In *Plessy* v. *Ferguson* the Court had said "separate" facilities for blacks could be "equal" to those provided for whites. The fact that such facilities were inferior was common knowledge, but for fifty years the Court had refused to determine whether the facilities were equal or not.

Sweatt v. Painter. This situation began to change in 1950 with the case of *Sweatt* v. *Painter*.[4] Sweatt had been denied admission to the University of Texas Law School because he was black. A trial court agreed that he had been denied equal protection of the law but continued the case for six months to give the state time to provide equal facilities for blacks. In 1947 Texas opened a makeshift law school for blacks with a faculty of five and a library of a few thousand books. Sweatt refused to accept this school as equal to a law school with a library of 65,000 books and a well-known faculty. He carried his case to the Supreme Court, which had no trouble finding that the whites-only University of Texas Law School had much better facilities. As Chief Justice Vinson put it,

> The law school to which Texas is willing to admit petitioner excludes from its student body members of the racial groups which number 85 percent of the population of the State and include most of the lawyers, witnesses, jurors, judges, and other officials with whom petitioner inevitably will be dealing when he becomes a member of the Texas bar.

Under such conditions, the Chief Justice argued, no school, whatever its facili-

[4] *Sweatt* v. *Painter* 339 U.S. 629 (1950).

ties, could offer Sweatt an equal chance to get the experience and social contacts he needed for successful participation in a nation dominated by whites.

Brown v. Board of Education of Topeka. The next step was to make clear to the general public how the Sweatt decision applied to segregation in the public schools. The NAACP believed it had found the ideal test case in *Brown* v. *Board of Education of Topeka.*[5] The schools for black children in Topeka, Kansas, were equal to those for white children in all ways—buildings and equipment, courses available, qualifications of teachers. The basic difference was that black children weren't allowed to go to school with white children. In 1954 the Court ruled that "in the field of public education the doctrine of 'separate but equal' has no place."

With this decision the Supreme Court reshaped the agenda of modern American politics. For another ten years, however, the judicial branch was left to struggle almost alone with the huge job of carrying out the government's legal and moral responsibility to black citizens. The executive branch did little until 1964.

The Warren Court: Judicial Activism

Earl Warren was Chief Justice from 1954 to 1969. During this period the Supreme Court was known as the Warren Court.[6] It was also known as an activist court, since in many areas the Court was at the center of major controversies. The Warren Court's landmark decision on school desegregation was only the first of a series of decisions that tried to reshape race relations in the United States.

ONE MAN, ONE VOTE

Race relations was one area in which the Warren Court took the lead over Congress and the Presidency. Another perhaps more controversial area of reform was political representation. Before the 1960s state legislatures drew the boundaries of state and congressional districts without taking into account the number of people in each district. A legislator elected from a farm district might represent only 25,000 voters, while one from a city district might represent ten times as many voters. In *Baker* v. *Carr* the Court ruled that equal protection of the law is denied when the number of representatives from a particular area is not determined by its population.[7] If half of the voters of Illinois lived in Chicago, then half the state legislators should come from Chicago, leaving the rest of the state to be represented by the other half.

[5] *Brown* v. *Board of Education of Topeka, Kansas* 347 U.S. 483 (1954).

[6] The Supreme Court is traditionally referred to by the name of the Chief Justice; hence Warren Court, Burger Court.

[7] *Baker* v. *Carr* 369 U.S. 186 (1962).

CRIMINAL DUE PROCESS

Earlier in this chapter we said that justice in the United States depends on an adversary process—someone argues for the person accused of a crime and someone argues against him. The judge and jury aren't fact finders; they listen to the facts presented in court.

Where do these facts come from? Very often they come from investigations carried out by the police. But what if the accused person is uneducated and poor, too uneducated to fully understand the ins and outs of the law and too poor to hire a lawyer? The Warren Court felt that it made no sense if only one party, the police and the prosecution, had the resources to make investigations. Moreover, if an accused person answered police questions he might easily hurt his own case. In *Gideon* v. *Wainwright* the Court ruled that if the defendant is too poor to hire a lawyer the government must supply him with one.[8] The Court also ruled that no evidence obtained in an illegal search could be used in a federal court and that wiretapping was "search and seizure" and couldn't be used as evidence unless it had been authorized by a warrant.

The Burger Court: Judicial Restraint

The role of the Warren Court in protecting the rights of accused people was strongly criticized. One of Nixon's favorite campaign promises in 1968 was that he would bring back law and order. He claimed that the Supreme Court was "coddling criminals" and "seriously hamstringing the peace forces in our society." He promised to appoint to the Court only judges who would be strictly bound by the Constitution. Shortly after Nixon's election Warren resigned from the Court. Nixon appointed Warren Burger, who was opposed to an activist role for the Court, as Chief Justice.

Within the first three years of his Presidency Nixon was able to make three more appointments to the Court. In each case he chose justices who

[8] *Gideon* v. *Wainwright* 372 U.S. 335 (1963).

TABLE 11.1 *Members of the Supreme Court, 1976*

Member	*Appointed by*	*Year*
William J. Brennan, Jr.	Eisenhower	1957
Potter Stewart	Eisenhower	1959
Byron R. White	Kennedy	1962
Thurgood Marshall	Johnson	1967
Warren E. Burger	Nixon	1969
Harry A. Blackmun	Nixon	1970
Lewis F. Powell, Jr.	Nixon	1971
William H. Rehnquist	Nixon	1971
John P. Stevens	Ford	1975

were conservative in outlook. Table 11.1 shows the current makeup of the Supreme Court.

Though the Burger Court has been in some ways more restrained than the Warren Court, it has not reversed the trends set by Chief Justice Warren. In fact in recent years the Court has approved the use of busing to integrate schools, has outlawed the death penalty in criminal cases, and has rejected the claim of the Nixon administration that it didn't have to get court approval to use wiretaps on supposed subversives.

The Supreme Court and American Politics

Some students of politics ask what a group of justices appointed for life is doing in a government based on popular election. They also ask why, in a government where one power is supposed to balance another, one group has "supreme" power over the interpretation of the Constitution. The answer may be seen in the history of the Supreme Court—the Court is not all-powerful.

LIMITS ON THE POWER OF THE COURT

For one thing the Supreme Court makes its decisions within the framework of the Constitution and the decisions on previous cases. This greatly limits its ability to write into a decision anything it wants. Some people claim that this makes the Court's actions automatic: The justices simply compare each law with the clear words of the Constitution and make their decisions on this basis.

Most students of the Supreme Court, however, would disagree. The Constitution is rarely clear. In fact it has survived largely because it *is* ambiguous—so that each generation can interpret it to fit the times. The Court is guided by the Constitution, but it still must *interpret,* and here it uses its own judgment. At times it has been criticized for interpreting the Constitution too loosely, at other times for not interpreting it loosely enough. Such criticisms will continue to be made, for the Court's actions aren't automatic.

Political Restraints. It's widely believed that the Supreme Court is isolated from the mainstream of American politics. In a way this is true. The justices aren't elected; they do stay out of party politics; they aren't visited by lobbyists or constituents. They are, as the founders intended them to be, above politics in this sense.

But the justices are not cut off from the currents of American politics and the preferences of the public. For one thing they are appointed by Presidents who are interested in particular policies. In the 1930s, for example, President Roosevelt appointed justices he believed would interpret the Constitution loosely in the area of expansion of federal power. President Nixon appointed justices he believed would be stricter in their interpretation of the Constitution in the area of criminal prosecution.

Even after being appointed, the justices stay in touch with the times. They don't just read the Constitution, they read the newspapers as well. It would be an exaggeration to say the justices write their opinions on the basis of the last election, but as the events of the 1930s show, they are affected by election results.

Other Limits on the Court. The power of the Supreme Court is limited in another way. Even after it has declared an act unconstitutional, it can be overruled. One way is by a constitutional amendment. This, as we have pointed out, is usually a slow and cumbersome process. Another limit on the Court is the fact that it can't enforce its decisions. Although government officials usually won't openly disobey the Court, when they disagree with a Court ruling they can be very successful in limiting its effect. This has happened in the cases of school desegregation and school prayers.

Finally, the powers of the Supreme Court are limited by the power of Congress to approve appointments and to impeach justices for misconduct.

The Court System

The Supreme Court is part of a complex system of federal, state, and municipal courts. This system is shown in Figure 11.1.

FEDERAL COURTS

The federal judicial system has three layers: the Supreme Court at the top, circuit courts in the middle, and district courts at the bottom. There are also special courts for cases involving customs, patents, and the military.

The Supreme Court has both original and appellate jurisdiction. *Original jurisdiction* means that cases can start, or originate, before the Supreme Court. The Court has original jurisdiction only in cases that involve ambassadors and other public ministers and in cases that involve disputes between states, for example, the case in which the Supreme Court determined which branch of the Red River was the boundary between Texas and Oklahoma.

Appellate jurisdiction is the right to try cases before the Supreme Court that have been appealed from lower courts. The Supreme Court hears cases appealed from lower federal courts and from state supreme courts.

Circuit Courts of Appeals. Most cases come to the Supreme Court on appeal from *circuit courts*. There are eleven circuit courts, each with jurisdiction over a particular area. The circuit courts were created to take some of the load off the Supreme Court and to make handling of cases in the federal judicial system easier. They have between three and fifteen judges, depending on the case load in the circuit or region. The circuit courts are called courts of appeal because they have no original jurisdiction; they hear only cases appealed from lower courts. Only the Supreme Court can review the decision of a circuit court.

District Courts. Ninety *district courts* and four territorial courts hear the great majority of the cases that come to the federal court system. Large states like California have as many as four district courts, and a large district court might have as many as twenty-four judges, though often only three judges will hear a case. District courts hear cases involving citizens from different states or transportation of stolen goods across state lines. They also hear cases involving violations of federal laws—immigration, counterfeit, antitrust, food and drug, income tax, and so on.

STATE COURTS

In addition to the federal judicial system, each state has its own judicial system. Some of these systems are very complicated. State systems are often decentralized, that is, organized on a county or district basis. Generally, however, a state court can be classified at one of three levels: trial court, intermediate court of appeals, and state supreme court.

SELECTION OF JUDGES

Because there are two different judicial systems, federal and state, there are two different kinds of judges. All federal judges are appointed by the Pres-

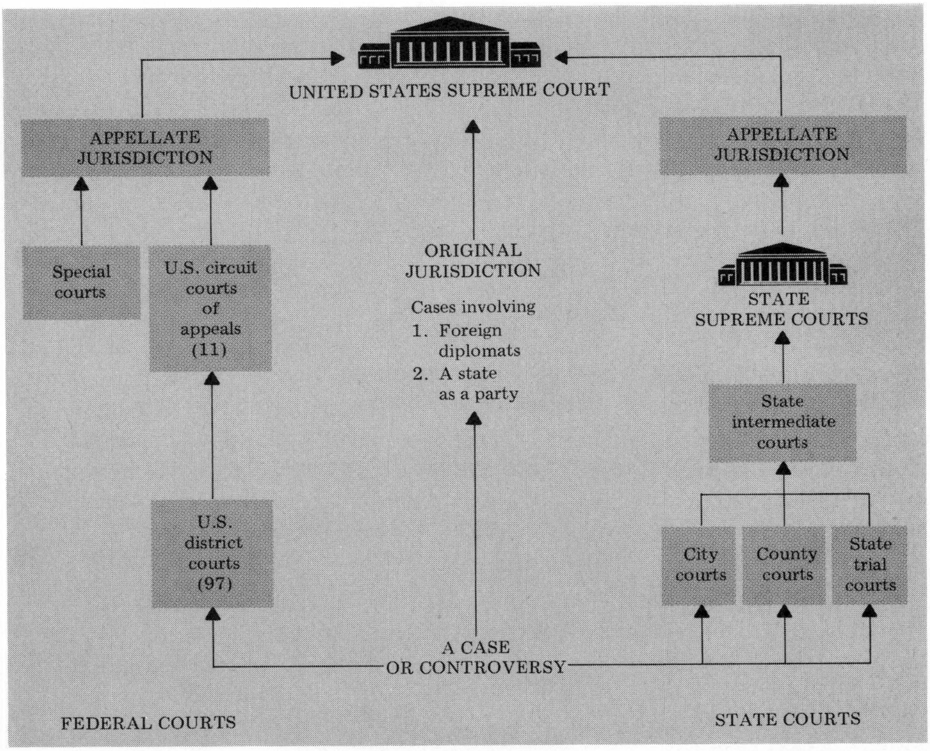

FIGURE 11.1
The Judicial System

ident, though they must be approved by the Senate. These appointments are usually made on a party basis—a Republican President appoints Republican judges and a Democratic President appoints Democratic judges. Law Professor Philip B. Kurland explains this situation as follows: "The judiciary has long been treated as the place to put political workhorses out to pasture. The great majority of America's judges have their posts because—and only because—of prior services rendered to the dominant political party."

Selection of judges at the state and local levels is done by appointment, election, or both. The most common arrangement, found in thirty-eight states, is popular election, with terms of office lasting anywhere from two years to life. However, few people are satisfied with the way judges are chosen in the United States, for it seems that no matter what arrangement is used, it's still the politicians who choose the judges. Judges selected in this way don't always have the respect of citizens. And the quality of the judges largely determines the quality of justice.

ATTEMPTS AT REFORM

The American judicial system is a complicated one, but very little has been done to try to straighten it out. One student of the American judicial system writes: "The most important observation about change in court structure is that . . . little of it has occurred in the last century."[9] Thus the judicial system struggles to deal with twentieth-century problems with the structures and processes of the nineteenth century. While the executive branch has divided itself into dozens of departments and hundreds of agencies and the legislative branch has organized itself into committees, the judicial branch has been very much the same for nearly 100 years. Judges are expected to hear cases ranging all the way from conspiracy to divorce. But in recent years the problems of justice in American society have grown. Pressures for change in the judicial system are very strong.

CONTROVERSY

Should the Supreme Court Enforce Busing to Integrate Schools?

In the 1970s the Supreme Court and the other federal courts became involved in an explosive controversy over the busing of schoolchildren to integrate public schools. *Brown* v. *Board of Education of Topeka* had ruled that legal segregation of the public schools was unconstitutional. But as the

[9] Herbert Jacob, *Urban Justice* (Englewood Cliffs, N.J.: Prentice-Hall, 1973), p. 91.

years went by it became clear that ending legal segregation wouldn't necessarily eliminate segregated schools. The reason for this was that in many parts of the country blacks and other minority groups lived in separate areas, usually in the center of the city, while whites lived in other areas and in the suburbs. If children went to neighborhood schools, they usually went to schools that were de facto segregated. Some courts therefore decided that only by busing schoolchildren from one neighborhood to another could segregation be eliminated.

One Side

Busing schoolchildren is the only way to end de facto segregation. Segregated schools violate the Constitution whether they are a result of state law or of housing patterns. To end such segregation white children must be bused into black neighborhoods and black children must be bused into white areas.

There is also the question of which branch of the government should enforce school desegregation. It's the courts' duty to do so. The President,

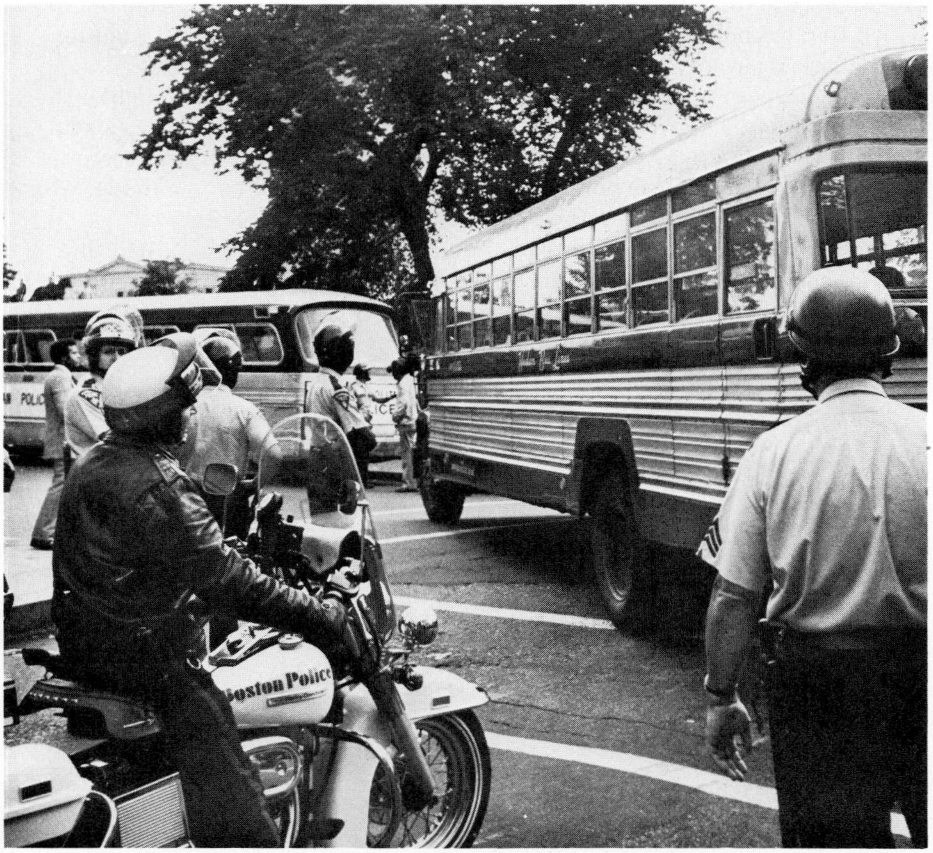

Boston police have enforced court ordered busing to desegregate Boston public schools.

Congress, and state legislatures are powerless to act effectively because of political pressures. The courts may not be the best place to make policy on racial integration, but if the other branches of the government won't take action, the courts are the only place where such action can be taken.

The Supreme Court is aware that it has taken on a big job alone, with little help from the other branches of the government. It hasn't made a final decision on desegregation, but perhaps this is because of the complexity of the problem and the strong feelings of citizens on this issue. It may be that because of the opposition to busing the Court is following its own directions to the federal courts: Require local officials to move toward integration "with all deliberate speed."

The Other Side

The only way to end de facto school segregation is to break down the barriers that force blacks and other minority groups to live in separate areas. The solution is to get rid of the ghettos. The Brown ruling, according to some courts, doesn't apply to de facto segregation.

The legislative and executive branches, not the courts, should enforce desegregation. If the courts rule that a district has to bus children from one neighborhood to another, they are taking over the lawmaking role of the legislative branch, ignoring the opinions of the community, and reading the Constitution any way they like.

Besides, court decisions can be avoided. Sociological decisions like the Brown ruling are hard to enforce; it's not easy to change a person's attitudes, beliefs, and way of living. And if, as some people think, the courts are the only place where policy on school desegregation can be made, why has the Supreme Court left the responsibility to the lower courts?

Finally, there are the views of the majority of the citizens. Whether or not the courts are moving against the current of public opinion is not yet clear. If this is the case we must ask the question, Does the Court have the right to enforce busing if such a policy goes against the will of the majority of the people?

How Institutions Work: V The Judicial Appeal Process

WHEN MAY A JUDICIAL DECISION BE APPEALED?

Appellate courts hear only cases that are appealed after a trial has been completed. Almost anyone who takes his case to court has the right to appeal.

HOW DOES AN APPEALS COURT DIFFER FROM A TRIAL COURT?

Appeals courts follow different rules from trial courts. The appeals court doesn't retry the case; rather, it works from the record of the original trial, from the appeal briefs, and from the oral arguments presented. To win a case on appeal, you have to show that the trial court misunderstood the case, made errors in the procedure, or came to a clearly mistaken conclusion. Besides preventing miscarriages of justice, appeals courts make the interpretation of the law more uniform.

WHAT IS THE STRUCTURE OF THE APPEALS COURT SYSTEM?

As Figure 11.1 shows, there are two levels of appeals courts—federal and state. The eleven U.S. circuit courts of appeals hear all appeals from federal district courts. The appeals courts each have from three to fifteen judges. Unlike trials, appeals are heard by a panel of judges, usually three. There is no jury. Although the circuit courts must hear all appeals brought to them from the district courts, only a small portion of the cases tried in district courts are actually appealed.

In fewer than half the states there are state intermediate courts. All states, however, have a highest court of appeals, usually called the state supreme court. Like the federal circuit courts, most state supreme courts must hear all cases brought to them. The procedures used in these courts vary widely, although in all states cases are decided by a majority vote of the justices.

HOW DO CASES REACH THE UNITED STATES SUPREME COURT?

As shown in Figure 11.1, appellate cases may come to the Supreme Court from the circuit courts, from the special courts, or from the state supreme courts. Cases generally reach the Supreme Court in two ways: appeal or certiorari. The appeal procedure is used when the case is a jurisdictional one between the states and the federal government. But most cases are brought to the Supreme Court by a *writ of certiorari* (from the Latin "to be made more certain"). The losing party in a federal court of appeals or a state supreme court, if his claim involves a question of federal law, may ask the United States Supreme Court to hear his case.

HOW DO THE JUSTICES DECIDE WHICH CASES TO TAKE?

Unlike most appeals courts, the Supreme Court can almost always decide which cases it will hear. After considering the cases brought to it, the justices vote on each one. If four justices vote in favor, a case is accepted; if not, the case is rejected and the decision of the lower court stands.

A case has little chance of being heard by the Supreme Court unless it involves major issues. The justices realize that they can't correct every judicial mistake. Instead, the Court serves as the highest point at which public policy conflicts can be settled. This is why it often accepts *amicus curiae* ("friend of the court") briefs. The federal government or private interest groups may use this method to argue the political and social as well as legal aspects of a case.

HOW MANY CASES DOES THE SUPREME COURT HEAR?

The Court is asked to hear over 4000 cases each year. The justices usually agree to hear fewer than 300 of these.

IS THE DECISION OF THE UNITED STATES SUPREME COURT THE FINAL ACTION IN A CASE?

It depends. When the Court upholds the lower court's action, the case is over. When it reverses a lower-court action, the case may be retried. Those who have won a case in the Supreme Court have sometimes lost their case in a retrial on the particular evidence presented.

Questions for Review

1. Describe the roles of the plaintiff, the defendant, the lawyer, and the judge in a court case.
2. What are some of the advantages and disadvantages of adjudication? What is its effect on social reform?
3. What is the significance of the Cherokee Nation and Steel Mill cases?
4. How did the Marbury and McCulloch cases contribute to the strength of the federal government?
5. Describe FDR's battle with the Supreme Court. Who won?
6. How has the Supreme Court responded to racial discrimination over the years?
7. What is the point of having justices appointed for life?
8. What are some of the limits on the power of the Supreme Court?
9. Describe the federal court system.
10. Define original jurisdiction and appellate jurisdiction.

Chapter 12

Separation of Powers

The writers of the Constitution faced a dilemma. They wanted to create a national government with the power to act, and they wanted to limit that power. How could this be done? One way, as we'll see in the next chapter, is to create a national government that can pass laws, but to put limits on the laws it can pass. But the Constitution limits the power of the government in another important way: It puts restrictions on each branch of the government. No one branch has absolute power over any other. This system of separation of powers or checks and balances works as a check on abuses of power.

The Constitutional Framework

The founders knew there could be no nation unless the government had certain powers—the authority to tax, to regulate the actions of citizens, to make binding contracts, to punish those who break the law. But they didn't want to give all this authority to any single group, so they created a complex system of divided powers. Each branch of the government was given ways of preventing the other branches from dominating it; thus no branch could gain complete authority over the government. *The Federalist* (No. 51) explains the principle of separation of powers in these words:

> Ambition must be made to counteract ambition. . . . If men were angels, no government would be necessary. If angels were to govern men, neither external nor internal controls on government would be necessary. In framing a government which is to be administered by men over men, the great difficulty lies in this: you must first enable the government to control the governed; and in the next place oblige it to control itself.

SEPARATION OF POWERS

As we have seen, the government was divided into three separate branches, legislative, executive, and judicial. According to *The Federalist*, this separation of powers had three goals:

1. The powers of government would be divided. This argument is stated in *The Federalist* (No. 51) as follows:

> In the compound Republic of America, the power surrendered by the people is first divided between two distinct governments (Federal government and the States), and then the portion allotted to each subdivided among distinct and separate departments. . . . The different governments will control each other, at the same time that each will be controlled by itself.

2. Through the system of *checks and balances* each branch of the government could limit the activities of the others. For example, Congress makes laws, but the President can veto them. Congress can override a veto, but this

takes a two-thirds vote. The President appoints judges, but they must be approved by the Senate. The judges are appointed for life, but they can be impeached and convicted by Congress. So it goes throughout the federal government and every state government as well. Table 12.1 shows how often some of these checks have been used.

3. Because of these checks, the various parts of the government must cooperate with one another. As a result a wider range of interests is reflected in governmental policy. Moreover, each branch has its own outlook; the blending of these different outlooks should result in better government. The system of checks and balances also requires the various groups to make a greater effort to communicate.

SEPARATION OF POWERS IN ACTION

The Constitution doesn't say how the branches of government are to relate. Although Congress, the Presidency, and the Supreme Court remain independent of one another, their relative power has varied. At times one has appeared to be stronger and the others weaker. But each has played an important role at various times in U.S. history.

In addition, the three branches haven't functioned the way the founders expected. Each was supposed to do a particular job: Congress to make laws, the President to carry them out, and the courts to interpret them. In fact, however, the three branches share these functions. Congress does pass laws, but the executive and judicial branches play an important part in this function. The President's legislative power goes beyond his power to veto laws. Much of the legislation passed by Congress begins as part of the President's program. In the same way the Supreme Court's legislative power goes beyond its power of judicial review. In some areas the courts have laws that control citizens as much as any law of Congress, as can be seen in the case of school desegregation.

Nor is the power to execute the laws limited to the executive branch. In many desegregation rulings the courts have included instructions on how to

TABLE 12.1
The use of checks and balances, 1789–1970

There were 2255 Presidential vetoes of congressional acts.
Congress subsequently overruled 75 of those vetoes.
The Supreme Court ruled 85 congressional acts or parts of acts unconstitutional.
The Senate refused to confirm 27 nominees to the Supreme Court (out of a total of 138 nominees).
Congress impeached 9 federal judges; of these, 4 were convicted. The Senate rejected 8 Cabinet nominations.

Source: Senate Library, Presidential Vetoes (New York: Greenwood Press, 1968); *Congressional Quarterly, Inc.;* and *Current American Government* (Washington, D.C.: *Comgressional Quarterly,* Spring 1973), p. 106.

carry out the ruling and have closely supervised local school boards. Congress, too, is involved in the execution of laws. Many of its committees keep a close watch on the way government agencies administer the laws.

Thus while the three branches set up by the Constitution remain strong and independent, their functions overlap. Perhaps the most important overlap is between the legislative powers of Congress and those of the President. In recent years legislation has tended to start in the executive branch. This suggests a passive Congress—but is this really the case?

CONGRESS VS. THE PRESIDENCY

The news media often exaggerate the power of the Presidency in making public policy. They talk about Johnson's War on Poverty, Nixon's revenue-sharing plan, or Ford's energy policy. But a major Presidential program is rarely passed without any changes; the final bill is usually a compromise between what Congress and the President want.

Influence of Congressional Leaders. When Congress doesn't like a President's program, not much of it will become law. For example, when Kennedy was running for President in 1960 he described his New Frontier in speech after speech. However, conservative southern senators like James Eastland of Mississippi headed major Senate committees. They had strong positions in Congress and voter support back home. Though he won the election, Kennedy had little success in getting his program passed against the opposition of such powerful congressional leaders.

Congress' Legal Powers. Congress also has certain legal powers over the executive branch. Of these powers, the following are the most important:

1. *Organization.* The departments and agencies of the executive branch are created by acts of Congress.
2. *Authorization.* The programs administered by executive agencies depend on congressional legislation. NASA, for example, can't design and carry out any space program it wants; its programs have to be authorized by Congress.
3. *Financing.* Congress controls the purse strings, and programs that aren't funded can't be carried out. In a bitter fight in 1970, Congress refused to provide funds for the development of a supersonic transport (SST), and Nixon had to drop the project.
4. *Review.* Congress has the right to supervise the activities of executive agencies. Public hearings by a hostile congressional committee can be embarrassing for an executive agency and may result in changes in policy.

In recent years Congress has not made full use of its powers. As a result some say Congress no longer acts as a check on the executive branch. According to the Ralph Nader Congress Project, "No matter how hard the Congress may struggle on one issue, it is overwhelmed by the vastly greater forces of the presidency."[1] And there is evidence for this. For example, even when Congress passes legislation the President doesn't like, the battle isn't over. The President can veto the legislation. The veto power was included in the Constitution as a Presidential check on unconstitutional legislation, but it has become an important policy tool: The President can threaten to veto acts of Congress that don't suit the Presidential program. Nixon, for example, sent the following message to Congress when it was getting ready to vote on major health and education bills:

> I will simply not let reckless spending of this kind destroy the tax-reduction we have secured and the hard-earned success we have earned in the battle against inflation. . . . With or without the cooperation of the Congress, I am going to do everything within my power to prevent such a fiscal crisis for millions of our people. . . . Let there be no misunderstanding: if bills come to my desk calling for excessive spending which threatens the federal budget, I will veto them.

Congress can override a Presidential veto with a two-thirds vote, but such a majority isn't easy to get. Franklin Roosevelt vetoed 631 congressional bills; Congress overrode 9 of those vetoes. Eisenhower vetoed 181 bills; only 2 were overridden. Recent Presidents have had more effective opposition, though. Of Nixon's 43 vetoes, 6 were overridden, and during Ford's first six months in office 4 of his 24 vetoes were overridden.

Earlier we discussed the growth of the executive branch. This growth, along with the apparent weakness and disorganization of Congress, has led some people to claim that the executive branch is taking over the legislative function of Congress. But two things should be kept in mind. First, what Congress gives, Congress can take away. The President depends on a large White House staff and a variety of executive agencies. Authorization and funds for these come from Congress.

Second, the complaint that the executive branch has replaced Congress as the major force in American politics comes out of a period when foreign-policy issues dominated the headlines. It's true that the Constitution gives Congress the power to declare war, but traditionally matters of defense and national security have been handled by the executive branch. Congress, on the other hand, plays a bigger role in bread-and-butter issues. No President,

[1] Mark J. Green, James M. Fallows, and David R. Zwick, *Who Rules Congress?* (New York: Bantam, 1972), p. 94.

for example, could push through a tax-reform bill on his own. It's to Congress, not the President, that we turn for action on matters like revenue sharing, aid to education, or minimum-wage policy.

The President and the Bureaucracy

The President, Congress, and the courts are independent of one another; governmental power is shared rather than unified. But the division of power goes further than that. We talk about the battle between Congress and the Presidency as if they were two individuals in conflict. In fact, however, neither Congress nor the executive branch is a single unit. The executive branch in particular is a huge bureaucracy; within it there are many other independent power centers.

PRESIDENTIAL CONTROL

The federal bureaucracy is a big, complicated organization; there are many layers between the President and the lowest clerk on the government payroll. The bureaucracy is made up of thousands of separate agencies and programs and millions of employees.

Bringing order to the executive branch is close to impossible. Johnson's Great Society program, for example, included 21 new health programs, 17 new educational programs, 15 new economic-development programs, 17 new resource-development programs, 4 new manpower-training programs, and 12 new programs to aid the cities. How was this legislation to be carried out? In committee hearings Senator Edmund Muskie found that there were 170 different federal aid programs, financed by 400 separate appropriations and administered by 21 departments and agencies.

The President is in charge of the executive branch, but he's lucky if he knows what's happening in even a tiny part of it. Look at the following news item, datelined Notasulga, Alabama, July 27, 1972:

> In 1932, Charlie Pollard, then a 26-year-old Macon County farmer, took advantage of a public health official's offer of a free blood test and was told a few days later that he had "bad blood."
>
> "They been doctoring on me off and on ever since then," Mr. Pollard, now 66, said yesterday. "And they give me a blood tonic."
>
> Mr. Pollard did not know until Tuesday that for the past 40 years he has been one of a constantly dwindling number of human guinea pigs in whose "bad blood" the effects of syphilis have been observed.
>
> U.S. Public Health Service officials revealed Tuesday that under a Public Health Service study, treatment for syphilis has been withheld from hundreds of afflicted Negroes for the 40-year period. For the past 25 years, penicillin has been generally available to treat it. The purpose of

the study was observation of the course of the disease in untreated persons over a long period of time.

This study had been carried out by officials of the U.S. government, with public funds, during the Presidencies of Roosevelt, Truman, Eisenhower, Kennedy, Johnson, and Nixon. Any of these Presidents would probably have stopped the program if they had found out about it. But how can one person know what's being done in the name of the U.S. government in hundreds of offices, laboratories, agencies, departments, and projects? This situation is illustrated by the following snatch of conversation between Franklin Roosevelt and one of his top advisers:

> "When I woke up this morning, the first thing I saw was a headline in the *New York Times* to the effect that our Navy was going to spend two billion dollars on a shipbuilding program. Here I am, the Commander-in-Chief of the Navy having to read about that for the first time in the press. Do you know what I said to that?"
>
> "No, Mr. President."
>
> "I said, Jesus Chr-rist![2]

When we think of the President of the United States and the bureaucracy he's in charge of, we imagine that the President gives orders and the agencies obey. But we forget how much top officials depend on their subordinates. The President depends on his subordinates for two important things: information and obedience.

Information. Only the federal agencies know which programs are working and which ones aren't. Take foreign policy. The State Department, the CIA, and the military have people on the spot. The President depends on them for information. The same is true of domestic affairs. The Agriculture Department has the facts and figures on grain production; the Nuclear Regulatory Commission has the details on the safety of nuclear power plants.

Control of such information can give executive agencies power over the President. Agencies that want more money for their programs will give him information showing why additional funds are needed. Or they'll try to make their programs look more successful than they are. The messages sent by field commanders during the Vietnam War made the situation look much better than it really was.

Moreover, failures can be covered up. An official investigation of the My Lai killings, in which a large number of Vietnamese civilians were killed by American troops, found that the number of reported victims got lower as the information travelled upward through the chain of command. By the time the report reached the top it didn't look bad at all.

[2] Cited in Sidney Hyman, ed., *Beckoning Frontiers* (New York: Knopf, 1951), p. 336.

Lower officials have good reason to send misleading information up the executive ladder. Their careers depend on what the higher officials think of them. In addition government agencies want to protect their programs; they want to make sure they get enough money each year, and they often adjust their reports to fit these needs.

Obedience. Article 2 of the Constitution requires the President to see that the laws are "faithfully executed." But the actual execution of the laws usually takes place at a much lower level. For example, the law says there must be safety regulations for air travel; the President is supposed to make sure the law is carried out. But the regulations are made by the Flight Standards Service of the Federal Aviation Administration. Thus the safety of air travel depends more on the rules worked out at the lower level than on the general principles set down by Congress.

The size of the executive branch and the fact that the lower levels control a lot of information make it impossible for the President and his staff to know what's going on in all parts of the government and to make sure their orders are obeyed. Many Presidents have complained that they had no real control over parts of the government. Kennedy, for example, complained that he couldn't count on the State Department to follow his foreign-policy guidelines.

CONGRESS AND THE BUREAUCRACY

Government agencies, supposedly subordinate to the President, often establish close ties with congressional committees. The various bureaus of the Agriculture Department work closely with the Senate and House Agriculture Committees. The U.S. Corps of Engineers, which is in charge of flood control on American rivers, is famous for its ties with Congress.

Such ties are a good example of the way separation of powers works. If the government were really divided into three separate branches, there would be a much greater gap between Congress and the bureaucracy. Congress would pass laws; these laws would go to the President; he in turn would direct the bureaus and agencies of the executive branch to carry them out. The connection between Congress and the bureaucracy would be indirect, going through the office of the President. In fact, however, the connection is often quite direct and doesn't go through the President's office.

Coordinating the Executive Branch

Every President has faced the problem of how to take and keep control of the executive branch. Some have depended on close personal advisers, some on the Cabinet, and some on agencies like the Office of Management and Budget.

THE PRESIDENT'S ADVISERS

Presidents often give a few top officials in the White House the job of coordinating domestic or foreign policy. In the area of foreign policy such advisers have been given a lot of power, as may be seen in the case of Henry Kissinger. At first Kissinger was asked to come to the White House to study long-term security and foreign-policy questions. He was given funds for a highly professional staff. Kissinger and his staff were soon involved in the day-to-day decisions of foreign policy. They set up the China and Russia summit meetings, negotiated the U.S. withdrawal from Vietnam, and participated in negotiations to end the conflict in the Middle East. In short, Kissinger became his own state department and sometimes his own defense department.

This kind of thing can create a lot of tension. Kissinger attracted hostility from the Departments of State and Defense. Nixon's domestic advisers, H. R. Haldeman and John Ehrlichman, were given control over various government programs; this, too, led to conflict. But tension between the White House staff and other government departments is nothing new. Here one of Johnson's advisers explains why Johnson gave control to his staff rather than to the Cabinet:

> Power, in the Presidential sense, is a very personal thing. It is invested in one man in the White House. Since power is his greatest resource, it is the instrument by which he works his will. It is not something he is likely to invest in people whose first allegiance is not to him. He is not likely to share what is his most precious resource with people whom he does not know well. Many Cabinet officers are men who are not well known to the President personally prior to his inauguration. They also become men with ties to their own departments, to the bureaucracy, to congressional com-

The President's economic policy board coordinates planning for the nation's economic problems.

mittees, rather than exclusively to the President, as is the case with White House assistants.[3]

THE CABINET

The Cabinet might help the President coordinate the executive branch, but as the quotation just given suggests, it hasn't often been used in this way. Each Cabinet member is in charge of a government department—Treasury, Commerce, Labor, and so on. The Cabinet members usually come from the President's party and nearly always have a lot of experience in the areas for which their departments are responsible. The Secretary of Agriculture, for example, will have been active in farm matters and will be acceptable to the large farmer organizations.

It's sometimes said that the Cabinet should meet regularly to coordinate governmental programs and advise the President on policy matters. Few Cabinets have done this. Most Cabinet members struggle to expand their own departments; while this is to be expected, it keeps the Cabinet from becoming a useful advisory group. For advice on policy, Presidents tend to use smaller, hand-picked groups.

THE OFFICE OF MANAGEMENT AND BUDGET

Each year the President sends a budget to Congress listing the programs he wants supported and the amount that should be spent on each. The Office of Management and Budget (OMB) prepares the budget and coordinates the various parts of the executive branch.

The OMB has been criticized for interfering with the administration of governmental programs. The critics claim that the OMB isn't well informed about the programs it's trying to control. This shows that the struggle between the office of the President and the various departments will continue. The President tries to coordinate, while the departments try to keep some independence. It's a struggle that neither side can win, though the balance may shift one way or the other.

Watergate and the Presidency

The relative power of the branches of the government has varied over the years since the writing of the Constitution. During the nineteenth century Congress often dominated the policy-making process. From the late nineteenth century to the 1930s the Supreme Court often played a dominant role, severely limiting the legislative power of Congress and the President. But since the 1930s there's been a great rise in Presidential power.

[3] Bill Moyers, taken from an interview conducted by Hugh Sidney, reprinted in Charles Peters and Timothy J. Adams, eds., *Inside the System* (New York: Praeger, 1970), p. 24.

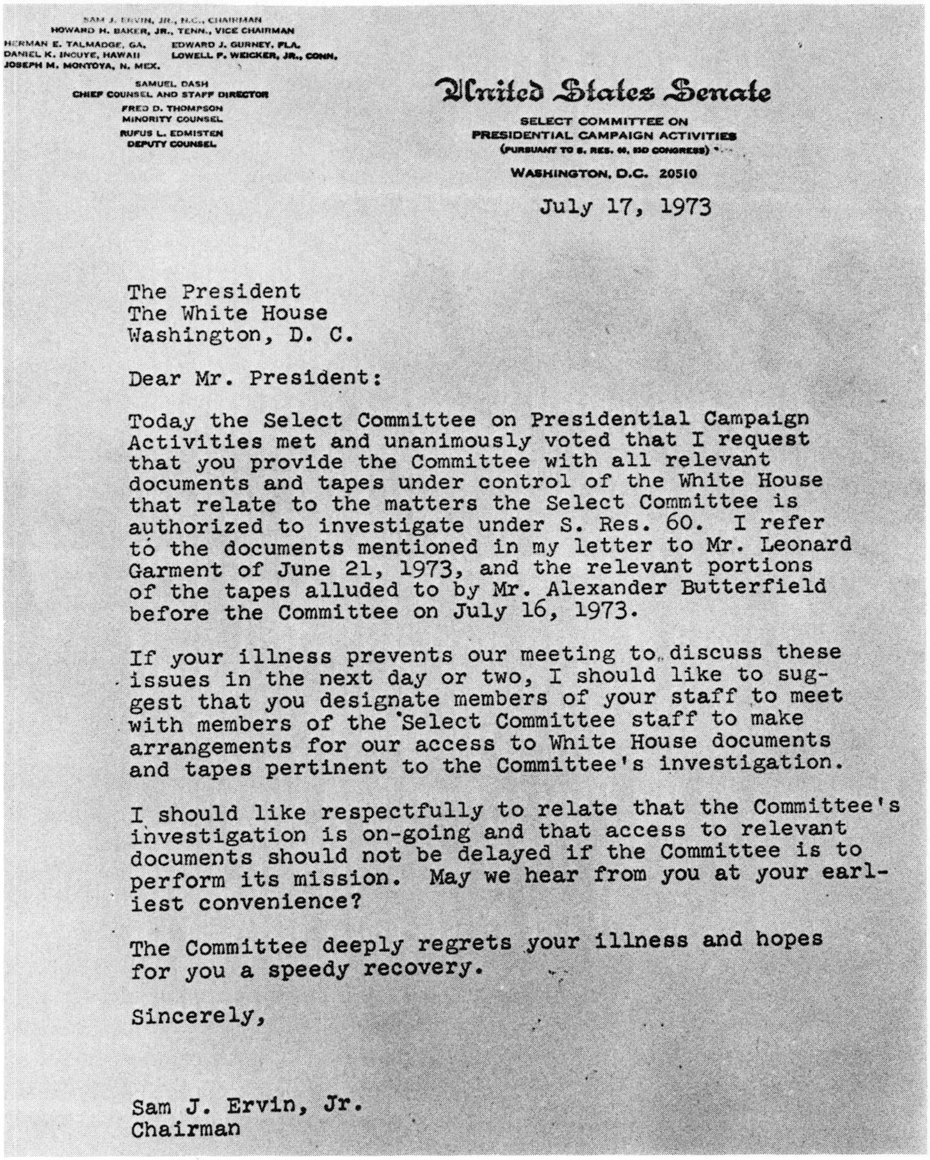

SAM J. ERVIN, JR., N.C., CHAIRMAN
HOWARD H. BAKER, JR., TENN., VICE CHAIRMAN
HERMAN E. TALMADGE, GA. EDWARD J. GURNEY, FLA.
DANIEL K. INOUYE, HAWAII LOWELL P. WEICKER, JR., CONN.
JOSEPH M. MONTOYA, N. MEX.

SAMUEL DASH
CHIEF COUNSEL AND STAFF DIRECTOR
FRED D. THOMPSON
MINORITY COUNSEL
RUFUS L. EDMISTEN
DEPUTY COUNSEL

United States Senate
SELECT COMMITTEE ON
PRESIDENTIAL CAMPAIGN ACTIVITIES
(PURSUANT TO S. RES. 60, 93D CONGRESS)
WASHINGTON, D.C. 20510

July 17, 1973

The President
The White House
Washington, D. C.

Dear Mr. President:

Today the Select Committee on Presidential Campaign Activities met and unanimously voted that I request that you provide the Committee with all relevant documents and tapes under control of the White House that relate to the matters the Select Committee is authorized to investigate under S. Res. 60. I refer to the documents mentioned in my letter to Mr. Leonard Garment of June 21, 1973, and the relevant portions of the tapes alluded to by Mr. Alexander Butterfield before the Committee on July 16, 1973.

If your illness prevents our meeting to discuss these issues in the next day or two, I should like to suggest that you designate members of your staff to meet with members of the Select Committee staff to make arrangements for our access to White House documents and tapes pertinent to the Committee's investigation.

I should like respectfully to relate that the Committee's investigation is on-going and that access to relevant documents should not be delayed if the Committee is to perform its mission. May we hear from you at your earliest convenience?

The Committee deeply regrets your illness and hopes for you a speedy recovery.

Sincerely,

Sam J. Ervin, Jr.
Chairman

PRESIDENTIAL POWER UNDER NIXON

President Nixon added further to the power of the Presidency, but he pushed it so far that he came into conflict with the other branches of the government. For example, Nixon claimed he had the right to the *impoundment* of funds, that is, not to spend money appropriated by Congress if he thought the appropriation was unwise. In this way he effectively refused to carry out laws passed by Congress.

But it wasn't clashes of this sort that led to Nixon's downfall. Rather, it was a series of illegal abuses of power summed up under the heading Watergate. The Watergate affair began with the discovery of an attempt to wiretap the headquarters of the Democratic National Committee in the Watergate building, an attempt that was later linked to the President's own campaign committee. In addition there was evidence of plans for a number of "dirty tricks" during the campaign, as well as illegal campaign contributions, including contributions by the milk producers in return for higher milk price supports and from International Telephone and Telegraph in return for favorable action on an antitrust suit. It was also discovered that the President and his staff had pressured the Internal Revenue Service to audit the tax returns of people who were opposed to the Nixon administration.

Furthermore, executive power had been used in an attempt to cover up the Watergate break-in. The President and his staff had tried to get the CIA and the FBI to limit their investigations.

These abuses formed the basis of the actions against President Nixon in the courts and in Congress. It's important to note that the movement to impeach the President didn't grow out of policy differences. Congress can't vote a President out of office because it disagrees with his policies. It may refuse to pass laws the President wants, or the President may veto laws passed by Congress. But the President remains in office.

REMOVING A PRESIDENT FROM OFFICE

Nixon was reelected by the largest majority in U.S. history. He held the most powerful office in the world. He controlled a huge executive branch whose activities affected all areas of American life. Less than two years later he resigned from office in the face of almost certain impeachment and conviction. How did this come about?

To find the answer we turn again to the Constitution. As *The Federalist* put it, we wouldn't need controls over the government "if angels were to govern men." But the writers of the Constitution didn't believe government officials were likely to be angels. Controls over their conduct would be needed. The Watergate scandal shows how right they were. And Watergate illustrates how a government made up of independent powers can limit the abuse of power by any branch of the government.

The Role of Congress. Article 1 of the Constitution gives Congress the power to remove a President.

Article 2 of the Constitution states that a President can be removed only if he is convicted of treason, bribery, or other "high crimes or misdemeanors." Much of the debate over the possible impeachment of President Nixon had to do with the interpretation of these terms. Some argued that the President could be impeached only if he had committed a crime for which an ordinary citizen would be convicted in court. Others argued that the President could be impeached for gross misconduct in office. This interpretation seemed to have greater support as the debate went on. The accusations in the articles of impeachment voted by the House Judiciary Committee in July 1974 included not only criminal activities but also other types of misconduct, such as failure to supervise the actions of subordinates, that would not be criminal acts.

The impeachment process wasn't completed in 1974; Nixon resigned after the Judiciary Committee had voted three articles of impeachment against him. The next step in the process would have been a House vote on these articles. If a majority of the House had voted for impeachment, the Senate would have conducted a trial of the President.

The role of the Judicial Branch. The court system also played a major role in the Watergate affair. The trials conducted by Judge John Sirica of the federal district court brought out many important facts about the break-in and cover-up.

At times of constitutional crisis the most significant interpretations are often made by the Supreme Court. In the case of Watergate, for example, a major conflict arose over tape recordings of the President's conversations. The tapes had been subpoenaed as evidence in the trial of some of Nixon's staff members, who were accused of trying to cover up the Watergate break-in. Nixon claimed that he alone could decide whether the tapes would be re-

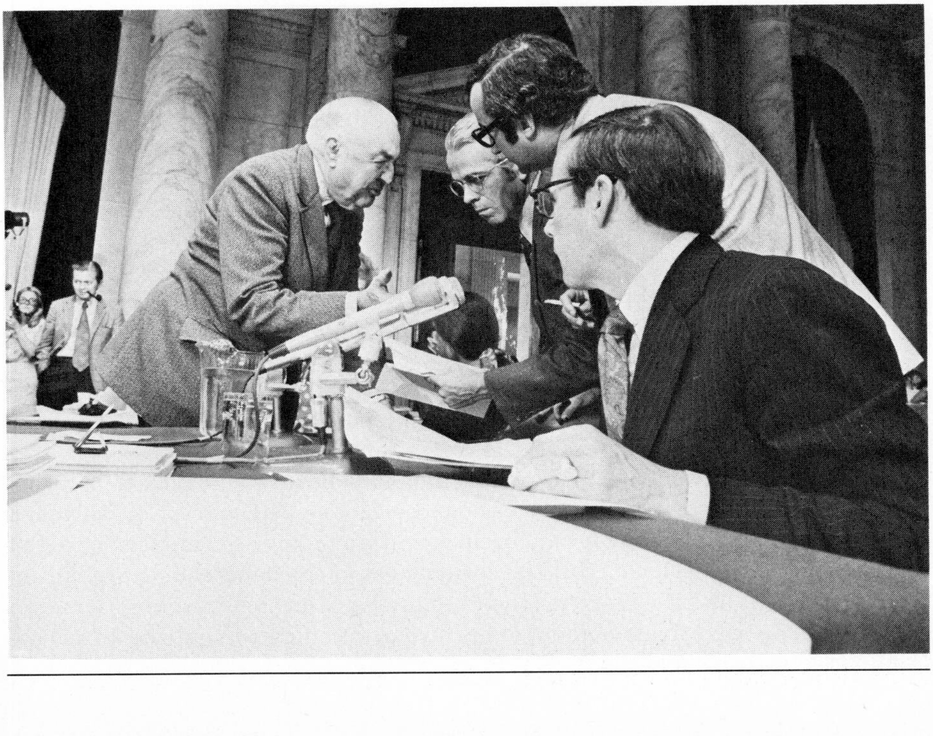

Chairman Sam Ervin of the Senate Watergate Committee talks to his staff and to former White House aide John Dean III.

leased; he argued that "executive privilege" gave him the right to keep his records secret.

The case went to the Supreme Court. The Court ruled that executive privilege didn't apply to criminal cases. The President could keep secret records if they were needed in his work, but if they were needed in a criminal case he couldn't hold them back.

This decision was an important step in the process that led to the President's resignation. He had resisted earlier attempts to get the tapes, but he couldn't ignore the Supreme Court. Several members of Congress made it clear that the President was sure to be impeached if he disobeyed the Court. Here the powers of Congress and the Court combined to limit the power of the President.

Watergate and the Constitution

The Watergate affair illustrates how constitutional principles like separation of powers adjust to new conditions. This adjustment isn't a mechanical process. The words of the Constitution need interpretation. A term like impeachment is by no means clear, and executive privilege isn't mentioned in the Constitution at all.

How do the members of Congress decide what impeachment really means? To begin with, when the Constitution is unclear they look further. They read other works by the men who wrote the Constitution; they study the records of the debate at the Constitutional Convention; they do research to find out how the term was used in earlier legal practice.

Perhaps most important, those who are trying to interpret the Constitution will consider how others have interpreted it in the past. How has impeachment been handled before? Congress spent a lot of time studying the records of the impeachment and trial of President Andrew Johnson after the Civil War; the Supreme Court considered the way earlier Presidents and earlier courts had interpreted executive privilege.

In addition there are political forces. The fact that the President was a Republican whose policies were offensive to many Democrats can't be ignored. It's no accident that the congressional members in favor of impeachment were likely to be Democrats and those opposed were likely to be Republicans. And members of Congress also pay attention to the views of their constituents. The fact that Nixon's public support faded during the summer of 1974 probably played a part in their decisions.

Some critics claim that the impeachment debate was a purely political process. Nixon's press secretary called the House Judiciary Committee a "kangaroo court," meaning it paid little attention to law or evidence but acted entirely on a political basis. But the seriousness of the debate on the meaning of impeachment and the fact that the final pressure on the President to resign came from conservative members of his own party suggest that the Judiciary Committee was not a kangaroo court after all.

AFTER WATERGATE

Some students of politics thought the Watergate affair would lead to a major change in the structure of the government. Some even thought it would destroy the Presidency as an effective political force.

The results weren't that dramatic. A strong Presidency is needed in the modern world. No sooner had Nixon left office than Ford and his staff were managing foreign policy and trying to cope with the nation's economic crisis.

On the other hand, Watergate seems to have had a major effect on the balance of power among the branches of the government. For one thing the crisis showed how important it is for the various branches to be independent. Congress called on its ultimate power—impeachment—and the President resigned. The Supreme Court and the President came into direct conflict over Presidential power, but when the Court ruled that the President had to turn over the Watergate tapes, he obeyed.

The Balance of Power

Watergate didn't destroy the Presidency. But it resulted in a more active and independent Congress. As we have seen, in the period since Watergate Congress has overridden Presidential vetoes more often than it did before. It has taken an active role in energy policy. It has begun to supervise government operations more fully. And, in what may be its biggest shift, it has played a larger role in foreign policy. It has limited U.S. aid to South Vietnam, Turkey, and Chile, and it has been deeply involved in trade negotiations with the Soviet Union and other countries. In contrast to its passive role in the early days of the Vietnam War, Congress took a much more active role in attempting to limit U.S. involvement in the conflict in Angola.

After Watergate, Congress began to assert more power over the executive branch. This Special Intelligence Committee investigated the FBI and the CIA.

It's important to note that Congress hasn't claimed new powers for itself. It's simply making better use of the powers it has always had under the Constitution, such as the power of the purse and the power to investigate. What has changed is not the constitutional powers of Congress but the attitudes of the members of Congress toward using those powers.

It's clear that these changes have somewhat reduced the dominant role of the Presidency. But the Presidency is still a powerful, independent force—probably the most powerful of the three branches. There's still a need for strong, unified authority to deal with complex problems. Though there are efforts under way to reorganize Congress to make it both more responsive and more coordinated, Congress probably can't reorganize itself enough to match the Presidency in its ability to coordinate policy.

CONTROVERSY

Should Congress or the Presidency Make National Policy?

One Side The executive branch should determine national policy. The President is elected by a national constituency rather than hundreds of local ones. The Presidential campaign focuses citizens' attention on broad choices for dealing with social issues. Each of the major candidates runs on a platform to which every region, race, or social class can respond favorably or unfavorably. Congressional campaigns present only partial programs aimed at a particular constituency, but a victory or defeat at the Presidential level reflects the preferences of the entire society.

Not only does the Presidency represent national public opinion, it can think and plan on a national level. Through careful selection of the White House staff, Cabinet members, and other top officials, the President brings together a group with a lot of experience and ability. Although there will be differences in opinion within the executive branch, there will also be a shared outlook. Out of this group can come a coordinated national program. In short, the executive branch is the truly national part of the government and therefore is the best place for meaningful policy making.

The Other Side Congress is the branch where national policy should be made. It has an important advantage over the White House: It is in continuous, direct contact with citizens. Members of Congress often make trips back home. They hear from constituents and lobbyists every day. The White House is more isolated. There are many layers between the President and the general public. The President deals with the public through his staff or through the news media; senators and representatives deal directly with the public.

A program worked out by Congress will be more democratic. It will reflect a compromise among the preferences of citizens across the nation. Congress may be tied to local interests, but these are the interests a government is supposed to protect. Citizens want jobs, clean air and water, crime control, social services, and dozens of other benefits. But they don't agree on how much of which of these benefits they want and at what cost. Only Congress can reach a compromise among the conflicting needs and preferences of over 200 million people.

A program developed by Congress will therefore be more practical. Congress will come up with a national program that is a compromise among dozens of competing interests. But such a program is realistic. A program that fails to account for these very real differences isn't likely to be accepted. And this is the danger to any program that comes from a staff of experts in the White House.

How Institutions Work: VI
The Federal Budget

WHAT IS THE SIGNIFICANCE OF THE FEDERAL BUDGET?

The annual budget determines how much money the government will spend and what it will be spent on. Figure 12.1 shows how President Ford's 1976 budget proposed to spend $350 billion. The budget is also a tool of fiscal policy; for example, it can be reduced in order to fight inflation or increased in order to stimulate the economy.

WHO MAKES UP THE ANNUAL BUDGET?

Each spring the agencies and departments of the government start planning their budget requests for the fiscal year beginning in October of the following year. These requests are sent to the Office of Management and Budget. The OMB reviews the budget requests and sends them to the President, who by this time has also been given economic forecasts and revenue estimates for the coming fiscal year. The President coordinates this information and sets budget guidelines.

Using these guidelines the various agencies then make detailed budget requests, which are analyzed by the OMB and passed on to the President. The final budget proposal is sent to Congress by the President, usually in January or February.

WHAT IS CONGRESS' ROLE?

The President's budget proposal is actually just a request; only Congress can vote to spend federal funds. This is a two-step process. First, Congress passes *authorizations*, or legislation that authorizes a particular program and sets a limit on spending for that program. Second, it passes *appropriations* bills to grant the actual funds. An authorization without an appropriation is meaningless.

HOW DOES CONGRESS MAKE BUDGET DECISIONS?

Usually the President's budget requests go to the House Appropriations Committee. After an appropriations bill has been passed by the House, it is sent to the Senate Appropriations Committee. Traditionally the Senate has been used as a court of appeals for agencies trying to restore budget cuts made by the House. But there are problems with this pattern. Congress usually goes over the President's budget by

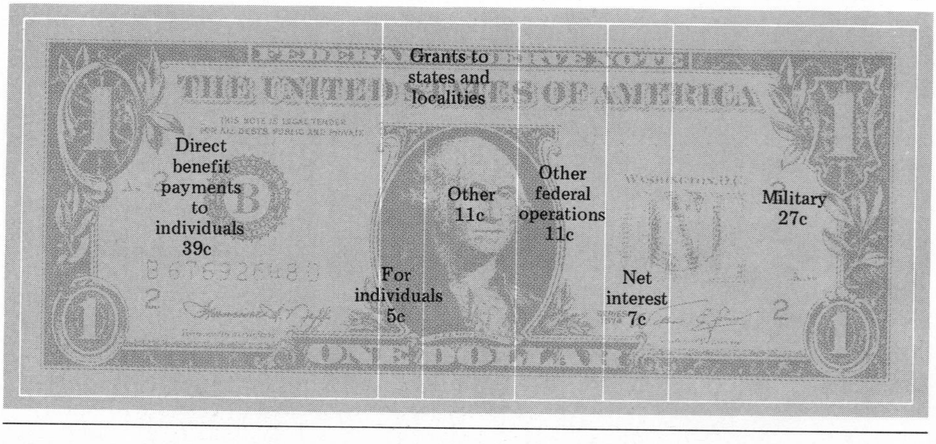

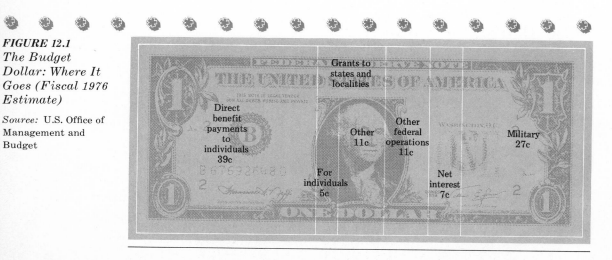

FIGURE 12.1
The Budget Dollar: Where It Goes (Fiscal 1976 Estimate)

Source: U.S. Office of Management and Budget

billions of dollars. Moreover, Congress looks at the budget piece by piece without ever seeing it as a whole. For these reasons Congress passed legislation in 1974 to reform its budget procedures.

WHAT CHANGES ARE CALLED FOR IN THE BUDGET-REFORM LAW?

The Congressional Budget Act created new House and Senate Budget Committees and a Congressional Budget Office. Under the new procedures Congress first sets an overall target for spending and then, after the appropriations process has been completed, settles any differences between the target amount and the total appropriations.

IS THERE ANY CHECK ON THE WAY THE FUNDS APPROVED BY CONGRESS ARE SPENT?

Each executive agency is responsible for making sure it doesn't go over its budget. The OMB also supervises all spending by the executive branch. In addition Congress gets an independent audit of all government spending from the General Accounting Office.

DOES THE PRESIDENT HAVE TO SPEND THE FULL AMOUNT APPROPRIATED BY CONGRESS FOR EACH PROGRAM?

There's been a lot of debate on this question, particularly when Nixon impounded funds for certain programs and refused to spend the amount called for by law. To avoid further conflict, the budget-reform act requires congressional approval for all Presidential impoundments.

CAN THE EXECUTIVE BRANCH GET MORE FUNDS FROM CONGRESS UNDER SPECIAL CONDITIONS?

Yes, such requests can be made in the form of supplemental appropriations.

Questions for Review

1. What is the purpose of separation of powers?

2. How does the system of checks and balances work in practice?

3. What resources does Congress have in its battle with the Presidency?

4. In what ways does the President depend on the executive bureaucracy?

5. Why doesn't the Cabinet play a major role in coordinating governmental programs?

6. How does the Watergate affair illustrate the importance of separation of powers?

7. Describe the impeachment process. Can a President be impeached for making unpopular policy decisions?

8. What role did the courts play in Nixon's resignation?

9. What effect did the Watergate affair have on the balance of power among the three branches of the government?

Chapter 13

The Government and the Individual

If you ask the average citizen how political decisions are made in the United States, he or she will probably answer "by majority vote." In some ways this is correct. A democracy is a government where the majority rules. Children learn about the majority rule very early, often from a homeroom teacher: "Today we're going to elect our student council representative. . . . We have two nominees, Susan and Larry. Write your choice on a piece of paper." When the ballots have been counted, the teacher announces the results: "Susan got 17 votes and Larry got 14. The majority rules, so Susan is our representative."

While it's true that the majority rule is basic to a democracy, there are variations on this rule. Among these variations are the following:

1. *The special majority.* Some issues are so important that a "50 percent plus 1" majority isn't enough. For example, if Congress passes a bill by a simple majority vote and the President vetoes it, Congress can override the veto by a "special" two-thirds majority. The Constitution doesn't give the President final power over legislation, but it does take his disapproval seriously. So it requires a special majority to override a Presidential veto.

2. *The voting unit.* As we'll see in the next chapter, the principle of federalism gives some responsibility to voting units much smaller than the entire population. Which voters should decide on the textbooks to be used in the Richmond, Virginia, public schools—the voters in Richmond, those in Virginia, or those in the entire United States? When the decision is left to the local community or the state, majority rule at the national level may be violated. When the decision is shifted to the national level, the preferences of a majority of the local citizens may be ignored.

3. *Plurality rule. Plurality* rule has the opposite effect from a special majority. It allows the preferences of a group smaller than a majority to prevail, as long as that group is larger than any other group. Nixon got only 43 percent of the vote in the 1968 Presidential election, but since Humphrey got 41 percent and Wallace got 14 percent, Nixon won the election.

4. *The intense minority.* Sometimes a small group of citizens feels very strongly about an issue, while the large majority doesn't care as much. Since "the squeaking wheel gets the grease," government officials often respond to the active minority rather than the indifferent majority. In day-to-day politics this informal rule is probably followed more often than strict majority rule.

5. *The rights of minorities.* The constitutional rights of minorities are so important that we'll devote the rest of this chapter to a discussion of these rights. Since the founding of the nation the principle of minority rights has been in conflict with the principle of majority rule. If "50 percent plus 1" were the only rule for democratic decision making, the majority would be free to do whatever it wanted to members of a minority group. It could take away their jobs, their homes, their rights, even their lives. And it would all be, by definition, democratic.

Majority Rule vs. Minority Rights

Many writers have warned of democratic tyranny—the so-called tyranny of the majority. In some ways such tyranny is more dangerous than the tyranny of a smaller group. There's less chance of successful resistance if a minority has a majority united against it. When public opinion is coupled with the strength of the government, that is, when the government is carrying out the will of the majority, it becomes a force that's hard to resist.

The writers of the Constitution were aware of this problem. They designed a government that would limit the power of the majority in many ways. Federalism, checks and balances, and the Bill of Rights all help prevent any single group—including the majority—from getting too much power.

The conflict between majority rule and minority rights is one of the great dilemmas of democracy. We've seen why the principle of majority rule has to be limited. But if you give all rights to all minorities, that is, give all minority groups in society the right to disobey the government, you no longer have a society. Where do you draw the line?

Much of the debate on the meaning of democracy centers on the question of minority rights. What rights are so important that they should be protected against majority rule? Historically these rights have included freedom of speech, press, and assembly; freedom of religion; property rights; and rights to a fair trial and fair procedure in criminal cases. A recent addition is the right of privacy.

Freedom of Speech, Press, and Assembly

Many people believe these three rights, known as civil liberties or First Amendment freedoms, are the basic ones that must be protected if democracy is to survive. They are set forth in the First Amendment to the Constitution: "Congress shall make no law . . . abridging the freedom of speech, or of the press, or the right of the people peaceably to assemble. . . ."

First Amendment freedoms are central to a democratic system. Only if there is freedom to present views on all sides of an issue can there be a real choice. And this is the key to effective majority rule.

These freedoms are very important to minority groups, too. The rights of free speech, press, and assembly give them a chance to persuade others to join them and form a new majority. Here the Supreme Court plays a major role. If the majority tries to silence its opponents or outlaw picketing or censor the press, the Court is supposed to block it.

Some people claim that the First Amendment freedoms are "absolute" rights that should never be limited by the majority or by the government speaking for the majority. According to this view, no one—neither a minority nor a majority—can legislate the truth. This will come only from a "free marketplace of ideas." Therefore a free society should never bar any group from expressing its views, no matter how unpopular they may be.

CONFLICTS OVER FREEDOM OF SPEECH

There are arguments against "absolute" freedom of speech. For one thing it clearly violates the principle of majority rule. Suppose a majority of the American people want to bar some group, such as communists or atheists, from expressing its views. What is the "democratic" thing to do—prevent the group from speaking and thus violate freedom of speech, or allow it to speak and thus violate the principle of majority rule? Some examples may help us understand why such conflicts arise.

Libel. The right to say what you want to may be a value, but the right of the citizen to be protected against unfair attacks is also a value. Therefore we have libel laws that limit freedom of speech in order to protect citizens from such attacks.

Like most political principles, these general guidelines aren't very useful in practice. You may believe in freedom of speech up to the point where some individual is unfairly offended or hurt; at that point libel laws should apply. But at what point does newspaper criticism of a government official become an unfair attack for which the official can sue the newspaper under libel laws? On this issue the courts have recently leaned toward allowing a wide range of criticism even if it might be harmful to the official. The right to criticize government officials is basic to a democracy, even at the risk of weakening the individual's right to be protected from unfair attack.[1]

Obscenity. This is another area where the Supreme Court has tried to balance conflicting interests. On one side is the First Amendment right to publish what you want to; on the other side is the right of citizens to protect themselves and their children from material they feel is offensive or harmful.

Most states have laws banning pornography, but it's hard to define what is pornographic. Some people think certain great literary works are so harmful to morals that they should be banned. Others say all writings and movies should be allowed, whatever their content.

At one time the Supreme Court held that a work was obscene if it had "no redeeming social value." Then it proposed that a work that might otherwise be labeled obscene would be allowed if it had "serious literary, artistic, political, or scientific value." The problem is that since these terms have no clear meaning, the Court has found itself deciding what is obscene on a case-by-case basis.

In 1973 the Court tried something new. It decided that the moral standards of the local area could apply: What might be pornographic in Kansas City might not be in San Francisco.[2] This seemed to clear the way for local censors. But the Supreme Court soon showed that it hadn't given up its right

[1] *New York Times* v. *Sullivan* 376 U.S. 254 (1964); *Gertz* v. *Robert Welch Inc.*

[2] *Miller* v. *California* 41 LW 4925 (1973).

to a final say in the matter. In a decision against a Georgia ban on the movie *Carnal Knowledge*, the Court made it clear that it would continue to see if local standards measured up to the First Amendment.

FREE SPEECH AND NATIONAL SECURITY

An important area of conflict from the point of view of democratic politics is the dispute between freedom of speech and national security. Freedom of speech is particularly important when it protects people with unpopular political opinions. But the right to express such opinions may conflict with the right of the society to protect itself.

As with libel and obscenity, it's easier to state the principle than to apply it. For example, the First Amendment guarantee of free speech doesn't give the citizen the right to commit sabotage or to use violence against government officials. This principle should be easy to apply, but actually the boundary between speech and action isn't clear. Some argue that speech itself can be violent. And there's no doubt that speech can be used to incite violence.

At times it's unclear whether we're dealing with speech or action. For one thing, it's hard to tell when speech incites action and when it doesn't. If I plan an act of sabotage with someone else, telling him where to plant the bomb and when to do it, I only "speak"—but it seems clear that I incite the action. But what if in a public speech I say people should sabotage government operations? What if I merely say "there are times when it would be justifiable to sabotage the government"? Am I inciting action? Even if someone hears my speech and then goes out and plants bombs in government buildings, it's hard to tell whether the action is a direct result of the speech.

In deciding on questions like these the courts have usually followed Oliver Wendell Holmes' doctrine of "clear and present danger."[3] Under this doctrine speech is punishable only when it may lead directly to illegal action and the connection between the speech and the action is clear. But this is just another way of stating the problem of deciding where speech ends and action begins. When does "clear and present danger" exist? The doctrine is not a clear principle that can be followed by the courts.

CONSPIRACY AND SUBVERSION

Drawing the line between civil liberties and the government's right to protect itself is made more difficult by the fact that attempts to limit these liberties often take place in time of war. At such times the dangers of sabotage and subversion loom large in the eyes of the government and the public. During World War II, for example, all Americans of Japanese ancestry, whether proved "subversive" or not, were moved from the West Coast to "relocation centers" in the Midwest, where they were kept until the war was over. The Supreme Court considered the government's action after the war was over but did not find it unconstitutional.

[3] *Schenck* v. *United States* 249 U.S. 47 (1919).

The Smith Act of 1940. Since World War II the issue of civil liberties vs. national security has centered on a series of laws dealing with conspiracy and subversion. These laws arose out of the United States' "cold war" against communism. The Smith Act made it a crime to teach or advocate the violent overthrow of the U.S. government. In 1951 the Supreme Court upheld the conviction of Eugene Dennis, head of the U.S. Communist party, under the Smith Act.[4] Critics of this decision argued that Dennis was convicted for speech, not action, but the Supreme Court held that the government had the right to protect itself against the actions he *advocated.*

The McCarran Act of 1950. The McCarran Act, passed at the beginning of the Korean War, required registration of communist organizations. In interpreting this act the Supreme Court held that although the registration requirement was constitutional, making party members register would mean making them testify against themselves, and this would violate the Fifth Amendment.[5] Thus the Court didn't challenge the act itself, but it interpreted it very narrowly.

The Antiriot Bill. A more recent attempt by Congress to legislate against subversion came in response to the urban riots of the late 1960s. A 1968 antiriot bill made it a crime to cross a state line to incite a riot. This was the basis of the trial of the "Chicago Seven," who were accused of conspiring to incite a riot at the 1968 Democratic Convention in Chicago. No conspiracy was proved, but five of the defendants were convicted under the antiriot bill. The convictions were reversed in 1972 by a federal appeals court because of the way their trial had been run. As in the case of the Smith and McCarran Acts, the courts interpreted the law narrowly so as to limit its impact on civil liberties but upheld the law itself, making it possible for the law to be used to limit freedom to speech.

The Free Press and the Pentagon Papers. The Pentagon Papers case arose when the government tried to prevent the *New York Times* and the *Washington Post* from publishing papers containing top-secret information on the Vietnam War, in which the nation was still involved. The government claimed that publication of the papers would do "grave and irreparable" damage to the national interest. The Supreme Court balanced this national security interest against the First Amendment guarantee of a free press and ruled against the government.[6] The newspapers were allowed to go on publishing the Pentagon Papers, which showed that the Kennedy and Johnson administrations had been involved in Vietnam long before Congress or the public knew what was going on.

[4] *Dennis et al.* v. *United States* 341 U.S. 494 (1951).

[5] *Communist Party* v. *Subversive Activities Control Board* 367 U.S. 1 (1961).

[6] *New York Times Co.* v. *United States* 403 U.S. 713 (1971).

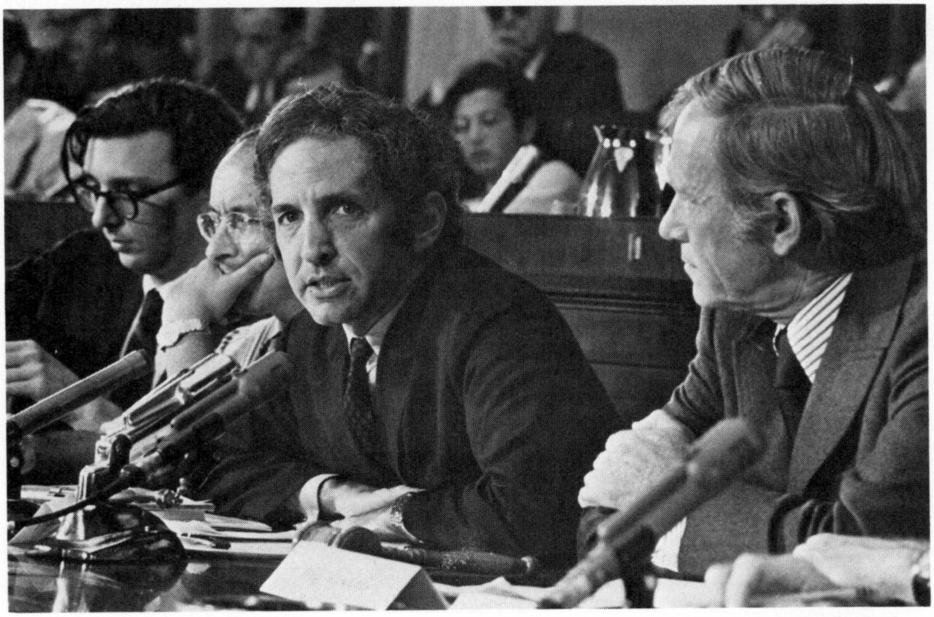

Daniel Ellsberg, who leaked the Pentagon Papers to the press, testifies before a special congressional panel.

The Supreme Court decision was praised as a victory for freedom of speech. But such victories are rarely clear-cut. The newspapers were allowed to publish the Pentagon Papers, but the Court left open the possibility that they might be barred from publishing similar material in the future.

Still, the Pentagon Papers case is an important example of the way the Supreme Court protects First Amendment freedoms. The administration used its strongest argument—national security—in trying to block publication of the papers. In most societies, even democratic ones, the government would be able to bar publication of material for such a reason. In this case, however, the Supreme Court said the newspapers, not the government, had the right to decide what to print.

Freedom of Religion

The First Amendment bars the government from interfering with the religious practices of the American people, whether by setting up a government-supported church or by favoring one religion over another. But, as in the case of freedom of speech, the wording of the First Amendment—"Congress shall make no law respecting an establishment of religion, or prohibiting the free exercise thereof . . ."—is ambiguous. How wide a separation must there be between church and state?

The government can't set up a church. But does this mean it can't give aid to private religious schools? Does it mean it can't provide buses for children going to such schools?

The government can't prohibit a citizen from practicing his religious beliefs. But what if his religion involves polygamy? What if it forbids him to pay taxes, serve in the armed forces, or salute the flag?

It can be seen that the Constitution leaves some questions unanswered. As a result the government follows a mixture of policies when it comes to separation of church and state. This mixture of policies stems from the need to balance one value (in this case freedom of religion) against other values. The problems involved can be seen in the following examples.

RELIGIOUS PRACTICES

Freedom of religion is clearly guaranteed in the First Amendment. But the principle of freedom sometimes comes into conflict with other principles. In the nineteenth century, for example, the Supreme Court upheld the government's prohibition of polygamy even though it was a fundamental practice of

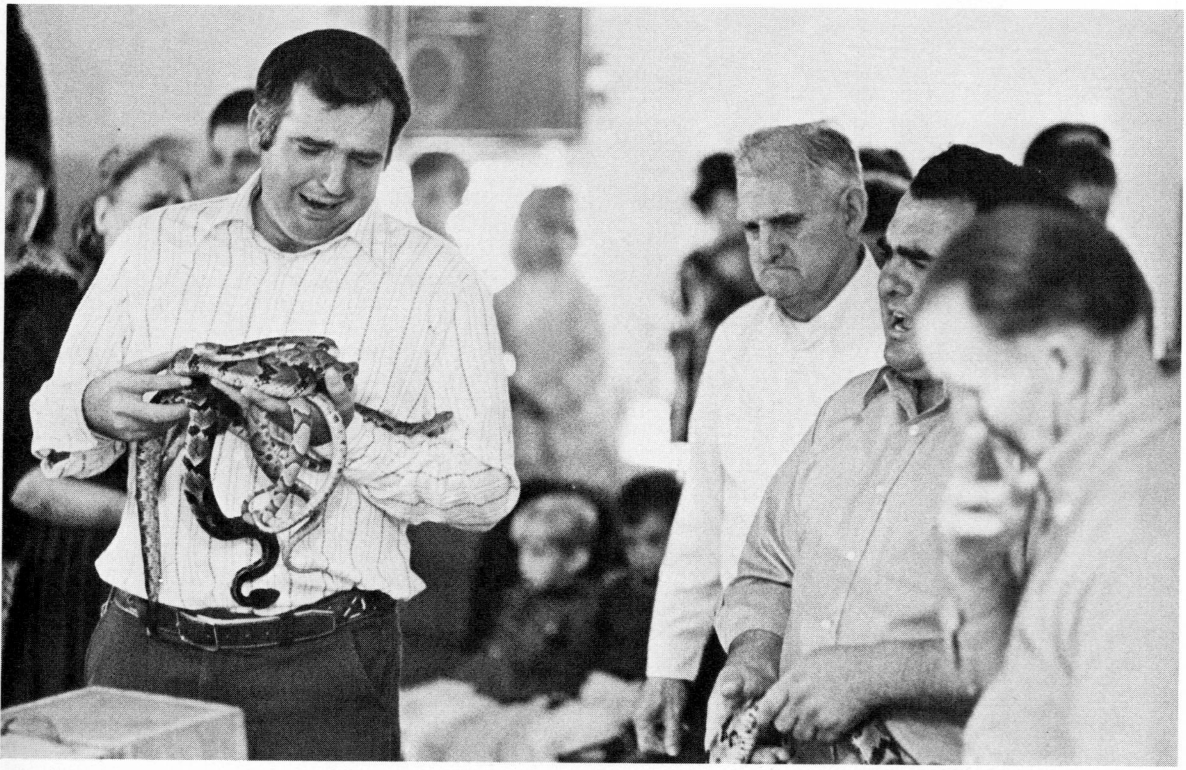

The First Amendment protects many religious practices that many people disapprove of.

the Mormon religion.[7] The Court reasoned that polygamy was so contrary to American moral standards that it couldn't be permitted even as a religious practice.

RELIGION AND EDUCATION

The field of education provides many examples of the delicate balance between freedom of religion and the requirements of law. The Supreme Court has ruled that compulsory education applies even to religious groups like the Amish, who are opposed to formal education. But parents are allowed to send their children to private religious schools, though such schools can't get government support.

Saluting the Flag. The so-called flag-salute cases are another example. The Jehovah's Witnesses don't allow their children to salute the flag. But until 1943 there were laws requiring children to salute the flag at the beginning of the school day. In 1940 the Supreme Court upheld such laws; Jehovah's Witnesses could be required to salute the flag.[8] Three years later the Court reversed itself, saying the government's interest in a flag salute wasn't as important as the right of a minority to follow its religious beliefs.[9]

School Prayers. Perhaps the most controversial problem of religious freedom is in the area of school prayers. Does it violate the freedom of nonbelievers if the government requires prayers in the public schools, even if the prayers are nonsectarian and parents can have their children excused? In 1962 the Supreme Court ruled that a New York State school district violated the Constitution by requiring that the school day begin with a nonsectarian prayer.[10] The school board had made it clear that parents could ask to have their children excused from the prayer. But the Court said such prayers violated the separation of church and state because they were required by the government.

There can be little doubt that the Court was taking the side of a small minority. Public-opinion polls show that a large majority favors school prayers. The parents who brought the case to court were a small and unpopular group. But their action led to a reinterpretation of the First Amendment to prevent the government from favoring religious citizens over nonbelievers.

Aid to Religious Schools. Does it violate the separation of church and state if the government gives aid to private religious schools? The argument in favor

[7] *Reynolds* v. *United States* 98 U.S. 145 (1879).

[8] *Minersville School District* v. *Gobitis* 310 U.S. 586 (1940).

[9] *West Virginia State Board of Education* v. *Barnette* 319 U.S. 624 (1943).

[10] *Engel* v. *Vitale* 370 U.S. 421 (1962) and *Abington School District* v. *Schempp* 374 U.S. 203 (1963).

of such aid is that these schools take some of the burden off the public schools. And since parents who send their children to religious schools are also taxed to support the public schools, they pay more because of their religious beliefs. On the other hand those who oppose aid to religious schools say such aid would discriminate in favor of particular religions.

The Supreme Court has generally ruled against aid to religious schools, but its position is by no means firm. Some aid to church-related colleges is allowed, as well as various kinds of indirect aid such as school buses.[11]

Property Rights

Protection of property rights is guaranteed by the Constitution and by law. The Constitution, for example, includes a just-compensation clause: The founders knew that private lands would be needed for public projects, but they made sure the owner would be fairly compensated out of the public treasury. The Constitution also prohibits the government from depriving a citizen of his property without due process of law. Based on these constitutional provisions are a wide range of laws protecting private property, and standing behind these laws is the police.

What do we mean by property rights? We mean the right to own something and keep other people from using it. We also mean the right to sell or trade the thing we own. But these rights are limited; the courts and the legislatures have put many restrictions on private property.

THE PROPERTY OWNER VS. THE PUBLIC INTEREST

Government restrictions on property are often based on the claim that the public interest is more important than property rights. You can't drive a car at its highest speed because that would threaten public safety. If you have a diseased elm tree in your front yard, you have to cut it down to keep the disease from spreading. You might say, "Who are they to tell me what to do with my property?" "They" is the government acting in the public interest.

It's hard to define the public interest; the definition varies from one place to another and from one time to another. A good example is billboards. The right of a property owner to lease some of his land to a billboard company went unchallenged for a long time. As a result our public highways are surrounded by private advertisements. But today the definition of public interest is changing, so state and local governments are beginning to restrict the use of billboards.

THE PROPERTY OWNER VS. HUMAN RIGHTS

In 1964 Californians were asked to vote on a proposed amendment to the state constitution stating that any property owner had the right to sell, lease, or

[11] *Everson* v. *Board of Education of Ewing* 330 U.S. 1 (1947).

rent his property to anyone he chose. This looks like a reasonable proposal, but actually it was a response to a bill passed by the California legislature banning racial discrimination in the sale and rental of property. This was a clear case of property rights (the right of a citizen to do what he wants to with his property) vs. human rights (the right of a black citizen not to be discriminated against). The California voters passed the amendment, but the state supreme court declared it unconstitutional, and this ruling was upheld by the United States Supreme Court.

This example illustrates how when two constitutional rights are in conflict, the courts have to make a final decision. As we saw in the case of school prayers, this sometimes puts the court on the side of the minority against the preferences of the majority. But despite limitations on property rights the American public has a strong respect for the rights of private ownership. In fact it's surprising that the restrictions on property are so few.

Criminal Rights

The area of criminal rights may be the hardest one in which to balance individual rights and majority preferences. Many people have blamed the Supreme Court for the high crime rate in American society. According to this view, if we put fewer restrictions on the police and the prosecutor we could reduce the crime rate.

This may be true, but a democratic society has other values besides protection against crime. Citizens in a free society are protected from excessive use of police power. This raises a dilemma: Do we have to buy more protection against crime at the price of a greater chance of abuse of power? The "no-knock" provision of the 1970 Drug Abuse Act illustrates this problem. The act allowed federal narcotics agents to break into homes without knocking if they could later show a judge that if they had given a warning the drugs would have been destroyed so they couldn't be used as evidence. But agents took advantage of the no-knock rule to break into homes in the middle of the night, destroy personal property, and so on—all without a warrant. So Congress repealed the rule in 1974.

Like the rights discussed earlier in this chapter, criminal rights are rooted in our constitutional system. An accused person is assumed to be innocent until proven guilty and has the same rights as all other citizens. Here the due process clause of the Fifth Amendment is basic, since it states that citizens cannot be denied legal recourse when their basic rights are violated. What are the rights involved?

CRIMINAL PROCEDURES

Arrest. To arrest a citizen, a police officer must have "probable cause" to believe the citizen has committed or is about to commit a crime. Most arrests are made without a warrant.

The right to be free from unreasonable arrest was upheld in a case stemming from the May 1971 Vietnam protests in Washington. Hundreds of demonstrators had marched to the Capitol for a rally; police arrested 1200 of them. Of these, only 8 were actually brought to trial, and the charges against them were eventually dropped. The demonstrators went to court, claiming that their rights had been violated. In 1975 they won their case.

Search and Seizure. Interpretation of the Fourth Amendment depends so much on particular conditions that Supreme Court rulings have varied almost as widely as police practices. In general the Court has limited the area that can be searched without a warrant to the person of the suspect and the area under his control. To search a suspect's home or office you usually have to get a warrant. A police officer may carry out a search without a warrant if there's reason to believe a crime has been committed and there's no time to get a warrant or if it's necessary to seize weapons or prevent destruction of evidence.

These rules are easy to apply in many cases, but the Court has found it hard to decide on general principles for dealing with "stop and frisk" laws. The Court has approved of searches when there is reason to suspect criminal activity but no reasonable ground for arrest. For example, in 1968 the Supreme Court ruled that it was reasonable for a detective to search three men he had seen repeatedly casing a store, and it upheld their conviction for carrying concealed weapons.[12] But in the same year the Court reversed a conviction on the grounds that the fact that the defendant was seen talking to a number of known drug addicts didn't justify his being searched and convicted for possession of heroin.[13]

THE RIGHT TO A FAIR HEARING

The courts have interpreted the constitutional right of due process to include prohibitions against self-incrimination, unreasonable bail, and double jeopardy (a defendant can be tried only once for a single act). The Constitution also guarantees a number of other rights such as the right to a speedy and public trial and the right to be told what the charges are. And while the Bill of Rights doesn't mention a right to appeal, the federal government and the states allow at least one appeal as a matter of legal right.

The Right of Privacy

Does the Constitution protect the individual when it comes to his private life? This is a new and interesting area of constitutional interpretation. In recent years the Supreme Court has begun to recognize a "right to privacy." This right isn't mentioned in the Constitution, but the Court has decided that it is

[12] *Terry* v. *Ohio* 392 U.S. 1 (1968).

[13] *Sibron* v. *New York* 392 U.S. 40, 64 (1968).

The Constitution guarantees a fair and speedy trial. Here Patty Hearst is escorted to federal court.

implied in the Fourth Amendment ban on "unreasonable searches and seizures," the Fifth Amendment protection against self-incrimination, and the undefined "other rights" mentioned in the Ninth Amendment.[14]

On this basis the Court overturned a Connecticut law making it illegal to

[14] *Griswold* v. *Connecticut* 381 U.S. 479, 490–492 (1965).

use any contraceptive drug or device.[15] Lower federal courts have challenged Virginia's sodomy law, ruling that states can't regulate, in the words of the Supreme Court, "intimate sexual relations between consenting adults, carried out under secluded conditions."[16] In a similar decision a federal district court recently ruled that a school district violated the right of privacy by refusing to hire homosexuals.[17] Here again the courts have protected the rights of the individual even though the behavior involved is viewed with disfavor by a majority of the population.

The most controversial issue involving the right of privacy is the issue of abortion. In 1973 the Supreme Court overturned antiabortion laws in forty-six states. It ruled that the right of privacy included the right of a woman to have an abortion during the first three months of pregnancy. Few Court decisions have aroused as much conflict. Many groups, including the Catholic Church, oppose abortion. They claim to represent the constitutional rights of another group: unborn children. It's likely that this controversy will continue, since both sides feel very strongly about the issue.

[15] Ibid.

[16] *Lovisi* v. *Slayton* 363 Fed. Supp. 620, 625–626 (1973).

[17] 41 LW 2691 (1973).

CONTROVERSY

Are School Prayers a Violation of Minority Rights?

The Constitution bars the government from favoring one religion over another. It's supposed to keep the government out of religion and religion out of the government. But this separation has never been complete. Take school prayers. The Supreme Court has ruled that such prayers are unconstitutional, but communities often try to get around this ruling.

One Side Communities should be allowed to require school prayers. Some communities may not want to pass such laws, but others are very religious. If the local citizens feel that a prayer is a good way to start the day, they should have the right to require school prayers. The schools can allow children to leave the room if they don't want to participate, and the prayer can be nonsectarian. In this way no one loses any freedom. But by forbidding school prayers the Supreme Court takes away the freedom of local communities to run their schools the way they want to.

The Other Side

It's true that many Americans want the school day to start with a prayer. In many communities a large majority would favor school prayers. But this is the kind of majority against which the minority has to be protected. The minority isn't protected if children who don't want to participate can leave the room, because children feel pressure to be like the majority. Contradictory pressures from home and school are hard on a child.

Prayer simply doesn't belong in the schools. It represents a breakdown of the constitutional separation of church and state and puts the support of the government behind religion.

Questions for Review

1. Name and describe some variations on the majority rule.

2. Why did the writers of the Constitution fear the "tyranny of the majority"?

3. What are the First Amendment freedoms? Why are they important in a democracy?

4. What are the arguments against freedom of speech?

5. Discuss the Smith Act, the McCarran Act, and the antiriot bill. How have the courts interpreted these laws?

6. What is the significance of the Pentagon Papers case?

7. What is the significance of the Supreme Court's ruling against school prayers?

8. What are some of the limits on property rights? Give illustrations.

9. Name the basic criminal rights.

Chapter 14

Federalism in America

A significant fact of American political life is that there are many governments in the United States. The federal government in Washington is the biggest and the most powerful, but it's just one of a large number of governments. There are also fifty state governments and a great variety of local governments.

Major Forms of Government

The major forms of government include unitary government, confederation, and federation. A *unitary government* is one in which all state and local governments are subordinate to the central government; in fact the central government could abolish the local governments if it wanted to. Policy decisions are made by the central government. Many European nations have such unitary systems.

In a *confederation* the central government is subordinate to the state governments. It has little direct power over the individual citizen; it acts only through the states. An example of a confederation is the government created by the Articles of Confederation in 1783.

A federal form of government is somewhere between a unitary government and a confederation. In a *federation* neither the central government nor the state governments are subordinate. Neither can abolish the other, and each is independent of the other in some areas. Both have direct power over citizens.

What form of government do we have in the United States? The traditional answer is that we have a federal form of government. But in practice it's hard to fit the United States neatly into any category. If in a federal form of government the central and state governments are equal, the United States is not a federation. The state governments are clearly subordinate to the central government in Washington. If in a federal form of government each level has certain powers that the other can't take away, again the United States is not a federation. Under the current interpretation of the Constitution, national laws (laws made by Congress) are the "supreme law of the land." In these ways the United States has what looks like a unitary form of government.

But the government of the United States is far from unitary. For one thing the states aren't created by the central government and can't be abolished by it. For another, the central and state governments can each raise and spend money. In addition each has important areas of activity and has direct control over citizens' lives.

Local Governments

The pattern of government in America would be fairly simple if we had to deal only with the national government and the states. After all, fifty-one governments isn't so very many. But there are many more governments in America—county governments, cities, towns, townships, as well as *special districts* for all sorts of purposes ranging from education to sewage disposal.

TABLE 14.1
Number and types of local governments, 1967

Counties	3,044
Municipalities	18,517
Townships	16,991
Special districts	23,885
School districts	15,781
All local governments	78,259

Source: U.S. Department of Commerce, Bureau of the Census, *Census of Governments, 1972.*

As can be seen from Table 14.1, there are almost 80,000 governments in America today.

Are all these units really governments? Some would say no. Only the national government and the states are guaranteed existence and independence by the Constitution. This means their power doesn't come from higher levels of government. Cities and counties, on the other hand, are set up by state governments and are subordinate to them.

Still, these units have many of the characteristics of government. Above all they have the power to raise money and spend it. Some (like city and county governments) raise funds and spend them on a wide range of programs; others (like the special districts) deal with special problems. But these problems are important ones and the districts act as real governments.

School districts are a good example of how special districts act as real governments. In terms of spending education is the largest domestic governmental activity. Over four-fifths of American public schools are controlled by independent school districts. These districts are run by independent school boards, often elected by the local citizens. They can impose taxes and float bonds to build and maintain schools and pay salaries. They have a say in curriculum and special programs. It's true that they have to operate within guidelines set by the states (and federal guidelines if they get federal funds). But by almost any standard these school districts are real governments.

Thus instead of two levels of government—the national government and the states—there are several levels covering the same territory and overlapping one another. Look at the number of units in the Chicago suburb of Park Forest: Cook County, Will County, Cook County Forest Preserve District, Village of Park Forest, Rich Township, Bloom Township, Monee Township, Suburban Tuberculosis Sanitarium District, Bloom Township Sanitary District, Non-High School District 216, Non-High School District 213, Rich Township High School District 227, Elementary School District 163, South Cook County Mosquito Abatement District.[1]

[1] Edward C. Banfield and Morton Grodzins, *Government and Housing in Metropolitan Areas* (New York: McGraw-Hill, 1958), p. 18; quoted in Advisory Commission on Inter-Governmental Relations, *Metropolitan America: Challenge to Federalism* (Washington, D.C., 1966).

Why so many governments? Why such a variety? How can they possibly get along with one another?

Centralization vs. Decentralization

In trying to answer these questions we'll start with the issue of centralization vs. decentralization. Again let's take education as an example. It used to be said that the French Minister of Education could look at his watch and say, "At this moment, every sixth-grade child in France is doing the following math problem . . . " and tell you the exact problem they were working on. This is an exaggeration, of course, but it shows that French education is a highly centralized system in which schedules, curriculum, standards, and the like are all set by the Ministry of Education in Paris and carried out in the local schools.

Compare this with the educational system in the United States. If you wanted to find out what pupils were doing in the sixth grade you could go to the Office of Education in the Department of Health, Education and Welfare in Washington. But you wouldn't find out there. Matters of schedule, curriculum, standards, and the like aren't decided in Washington. The American tradition in education is local control. Such matters are usually decided by the states or by the school boards of counties, cities, towns, or school districts.

Decentralization gives local citizens more chance to voice opinions about their schools.

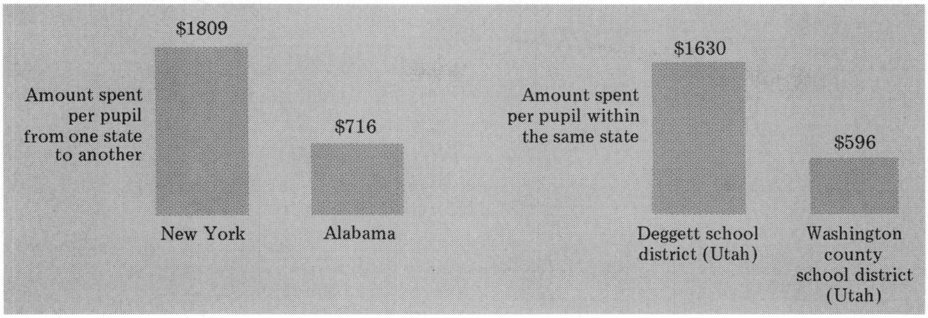

FIGURE 14.1 *Variations in State Expenditures for Education*

Source: Based on data from *Financial Status of the Public Schools, National Education Association, 1974.*

THE ARGUMENT FOR DECENTRALIZATION

There's a strong argument for decentralization. After all, pupils differ in different parts of the country. They have different interests, needs, and backgrounds. If some central government official tried to set up a uniform curriculum for the ghetto school in Harlem, the suburban school in Grosse Pointe, Michigan, and the rural school in Towner County, North Dakota, that curriculum wouldn't fit any of those schools very well. Only the local citizens and their school boards understand the educational needs of their district and can create programs to fit those needs.

Those who defend the present system point to the huge, complex bureaucracy that would be needed to run a nationwide school system—a bureaucracy that would put the schools beyond the control of the parents. Studies have shown that average citizens feel they understand local politics better than national politics and that they can have more influence on the local level. And citizens are more likely to be politically active when the political unit is small and more or less independent.

THE ARGUMENT FOR CENTRALIZATION

Those who argue for a centralized system point out that local control is uncoordinated and wasteful. Communities vary widely in their ability to provide a good education. As a result some pupils get a much better education than others who happen to be born in the wrong place. New York spends about two-and-a-half times as much on education as Alabama. And there are even greater variations within the states. Rich communities spend a lot more per pupil than poorer ones. (See Figure 14.1.)

The defender of centralization might also argue that local districts don't have the highly skilled teachers and facilities needed for a modern educational system. A local school district can't design a new physics curriculum; sometimes it can't afford laboratory facilities. These could be provided by a centralized school system.

It can also be argued that the present system is completely uncoordinated. A degree from a French *lycée* (high school) means something specific—you know what the student has studied and what he can do. In the United States a high school diploma has no standard meaning. In some cases it means the student is ready for college, in some cases not. How can you run a complex society that way?

Finally, the defender of centralization might point out that many serious urban problems are due to differences in school quality. If suburban schools were no different from inner-city schools, richer citizens wouldn't move to the suburbs in order to send their children to better schools, leaving the cities to the poor.

THE DILEMMA

Thus there's a real dilemma when it comes to the issue of centralization vs. decentralization—when you argue about federal power vs. states' rights or big government vs. local government. Decentralization can be criticized because coordination is lacking; centralization can be criticized because it doesn't pay enough attention to local needs and preferences. Suppose you could create a government as big or as small as you wanted. Clearly any proposal for a government bigger than, say, the small town or neighborhood would be criticized because there's little chance for citizens to participate effectively. But it's also clear that any government smaller than the whole world would be criticized as too small; after all, isn't the world one large, interdependent system?

Tension between these two principles is almost automatic. And it can be seen in much of our political history as well as in modern politics. In fact the crazy-quilt pattern of American government—the big governments in the states and big cities, the bigger government in Washington, the little governments overlapping these—can be seen as one response to the dilemma of centralization vs. decentralization: If neither solution is right, try both at the same time. So we have little governments (like school districts) to deal with local problems and big governments (like the national and state governments) to coordinate things and deal with larger problems.

The Variety of Governments

The mixed pattern of government in America is a result not of careful planning but of a long historical process. The history of federalism is largely the history of the clash between various interests. Since those interests have put pressure on the American political system from both sides, a mixed pattern has evolved. To see how this has happened, we must go back to the Constitution.

THE EVOLUTION OF FEDERALISM

We saw earlier how the writers of the Constitution tried to shift the balance of power between the states and the central government away from the state-dominated system of the Articles of Confederation. They created a federal executive branch, gave Congress the power to pass laws directly affecting the lives of citizens (including the power to tax), and set up a federal court system. Thus they created a truly national government. At the same time they set limits on the central government by means such as equal representation for all states in the Senate.

The balance seemed a good one, and few criticized it at the time. In fact, however, the division of powers between the central government and the states still had to be worked out in numerous court decisions, in the pressures of a changing nation, and—in several basic areas—on the battlefields of the Civil War.

WHY THE STATES GAVE UP THEIR POWER

It's dangerous to give up power—it may be hard to get back; it may be used against you. For generations people have been talking about a world federation, a European federation, a federation of African states—new centralized governments that would replace the various member nations. But except for unions created by force (in which the various parts don't give up their independence but have it taken away from them), there are few successful federations.

Why were the states willing to give up their power in 1787? There are several answers.

There Was Something to be Gained. The first answer has already been mentioned. The states had something to gain from union. There had been commercial and administrative confusion under the Articles of Confederation; trade among the states was hampered; trade with other nations was difficult without a central power that could make treaties; the rich new territories to the west couldn't be used without some central authority. The delegates to the Constitutional Convention were men of affairs, and their affairs weren't going very well. A central government would help.

There Was Little to Lose. As important as the gains from union was the question of what might be lost. As we have seen, no group is likely to give up power to another if it feels that its vital interests will suffer. One thing that has prevented the union of nations throughout history is that they have different basic cultures—different languages, different religions, different ways of life. One independent political unit is unlikely to give up its independence to a larger unit if it feels that the larger unit won't respect its vital interests. If an independent unit has such interests, it will join a union only if it can be guaranteed that its interests will be protected. Of course the more such interests there are, the more limits will be put on the central government and the less meaningful the union will be.

The states had few such vital interests to protect. They had a common language and a fairly common culture; they weren't sharply divided over religion. So they were willing to join the new central government.

The South's Interests Were Protected. There was, however, one vital interest that had to be protected. The most basic conflict of interest among the states was between the economies and social systems of the North and the South. The North had a growing economy based on manufacturing. The South's economy was solidly based on cotton and organized around slavery. Southern whites had a vital interest that they feared might be hurt by a government dominated by northern states.

To protect these interests the Constitution barred the government from taxing exports, since the South depended on finding markets for its cotton. Also the representation of southern states in the House of Representatives was increased by counting slaves as part of the population (at three-fifths of their actual number). And the Constitution barred Congress from interfering with the slave trade until 1808.

The issue of North vs. South and the related issue of slavery make it quite clear that the Constitution only temporarily settled the question of the relationship between the states and the national (or "federal") government. This question wasn't settled until the Civil War, and then only in part. How the powers of the national and state governments are to be divided—on racial matters and on other matters as well—remains open.

State and Nation

As with so many other issues in American political life, the Constitution didn't settle the issue of centralization vs. decentralization. Rather it provided a framework within which changes could be worked out. The basic framework was the federal principle: a unified central government and a set of partially independent states. Thus the Constitution supported both principles without facing the fact that they were contradictory. And perhaps this is why the federal system has evolved the way it has. The balance of power between the nation and the states has changed over time, but the framework of a central government and a set of independent states has survived.

IMPLIED POWERS

During the period from the writing of the Constitution to the Civil War a series of major Supreme Court decisions firmly established federal power over taxes, interstate commerce, and many other matters. In 1819 Chief Justice Marshall spelled out the doctrine of *implied powers*. He ruled that Congress wasn't limited to the powers listed in the Constitution. Rather, it had all the powers necessary to carry out those that were listed. This decision made it clear that the federal government was not simply a creation of the states.

CONCURRENT MAJORITY

Meanwhile the pull of decentralization led the nation to the Civil War. The issue centered on the vital interests of the various regions. During this period John Calhoun, a leading southern senator, developed the idea of *concurrent majority:* No majority of the citizens of the United States, nor a majority of the states themselves, could tell the others what to do. Policies had to be based on the agreement of a majority within the region involved; that is, each area would have to agree on policies affecting it. This principle was quite contrary to a strong federal government.

The Civil War settled the issue of secession. Decentralization could never go as far as to let a state or group of states leave the Union. But the war didn't settle the conflict between state and nation, nor did it do away with the idea of concurrent majority. Interest groups still have a strong voice in policies that affect them. Often these groups are economic interest groups rather than regional interest groups. But the principle of decentralization remains.

DUAL FEDERALISM

In the years from the Civil War to 1937, the Supreme Court developed a doctrine that has been labeled *dual federalism.* According to this doctrine the states and the national government each had a separate area of responsibility. The Constitution's commerce clause was interpreted as barring the states from regulating interstate commerce; the Tenth Amendment, on the other hand, was interpreted as limiting Congress by reserving some powers to the states.

Dual federalism was a negative doctrine. National power was limited to protect state power, and state power was limited to protect national power. As a result the Supreme Court often blocked both levels of government from carrying out social-reform legislation. Since 1937 the Court has not upheld this doctrine.

Where Does Power Lie?

As currently interpreted the Constitution doesn't treat the states and the nation as equals. Supreme Court decisions since the late 1930s have stressed the Constitution's statement that national laws are the "supreme law of the land . . . anything in the Constitution or laws of any state to the contrary notwithstanding" (Article 6, Section 2). Thus the laws of the national government are clearly superior. If Congress passes a law that conflicts with a state law, the congressional law prevails.

The only constitutional limitation on the national government in relation to the states is that it can't abolish the states or change their boundaries without their consent (Article 4, Section 3). But it's clear that Congress could take all effective power away from the states. The federal government has become active in many areas where state law once ruled, and in those areas federal law has replaced state law. Matters of business regulation, ecology, civil rights, and voting once were largely under state control. The states are still active in these areas, but the federal government has moved in. When you add the new programs that have become important since the 1930s, such as defense spending and atomic energy, you can see how the balance of power has shifted toward Washington.

THE FINANCIAL CRISIS

The weakness of state and local governments compared to the federal government is increased by the fact that the state and local governments can't raise enough money to meet their needs. The federal government gets over four-fifths of its revenue from income taxes; state governments get about two-thirds of their revenue from sales taxes; and local governments depend almost entirely on property taxes. The federal income tax provides more money than sales and property taxes because it taps personal income directly. Also, since it's a progressive tax it falls more heavily on the rich, though not by very much. Sales and property taxes are regressive; they fall more heavily on poorer citizens. And income taxes are more flexible: The amount they bring in goes up when the economy expands; sales and property taxes respond more slowly to the economy.

Sales and property taxes have another disadvantage: They lead to inequality among states and localities. This is particularly true of property taxes. Richer communities can raise much more in property taxes than poorer ones, but the needs of the poorer communities may be greater.

Many states have tried to get around these problems with income taxes of their own. But in most cases political pressures have kept the tax rates very low. State income taxes are unpopular largely because the federal government has already taken such a large bite out of personal income.

FEDERAL AID

State and local governments have come to depend more and more on federal funds. In the ten years between 1962 and 1972 federal aid to state and local governments rose from about $8 billion to over $35 billion per year. In 1973 it was estimated that federal aid provided 22 percent of all state and local revenues.

The two main forms of federal aid are grants-in-aid and revenue sharing. A *grant-in-aid* is given for a special purpose and usually comes with regulations on how the funds are to be used. *Revenue sharing* gives the states and localities more freedom in the use of the funds. Under this program, which began in 1972, $30 billion is being distributed to the states and to local governments over a five-year period. There are few strings attached. However, local governments are supposed to use the funds in the areas where they're needed most, such as health, public safety, and recreation.

Revenue sharing is an attempt to increase the powers of the states and localities compared to the federal government. And therefore it's controversial. Critics of revenue sharing (including some members of Congress) claim that local governments don't give funds to important programs like health and welfare. And many local governments haven't spent the federal funds on new projects but instead have used them to replace local funds so they could cut taxes. In addition civil-rights groups complain that the program doesn't include enough protection against racial and sexual discrimination.

It can be argued that revenue sharing has been attacked *because* it has succeeded in giving more power to local governments. The critics don't like the way that power is being used. They claim that local government officials are less willing to listen to minority groups or to citizens who need welfare programs. It's at the national level that such groups have been most effective.

Thus revenue sharing seems to represent a return of power to states and localities. But its long-term effects will depend on whether Congress remains committed to the program and whether it begins to restrict the use of the funds. A leading writer on federalism has claimed that in the long run revenue sharing will actually make state and local governments more dependent on the federal government. As Congress becomes more dissatisfied with the way the states and localities spend the funds, it will put more restrictions on them. The federal government will end up with even more control.[2]

STATE AND LOCAL GOVERNMENTS IN ACTION

The federal government may be more and more important, but you can't write off the state and local units. Counting only domestic programs (i.e., not counting defense, foreign affairs, or space programs), states and localities account for over 60 percent of government spending. And the states and localities still have a lot of power over many of the most important areas of public policy: protection of life and property; laws affecting marriage, divorce, and abortion; control of land use through zoning restrictions and the like. In fact most governmental activities that affect our daily lives are under the control of local or state governments. States and localities build highways, create and maintain most parks and recreation facilities, make laws that affect the environment, and educate children. It's true that in each of these areas funds often come from the federal government, along with some controls. But the states and localities have survived despite these controls.

COOPERATIVE FEDERALISM

The complex mixture of federal, state, and local powers we have today is called *cooperative federalism.* Government powers are shared across the

[2] Michael D. Reagan, *The New Federalism* (New York: Oxford University Press, 1972), pp. 104–105.

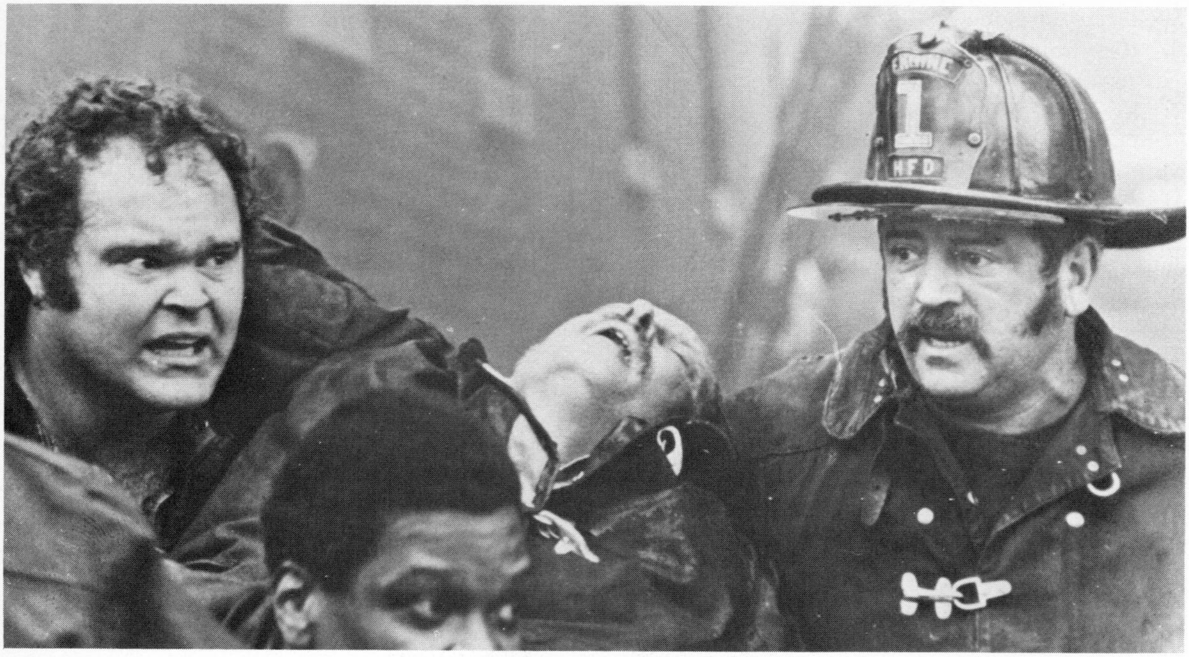

Many basic services are in the hands of local government.

various levels of government. One student of federalism has described this system as a marble cake rather than a layer cake.[3]

Public education, for example, has traditionally been under local and state control. Most of the funds for education are raised and spent locally. But the federal government has been involved in one way or another from the very beginning. A law passed in 1785 provided for federal grants to local governments to build schools. Federal aid continued in the nineteenth century, when the Morrill Land Grant Act allowed federal land grants to be given to the states to set up agricultural and mechanical colleges.

Since then various federal programs have expanded federal aid to education. During World War II federal funds were used to build and operate schools in places where defense activity (such as a military base) put pressure on the local school system. These programs continued after the war. In addition when Sputnik, the first artificial satellite, was put into orbit, the federal government decided that the United States must make a major effort to keep up with the Russians in technological education. The 1958 National Defense Education Act gave aid to local school districts to improve education in mathematics, science, and foreign languages. And the Elementary and Secondary

[3] Morton Grodzins, "Centralization and Decentralization in the American Federal System," in Robert A. Goldwin, ed., *A Nation of States* (Chicago: Rand McNally, 1963).

Education Act of 1965 involved fairly large grants of federal funds to school districts with large numbers of pupils below the poverty line.

Sharing of Functions. The history of government involvement in education illustrates how the states and the nation share functions. State and local control over education has not been eliminated by the growth in the role of the federal government. The government doesn't take over the schools. Rather, federal involvement takes the form of grants-in-aid to state educational commissions or local school boards. Such aid usually has strings attached, though, generally in the form of guidelines that must be followed if aid is to be given. (Note, however, that these guidelines are often set up after consultation with the states and school districts themselves.)

The federal government's role in the educational process again shows how the general principles of centralization vs. decentralization interact with particular interests. Opposition to federal involvement is often stated in terms of general principles. On the one hand it's argued that locally controlled education is better than education dominated by a Washington bureaucracy. On the other hand those who argue for centralization claim that national standards and equal educational opportunity are more important values. But how you feel about federal involvement in education often depends not on general principles but on where you stand on other issues. At times federal

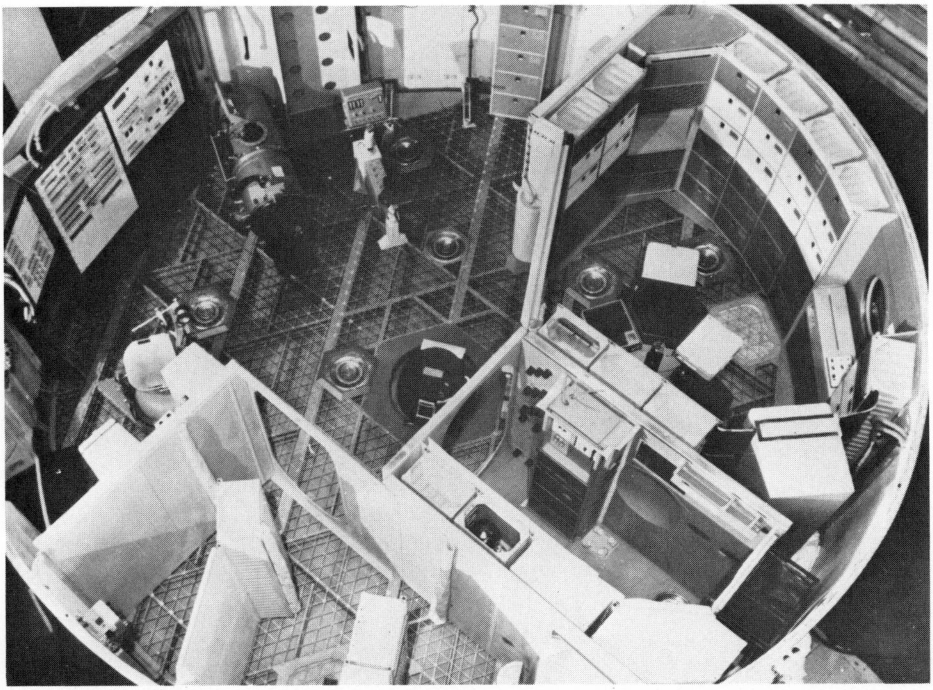

Federal aid for technical education grew in response to Russia's first advance in space. A mockup of Skylab crew quarters is shown here.

aid programs to local schools have included desegregation requirements. So your position on school desegregation is likely to affect your attitude toward federal aid that comes with such requirements.

The result is a mixed system. The federal government provides grants and guidelines, but the power over the educational system is shared with the states. The same pattern can be found in many areas. What about unemployment insurance—is it a federal or a state program? In most cases it's a state program. The states impose a payroll tax, and with the money raised in this way they provide unemployment insurance. But the states are *required* to impose such a tax; under federal law the national government would impose the tax if the states didn't do so. In addition, though they run their own programs the states have to meet federal standards. Thus the actual program is a complex pattern of shared powers and overlapping functions.

The Historical Development of Federalism

We can't give a full description of the forces that led to the pattern of federal-state-local relations that exists today. But we'll try to answer two important questions: Why has federal power grown so much beyond what the founders intended? And why, despite this growth, have state and local governments remained major centers of power?

GROWTH OF FEDERAL POWER

The answer to the first question lies in the development of America as a nation. The writers of the Constitution wanted to create a unified nation, particularly in the areas of interstate commerce and foreign affairs. And these were two very basic powers. As the nation became a large continental economy and a world power, the federal government's power also grew.

Development of a National Economy. As the nation developed a unified economy, the role of the federal government increased. A national economy makes it impossible for any one state to take control. If a state tries to regulate businesses and the businesses object to such regulation, they can move to another state. This reduces state control over business and makes federal regulation more likely.

The major economic problems of the United States are ones that affect the entire nation and need to be solved at the national level. Inflation and unemployment don't stop at state borders. The food in Chicago supermarkets comes from all over the country; unemployment rises in Detroit when car sales fall in California and New York; and unemployment in Detroit affects employment in every state. The economy is a highly interdependent system, and only national policy can deal with it.

Growth Through Defense Power. Another source of federal power is the United States' role as a world power. Federal power has always grown in wartime, and high military budgets maintain that power. This shows why the Constitution isn't a good guide to the powers of the federal government. Imagine that the power over national defense was the only *specific* power given to the federal government. It's easy to see how that power could lead to all the other powers of the government as long as there's a flexible interpretation of *implied* powers. The power to defend the nation is meaningless without the power to raise necessary funds, so the government has the power to tax. You can't defend the nation without advanced technology, so the government is involved in education. Good defense requires good roads, so the government spends billions of dollars to build roads. And so on.

Group Pressures for Equal Treatment. Pressure for equality almost always involves federal power. Since equality applies to citizens in all parts of the country, federal law is the best way to enforce it. For example, the "equal protection of the laws" provision of the Fourteenth Amendment was used by the Supreme Court to ban school segregation[4] and equalize voting rights,[5] and by lower federal courts to equalize treatment of the sexes.[6] As a result in recent years we have seen the growth of federal power in such areas as voter registration, which used to be under state or local control.

WHAT PRESERVES THE STATES AND LOCALITIES?

The Constitution puts no limits on federal expansion. Taxes give the federal government the money it needs for continued growth, while the states and localities are financially weak. And more and more problems need national solutions. So what preserves the states and localities?

The answer lies mainly in the structure of American politics, particularly the political parties. As we have seen, the parties are basically state and local organizations. They may develop national unity when it comes to Presidential elections, but this is only temporary. Besides, the White House and the state houses or city halls aren't always controlled by the same party. And even when they are, this doesn't mean the local party is controlled by the national party leadership (as it would be in some countries). Candidates for state and local elections—even for Congress—are chosen locally, not nationally. This gives the local party independence from national control. The result is that states and localities remain independent governments because they have political power, not because of the Constitution.

An example of the strength of local political power is the social-security legislation of the 1930s. The original plan was for a fully federal program. The program had been planned in Washington, and many people felt that it would

[4] *Brown* v. *Board of Education of Topeka* 347 US 483 (1954).

[5] *Baker* v. *Carr* 369 US 186 (1962).

[6] See the cases listed in Eduard S. Corwin, *The Constitution and What It Means Today*, revised by Harold W. Chase and Craig R. Ducat (Princeton, N.J.: Princeton University Press, 1974), pp. 645–646, footnotes 235–244.

be more effective if it was administered there. In fact, however, the program passed by Congress involved a lot of sharing with the states. Much of the program was administered by the states following federal guidelines—a pattern found in many other areas. The main reason was that the Roosevelt administration knew Congress would accept only a proposal that involved participation by the states. If Roosevelt, as head of the Democratic party, had controlled congressional votes, he wouldn't have had to worry. But members of Congress, though part of the federal government, are elected from particular states or districts and often feel a need to defend the locality they represent.

Washington, the States, and the Cities

The greatest challenge to the American mixture of governments is the situation of today's large cities. Can a Constitution written for a nation of farmers deal with the modern city? In the large metropolitan areas we see all the problems of central vs. local control, of many governments with overlapping functions, of federal-state relations and federal-local relations.

METROPOLITAN AREAS

Two things are clear about today's metropolitan areas: They are socially and economically interdependent, and they are politically divided. The interdependence takes many forms. People move easily from one part to another; they live in one area and work in another. They share roads, mass-transit systems, and shopping areas. They depend on the same clean water, pure air, and space for recreation.

We use the word "spillovers" to describe the ways the activities of one community affect its neighbors. There are many spillovers in a metropolitan area. Smoke from a factory in one community pollutes the air in the next community. If one community has an effective mosquito-abatement program but its neighbors don't, it will still suffer during the summer. If a suburb zones its land for single-family houses, it will keep out poor citizens and force them to find homes somewhere else, usually in the inner city.

Some spillovers can benefit other communities. One community may provide parks that are open to everyone. Or the inner city may keep its streets clean, and those streets may be used by people who live in the suburbs.

Thus the metropolitan areas are social and economic units that share problems and benefits. But on top of this interdependence is the disorder of American local government. It's estimated, for example, that there are about 1500 governmental units in the New York metropolitan area. There's the government of the central city and separate governments for satellite cities and small and large suburbs. These are overlapped by county governments, special districts, and various state and federal jurisdictions.

What this means is that while the problems may cover a wide area, the solutions are applied in small parts of that area. It also means there's a wide gap between those who pay for services and those who benefit from them. The inner city provides clean streets and pays for them with taxes paid by those who live there. The streets are used by people who live in the suburbs and pay their taxes to a suburban government. This helps explain why cities try to tax suburban residents who work in the city. Since they don't always succeed, many cities have dirty streets and most don't have good mass-transit systems.

The Urban Crisis. It's common knowledge that the inner cities are decaying and are being left to the largely nonwhite poor. The suburbs are white, richer—and fearful about the cities. This situation is partly a result of the American mixture of local governments with overlapping boundaries, of state government and federal government. When it leaves the city the white middle class crosses a political boundary into another community. Suburban residents no longer vote or otherwise take part in the government of the city; they no longer share its problems; above all, they no longer pay taxes to the city.

As a result there's a lot of pressure on the city to provide services for a growing population that needs those services badly—welfare services as well as the other needs of urban life. But the cities are feeling this pressure just when the tax revenue needed to provide money for those services is decreasing.

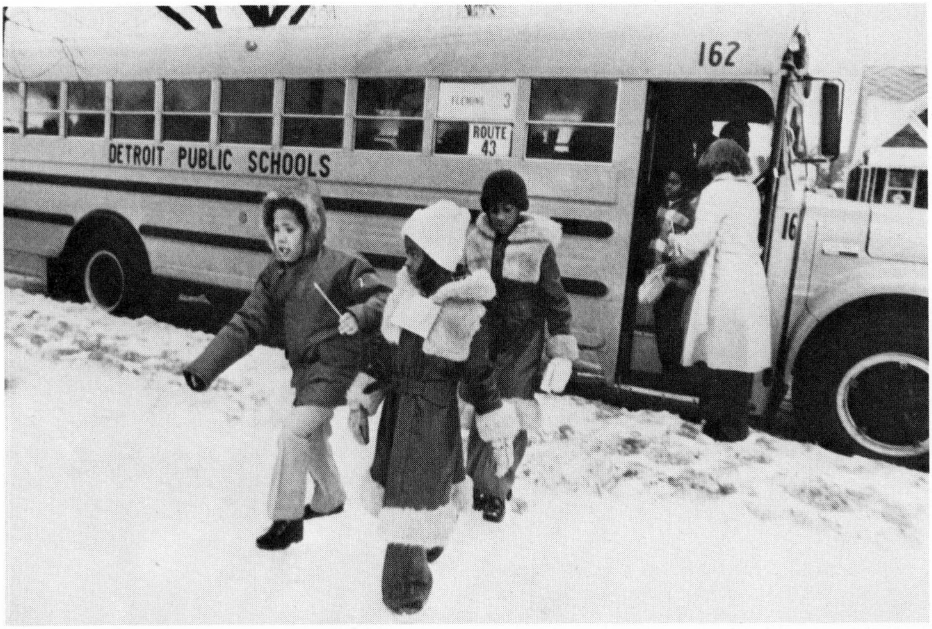

In many major cities the majority of public school children are nonwhite.

In addition the school-age population in the inner cities includes larger and larger percentages of nonwhites. (See Table 14.2.) This makes it hard to integrate the schools—there aren't enough white pupils to go around. It also makes the problem worse, since more and more whites move away from "ghetto schools."

Suppose the boundaries were different. Suppose moving to the suburbs didn't involve crossing the political boundary to another community. It's true that this wouldn't end the problems, but things would look a little different. The cities' tax revenues would not be affected by movement to the suburbs. The suburbs would still be part of the same political unit. And it would be easier to integrate the schools, which might weaken the desire of the white middle classes to move to the suburbs for the sake of better schools. In short, though the cities would still have their problems, those problems wouldn't be made worse by the existence of political boundaries.

The Federal Government and Housing. Another solution is for the federal government to become more involved in the problems of metropolitan areas. The government has long been involved in programs in urban areas, particularly housing programs. But this involvement has its problems. The first major federal program was the Housing Act of 1937, which set up the FHA mortgage-insurance program. This allowed many more people to build and own their

TABLE 14.2
Black student population in the big cities

School district	*Number of black students*	*Percent of all students*
Washington	133,638	95.5%
Atlanta	73,985	77.1
New Orleans	77,504	74.6
Newark	56,736	72.3
Richmond	30,746	70.2
Gary	31,200	69.6
Baltimore	129,250	69.3
St. Louis	72,629	68.8
Detroit	186,994	67.6
Philadelphia	173,874	61.4
Oakland	39,121	60.0
Birmingham	34,290	59.4
Memphis	80,158	57.8
Cleveland	83,596	57.6
Chicago	315,940	57.1
Kansas City, Mo.	35,578	54.4
Louisville	25,078	51.0

Source: U.S. Department of Health, Education and Welfare, *Directory of Public, Elementary and Secondary Schools in Selected Districts,* Fall 1972.

own homes than would otherwise have been possible. But this program was of greatest value to middle-class homeowners, resulting in stimulated growth of the suburbs at the expense of the inner city. The FHA program was balanced by federal support for low-rent housing, almost always in the inner city. Thus the federal programs helped create the urban crisis.

The Federal Government and Urban Renewal. The purpose of urban renewal was to renew the inner city. Local officials were given federal money to buy up blighted property (usually downtown slums where nonwhites were living) and clear the land. The land was then sold to developers. The result wasn't beneficial to the poor population of the inner cities; what was supposed to be urban renewal turned out to be black removal.

Local vs. Federal Control. The story of urban renewal illustrates one of the problems of the centralization vs. decentralization issue. When you decentralize power, to whom do you give it? The federal urban-renewal program was a decentralized one; federal funds were given to local officials, who planned the local renewal programs. Who benefits from such a program? It depends on who is in power locally—and this is not likely to be the poor residents of the inner city.

Local control means control by whoever controls the local area. Citizens often want local control when it means *they* can control. If they aren't in control locally, they may prefer outside control. Thus inner-city blacks sometimes call for local control over schools or the police, since they form a majority of the population. But where they are a minority they may prefer federal control.

This leaves us with some unanswered questions. Should the cities come under direct federal control? Should there be large metropolitan governments? Should there be local governments as there are now, or should there be even more local governments on a neighborhood basis? The situation of the metropolitan areas shows how all governmental units are too big and all are too small. Big units don't adjust easily to the problems of local citizens or give them enough control over their own lives. But small units need to be coordinated with the larger ones.

Suppose we have federal control or big metropolitan governments. Many of the problems of coordination would be solved and tax revenues would be equalized. But could such a government adjust its policies to the needs of citizens in various parts of the metropolitan area? Doesn't each part know best what it needs, and doesn't it have the right to run its own affairs? This question might be asked by a rich white suburban resident who would like to ignore the problems of the inner city, but it might also be asked by a black inner-city resident who wants local control.

But will the opposite solution work—a system of small governments like the one that already exists or one divided even further into neighborhood governments? This would give local residents more control over their own lives—or would it? The problems they would have to deal with—transportation, housing, pollution, even education—go beyond the neighborhood. The citizen would have more control over his government, but it would be a government that couldn't handle today's problems.

Thus it looks as if the dilemma of centralization vs. decentralization will be around for many years to come. The solutions tried at any particular time will depend more on the interests involved and the political power of various groups than on general principles of government.

How Institutions Work: VII The Structure of State and Local Governments

WHAT IS THE LEGAL AND POLITICAL FRAMEWORK OF STATE GOVERNMENT?

The basic structure of each state government is set forth in that state's constitution. All state constitutions are based on the principles of separation of powers and checks and balances; all provide for legislative, executive, and judicial branches. In all three branches the actions of the state must conform to the federal Constitution.

HOW ARE THE THREE BRANCHES OF GOVERNMENT ORGANIZED AT THE STATE LEVEL?

Executive

The chief executive of each state is the governor, elected for a two-year or four-year term. Like the President, the governor makes an annual budget proposal and largely sets the legislative agenda. Most governors can call special sessions of the legislature, and all but one have veto power. Even so, the role of the executive branch has traditionally been secondary to that of the legislature.

In almost all states the governor shares power with other elected officials—lieutenant governor, secretary of state, treasurer, attorney general, auditor, superintendent of education.

Legislative

In all states except Nebraska there are two houses in the legislature. In accordance with Supreme Court rulings, seats in both houses must be assigned on the basis of population. The size of state legislatures ranges from less than 60 to more than 400 members. As in Congress, the legislatures work through committees, and except in Minnesota and Nebraska, state legislatures are organized along party lines.

Only about half the state legislatures meet on an annual basis; the others meet only every two years. Many states also limit the length of legislative sessions, pay low salaries, and provide little staff. As a result, for many state legislators public service is a part-time job.

Judicial

Most state judicial systems are organized along similar lines. At the bottom are justices of the peace and municipal courts; in the middle layer are county or trial courts and special courts for juveniles, probate, and the like; at the top are courts of appeals or state supreme courts. In two-thirds of the states judges are elected. In the other states they are chosen either by appointment or through a merit system that combines appointment and election.

WHAT ARE THE MAIN FUNCTIONS OF STATE AND LOCAL GOVERNMENTS?

The states have the major responsibility for education and public health, transportation, welfare, and the administration of justice. They also have authority over corporations, public utilities, and financial institutions, and they regulate political parties and elections. These responsibilities are shared with local governments. Together, state and local governments spend more than $200 billion a year and employ over 10 million people.

WHAT IS THE LEGAL BASIS OF LOCAL GOVERNMENTS?

All local governments are created by the state and derive their power from the state. City charters are granted by the state, while other local units such as counties and special districts are subdivisions of the state or are created by the legislature. They have only the powers given them by the state. However, about half the states have "home rule," in which cities may run many of their own affairs.

WHAT ARE THE THREE BASIC FORMS OF CITY GOVERNMENT?

Most larger cities use the mayor-council form of government, in which the mayor shares power with an elected city council. A second form is the commission plan, in which a small board of elected commissioners serve both as a legislative council and as heads of city departments. There is also the council-manager plan, in which the council hires a professional city manager who runs the city subject to the council's approval.

WHAT ARE THE OTHER UNITS OF LOCAL GOVERNMENT?

Counties

All but three states are divided into counties. Counties are the most important unit of local government in rural areas. They are intended to serve as administrative and judicial units and are run by elected officials such as the sheriff, prosecutor, treasurer, and clerk, as well as a board of commissioners.

Townships

Townships are unincorporated, usually rural units of government found in less than half the states. They are run by a board of supervisors.

Special and School Districts

These districts are created for special purposes. They handle problems that may go beyond the boundaries of existing political units. The most important of these are school districts, which can tax, borrow, and spend public funds. There are also over 20,000 special districts for particular purposes such as soil conservation, fire protection, and recreation.

Questions for Review

1. What form of government do we have in the United States?
2. Why are counties and special districts "governments"?
3. Think about the place where you live. Name as many governmental units as you can that have jurisdiction in your area.
4. Discuss the issue of centralization vs. decentralization. How did the Constitution deal with this issue?
5. Why were the states willing to give up power to the central government?
6. What is meant by implied powers? Concurrent majority? Dual federalism?
7. Why is revenue sharing controversial?
8. Describe cooperative federalism. Give examples.
9. What factors led to the growth of federal power? Why have the states remained strong in the face of this expansion?
10. Could a metropolitan form of government help solve the problems of the cities, or should the federal government become more involved? Explain.

Chapter 15

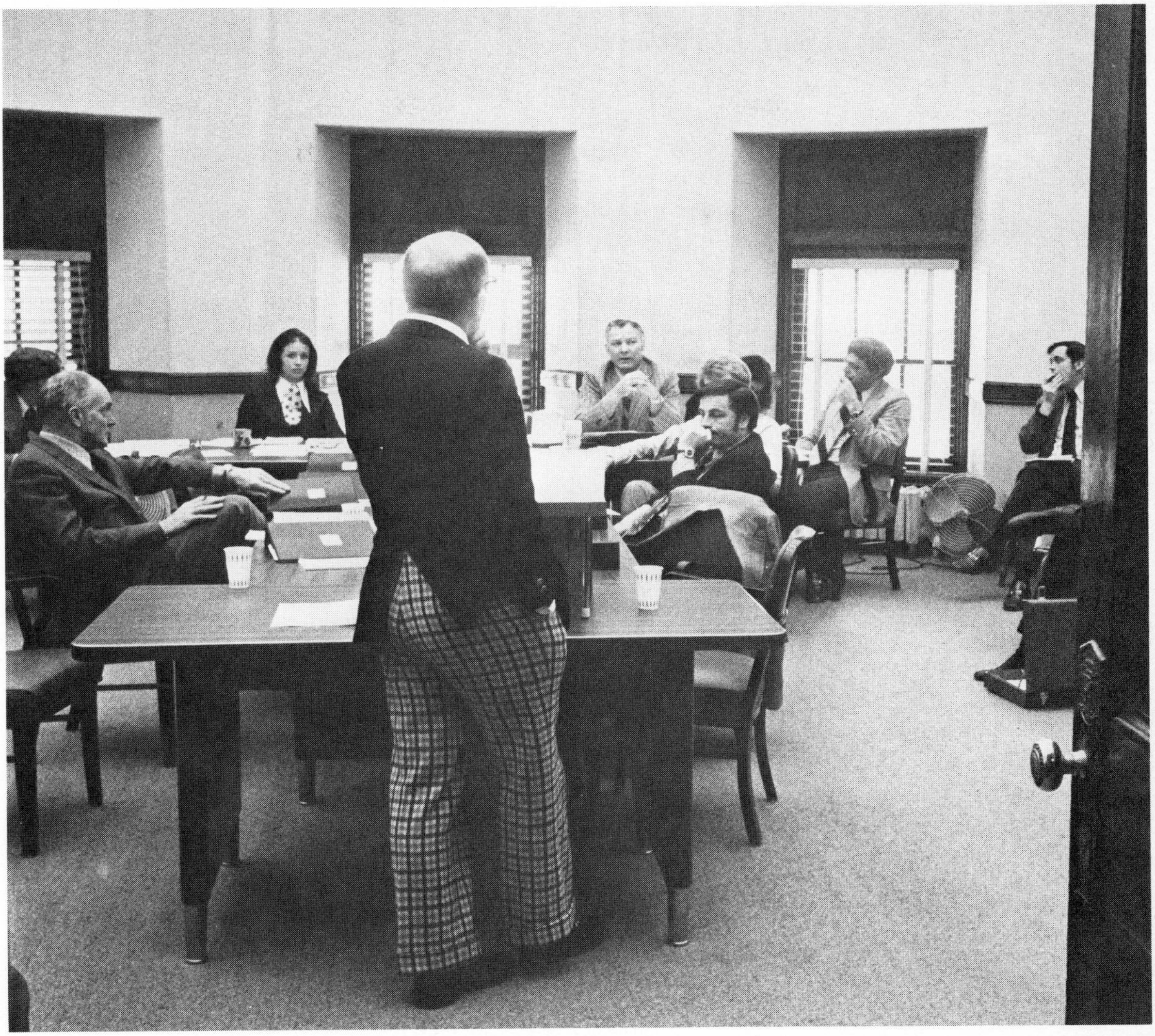

How Public Policy Is Made

How is policy made in America? Who decides what the government does? Throughout this book we've looked at the various actors and institutions in American politics with these questions in mind. Now we'll try to tie everything together by looking at the way policy is actually made.

What Is a Policy?

The activity of the government can be understood in terms of policies and decisions. Policies are long-term patterns of activity. Decisions are the points where that pattern changes. The United States had a hostile policy toward China from 1949 to 1971. It didn't recognize the government of mainland China, it put limits on trade with China, and it supported the Taiwan government. In 1971 President Nixon made a decision to go to Peking; this meant a change in policy.

Some policies continue for a long time while no decisions are made about them. Some are maintained by periodic decisions; an example is the decision to oppose China's entry to the United Nations year after year. And some policies are constantly being changed by decisions; an example is governmental policy on busing of schoolchildren, changed many times by decisions of the courts, the executive branch, and the states.

UNDERSTANDING GOVERNMENTAL POLICY

To understand how governmental activities affect the lives of Americans, you have to understand the roots of long-term policies as well as the sources of the decisions that change those policies. And since a policy is a long-term pattern of activity, we're interested in what the government actually does, not just in what it says it's going to do.

Study the Details. General statements of policy may be hopes rather than descriptions of reality. Congress may pass a law stating that all children have the right to an equal education, but that law will be meaningless without funds to carry it out. In addition there's often a gap between the general statement of a law and its details. A major tax bill, for example, may be intended to raise revenue, control inflation, and perhaps redistribute wealth. But the real policy is found in the details of the bill, and these may lead to results quite different from those set forth in the general statement.

Administration. We've been told that Congress makes policies and executive agencies carry them out. But this isn't always the way it works. How the policy is carried out may determine how effective it is. For example, Congress may pass a law to improve inner-city schools; it may even appropriate funds for that purpose. But if local school officials use the funds for other purposes, the policy does nothing for inner-city children.

The point is that a policy doesn't administer itself. Someone has to carry it out. And in the process it can be changed. Congress often passes laws that

Our policy *toward China was changed by a* decision *by President Nixon to travel to China.*

are quite vague because it wants executive agencies to give them more precise meaning. This increases the need to look at a policy in action rather than the statement of a policy.

Implementation. The more complicated the process of carrying out a law, the more likely it is that there will be a wide gap between the intentions of the law and its results. A study of voting-rights bills passed in the late 1950s and early 1960s illustrates this. Bills passed in 1957, 1960, and 1965 all had the same purpose: to outlaw voting discrimination against blacks, particularly in the South. The first law had little effect because it required that blacks sue in federal courts if they felt that their rights had been violated. This is a long, expensive, and cumbersome process. The 1960 law made things a bit easier; the Justice Department was allowed to bring suit. But each violation still had to be taken to court, so few blacks were registered under this law. The 1965 law, on the other hand, was much more effective. One of the main reasons was that it was easier to carry out; the Justice Department could enforce the law without going to court.[1]

Unintended Results. Not all policies work out the way the people who design or administer them intend them to. Often they have additional results that weren't planned. School districts' testing policies weren't intended to discrim-

[1] Frederick M. Wirt, *The Politics of Southern Equality* (Chicago: Aldine, 1970), chap. 3.

inate against blacks. But if the tests ask questions about aspects of life that are more familiar to middle-class whites or use language more like that used in white homes, they discriminate against blacks. Unintended results aren't always bad, however. Sometimes a policy with one goal can achieve other goals at the same time. In response to the energy crisis, for example, speed limits were lowered. The purpose was to save gasoline, but the policy also saved lives.

LIMITS ON WHAT THE GOVERNMENT CAN DO

There are many areas in which the government seems unable or unwilling to make policy. But even where it is able and willing, a general policy isn't enough. There's a long and difficult road from the creation of general policy to the actual results of that policy. Let's look at some of the reasons why governmental policy doesn't always do what it sets out to do.

Goals Are Sometimes Unclear. Policy goals are sometimes vague. Often this is simply because Congress isn't sure what it's trying to do. Or the goals of a law may conflict with other goals. In recent years there's been a lot of conflict over the use of busing to achieve school integration. The conflict is not between those who favor integration and those who oppose it. Rather it's between the goal of school integration and the goal of local control of the schools.

Sometimes We Don't Know How to Achieve Our Goals. In 1975 the Ford administration proposed a tax cut. The purpose was to increase consumer spending in order to stimulate the economy. There were two choices: a lump-sum tax rebate or a reduction in withholding from paychecks. One would give people a large amount all at once; the other would give them a bit more each month. Which would lead to more spending rather than more saving? Economic planners simply didn't know.

Some Things Can Be Changed More Easily than Others. Some changes aren't easy to achieve by governmental action. It's easier to reduce the size of classes in inner-city schools than to bring in better teachers. But it may be easier to improve the quality of teachers than to change the values children learn at home. If the values learned at home are the basic factor determining success in school, governmental programs can do little. They will do something about class size, since this is an area where something can be done, even though this may not get to the root of the problem.

Other Conditions May Be Wrong. The success of a policy often depends on other conditions beyond the control of the policy maker. If the conditions are right, the policy works; if not, the policy fails. In recent years, for example, there has been an increase in governmental action to end racial and sexual discrimination. Employers have been required to take *affirmative action* to open more and better jobs to women and minority groups. But in the mid-1970s the economic slump made it harder to carry out such a program.

It's Often Hard to Tell if a Program Has Succeeded. Is a program successful? It's often hard to tell. The standards of success may be unclear. Let's say the government sets up a retraining program for workers laid off from their jobs. What is the standard of success for such a program? The amount spent on training? The number of people who participate? The number who complete the program? Their success in finding jobs after completing the program? How long they hold those jobs? A program may be successful by one standard (lots of people complete the program) but unsuccessful by another (they can't find jobs in which they can use their new skills).

ACTION AND INACTION

To fully understand governmental policy, you have to look at what the government *doesn't* do as well as what it does do. If the government is inactive in some area, that is a policy, though it may not have been planned that way. There may not have been a decision to do nothing, but the lack of action has an effect anyway.

A visitor from a country like Belgium or Canada, where there is constant conflict over language policy, might ask about the American government's language policy. "What do you mean by a language policy?" most Americans would reply; "there's no language problem here." But this answer would be incorrect. Most Americans speak English, but a large minority speak Spanish. Government business is conducted in English; civil-service examinations are in English; school is taught in English. This works to the disadvantage of those whose native language is not English. In fact in recent years this problem has been recognized, and in New York City and California policy decisions have been made to deal with the problem.

How Issues Become Issues

The impact of governmental policy on the lives of citizens depends in part on how decisions are made about issues. But even more basic is the question of how issues get on the *agenda,* the list of topics that will be considered at any given legislative session, in the first place. How does the issue of roads vs. mass transit get on the government's agenda? Why should the government have a policy in this area?

SETTING THE AGENDA

The first step in dealing with a problem is to recognize that it is a problem. Once a problem has been recognized—"put on the agenda"—citizens can pressure the government; the issue can be debated in the news media, in

Congress, in the executive branch; proposals can be made for solving the problem.

The process by which problems come to the attention of the public and the government hasn't been studied much. One reason is that it's hard to identify "nonissues," that is, problems that have not yet been recognized. (If this was easier, the problems would be recognized earlier.) Issues can come up very suddenly. The women's liberation movement caught most people off guard, as did many of the first black protest activities. Looking back we can say these were issues that were bound to arise sooner or later. But that's looking back.

Does the Agenda Reflect Reality? One view of how problems get on the agenda is that they get on automatically. If the economy is going badly, economic problems automatically get on the political agenda; if it's going well, they get little attention. In earlier years, when our rivers were pure, pollution wasn't on the agenda. Now they are filthy, and pollution is a major political issue.

There's some truth to this view. It's hard to imagine pollution as an issue if the air and water are pure. But the "political" agenda doesn't merely reflect the "real" problems of a society. Our lakes and rivers were polluted long before we became concerned about the problem. Lake Erie became almost hopelessly polluted without anything being done about it. Now that the same thing is happening to some of the other Great Lakes, it's an issue. Surely something besides the problem itself is responsible. In the 1950s and 1960s the issue of race relations exploded on the American scene. Does this mean there was no problem in earlier years? Quite the opposite. The conditions in which American blacks lived were improving at the same time that their demands for equal rights became stronger. What had to be added to the problem itself was awareness of the problem.

Can Anyone Put a Problem on the Agenda? A second view is that anyone can put a problem on the agenda. In a way this is true, but it's also a little misleading. The Constitution guarantees the right to petition Congress or to form a political group. These things are often done. But not all social groups are equally organized. And unorganized interest groups have less chance of getting their problems on the political agenda than organized ones.

The fact that a serious problem exists doesn't make the average citizen active in trying to get the government to deal with that problem. This can be seen from a study that found black Americans more likely than whites to say they had serious problems—jobs, housing, income—that could be solved by governmental action. Thus blacks recognize their problems as political, that is, problems the government would be most likely to solve. Yet they are less likely than whites to put pressure on the government about such problems. When asked why, the usual reason is that they doubt their own political efficacy and the government's responsiveness.[2]

[2] Sidney Verba and Norman H. Nie, *Participation in America: Political Democracy and Social Equality* (New York: Harper & Row, 1972), chap. 10.

Can Any Problem Get on the Agenda? Just as some people are less likely than others to put their problems on the agenda, there are certain types of problems that are less likely than others to get on the agenda. For example, the tradition of free enterprise in America makes it unlikely that an issue involving government ownership of industries will be raised or, if it is raised, will be taken seriously. Such an issue might be so far "out of the question" that no one would think of raising it. Of course what is "out of the question" may be hard to tell until the issue is actually raised.

Comprehensive vs. Incremental Planning

Imagine government officials faced with a policy problem. Suppose they're trying to write legislation to deal with auto pollution. There are two ways they can approach the problem. One we call the comprehensive approach, the other the incremental approach.

THE COMPREHENSIVE APPROACH

If they use *comprehensive planning,* the government officials will consider all possible ways of handling the issue. They will state the goal they are trying to achieve and relate it to other goals they think are important. They will then choose the best possible way of achieving that goal.

A comprehensive approach to auto pollution might involve the following:

1. The past is no limitation. The planners won't be limited by what has been done before. The past design of cars, the number of older cars on the road, the evolution of the auto industry, and the pattern of auto use won't interfere with a new comprehensive plan.
2. All possible policies will be considered. The planners won't just consider ways to modify current cars; they will consider all possible solutions. Nor will they limit themselves to the existing means of transportation. They may consider the possibility of replacing the car with mass transit.
3. Connections with other policies will be considered. The planners will see the relation of their goal to other policies, and they won't be afraid to plan for changes in those policies if they are related to auto pollution. Does private ownership of cars lead to greater pollution? Then perhaps private ownership should be barred. Perhaps government ownership of the auto industry would increase control over pollution. If so, that possibility should be considered as well.
4. All values are considered. The planners don't consider only auto pollution. They are fully aware that we have other values besides controlling pollution. Pollution could be stopped by banning all cars, but that would hurt other values such as a functioning economy and full employment, or our desire to get from place to place. Comprehensive planners take these other values into consideration.

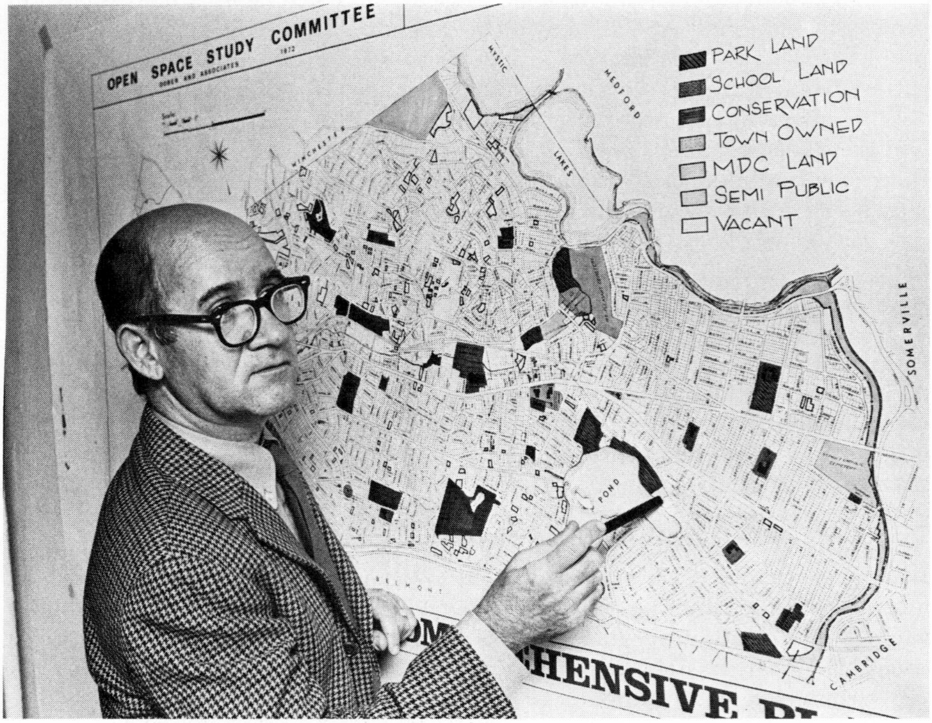

Comprehensive planning attempts to consider all aspects of a plan.

5. All effects are considered. What effect does a policy have on jobs, on housing, on other means of transportation? Maybe a reduction in pollution will improve health. The planners might even consider the need for new facilities for the aged, who will probably live longer in a pollution-free atmosphere.

THE INCREMENTAL APPROACH

Incremental planning differs from the comprehensive approach in every way:

1. The past is a major limitation. The planners consider the current situation—how many cars are on the road, their economic importance, current patterns of auto use. Past policies, such as the policy not to support mass transit, will be considered as a framework within which they must work.
2. Rather than considering all possible ways of dealing with the problem, the planners will consider cars as currently designed and changes that could fit into those designs.
3. They will stick fairly closely to the technical problem of standards for auto pollution and ignore larger changes in the economy. Such major

changes as the banning of private cars or the nationalization of the auto industry probably won't even enter their minds.

4. The planners won't worry much about the effects of their plan in other areas. Their area of concern is auto pollution; they'll let other government agencies worry about inflation or full employment. They won't consider other important values. Rather they'll ignore most other values and think only about auto pollution.

The results of these two approaches to policy making would be very different. The comprehensive planners could almost redesign the world from scratch. The incremental planners would create a policy designed to deal with a specific problem, modifying but not eliminating current practices.

Despite the apparent advantages of the comprehensive approach, most governmental policy takes the incremental approach. Policies tend to be based on previous policies and are worked out step by step, focusing on one aspect of the problem at a time. For example, a major study of government spending on various programs asked how you could predict what any state or city would spend on things like welfare, education, parks, and the like. What would you base your prediction on—the party that won the last election? The major social groups in the state or city? The kinds of problems the government faced? No. The best way to predict how a government will spend its funds this year is to look at how it spent them last year. There may be changes, but they will be incremental changes. Last year's budget tends to be the starting point for this year's.[3]

THE ARGUMENT FOR INCREMENTAL PLANNING

Incremental planning is a fact of American politics. It's the way most policy is made. Those who defend this approach argue that it's an effective way of making policy. For one thing, focusing on one aspect of a problem isn't a bad way of doing things. Other values and issues aren't ignored; there are other government agencies worrying about them. If separate parts of the government worry about separate problems, all the problems will be taken care of.

Furthermore, it's a good idea to make policy without considering all possible effects, otherwise nothing would ever get done. It would take a lifetime to study all the possible effects of a policy.

However, there are flaws in this argument. It assumes that every problem has a government agency working on it. But this isn't the case; some interests just aren't considered. It's only in recent years that a government agency has been set up to deal with consumer interests, and that agency is much weaker than most others. Also, while it's true that a comprehensive approach to policy making might lead to no policy at all, there are too many examples where unintended effects have made the results of a policy almost the opposite of what was planned.

[3] Ira Sharkansky, *Spending in the American States* (Chicago: Rand McNally, 1968).

KEEPING "POLITICS" OUT OF POLICY

When people talk about freeing some area of public policy such as schools or medical care from "politics," they usually mean *party* politics. They think such matters shouldn't be the concern of the political parties, with each party using the issue to get votes. And they think the policy should be removed from the control of Congress.

How, then, should such policy be made? The answer they give is that such policies should be decided on by unbiased experts. Regulation of the airwaves, for example, is a technical problem. You need experts in communications policy. The granting of a new TV license shouldn't be the subject of party conflict, with the license going to the side that can get the most congressional support. Education of children, too, should be free from the pressures of party politics and under the control of experts in education.

The attempt to remove policy making from party politics is found in the executive branch with its many agencies, in Congress with its committees, and in state and local governments. But removing some governmental activity from party politics doesn't remove it from politics in general. The decisions of experts remain "political" as long as they have the force of the government behind them, as long as they involve regulation of citizen life or the spending of tax money. What removing an issue from party politics does, however, is to turn it over to a narrow constituency. Removing communications policy from party politics means turning it over to the communications industry. The industry becomes the constituency of the government agency making the policy. The same is true of education policy. The role of organized educational interests—colleges of education, the educational bureaucracy, teachers' organizations—increases as the pressures of a wider constituency decrease.

It should be clear that this kind of decision making leads to incremental planning. Those who make policy don't take a comprehensive view of social problems. Rather their attention is focused on the group for which they are making policy—their particular constituency.

CENTRALIZED PLANNING

As we have seen in many areas of American politics, one tendency is balanced by another. The forces of decentralization pull against the forces of centralization; Congress pulls against the President; individual liberties pull against national security. The same is true in policy making. The tendency toward incremental, decentralized policy making is constantly offset by attempts to develop more comprehensive and centralized planning procedures.

Both Congress and the executive branch have tried to create institutions for comprehensive policy making, institutions that go beyond the committees of Congress and the departments of the executive branch.

The OMB. The Office of Management and Budget is directly under the control of the President. Its purpose is to improve the coordination of governmental policy. It prepares the federal budget and tries to make sure the budget proposals coming from the various departments fit into the President's program. In addition it tries to oversee the way programs are carried out.

The Council of Economic Advisers. This three-member council was set up under the Full Employment Act of 1946. Its purpose is to help the President make overall economic policy. The members of the council are usually professional economists, but they share the President's general economic views.

The National Security Council. This council brings together the top officials from the various departments that deal with foreign affairs: the Department of State, the Department of Defense, and the CIA. It tries to coordinate U.S. foreign policy. Over the years it has grown from a committee of top officials to an agency with a large professional staff.

Budget Committees in Congress. The budgetary process in the House and Senate has traditionally been incremental and decentralized. The President would submit his budget to Congress, and separate committees would work on separate parts. No committee looked at the budget as a whole. In 1974 Congress set up new budget committees in both houses. These new committees will allow the members of Congress to look at the overall budget and set target figures before working on the various parts.

Actors in the Policy-Making Process

Who are the influential actors on a particular policy? They may be individuals and groups within the government or outside it.

One possible actor is the mass public. Its opinion can be expressed in public-opinion polls and in letters to members of Congress, perhaps at election time. Or the actors may be special publics. Such groups are likely to have an interest in a particular policy. Union members, for example, are a special public in the area of labor legislation, farmers in the area of farm legislation, and so on. Or the actors may be organized groups—those with broad constituencies (such as associations, like the National Association of Manufacturers, that represent industry as a whole) and those with narrow constituencies (such as the Auto Workers, the Teamsters, the National Association of Retail Druggists).

Policy makers can also come from the party system. They might include members of the national committees or groups like the Young Democrats or the Ripon Society (a group of liberal Republicans), as well as state and local party groups.

The states, through their governors or other representatives, take part in federal policy making. And so do the cities and other local governments. But the most important actors in the making of federal policy tend to come from within the federal government itself. The office of the President is very important. This includes the President and his close advisers on the White House staff, as well as the OMB, the Council of Economic Advisers, and the National Security Council. The departments of the executive branch—Agriculture, Commerce, State, and so on—and the independent regulatory commissions such as the Interstate Commerce Commission and the Federal Communications Commission participate also.

How Is Policy Made?

The federal government is active in almost all areas of citizen life. To see how policy is made, we might have to look at thousands of issues and at the activities of hundreds of bureaus, committees, and agencies. We can't do this, but we can give an overview of the various ways policy is made and the actors involved. In the rest of this chapter, therefore, we present a few case studies of governmental policy making.

Government Regulation of Business

Government regulation of business illustrates a pattern of policy making that's common in many areas where the government is active. Despite our free-enterprise tradition, the government has long been active in regulating business activity. For some industries, such as airlines, the government sets rates. In addition the government controls certain businesses by granting them limited franchises. For all kinds of businesses it sets standards—standards of purity for drugs, safety for cars, and the like. The government also enforces the antitrust laws.

As we've pointed out before, the laws passed by Congress are often vague. They take on meaning only when they are administered. Most of the major laws dealing with regulation of industry are of this type. They tell the agency administering the law to follow "public interest and necessity" or "public convenience" or to see that rates are "just and reasonable." These are very general guidelines. What's important is who administers the law and how.

INDEPENDENT REGULATORY COMMISSIONS

Over the years Congress has created an "alphabet soup" of *independent regulatory commissions* to control various businesses: the Civil Aeronautics Board (CAB), the Federal Trade Commission (FTC) to administer the antitrust laws, the Federal Power Commission (FPC), the Federal Communications Commission (FCC), the Interstate Commerce Commission (ICC), the Securities and Exchange Commission (SEC) to regulate the stock market, and so on.

Although they deal with different areas, the commissions have many things in common. They are not directly under the control of the President or Congress. They are supposed to be free from party politics. Their boards of directors must come from both parties, and they are appointed for fixed terms so they can't be removed by a new President.

Instead of serving the general public interest, however, the regulatory commissions have become separate from the rest of the government. They deal only with the industries they regulate—the FCC with the broadcast industry, the ICC with the railroads and truckers, the CAB with the airlines. Over time these industries have become the constituencies of the various commissions; that is, the commission works closely with the industry it's supposed to be regulating. Thus in a way the regulator and the regulated become one and the same.

In such cases policy making becomes completely decentralized: Policy for each industry is made by a separate agency responsible only for that industry. Congress and the Presidency—the branches of the government that have broad constituencies—are left out. Often the regulatory commission *responsible for* a particular industry ends up being *responsive to* that industry. The result is usually a regulatory policy that favors the industry being regulated. For example, the CAB regulates air fares and assigns air routes. The result, according to one economist, is that air fares are 35 percent higher than they would be otherwise.

This pattern of regulation is found throughout the federal government. It may be found in the Department of the Interior in relation to regulation of the oil industry, in the Treasury Department in relation to regulation of banking, in the Department of Agriculture in relation to farm interests. In each case the separation between public and private, between the government agency and the interest being regulated, becomes hopelessly blurred.

These agencies go through an interesting "life cycle" that illustrates the process of policy making in many areas of American life.[4]

CREATION OF AN AGENCY

It all starts with a demand for the correction of some abuse. The ICC was created to cope with major abuses by the railroads, the SEC to cope with stock-market abuses. At this stage there are many actors involved: the public and the news media; groups of citizens with a particular interest in regulation (such as the farmers who didn't like the railroads' rate policy); the political parties that make reform part of their platform; and the President and Congress, who create the legislation. The business to be regulated is involved too, of course.

At this point the new agency is born. Congress gives it its blessing, but little guidance.

The Young Agency. At first the new agency is active. The businesses being regulated resist it. The power of the agency is not completely clear, since it wasn't spelled out by Congress. Often it takes years for the courts to decide on

[4] The notion of a life cycle is developed by Marver Bernstein, *Regulating Business by Independent Commissions* (Princeton, N.J.: Princeton University Press, 1965).

those powers. The businesses have good technical information and legal advice. They may be better staffed than the agencies that are trying to regulate them.

The Mature Agency. In the end the reforming energy of the agency fades. New people come in. The agency becomes the protector of the industry and works closely with it. The regulation is no longer in the public interest but in the interest of the industry itself. The number of actors involved has been reduced to those who are most directly affected.

One reason a close relationship can develop between the regulator and the regulated is that there are no effective opposition groups. For this reason the recent growth of consumer-protection organizations is of great political interest. Public-interest lobbies such as Common Cause can oppose the regulating agency. These new lobbies have two resources not available to the general public: a professional staff and the willingness to fight. With these resources they can help make business regulation responsive to other needs besides those of the regulated industry. Thus they are an important new actor in this policy area.

Tax Policy

Taxes are the key to all other governmental programs. They provide the funds for almost everything else the government does. They touch the lives of all citizens. In terms of impact, everyone in America is an actor on tax policy.

HOW IS TAX POLICY MADE?

At first glance tax policy doesn't look like a good area for decentralized policy making. Taxes affect all citizens and all parts of the economy. Because they redistribute income, they can become the subject of major clashes over the principle of free enterprise and the proper role of the government in relation to the poor. But even in this area we find the tendency to make policy in a series of narrow decisions. One reason for this is the complexity of the tax system. Federal income taxes are the largest items on citizens' tax bills, but they pay many other kinds of taxes as well. And these items are decided on by the states, by localities, and by special districts. As a result decisions are made for narrow constituencies without consideration of their impact on other groups.

Let's look more closely at how federal tax policy is made. The public is involved in tax policy because of its concern about high taxes and because of government officials' concern about the next election. The President is concerned as well, particularly when higher taxes are needed to support programs he favors or when he wants to use tax policy to slow down or speed up the economy.

The Role of Congress. When it comes to a particular tax policy, Congress plays a major role. It supervises tax policy more than most other policies. However, it's not Congress as a whole but two committees—the House Ways and Means Committee and the Senate Finance Committee—that we have to study when looking at tax policy.

The procedure isn't very different from the procedure used in business regulation. The independent regulatory commissions are separate agencies, while the House Ways and Means Committee and the Senate Finance Committee are parts of Congress. But a similar pattern can be seen. Congress starts with a vague general principle—a progressive income tax. The committee fills in the blanks. And here again decisions are made with particular constituencies in mind and little concern for overall public policy.

How Tax Laws Are Written. Tax laws are a series of specific decisions about specific types of income. Various industries, businesses, and other types of economic interests make requests for relief through *tax deductions, tax exemptions*, lower tax rates, and the like. In this they are often represented by a member of Congress whose constituents have a strong interest in that area.

The procedures for writing tax laws make it easy to respond to such requests. To begin with, the law is complicated and contains a wide range of choices. For example, income can be taxed as regular income or as capital gains (at a much lower rate). Congress would be severely criticized if it made a certain kind of income completely exempt from taxes or even gave it a lower tax rate. But moving one kind of income from regular salary to capital gains appears to be a technical decision, and people are less likely to object to such a decision.

Furthermore, the decisions are made on an "interest-by-interest" basis. When the question of tax policy for a particular interest group comes up, Congress deals with it in terms of what is fair in that case. It seems easy, and not harmful to others, to offer a particular group relief from a tax rate it feels is too high. There are more general principles involved: Who will have to pay higher taxes to replace the revenue lost in this way? What programs will have to be cut? Is the advantage offered to this group equal to advantages given to others? But since each group is considered separately, these broader questions aren't asked.

One result of this process is that tax benefits usually go to wealthier citizens. As we have seen, those with higher income and education are more likely to pressure Congress for tax relief. Also they are more likely to have the kind of income that will benefit from exemptions and special rates. Table 15.1 shows that the benefits from capital-gains tax rates are more likely to go to those with high incomes.

Congress as a whole doesn't play much of a role in this process. Tax bills often come up as "members' bills" dealing with special cases rather than general tax law. Each year the Ways and Means Committee brings a long list of members' bills before the House under a rule allowing them to pass without debate. Only later is it discovered that some of these bills have given a particular industry a major tax break not available to others, a benefit that costs the U.S. Treasury millions of dollars.

The final result is a hodgepodge of separate benefits with no overall structure. This can be seen by looking at the *depletion allowance*, which for many years gave the oil industry a 22 percent deduction from gross earnings because its resources were being used up. This allowance was supposed to stimulate exploration for new sources of oil needed for national defense, among other things. Over time similar allowances have been given to other industries using natural resources that may disappear. Allowances are made for the gravel and sand industry, though no one has argued that we need more gravel and sand for national defense. On the other hand the coal industry has been given an allowance because there's *too much* coal—it can't be sold because of the competition from gas and oil! In short the various allowances to industries using natural resources follow no general plan but are made on a case-by-case basis.

Thus tax policy is worked out in ways similar to the regulation of business. The public is somewhere in the background pushing for lower taxes. But its voice isn't heard when it comes to the details of tax law. The President is involved when there's a need for more tax revenue or when the Treasury wants to use tax policy to regulate the economy. But this involvement is rather general; it doesn't determine how the tax burden is divided among various groups. Congress, too, is involved only in a general sense. It sets overall guidelines for tax policy. But the most effective actors on tax policy are the businesses and other interests that work closely with congressional committees and particular members of Congress.

The result is tax loopholes that exempt many billions of dollars from federal taxes. In 1972 it was estimated that $166 billion of income was exempt from taxes and that the federal government lost $55 billion in tax revenue by not taxing that income. (See Table 15.2.)

RETURNING TAX POLICY TO PUBLIC VIEW

There are times when tax policy comes into public view, when concern for the public interest is balanced against the narrow interests that usually control

TABLE 15.1
Capital gains benefit the rich

Adjusted gross income	*Average amount saved through capital-gains tax exemption*
Under $3,000	$ 1.66
$5,000–7,000	7.44
$10,000–15,000	16.31
$50,000–100,000	2,616.10
Over $100,000	38,126.29

Source: Reprinted with permission from *The Washington Monthly*. Copyright by the Washington Monthly Co., 1028 Connecticut Ave., N.W., Washington, D.C. 20036.

policy. In 1974 and 1975 a number of events took tax policy out of congressional committees and brought it to the attention of the public as well as the executive branch: (1) The energy crisis made the oil industry and its 22 percent depletion allowance a matter of public concern; (2) the recession led the Ford administration to use tax policy to try to stimulate the economy; and (3) the discovery of President Nixon's attempts to avoid taxes led to public concern with tax reform. Under these conditions there was a greater chance for more general tax reform. It seemed likely, for example, that Congress would abolish the oil-depletion allowance.

This tells us something important about decentralized policy making: It is successful when few people pay attention to it. When some area of public policy becomes a matter of general public concern, the dominant position of narrow interests is challenged.

TABLE 15.2 *Income that escapes federal taxes*

	(BILLIONS OF DOLLARS)	
Form of tax relief	*Estimated income removed from tax base in 1972*	*Estimate loss in tax revenue*
Tax exemption for transfer payments, including social-security pensions	$ 55.1	$13.1
Special deductions, double exemptions for the aged and blind, and the retirement income credit	42.2	14.2
Special benefits for homeowners, including deductions of mortgage interest	28.7	9.6
Special tax treatment of capital gains on sales of securities, etc.	26.0	13.7
Exemption of interest earned on life insurance investments	9.1	2.7
Tax exemption of interest on state and local bonds	1.9	1.2
Tax exemption of up to $100; in annual dividends per person	1.9	0.7
Excess depletion and depreciation allowances	1.1	0.6
Total	$166.0	$55.8

Source: "Individual Income Tax Erosion by Income Classes," a study by Joseph A. Pechman and Benjamin A. Okner, Brookings Institution, published by the Joint Economic Committee of Congress on May 8. Reprinted from *U.S. News and World Report,* May 22, 1972. Copyright © 1972, U.S. News and World Report, Inc.

Medical Care

In the summer of 1965 President Johnson signed into law the medicare program, a program of government support for the medical expenses of citizens over 65. This was a major step in a long battle over the role of the government in relation to medical costs. The issue had been on the agenda since the 1930s. But in the face of a strong campaign by the American Medical Association, which labeled any program of government health insurance "socialized medicine," none of the earlier programs had been able to get through Congress.

This situation shows how the absence of governmental action is still a policy. Medical costs for Americans had been rising rapidly with the improvement in medical care. And this improvement itself was one of the sources of higher medical costs. People live longer, and medical costs are particularly high for the aged. (See Table 15.3.) By the 1940s the United States was the only industrial nation in the world with no government health-insurance program.

The program passed in 1965 was a real breakthrough for government health insurance. But it was limited to medical expenses for the aged. Thus it's a good example of incremental policy making. The supporters of federal medical assistance would have preferred a broader program. They supported the narrower one because it was possible to get it passed in 1965 and because they thought it could be used as a base on which to build toward a more comprehensive program. Each incremental step becomes a takeoff point for the next.

ACTORS ON MEDICAL-CARE LEGISLATION

The Public. For many years public-opinion polls had found that the American people strongly favored government health insurance, despite the AMA's campaign against it. But this public support was not the same as strong pres-

TABLE 15.3
Medical costs are highest for the aged

	HEALTH SPENDING PER PERSON IN 1971		
	65 and Over	*Ages 19–64*	*Under 19*
Hospital care	$410	$158	$ 41
Nursing home	151	2	—
Physicians' services	144	69	45
Drugs	87	37	20
Dentists' services	19	27	16
Other health services	50	30	18
Total	$861	$323	$140

Source: U.S. Department of Health, Education and Welfare. Reprinted from *U.S. News and World Report,* January 22, 1973.

sure on the government. Much more is needed to carry a program through Congress.

The Aged. It's interesting to note that even after the issue began to focus on medical care for the aged, there was little direct involvement of the aged as a cohesive group. There were some organizatios such as senior citizens' councils and golden age clubs, but these were small compared with the major lobbying groups such as the AMA. This illustrates again how hard it is to get organized pressure from consumer groups. Although the aged were major consumers of medical services and would be greatly helped by this legislation, they were not a self-conscious, organized group.

Interest Groups. The major public actors on the issue of medical assistance were organized groups. These included the AFL-CIO, other labor unions, and charitable organizations. They were opposed by the AMA, the American Hospital Association, the Life Insurance Association of America, and other more general organizations such as the U.S. Chamber of Commerce. It was these organizations—because they were *organized*—that could carry on the battle, particularly in Congress.

The AMA had several advantages. It was well financed. Medical problems were its main concern. And it could call on its membership. Doctors are members of a highly respected profession; they are spread throughout the country and are likely to be important citizens in their localities—just the kind of constituency to catch the attention of members of Congress.

The Presidency. If the battle had been between the interest groups alone, the stalemate might never have been broken. But there were other important actors, both in the White House and in Congress. Much of the pressure for medical-care legislation came from the Presidency. Truman made medical insurance one of his major legislative goals. His program was blocked by a hostile coalition of Republicans and conservative Democrats, but his support kept the issue alive. During the Eisenhower years the program had little Presidential support, but it came alive again under President Kennedy and the medicare bill was passed during the Johnson administration. Without this strong push from the White House, no progress would have been made.

Congressional Committees. The two powerful committees in this case, as in the tax case, were the House Ways and Means Committee and the Senate Finance Committee, with the chairman of the House committee, Wilbur Mills, playing a major role. The annual hearings before his committee were the main public battleground in the war over medical insurance. It was here that the various interest groups testified, and it was here that legislation would have to be introduced if it was to be successful in the House of Representatives.

The story of medicare points up the fact that Congress is organized in such a way that it rarely acts as a unit. Rather the key roles are played by

Labor leaders, like Teamster head Frank Fitzsimmons, are important actors in the policy process.

particular congressional members and committees. In 1961 President Kennedy, who favored a medical-assistance program, had a Democratic majority in Congress. But this majority wasn't enough to push through a legislative program. It included many conservative southern Democrats who often joined the Republicans to oppose the administration. It was only when Representative Mills decided to support the medicare plan that it was passed. The public did play a role in his change of mind, though it was an indirect role. Johnson's landslide victory in 1964 brought with it both a larger Democratic majority and an apparent demand from the people for some new legislation.

CONCLUSIONS

The medicare legislation shows how, as we've seen before, what may really count is not the decision to write new legislation but the details of that legislation and how they are applied. In working out these details Mills "called on committee members, HEW officials, and interest group representatives to lend their aid in drafting a combination bill."[5] In this way interest groups like the AMA, though they may have lost the battle against the new legislation, did have some influence on the details of the bill. For example, one of the effects of the bill has been a large increase in the income of doctors, mainly because it didn't define "reasonable charges."

What can be said about the actors on the medicare issue? For one thing it shows that no one is all-powerful. The AMA didn't have its way; it would have preferred no legislation at all. The President—even with a majority from the same party in Congress—couldn't push through the legislation he wanted. The public, though according to the polls it favored some medical-assistance program, was unable to make Congress act.

The House Ways and Means Committee and its chairman seemed to have the power to make or break medicare. But even Mills changed his mind when the pressures on him changed. And he probably wouldn't have held the line against a medical program as long as he did if he hadn't had the support of the AMA.

Medicare represented an incremental change in the government's involvement in health insurance. And as such it became the basis for the next step. A number of plans for a more comprehensive national health-insurance program are currently under consideration. The AMA no longer opposes all such programs. Rather the debate is about the kind of program: How comprehensive? Paid for in what way? Run by whom? These aren't minor questions. As we have seen, the details of a policy may be more important than its overall goals. But the issue is no longer "whether" but "what kind" of program.

America's Vietnam Policy

The histories of U.S. involvement in Vietnam have been and will continue to be written, and we can only touch lightly on this complex issue here. But the history of Vietnam policy can tell us a lot about how foreign policy is made. Vietnam shows how foreign policy is made in "ordinary" times and how it's made in the unusual situation in which a foreign-policy issue has aroused major public controversy.

Vietnam policy under President Kennedy and during the first years of the Johnson administration was made the way foreign policy is usually made—with little attention from Congress or the public. Vietnam policy after 1964 was a much more public issue. Yet even then it took quite a while for Congress to get much control over it.

[5] Theodore R. Marmor, "The Congress: Medicare Politics and Policy," in Allan P. Sindler, ed., *American Political Institutions and Public Policy* (Boston: Little, Brown, 1969), p. 52.

VIETNAM UNDER KENNEDY

According to Roger Hilsman, Kennedy's Assistant Secretary of State for Far Eastern Affairs, "any discussion of the making of United States foreign policy must begin with the President."[6] Despite Congress' power to declare war and to appropriate funds and the power of the Senate to approve treaties, foreign affairs have traditionally been handled by the President. Only the executive branch has the information and skills needed for foreign policy making. Besides, the powers of Congress haven't limited the President: Truman sent American troops to Korea without a congressional declaration of war, and the American involvement in Vietnam took place largely through a series of Presidential decisions.

But the President isn't a completely free agent when it comes to foreign policy. To begin with, policies have a history. The President must make his decisions in the light of what has happened in the past. When Kennedy took office in 1961 he inherited commitments made by the Eisenhower administration to support the government of South Vietnam. There were already several hundred American military men in Vietnam working directly with the South Vietnamese government.

The President is limited in another way. He depends on the foreign-policy bureaucracy. They give him advice and control the information coming to him. In "ordinary" foreign policy the major actors are the Presidency and the agencies that give the Presidency information: the State Department, the CIA, and the military.

Thus in 1962, using information from the CIA on the needs of the South Vietnamese government, President Kennedy ordered an increase in American troops in Vietnam from a few hundred men to 12,000 men. This was considered a limited response to a particular issue, not a commitment to preserve the South Vietnamese government at any cost. In this way it was an incremental policy, one that modified an earlier policy.

But Vietnam policy was also guided by an overall strategy based on the desire to keep communism from spreading. According to the "domino theory," if South Vietnam was lost the other Asian nations would also fall. So Vietnam policy in the 1960s took the form of small, incremental steps guided by the desire not to "lose" South Vietnam.

The Role of Congress. The role of Congress during this period was minimal. From 1961 to 1963 Congress had little to do with Vietnam. Its first major involvement came in the summer of 1964, during President Johnson's first year in office. In response to a Presidential request Congress passed the so-called Tonkin Gulf resolution, which expressed support for the President in Vietnam and allowed him "to take all necessary measures to repel any armed attack against the armed forces of the United States and to prevent further aggression."

[6] Roger Hilsman, *The Politics of Policy Making in Defense and Foreign Affairs* (New York: Harper & Row, 1971), p. 17.

This event illustrates the roles of the President and Congress in foreign affairs. The fact that the President asked for the resolution shows that there is some sharing of power over foreign affairs. But the resolution itself shows how little sharing there was. The President, as well as many members of Congress, felt that the President already had the powers given to him by the resolution. In other words the President didn't need congressional support, but such support was a way of strengthening his position.

VIETNAM UNDER JOHNSON

The "second stage" of the Vietnam War dates from sometime in 1965. There were two changes. For one thing the American involvement grew steadily. In 1968 there were over half a million American troops in Vietnam and large-scale bombing of North Vietnam. At the same time Vietnam came to public attention. In 1964, when the American people were asked to name the most important problem facing the nation, 8 percent mentioned Vietnam. By 1966 that figure had risen to 46 percent, and during the late 1960s almost everyone agreed that Vietnam was the nation's most important problem. Some groups showed their concern in a growing number of protest marches and demonstrations.

Protest against the war also moved to the floor of the Senate, where senators like Fulbright, McGovern, Kennedy, and McCarthy spoke out against Vietnam policy. And in 1968 first McCarthy and then Kennedy entered the Presidential primary campaigns against President Johnson. The result was the President's withdrawal from the campaign.

But in some ways things didn't change much. Vietnam became an explosive issue in American politics. Congress was aroused, the public was concerned, and large groups became active in opposing the administration's policy. But Vietnam policy was still shaped by the President with the advice of his staff.

There are many reasons for the comparatively weak position of Congress when it comes to foreign policy. For one thing the Constitution gives the President more power. The President's role as Commander-in-Chief of the armed forces was the main basis for sending troops to Korea and Vietnam. But more important than constitutional power is the administration's greater ability to coordinate policy, to get information on foreign affairs, and to present its views to the American people. The President controls the bureaucracy in the State Department, the Defense Department, and the CIA, as well as a large White House staff. Congress has few resources like these.

VIETNAM'S IMPACT ON FOREIGN POLICY

During the period when the United States was directly involved in the Vietnam War, Congress complained but did little to change U.S. policy. After direct American involvement ended with the ceasefire early in 1973, Congress took a more active role. It put limits on the use of American military forces in

Foreign policy is directed by the executive branch. Here Secretary of State Kissinger tours the Middle East.

Vietnam and Cambodia. In 1973 it passed, over the President's veto, a law setting a limit of sixty days on the President's ability to send U.S. forces to foreign countries without the consent of Congress. (In the Korean and Vietnam Wars the President had sent troops without the consent of Congress.)

Congress was able to play a more active role in foreign policy because of the weakness of the Presidency during the Watergate affair and because it was revealed that the administration had misled Congress and the public about the bombing of Cambodia four years earlier. Secretary of State Kissinger complained that "the growing tendency for Congress to legislate in detail the . . . conduct of our foreign affairs raises grave issues." He wondered if the United States could carry out an effective foreign policy if it could not speak with a unified voice. He argued that Congress should limit its involvement in foreign policy in order to give the administration the flexibility it needs.[7]

Many members of Congress agreed with Kissinger. Congress isn't organized to supervise the day-to-day operation of foreign policy, nor is it effective in making more general policy. The information and skills needed are found largely in the executive branch. But Congress was so dissatisfied with the administration that it seemed unlikely to return the powers it had taken away.

[7] *New York Times*, January 25, 1975.

How We Find Out About Politics: III Policies and Leaders

In studying public policy—both the institutions where policy is made and the people who make it—many political scientists do what can be called *documentary research*. For this they use the records the government keeps on itself and the records others outside the government publish about government activities and personnel.

The government describes its personnel, activities, and policies in hundreds of documents and reports. It also keeps records on many other aspects of American life. You can learn from government documents the number of scientists being trained in various universities, the number of private airplanes sold each year, the number of beds in private nursing homes, and the like. Very few activities in American society, whether public or "private," escape this record-keeping process.

In addition, because the government is involved in such a wide range of activities, many agencies outside the government keep records about the government. The AFL-CIO, for example, publishes congressional voting records on bills that are important to labor unions.

This documentation, though extensive, must be used carefully. There are several things that should be kept in mind:

1. Bias. Many government records are the result of self-reporting. Records of campaign contributions are kept by the political parties that collect the contributions. Records of crimes are kept by the FBI and local police. But self-reporting is often biased. It tends to exaggerate facts that make those who keep the records look good and play down facts that make them look bad. A city police department that thinks it's short-handed and wants a budget increase might report crime statistics in such a way as to show an increase in crime. (It might call every loss of property "suspected theft.") Another police department that has just had a budget increase will report statistics in such a way as to show a decrease in crime. (It might report only clear-cut cases of theft.)

2. Durability. Records can be lost or destroyed. The researcher who depends on documents may discover that the records he needs were destroyed in a fire or were never even kept in the first place. Say you wanted to compare the voter turnout in city elections with the turnout in national elections for the past 100 years. You would have no trouble finding the information for national elections, but for some communities you might be able to find records of turnout in local elections only for the past ten or twenty years.

3. Secrecy. In a democracy the business of government is supposed to be public. And compared to many nations the amount of information the U.S. government makes public is large. But even in the United States much government business is conducted secretly. It is particularly true in matters involving national security. Governmental secrecy, however, goes far beyond this. Nearly everything that goes on inside the White House has traditionally been made public only if the President or his staff felt that it should be made public. Although floor debate in Congress is public, congressional committees often meet in private. Supreme Court decisions are announced publicly, but the meetings of the justices take place in private. In short, it's much easier to get information on the finished product of a legislative, executive, or judicial agency than to get information on the political process leading to that product. So the study of public documents is always the study of what the government chooses to let the outsider know.

To give you an idea of the types of studies that can be carried out using these kinds of materials, here are a few examples:

1. Political representation. It's possible to combine several kinds of information to give an overall picture of political representation. Census records can show whether the citizens in a particular district are generally poor or rich, Catholic or Protestant, rural or urban. On this basis we can make some guesses about how the representative they elect might vote on various public policies. We might guess, for example, that representatives from rural districts would favor farm price supports, while representatives from urban districts would favor support for mass transit. And since there are records of the actual votes, we would be able to check out our guesses.

2. The Legislative Process. A particularly useful source of information about Congress is the weekly *Congressional Quarterly*. It reports the roll-call votes of all members of Congress. It also gives a variety of information about major bills: their subject matter, their sponsors, what was said in committee hearings, the action on the floor of Congress. It tells you who heads the various committees, what lobbyists are active on which bills, and how any piece of legislation fits into the President's program.

This kind of material is valuable for studying a great variety of questions about the legislative process. Is a committee headed by a southern Democrat likely to handle a civil-rights bill differently than a committee headed by a northern Democrat? Which pressure groups are most likely to get legislation favorable to them? Are cohesive subcommittees more successful in getting their bills passed than divided ones? Political scientists have used documentary information about Congress to study all of these issues and have developed a very detailed understanding of the legislative process.

3. Political Leaders. For those who want to know about the people who lead our society, a lot of material on the social and educational backgrounds and the careers of people who reach top governmental positions is available in publications such as the *Congressional Directory*, the State Department *Biographical Register*, *Who's Who in America*, or various biographical directories to special groups such as blacks, lawyers, or corporation officials.

Using such information we could answer several kinds of questions. We could try to figure out how much overlap there is between the various power groups in American society. For example, do the same people who serve on the boards of trustees of large universities also direct major corporations? And are these the same people who move in and out of government, serving as advisers to important political leaders? Or we could use such information to find out about the social backgrounds of leaders. We might want to know whether a large percentage of congressional members graduated from Ivy League colleges, whether there are more top officials who are black or female than there used to be, or whether the percentage of lawyers in the Senate has changed in the past 100 years.

4. Priorities in public policy. Government budgets and reports give detailed information about public policy. This kind of information is important, since it shows the priority given different programs. We know, for example, that for a long time military and national-security affairs have accounted for more than three out of every five dollars spent by the federal government, leaving all other programs to be funded out of the remaining 40 percent. We could also use this kind of information to compare the priorities of different governmental units. For example, we could see whether some states stress elementary education more than others by comparing not only spending per pupil put also the percentage of the tax dollar spent on elementary education.

Questions for Review

1. What is the difference between a policy and a decision? Give examples.
2. Why don't some policies achieve what they set out to achieve?
3. Does the federal government have a language policy?
4. How do issues get on the political agenda?
5. Contrast the comprehensive approach to policy making with the incremental approach.
6. What are some of the advantages and disadvantages of incremental planning?
7. Who are the main actors in the policy-making process?
8. Why is an independent regulatory commission, which is free from Presidential or congressional control and from party politics, still a *political* unit? Describe the "life cycle" of such a commission.
9. What effect does decentralized decision making have on tax policy?
10. How does medicare illustrate incremental policy making? Who were the major actors on medicare legislation?
11. Discuss the significance of the Vietnam War in terms of governmental policy making.

Postscript: A Glimpse of the Future

It is never easy to predict the future, especially the future of a complex nation of 300 million people. But we have learned enough about American politics and government to make reasonable guesses about what might happen as today's college students become tomorrow's parents, teachers, workers, and voters. In the future we see a larger, more powerful government. At the same time we see more social conflict over the role of government.

The responsibilities and powers of government are growing. Although this has been true for the past 200 years, today the point takes on special meaning. There is an increasing *rate* of growth. Less and less is government one of many institutions in society, sharing responsibilities and powers with business, education, and the rest. More and more government is becoming *the* dominant institution in America.

What accounts for this dominance? What are its implications? Three ideas help us understand why government is the central force in society today: the demand for equality, the number of benefits viewed as collective goods, and planning for scarcity. As we briefly review each of these ideas, we see that social conflict is one of the major implications of a growing government.

The Demand for Equality

Americans are proud that their nation was built on principles of equal opportunity and treatment. Although every citizen does not deserve the same rewards, each should have a fair chance to get them.

If this is the principle, we know that the practice has sometimes been flawed. The list of groups denied equal treatment and equal opportunity is long: Irish, Italian, and Eastern European immigrants; American Indians and Spanish-speaking Americans; blacks and women; the poor and the physically disabled.

Where do disadvantaged groups go when they are treated unfairly? Increasingly they have been going to the government. Not the church, not private business, not charity, but the government is looked upon as the institution that will bring about equal opportunity. The government has responded with programs, policies, and laws. And the government grows accordingly. Thus the more pressure that is put on the government, the larger the budget and bureaucracy it needs.

EQUALITY AND CONFLICT

Increasing the scope of government also increases the scope of political conflict. It's not that Americans disagree with the principle of equal opportunity, but in two ways they disagree about how far the principle should be extended.

First, there are citizens who are bothered by the sheer growth of the government. They feel that government, however well intentioned, is an awkward and costly tool for social reform. The government tries to help but may do as much harm as good. For example, a government medical program seems like a good idea, particularly if it means health care for people too poor to pay for doctors and hospitals. But then we have a new and costly government bureaucracy to deal with. And it's possible that the quality of medical service will decline if doctors and hospital administrators feel cramped by government regulations and paperwork.

Second, and more basic, is the tension between the principles of equality and freedom. Protecting the equality of one group can interfere with the freedom of another. Busing schoolchildren may increase equality of educational opportunity, but it may also decrease the freedom of parents to choose the kind of school they want for their children. Programs designed to provide equal rights for women are viewed by some as destroying the traditional freedom of institutions to run their own affairs.

As the government takes on more and more responsibility, it also becomes the scene of conflict over the principles and programs of equality. Some of the battles will be over the programs themselves; others will be over the merits of greater government power.

Here we see a pattern that will repeat itself in many areas of American social and political life in coming years. Inequality of opportunity, industrial pollution, unemployment, a poor international trade balance—the government is seen as the source of programs and policies to deal with such problems. Therefore it grows in the number of people it employs, the share of the national income it needs, and the amount of regulations and laws it passes. As it grows it becomes the place where different viewpoints about the problems are expressed. Thus there is an increase in political conflict.

Collective Goods

We have learned that certain social benefits are not likely to be produced if left up to individuals or workings of the free marketplace. Such benefits are called collective goods. A useful example of a collective good is the clean air that results if cars are equipped with antipollution devices. Clean air is a social benefit. Moreover, it is a benefit from which it is nearly impossible to exclude any particular person. All people get to breathe the clean air, even if some of them do not install the antipollution device. In fact the rational person would *not* install it and would still have the benefit of clean air produced by others who do use the device. If everyone acted rationally, however, no one would install the device, and there would be no social benefit.

A collective good, then, is one from which you can't exclude people who don't contribute. Because noncontributors can't be excluded, binding arrangements are needed to see that everyone does contribute. This, of course, means government. The government provides collective goods through regulations and taxes. It doesn't depend on the voluntary contributions of individuals.

We originally introduced the idea of collective goods in order to answer the question, Why government? We repeat the idea in order to answer another question, Why does government grow? The more benefits that become defined as collective goods, the greater become the powers and responsibility of the government.

As we enter the last part of the twentieth century, more and more social goals or benefits are defined as collective goods. National defense has always been considered one. (It's hard to exclude a citizen from the protection of a military security system; you can't let an enemy bomb only the houses of noncontributors.) But there are now also a number of things that weren't considered collective goods a few decades ago. One example is a clean environment, which has been considered a collective good only very recently and therefore has become a government responsibility. Another example is medical research. If cures for diseases are found, every citizen will benefit. A public highway system is considered a collective good; so are public parks and a stable economy.

Defining certain benefits as collective goods means expanding the powers of the government. It is the justification for government involvement in the economy, in social and family life, and in research and education. Creating a collective good such as national defense requires laws, programs, and agencies. Government powers expand, and the government grows.

COLLECTIVE GOODS AND CONFLICT

It might seem that there would be no conflict over whether government should provide collective goods. Who could oppose national security, clean air and water, or a highway system? But there *is* conflict—serious conflict, primarily, over what comes first. Should taxpayers' money be spent on building a faster fighter plane, cleaning polluted rivers, or improving the highway system? There's no way of knowing if one collective good is better than another. Calling things collective goods doesn't eliminate conflict; it increases it. And as a result there is conflict over what comes first.

A second source of conflict is that there are differences of opinion about what can be called a collective good. Some economists believe too many benefits are being defined as collective goods. They argue that the present trend toward collective goods is really the result of a government bureaucracy trying to expand its powers. And this trend is not producing the kind of society Americans want. The free-market system is more likely to produce such a society. For example, when enough citizens prefer clean air to fast cars (or jobs in the factories that produce those cars), they will use their purchasing power to punish the polluters. The market will respond; cars that pollute will no longer be manufactured.

The government trying to take over the job of the marketplace only messes things up. It creates a bureaucracy that justifies itself by spending taxpayers' money and regulating the lives of individual citizens. The people who stick to this view oppose the way in which the government, not the individual, decides how best to spend the money an individual earns by his or her own labor.

Planning for Scarcity

Another trend in American society is contributing to the growth of government. This is the trend toward increased planning—the attempt to be ready for the future. Will there be enough doctors in the year 2000? If not, start spending more money on medical education now. Will there be enough wood pulp to satisfy our needs for paper in the year 2000? If not, support research that might discover new methods of making paper. Will there be too few open spaces for wildlife in the year 2000? If so, now is the time to stop the developments that destroy wilderness areas.

Whose job is it to plan for the future? The simple answer is that it is everyone's job. But this won't work. So we give the job to an institution large, rich, and powerful enough to think about the future and to try to control things that may affect the future. That institution is the government. Planning means a growth of government powers.

The planning job of the government has recently taken on increased importance because of the shift from abundance to scarcity. The period from the end of World War II (1945) until the early 1970s convinced many Americans that ours was a society of abundance. There was a great increase in educational opportunities, and hundreds of new colleges and universities were started. There was a large increase in the buying power of many Americans. And there were nice things to buy. American technology mass-produced such important labor-saving devices as automatic washing machines and dishwashers. It also produced entertainment through television and movies. Even work seemed to be easier. Shorter working hours and longer (paid) vacations became the custom. And there was an increase in the number of "high-status" jobs as professional and technical positions became available in the government, education, and some of the newer industries. The result was a growing and largely satisfied middle class.

Few Americans noticed that the "American way of life" was based in part on cheap labor, some provided in this country by the rural poor and the underpaid blacks, the remainder provided by cheap labor abroad. Some of the minerals needed by American industry were mined by cheap labor in South America and parts of Africa; the fresh fruit enjoyed by Americans was picked by migrant workers in California or local workers in Honduras.

Even less noticed by Americans was the importance of a constant supply of cheap energy; energy that filtered swimming pools and lit theater marquees; heated university libraries in the winter and air-conditioned them in the summer; drove motor boats and campers; brought big-time sports into everyone's living room. The major source of this cheap energy was cheap oil.

Energy is no longer cheap. Neither is the labor that provided many of the services and products enjoyed by middle-class America in the 1950s and 1960s. The world does not have an unending supply of resources and labor available to support the way of life to which many Americans have become accustomed.

Thus we enter a period in which abundance has become scarcity, or at least a period in which we can no longer assume a steadily increasing standard of living. There is now concern about how best to hold onto what we have. One result has been to place more emphasis on planning—individual planning at the family level and social planning at the government level. The energy crisis is the best—but not the only—example of what we mean. The sharp increase in the cost of imported oil has led the government into long-range planning about future energy needs and energy sources.

PLANNING, SCARCITY, AND CONFLICT

A time of scarcity is a time when those who already have the advantage battle to hold onto what they have, to expand their wealth and security if possible, and to pass it along to their children. The less-advantaged groups in society shout "foul." In a time of limited growth, fewer jobs, and sacrifices for the future, it does not seem fair that those who are already well off should continue to have the advantage.

The government is in the middle of this conflict. It tries to distribute national wealth and yet plan for the future in the midst of conflicting claims. Once again we find conditions that appear to lead to both greater government power and greater political conflict.

The 1976 Election in Historical Perspective

A New President

In January 1977 James E. Carter ("Jimmy") became the thirty-ninth President of the United States. Carter, an ex-governor of Georgia and a peanut farmer by occupation, had won the fall 1976 Presidential election. He had defeated incumbent President Gerald Ford.

Ford was the first incumbent President to fail to win reelection since Herbert Hoover was defeated by Roosevelt in the Depression election of 1932. Ford had replaced President Nixon after Nixon had practically been thrown out of office. Facing impeachment proceedings because of his role in the Watergate cover-up, Nixon had resigned in disgrace. Nixon's predecessor in the White House was Lyndon Johnson, who had been scared out of office by his political opposition. In 1968 he decided not to run for reelection when challengers within his own party appeared likely to deny him the nomination. And before Johnson came Kennedy, a President who had been assassinated. Thus the last two decades have not been easy times for the men holding what is supposed to be the most prestigious and powerful position in the world.

What manner of man now sits in the White House? How did he come to occupy this powerful political office? Carter began his campaign for the Presidency as an unknown. He faced two major challenges. First, he had to win his party's nomination. This he did in the summer of 1976, when the Democratic party nominated him after an exhausting series of primary campaigns. Second, he had to win the Presidential election itself, never an easy task when your opponent is an incumbent President, and particularly difficult when you are, as Carter was, an outsider in American politics. Before reaching the White House Carter's only political office had been a one-term governorship of Georgia. This is not a position that provides national visibility or a national constituency. (How many people outside of Georgia know anything about its present governor?) And Carter is from the Deep South, an area of the country that had not sent a President to the White House in a century.

Three Ways of Voting

To understand Carter's remarkable rise from Plains, Georgia, to the White House we have to place the 1976 election in a broader context. The first thing to look at is how voters decide whom to vote for.

There are three ways in which voters make up their minds how to vote: (1) They can vote along party lines, supporting the candidate of the party they are loyal to. (2) They can stress the issues, supporting the candidate who comes closest to taking the positions they favor. (3) They can decide on the basis of the candidates' personal qualities, supporting the one they think is more honest or has greater leadership ability. Here are some illustrations of how voters might have used these three approaches in deciding whether to support Democrat Jimmy Carter or Republican Gerald Ford.

Party loyalty. "I am a loyal Democrat, just as my parents were before me. The Democratic party has always been good for working people like me. I don't know much about that Carter guy. But I know that he is a Democrat, and that's good enough for me. He gets my vote."

Issues. "It seems like the country is going to have to do something about inflation. Carter has got some ideas, but I don't see how his big spending programs will slow down inflation. Ford seems to have a better understanding of what is needed. My paycheck won't amount to much unless inflation is stopped, so I think I'll vote for Ford."

Personal qualities. "I want a man in the White House who is honest and fair to all groups. And I want him to be someone who understands the kind of problems people like me are having today. Ford seems cold and aloof. I think I'll go along with Carter."

PARTY LOYALTY

In earlier chapters we noted that millions of American citizens are loyal to either the Democratic or the Republican party. This loyalty is not a formal membership in a political party. Instead, it is a feeling of belonging, a sense that one is a Republican or that one generally prefers the Democrats. This party identification is often inherited from one's parents. It's rather like being a Catholic or a Jew or a Protestant because your parents were of that religion, even if you're not a church member.

Party voting is the simplest, least costly way of deciding whom to support in an election. You don't have to collect and understand a lot of information about complex issues of foreign or domestic policy. You don't even have to pay too much attention to the personal qualities of the candidate. It's enough to know that the candidate has been nominated by the political party to which you are loyal. In effect, when party voting is high, citizens are trusting their political leaders to nominate candidates who stand for the same things they do and who are decent, honorable people.

No doubt there was a lot of party voting in the election that sent Carter to the White House. For one thing, Carter won the votes of groups that have usually been loyal to the Democratic party for the past 40 years: blue-collar workers, especially union members; blacks and other racial minorities; Jews and Catholics; the less well-off members of society. And Carter won the support of almost every southern state. His victories in the South, however, were due to the overwhelming support he received from black voters. This is not the same "solid South" that had been supporting Democrats ever since the Civil War and Reconstruction.

In contrast to Carter, Ford won the votes of the western and midwestern states, which usually vote Republican. And he gained the votes of farmers, professional and business groups, wealthier citizens, Protestants, and a majority of white citizens.

Party voting alone, however, doesn't fully explain the Carter victory. For one thing, about 40 percent of American citizens now call themselves "Independents." They claim that neither of the two major parties has their loyalty. In addition, there is evidence that voting on the basis of issues and on the basis of candidates' personal qualities has been increasing in recent years.

ISSUES

The 1960s were dramatic years in several ways. These were the years in which new social movements entered the political arena: women's liberation, black power, environmental action groups, antiwar demonstrations. A flood of new political issues arose along with these social movements: legalization of marijuana, abortion, amnesty for draft dodgers, urban unrest and conflict, street crime, protection of the environment, consumer demands. Often we call these issues "social issues" in order to tell them apart from "economic issues" such as taxes, jobs, social welfare, and the like. One of the most important things about the new social issues of the 1960s is that they were not Democratic or Republican party issues. The stands that citizens took on the Vietnam War or on criminal justice or on women's rights were not likely to be related to being a Democrat or a Republican. The social issues cut across traditional party lines.

Although the issues that seemed so pressing in the late 1960s and early 1970s have faded in political importance, their effects on the political parties can still be seen. A large number of new voters entered the voting public in the 1960s. These younger voters were highly aware of the social issues. But because these issues were not seen as particularly Republican or Democratic, these new voters entered the electorate not as party members but as independents. The hold of the political parties on the voting public was weakened by the social movements and issues of the 1960s.

This is the opposite of what happened in the 1930s. Those were also years of political change. And they were years in which new voters entered the electorate—not only young voters but also European immigrants working in cities and blacks who had recently migrated to the North to find industrial jobs. The major issues of the Depression years were economic ones: jobs, unemployment, financial security. The new voters felt strongly about these issues. And they liked the way the Democratic party was trying to do something about them. They became loyal Democrats, and today they continue to give the Democratic party their support.

However, these staunch Democrats (and the equally staunch Republicans who disliked the Democrats' New Deal programs) are a smaller and smaller part of the electorate. They are being replaced by newer voters who don't have those old party ties.

All of this adds up to an electorate with an increasing number of independent voters and a decreasing number of party voters.

PERSONAL QUALITIES

We said earlier that when a citizen votes along party lines he is saying, in effect, "I trust the leaders of my party to nominate a candidate who supports the right policies and is able to give the country leadership. I don't have to do any checking on the issue positions of the candidate or on his personal qualities. It's enough that he was chosen by my party."

Events of the past ten years have badly shaken the average citizen's confidence in the nation's political leaders. Cynicism has replaced trust. Doubts have replaced confidence. This decline in confidence began in 1964, when the Democratic party's candidate, Johnson, vowed not to send American boys to fight on Asian soil. Yet at the same time, unknown to the voters or even to Congress, Johnson and his advisers were planning to expand American involvement in Vietnam. As this involvement became known and the United States sent more troops and weapons to Vietnam, Johnson suffered a "credibility gap." People didn't believe he was doing what he said he was doing.

Americans' trust in their national leaders dropped more rapidly and more sharply during the Watergate scandal. Nixon promised to restore confidence in the Presidency but instead became involved in a series of secret and illegal acts. When these acts became known, Nixon and his close advisers denied any knowledge of them. Eventually, of course, the entire story came out. Nixon left the White House in disgrace, and several of his chief advisers were jailed.

Johnson's "secret war" and Nixon's "Watergate cover-up" didn't leave the American people feeling very comfortable about their leaders. Nor have more recent revelations of domestic spying by the FBI and the CIA, sex scandals in Congress, illegal campaign gifts by giant corporations, and bribes by corporations looking for government contracts.

The American electorate has had good reason to ask whether the political recruitment and nomination processes in American society are resulting in leaders of high moral quality. As trust and confidence in the selection process itself, as well as in the leaders chosen, have declined, the voter has become more aware of the importance of "personal qualities." Jimmy Carter was able to take advantage of this awareness. There is some evidence that a large number of people voted for Carter because of their feelings about him as a person.

The 1976 Election

Before we pull together the various points we have made about the 1976 election, two additional facts should be mentioned. The 1976 Presidential election was the first ever to be financed with public money. And the 1976 election was more of a "media event" than any previous election.

PUBLICLY FINANCED CAMPAIGNS

In 1976 each Presidential candidate received $21.8 million from the public treasury. This money came from a $1 voluntary check-off on individual federal income tax returns. The campaign finance bill that set up this program was in direct response to the abuses that had been revealed in the Watergate investigations: Corporations and wealthy individuals bought political favors by contributing heavily to the campaigns of political candidates.

The amount of money available to the Presidential candidates, however, was a good deal less than in previous years. Fewer traditional campaign activities were possible. There were fewer bumper stickers, buttons, billboards, posters. There were fewer storefront campaign headquarters. And because the money to finance the campaign came from the public treasury, there was no need for fund-raising dinners, picnics, or cocktail parties. All in all, there were fewer reasons for local Democrats or local Republicans to get together.

The campaign was not very visible on the streets, in shopping centers, on college campuses, or in union halls. Some commentators called the campaign a non-event, and blamed public financing for this. But the campaign was not so much a "non-event" as it was a "media event." The candidates were very visible, but most citizens saw them or heard about them only as they appeared on the television screen.

THE ROLE OF THE MEDIA

Two things contributed to the role of the media in the 1976 election. First, what money the candidates did have they spent on TV, newspaper, and radio advertising. One estimate of Ford's expenditures, for example, says he spent $12 million on television, or more than half of his total budget. Carter's media expenses also amounted to about half of his total spending.

Second, the Presidential candidates appeared in three television debates.

These debates were watched by 70 to 80 million Americans. Much of what the voters learned about the candidates they learned from the debates.

What effect did the debates and other television campaigning have on the election? To answer this question we must first remember the three ways voters make up their minds about whom to support: party loyalty, issues, and personal qualities. We saw that party voting has traditionally been used by voters who don't want to take the trouble to learn very much about the candidates. The easiest thing is just to vote along party lines.

But the advantages of party voting are reduced when the campaign takes place in the media. A great deal of information about the candidates and their positions on the issues is as close as the TV's on–off switch. The typical voter no longer depends on party leaders as sources of information about the candidate.

The media are particularly important when the voters are in a mood to stress the candidates' personal qualities. Television allows the voters to take a good look at a candidate and to form an opinion about the kind of person he is. Does he speak with conviction? Is he the kind of person who can be trusted? Does he seem to care about people like me? Does he have leadership qualities? In asking these kinds of questions, the voter is looking at the personal qualities of the candidate, not his party.

THE CARTER VICTORY

Several different political conditions favored Jimmy Carter in 1976. Weakened party loyalties at the level of the individual voter and weakened control over the party structure at the leadership level made it easier for an "outsider" to win the party's nomination. Public campaign financing made Carter less dependent on the party for money. The role of the media in the campaign made it possible for Carter to emphasize his personal qualities directly to the voters. There was a mood of dissatisfaction with the federal government and with "those guys in Washington." This, again, helped Carter, the outsider, in his campaign against Ford, the insider.

No one of these things could have elected Carter. Taken together, however, they added up to remarkable victory for a man who just two years before was practically unknown in national politics.

The Carter Administration

It's too early to know much about the kind of President Carter will be. But he did enter the White House with one enormous advantage over recent Presidents. He is a member of the political party that is in control in Congress. In the Senate there are 61 Democrats and only 38 Republicans (there is one Independent). In the House of Representatives the Democratic party controls approximately 70 percent of the seats. The Democratic party's dominance is reflected in the state legislatures and in the state governorships. There are 37 Democratic governors and only 12 from the Republican party (and one Independent).

In both the Nixon and Ford Presidencies the executive branch, controlled by the Republican party, faced a lot of opposition in Congress, controlled by the Democratic party. This led to a large number of Presidential vetoes of Democratic legislation, as well as many changes in Presidential programs. The tension between the Democratically controlled Congress and the Republican White House had been aggravated by the large number of younger, more liberal members of Congress elected during the Watergate years.

Now, for the first time in nearly a decade, the nation has a President and a Congress of the same general political outlook. Thus, there is an opportunity for a new partnership between the executive and legislative branches. Whether Carter, the "outsider," will be able to take advantage of this opportunity is still an unknown. The student of American politics should pay close attention to the way in which Congress and the White House work together over the next few years.

The Constitution of the United States

[PREAMBLE]

We the people of the United States, in Order to form a more perfect Union, establish Justice, insure domestic Tranquility, provide for the common defence, promote the general Welfare, and secure the Blessings of Liberty to ourselves and our Posterity, do ordain and establish this Constitution for the United States of America.

ARTICLE 1

Section 1

[LEGISLATIVE POWERS]

All legislative Powers herein granted shall be vested in a Congress of the United States, which shall consist of a Senate and a House of Representatives.

Section 2

[HOUSE OF REPRESENTATIVES, HOW CONSIDERED, POWER OF IMPEACHMENT]

The House of Representatives shall be composed of Members chosen every second Year by the People of the several States, and the Electors in each State shall have [the] Qualifications requisite for Electors of the most numerous Branch of the State Legislature.

No Person shall be a Representative who shall not have attained to the Age of twenty five Years, and been Seven Years a Citizen of the United States, and who shall not when elected, be an Inhabitant of that State in which he shall be chosen.

Representatives and direct Taxes shall be apportioned among the several States which may be included within this Union, according to their respective Numbers, which shall be determined by adding to the whole Number of free Persons, including those bound to Service for a Term of Years, and excluding Indians not taxed, three fifths of all other Persons. The actual Enumeration shall be made within three years after the first Meeting of the Congress of the United States, and within every subsequent Term of ten Years, in such Manner as they shall by Law direct. The Number of Representatives shall not exceed one for every thirty Thousand, but each State shall have at Least one Representative; and until such enumeration shall be made, the State of New Hampshire shall be entitled to chuse three, Massachusetts eight, Rhode-Island and Providence Plantations one, Connecticut five, New York six, New Jersey four, Pennsylvania eight, Delaware one, Maryland six, Virginia ten, North Carolina five, South Carolina five, and Georgia three.

When vacancies happen in the Representation from any State, the Executive Authority thereof shall issue Writs of Election to fill such Vacancies.

The House of Representatives shall chuse their Speaker and other Officers; and shall have the sole Power of Impeachment.

Section 3

[THE SENATE, HOW CONSTITUTED, IMPEACHMENT TRIALS]

The Senate of the United States shall be composed of Two Senators from each State, chosen by the Legislature thereof, for six Years; and each Senator shall have one Vote.

Immediately after they shall be assembled

in Consequence of the first Election, they shall be divided as equally as may be into three Classes. The Seats of the Senators of the first Class shall be vacated at the Expiration of the second Year, of the second Class at the Expiration of the fourth Year, and of the third Class at the Expiration of the sixth Year, so that one third may be chosen every second Year; and if Vacancies happen by Resignation, or otherwise, during the Recess of the Legislature of any State, the Executive thereof may make temporary Appointments until the next Meeting of the Legislature, which shall then fill such Vacancies.

No Person shall be a Senator who shall not have attained to the Age of thirty Years, and been nine Years a Citizen of the United States, and who shall not, when elected, be an Inhabitant of that State for which he shall be chosen.

The Vice-President of the United States shall be President of the Senate, but shall have no Vote, unless they be equally divided.

The Senate shall chuse their other Officers, and also a President pro tempore, in the Absence of the Vice-President, or when he shall exercise the Office of President of the United States.

The Senate shall have the sole power to try all impeachments. When sitting for that Purpose, they shall be on Oath or Affirmation. When the President of the United States [is tried] the Chief Justice shall preside: And no Person shall be convicted without the Concurrence of two thirds of the Members present.

Judgment in Cases of Impeachment shall not extend further than to removal from Office, and disqualification to hold and enjoy any Office of honor, Trust or Profit under the United States: but the Party convicted shall nevertheless be liable and subject to Indictment, Trial, Judgment and Punishment, according to Law.

Section 4

[ELECTION OF SENATORS AND REPRESENTATIVES]

The Times, Places and Manner of holding Elections for Senators and Representatives, shall be prescribed in each State by the Legislature thereof; but the Congress may at any time by Law make or alter such Regulations, except as to the Places of chusing Senators.

The Congress shall assemble at least once in every Year, and such Meeting shall be on the first Monday in December, unless they shall by Law appoint a different Day.

Section 5

[QUORUM, JOURNALS, MEETINGS, ADJOURNMENTS]

Each House shall be the Judge of the Elections, Returns and Qualifications of its own Members, and a Majority of each shall constitute a Quorum to do Business; but a smaller Number may adjourn from day to day, and may be authorized to compel the Attendance of absent Members, in such Manner, and under such Penalties as each House may provide.

Each House may determine the Rules of its Proceedings, punish its Members for disorderly Behaviour, and, with the Concurrence of two thirds, expel a Member.

Each House shall keep a Journal of its Proceedings, and from time to time publish the same, excepting such Parts as may in their Judgment require Secrecy; and the Yeas and Nays of the Members of either House on any question shall, at the Desire of one fifth of those Present, be entered on the Journal.

Neither House, during the Session of Congress, shall, without the Consent of the other, adjourn for more than three days, nor to any other Place than that in which the two Houses shall be sitting.

Section 6

[COMPENSATION, PRIVILEGES, DISABILITIES]

The Senators and Representatives shall receive a Compensation for their Services, to be ascertained by Law, and paid out of the Treasury of the United States. They shall in all Cases, except Treason, Felony and Breach of the Peace, be privileged from Arrest during their Attendance at the Session of their respective Houses, and in going to and returning from the same; and for any Speech or Debate in either House, they shall not be questioned in any other Place.

No Senator or Representative shall, during the Time for which he was elected, be appointed to any civil Office under the Authority of the United States, which shall have been created, or the Emoluments whereof shall have been encreased during such time; and no Person holding any Office under the United States, shall be a Member of either House during his Continuance in Office.

Section 7

[PROCEDURE IN PASSING BILLS AND RESOLUTIONS]

All Bills for raising Revenue shall originate in the House of Representatives; but the Senate may propose or concur with Amendments as on other Bills.

Every Bill which shall have passed the House of Representatives and the Senate, shall, before it becomes a Law, be presented to the President of the United States; if he approves he shall sign it, but if not he shall return it, with his Objections to that House in which it shall have originated, who shall enter the Objections at large on their Journal, and proceed to reconsider it. If after such Reconsideration two thirds of that House shall agree to pass the Bill, it shall be sent, together with the Objections, to the other House, by which it shall likewise be reconsidered, and if approved by two thirds of that House, it shall become a Law. But in all such Cases the Votes of both Houses shall be determined by Yeas and Nays, and the Names of the Persons voting for and against the Bill shall be entered on the Journal of each House respectively. If any Bill shall not be returned by the President within ten Days (Sundays excepted) after it shall have been presented to him, the Same shall be a Law, in like Manner as if he had signed it, unless the Congress by their Adjournment prevent its Return, in which Case it shall not be a Law.

Every Order, Resolution, or Vote to which the Concurrence of the Senate and House of Representatives may be necessary (except on a question of Adjournment) shall be presented to the President of the United States; and before the Same shall take Effect, shall be approved by him, or being disapproved by him, shall be repassed by two thirds of the Senate and House of Representatives, according to the Rules and Limitations prescribed in the Case of a Bill.

Section 8

[POWERS OF CONGRESS]

The Congress shall have the Power To lay and collect Taxes, Duties, Imposts and Excises, to pay the Debts and provide for the common Defence and general Welfare of the United States; but all Duties, Imposts and Excises shall be uniform throughout the United States.

To borrow Money on the credit of the United States;

To regulate Commerce with foreign Nations and among the several States, and with the Indian Tribes;

To establish an uniform Rule of Naturalization, and uniform Laws on the subject of Bankruptcies throughout the United States;

To Coin Money, regulate the Value thereof, and of foreign Coin, and fix the Standards of Weights and Measures;

To provide for the Punishment of counterfeiting the Securities and current Coin of the United States;

To establish Post Offices and post Roads;

To promote the Progress of Science and useful Arts, by securing for limited Times to Authors and Inventors the exclusive Right to their respective Writings and Discoveries;

To constitute Tribunals inferior to the supreme Court;

To define and punish Piracies and Felonies committed on the high Seas, and Offences against the Law of Nations;

To declare War, grant Letters of Marque and Reprisal, and make Rules concerning Captures on Land and Water;

To raise and support Armies, but no Appropriation of Money to that Use shall be for a longer Term than two Years;

To provide and maintain a Navy;

To make Rules for Government and Regulation of the land and naval Forces;

To provide for calling forth the Militia to execute the Laws of the Union, suppress Insurrections and repel Invasions;

To provide for organizing, arming, and disciplining the Militia, and for governing such Part of them as may be employed in the Service of the United States, reserving to the States respectively, the Appointment of the Officers, and the Authority of training the Militia according to the discipline prescribed by Congress;

To exercise exclusive Legislation in all Cases whatsoever, over such District (not exceeding ten Miles square) as may, by Cession of particular States, and the Acceptance of Congress, become the Seat of the Government of the United States, and to exercise like Authority over all Places purchased by the Consent of the Legislature of the States in which the Same shall be, for the Erection of Forts, Magazines, Arsenals, dock-Yards, and other needful Buildings—And

To make all Laws which shall be necessary and proper for carrying into Execution the foregoing Powers, and all other Powers vested by this Constitution in the Government of the United States, or in any Department or Officer thereof.

Section 9

[LIMITATION UPON POWERS OF CONGRESS]

The Migration or Importation of such Persons as any of the States now existing shall think proper to admit, shall not be prohibited by the Congress prior to the Year one thousand eight hundred and eight, but a Tax or duty may be imposed on such Importation, not exceeding ten dollars for each Person.

The Privilege of the Writ of Habeas Corpus shall not be suspended, unless when in Cases of Rebellion or Invasion the public Safety may require it.

No Bill of Attainder or ex post facto Law shall be passed.

No Capitation, or other direct, Tax shall be laid, unless in Proportion to the Census or Enumeration herein before directed to be taken.

No Tax or Duty shall be laid on Articles, exported from any State.

No Preference shall be given by any Regulation of Commerce or Revenue to the Ports of one State over those of another; nor shall Vessels bound to, or from, one State, be obliged to enter, clear, or pay Duties in another.

No Money shall be drawn from the Treasury, but in Consequence of Appropriations made by Law; and a regular Statement and Account of the Receipts and Expenditures of all public Money shall be published from time to time.

No title of Nobility shall be granted by the United States: And no Person holding any Office of Profit or Trust under them, shall, without the Consent of the Congress, accept of any present, Emolument, Office, or Title, of any kind whatever, from any King, Prince, or foreign State.

Section 10

[RESTRICTIONS UPON POWERS OF STATES]

No State shall enter into any Treaty, Alliance, or Confederation; grant Letters of Marque and Reprisal; coin Money; emit Bills of Credit; make any Thing but gold and silver Coin a Tender in payment of Debts; pass any Bill of Attainder, ex post facto Law, or Law impairing the Obligation of Contracts, or grant any Title of Nobility.

No State shall, without the Consent of the Congress, lay any Imposts or Duties on Imports or Exports, except what may be absolutely necessary for executing its inspection Laws: and the net Produce of all Duties and Imposts, laid by any State on Imports or Exports, shall be for the Use of the Treasury of the United States; and all such Laws shall be subject to the Revision and Control of [the] Congress.

No State shall, without the Consent of Congress, lay any Duty of Tonnage, keep Troops, or Ships of War in time of Peace, enter into any Agreement or Compact with another State, or with a foreign Power, or engage in War, unless actually invaded, or in such imminent Danger as will not admit of delay.

ARTICLE 2

Section 1

[EXECUTIVE POWER, ELECTION, QUALIFICATIONS OF THE PRESIDENT]

The executive Power shall be vested in a President of the United States of America. He shall hold his Office during the Term of four Years, and, together with the Vice-President, chosen for the same Term, be elected as follows:

Each State shall appoint, in such Manner as the Legislature thereof may direct, a Number of Electors, equal to the whole

Number of Senators and Representatives to which the State may be entitled in the Congress: but no Senator or Representative, or Person holding an Office of Trust or Profit under the United States, shall be appointed an Elector.

The Electors shall meet in their respective States, and vote by Ballot for two Persons of whom one at least shall not be an Inhabitant of the same State with themselves. And they shall make a List of all the Persons voted for, and of the Number of Votes for each; which List they shall sign and certify, and transmit sealed to the Seat of the Government of the United States, directed to the President of the Senate. The President of the Senate shall, in the Presence of the Senate and House of Representatives, open all the Certificates, and the Votes shall then be counted. The Person having the greatest Number of Votes shall be the President, if such Number be a Majority of the whole Number of Electors appointed; and if there be more than one who have such Majority, and have an equal Number of Votes, then the House of Representatives shall immediately chuse by Ballot one of them for President; and if no Person have a Majority, then from the five highest in the List the said House in like Manner chuse the President. But in chusing the President, the Votes shall be taken by States, the Representation from each State having one Vote; A quorum for this purpose shall consist of a Member or Members from two thirds of the States, and a Majority of all the States shall be necessary to a Choice. In every Case, after the choice of the President, the Person having the greatest Number of Votes of the Electors shall be the Vice-President. But if there should remain two or more who have equal Votes, the Senate shall chuse from them by Ballot the Vice-President.

The Congress may determine the Time of chusing the Electors, and the Day on which they shall give their Votes; which Day shall be the same throughout the United States.

No person except a natural born Citizen, or a Citizen of the United States, at the time of the Adoption of this Constitution, shall be eligible to the Office of President; neither shall any Person be eligible to that Office who shall not have attained to the Age of thirty five Years, and been fourteen Years a Resident within the United States.

In Case of the Removal of the President from Office, or of his Death, Resignation, or Inability to discharge the Powers and Duties of the said Office, the Same shall devolve on the Vice-President, and the Congress may by Law provide for the Case of Removal, Death, Resignation or Inability, both of the President and Vice-President, declaring what Officer shall then act as President, and such Officer shall act accordingly, until the Disability be removed, or a President shall be elected.

The President shall, at stated Times, receive for his Services, a Compensation, which shall neither be encreased nor diminished during the Period for which he shall have been elected, and he shall not receive within that Period any other Emolument from the United States, or any of them.

Before he entered on the Execution of his Office, he shall take the following Oath of Affirmation:—"I do solemnly swear (or affirm) that I will faithfully execute the Office of the President of the United States, and will to the best of my Ability, preserve, protect and defend the Constitution of the United States."

Section 2

[POWERS OF THE PRESIDENT]

The President shall be Commander in Chief of the Army and Navy of the United States, and the Militia of the several States, when called into the actual Service of the United States; he may require the Opinion, in writing, of the principal Officer in each of the executive Departments, upon any subject relating to the Duties of their respective Offices, and he shall have Power to grant Reprieves and Pardons for Offences against the United States, except in Cases of Impeachment.

He shall have Power, by and with the Advice and Consent of the Senate, to make Treaties, provided two thirds of the Senators present concur; and he shall nominate, and by and with the Advice and Consent of the Senate, shall appoint Ambassadors, other public Ministers and Consuls, Judges of the supreme Court, and all other Officers of the

United States, whose Appointments are not herein otherwise provided for, and which shall be established by Law: but the Congress may by Law vest the Appointment of such inferior Officers, as they think proper in the President alone, in the Courts of Law, or in the Heads of Departments.

The President shall have Power to fill up all Vacancies that may happen during the Recess of the Senate, by granting Commissions which shall expire at the End of their next Session.

Section 3

[POWERS AND DUTIES OF THE PRESIDENT]

He shall from time to time give to the Congress Information of the State of the Union, and recommend to their Consideration such Measures as he shall judge necessary and expedient; he may, on extraordinary Occasions, convene both Houses, or either of them, and in Case of Disagreement between them, with Respect to the Time of Adjournment, he may adjourn them to such Time as he shall think proper; he shall receive Ambassadors and other public Ministers; he shall take Care that the Laws be faithfully executed, and shall commission all the Officers of the United States.

Section 4

[IMPEACHMENT]

The President, Vice-President and all civil Officers of the United States, shall be removed from Office on Impeachment for, and Conviction of, Treason, Bribery, or other high Crimes and Misdemeanors.

ARTICLE 3

Section 1

[JUDICIAL POWER, TENURE OF OFFICE]

The judicial Power of the United States, shall be vested in one supreme Court, and in such inferior Courts as the Congress may from time to time ordain and establish. The judges, both of the supreme and inferior Courts, shall hold their Offices during good Behavior, and shall, at stated Times, receive for their Services, a Compensation, which shall not be diminished during their Continuance in Office.

Section 2

[JURISDICTION]

The judicial Power shall extend to all Cases, in Law and Equity, arising under this Constitution, the Laws of the United States, and Treaties made, or which shall be made, under their Authority;—to all Cases affecting Ambassadors, other public Ministers and Consuls;—to all Cases of admiralty and maritime Jurisdiction;—to Controversies to which the United States shall be a Party;—to Controversies between two or more States;—between a State and Citizens of another State;—between Citizens of different States;—between Citizens of the same State claiming Lands under Grants of different States, and between a State, or the Citizens thereof, and foreign States, Citizens or Subjects.

In all Cases affecting Ambassadors, other public Ministers and Consuls, and those in which a State shall be Party, the supreme Court shall have original Jurisdiction. In all the other Cases before mentioned, the supreme Court shall have appellate Jurisdiction, both as to Law and Fact, with such Exceptions, and under such Regulations as the Congress shall make.

The Trial of all Crimes, except in Cases of Impeachment, shall be by Jury; and such Trial shall be held in the State where the said Crimes shall have been committed; but when not committed within any State, the Trial shall be at such Place or Places as the Congress may by Law have directed.

Section 3

[TREASON, PROOF AND PUNISHMENT]

Treason against the United States, shall consist only in levying War against them, or in adhering to their Enemies; giving them Aid and Comfort. No Person shall be convicted of Treason unless on the Testimony of two Witnesses to the same overt Act, or on Confession in open Court.

The Congress shall have Power to declare the Punishment of Treason, but no Attainder of Treason shall work Corruption of Blood, or Forfeiture except during the Life of the Person attainted.

ARTICLE 4

Section 1

[FAITH AND CREDIT AMONG STATES]

Full Faith and Credit shall be given in each State to the public Acts, Records, and judicial Proceedings of every other State. And the Congress may be general Laws prescribe the Manner in which such Acts, Records and Proceedings shall be proved, and the Effect thereof.

Section 2

[PRIVILEGES AND IMMUNITIES, FUGITIVES]

The citizens of each State shall be entitled to all Privileges and Immunities of Citizens in the several States.

A Person charged in any State with Treason, Felony, or other Crime, who shall flee from Justice, and be found in another State, shall on Demand of the executive Authority of the State from which he fled, be delivered up, to be removed to the State having Jurisdiction of the Crime.

No person held to Service or Labour in one State, under the Laws thereof, escaping into another, shall, in Consequence of any Law or Regulation therein, be discharged from such Service or Labour, but shall be delivered up on Claim of the Party to whom such Service or Labour may be due.

Section 3

[ADMISSION OF NEW STATES]

New States may be admitted by the congress into this Union; but no new State shall be formed or erected within the Jurisdiction of any other State; nor any State be formed by the Junction of two or more States, or Parts of States, without the Consent of the Legislatures of the States concerned as well as of the Congress.

The Congress shall have Power to dispose of and make all needful Rules and Regulations respecting the Territory or other Property belonging to the United States; and nothing in this Constitution shall be so construed as to Prejudice any Claims of the United States, or of any particular State.

Section 4

[GUARANTEE OF REPUBLICAN GOVERNMENT]

The United States shall guarantee to every State in this Union a Republican Form of Government, and shall protect each of them against Invasion; and on Application of the Legislature, or of the Executive (when the Legislature cannot be convened) against domestic Violence.

ARTICLE 5

[AMENDMENT OF THE CONSTITUTION]

The Congress, whenever two thirds of both Houses shall deem it necessary, shall propose Amendments to this Constitution, or, on the Application of the Legislatures of two thirds of the several States, shall call a Convention for proposing Amendments, which, in either Case, shall be valid to all Intents and Purposes, as Part of this Constitution, when ratified by the Legislatures of three fourths of the several States, or by Conventions in three fourths thereof, as the one or the other Mode of Ratification may be proposed by the Congress; Provided that no Amendment which may be made prior to the Year One Thousand eight hundred and eight shall in any Manner affect the first and fourth Clauses in the Ninth Section of the first Article, and that no State, without its Consent, shall be deprived of its equal Suffrage in the Senate.

ARTICLE 6

[DEBTS, SUPREMACY, OATH]

All Debts contracted and Engagements entered into, before the Adoption of this Constitution, shall be as valid against the United States under this Constitution, as under the Confederation.

This Constitution, and the Laws of the United States which shall be made in Pursuance thereof; and all Treaties made, or which shall be made, under the Authority of the United States, shall be the supreme Law of the Land; and the Judges in every State be bound thereby, any Thing in the Constitution or Laws of any State to the Contrary notwithstanding.

The Senators and Representatives before mentioned, and the Members of the several

State Legislatures, and all executive and judicial Officers, both of the United States and of the several States, shall be bound by Oath or Affirmation, to support this Constitution, but no religious Test shall ever be required as a Qualification to any Office or public Trust under the United States.

ARTICLE 7

[RATIFICATION AND ESTABLISHMENT]
The Ratification of the Conventions of nine States, shall be sufficient for the Establishment of this Constitution between the States so ratifying the Same.

Done in Convention by the Unanimous Consent of the States present the Seventeenth Day of September in the Year of our Lord one thousand seven hundred and Eighty seven and of the Independence of the United States of America the Twelfth In witness whereof We have hereunto subscribed our Names.

Go. Washington
Presidt and deputy from Virginia

New Hampshire	*John Langdon* *Nicholas Gilman*	*Delaware*	*Geo. Read* *Gunning Bedford jun* *John Dickinson* *Richard Bassett* *Jaco: Broom*
Massachusetts	*Nathaniel Gorham* *Rufus King*	*Maryland*	*James McHenry* *Dan of St Thos. Jenifer* *Danl Carroll*
Connecticut	*Wm Saml Johnson* *Roger Sherman*	*Virginia*	*John Blair* *James Madison Jr.*
New York	*Alexander Hamilton*	*North Carolina*	*Wm Blount* *Richd Dobbs Spaight* *Hu Williamson*
New Jersey	*Wil: Livingston* *David Brearley* *Wm Paterson* *Jona: Dayton*	*South Carolina*	*J. Rutledge* *Charles Cotesworth Pinckney* *Charles Pinckney* *Pierce Butler*
Pennsylvania	*B. Franklin* *Thomas Mifflin* *Robt. Morris* *Geo. Clymer* *Thos. FitzSimons* *Jared Ingersoll* *James Wilson* *Gouv Morris*	*Georgia*	*William Few* *Abr Baldwin*

Amendments of the Constitution

[THE FIRST TEN AMENDMENTS, KNOWN AS THE BILL OF RIGHTS, WERE PROPOSED BY CONGRESS ON SEPTEMBER 25, 1789; RATIFIED AND ADOPTION CERTIFIED ON DECEMBER 15, 1791.]

AMENDMENT I

[FREEDOM OF RELIGION, OF SPEECH, OF THE PRESS, AND RIGHT OF PETITION]
Congress shall make no law respecting an establishment of religion, or prohibiting the free exercise thereof; or abridging the freedom of speech, or of the press; or the right of the people peaceably to assemble, and to petition the Government for a redress of grievances.

AMENDMENT II

[RIGHT TO KEEP AND BEAR ARMS]
A well regulated Militia being necessary to the security of a free State, the right of the people to keep and bear Arms, shall not be infringed.

AMENDMENT III

[QUARTERING OF SOLDIERS]
No Soldier shall, in time of peace be quartered in any house, without the consent of the Owner, nor in time of war, but in a manner to be prescribed by law.

AMENDMENT IV

[SECURITY FROM UNWARRANTABLE SEARCH AND SEIZURE]
The right of the people to be secure in their persons, houses, papers, and effects, against unreasonable searches and seizures, shall not be violated, and no Warrants shall issue, but upon probable cause, supported by Oath of affirmation, and particularly describing the place to be searched, and the persons or things to be seized.

AMENDMENT V

[RIGHTS OF ACCUSED IN CRIMINAL PROCEEDINGS]
No person shall be held to answer for a capital, or otherwise infamous crime, unless on a presentment or indictment of a Grand Jury, except in cases arising in the land or naval forces, or in the Militia, when in actual service in time of War or public danger; nor shall any person be subjected for the same offense to be twice put in jeopardy of life or limb; nor shall be compelled in any criminal case to be a witness against himself, nor be deprived of life, liberty, or property, without due process of law; nor shall private property be taken for public use, without just compensation.

AMENDMENT VI

[RIGHT TO SPEEDY TRIAL, WITNESSES, ETC.]
In all criminal prosecutions, the accused shall enjoy the right to a speedy and public trial, by an impartial jury of the State and district wherein the crime shall have been committed, which district shall have been previously ascertained by law, and to be informed of the nature and cause of the accusation; to be confronted with the witnesses against him; to have compulsory process for obtaining witnesses in his favor, and to have the Assistance of Counsel for his defence.

AMENDMENT VII

[TRIAL BY JURY IN CIVIL CASES]
In Suits at common law, where the value in controversy shall exceed twenty dollars, the right of trial by jury shall be preserved, and no fact tried by a jury, shall be otherwise reexamined in any Court of the United States, than according to the rules of the common law.

AMENDMENT VIII

[BAILS, FINES, PUNISHMENTS]
Excessive bail shall not be required, nor excessive fines imposed, nor cruel and unusual punishments inflicted.

AMENDMENT IX

[RESERVATION OF RIGHTS OF THE PEOPLE]
The enumeration in the Constitution, of certain rights, shall not be construed to deny or disparage others retained by the people.

AMENDMENT X

[POWERS RESERVED TO STATES OR PEOPLE]
The powers not delegated to the United States by the Constitution, nor prohibited by it to the States, are reserved to the States respectively, or to the people.

AMENDMENT XI

[PROPOSED BY CONGRESS ON MARCH 4, 1793; DECLARED RATIFIED ON JANUARY 8, 1798.]
[ELECTION OF PRESIDENT AND VICE-PRESIDENT]
[RESTRICTION OF JUDICIAL POWER]
The Judicial power of the United States shall not be construed to extend to any suit in law or equity, commenced or prosecuted against one of the United States by Citizens of another State, or by Citizens or Subjects of any Foreign State.

AMENDMENT XII

[PROPOSED BY CONGRESS ON DECEMBER 9, 1803; DECLARED RATIFIED ON SEPTEMBER 25, 1804.]

[ELECTION OF PRESIDENT AND VICE-PRESIDENT]

The Electors shall meet in their respective states, and vote by ballot for President and Vice-President, one of whom, at least, shall not be an inhabitant of the same state with themselves; they shall name in their ballots the person voted for as President, and in distinct ballots the person voted for as Vice-President and they shall make distinct lists of all persons voted for as President, and of all persons voted for as Vice-President, and of the number of votes for each, which lists they shall sign and certify, and transmit sealed to the seat of the government of the United States, directed to the President of the Senate;—The President of the Senate shall, in the presence of the Senate and House of Representatives, open all the certificates and the votes shall then be counted;—The person having the greatest number of votes for President, shall be the President, if such number be a majority of the whole number of Electors appointed; and if no person have such majority, then from the persons having the highest numbers not exceeding three on the list of those voted for as President, the House of Representatives shall choose immediately, by ballot, the President. But in choosing the President, the votes shall be taken by states, the representation from each state having one vote; a quorum for this purpose shall consist of a member or members from two-thirds of the states, and a majority of all the states shall be necessary to a choice. And if the House of Representatives shall not choose a President whenever the right of choice shall devolve upon them, before the fourth day of March next following, then the Vice-President shall act as President, as in the case of the death or other constitutional disability of the President.—The person having the greatest number of votes as Vice-President, shall be the Vice-President, if such number be a majority of the whole number of Electors appointed, and if no person have a majority, then from the two highest numbers on the list, the Senate shall choose the Vice-President; a quorum for the purpose shall consist of two-thirds of the whole number of Senators, and a majority of the whole number shall be necessary to a choice. But no person constitutionally ineligible to the office of President shall be eligible to that of Vice-President of the United States.

AMENDMENT XIII

[PROPOSED BY CONGRESS ON JANUARY 31, 1865; DECLARED RATIFIED ON DECEMBER 18, 1865.]

Section 1

[ABOLITION OF SLAVERY]

Neither slavery nor involuntary servitude, except as a punishment for a crime whereof the party shall have been duly convicted, shall exist within the United States, or any place subject to their jurisdiction.

Section 2

[POWER TO ENFORCE THIS ARTICLE]

Congress shall have the power to enforce this article by appropriate legislation.

AMENDMENT XIV

[PROPOSED BY CONGRESS ON JUNE 16, 1866; DECLARED RATIFIED ON JULY 28, 1868.]

Section 1

[CITIZENSHIP RIGHTS NOT TO BE ABRIDGED BY STATES]

All persons born or naturalized in the United States, and subject to the jurisdiction thereof, are citizens of the United States and of the State wherein they reside. No State shall make or enforce any law which shall abridge the privileges or immunities of citizens of the United States; nor shall any State deprive any person of life, liberty, or property, without due process of law; nor deny to any person within its jurisdiction the equal protection of the laws.

Section 2

[APPORTIONMENT OF REPRESENTATIVES IN CONGRESS]

Representatives shall be apportioned among

the several States according to their respective numbers, counting the whole number of persons in each State, excluding Indians not taxed. But when the right to vote at any election for the choice of electors for President and Vice-President of the United States, Representatives in Congress, the Executive and Judicial officers of a State, or the members of the Legislature thereof, is denied to any of the male inhabitants of such State, being twenty-one years of age, and citizens of the United States, or in any way abridged, except for participation in rebellion or other crime, the basis of representation therein shall be reduced in the proportion which the number of such male citizens shall bear to the whole number of male citizens twenty-one years of age in such State.

Section 3

[PERSONS DISQUALIFIED FROM HOLDING OFFICE]

No person shall be a Senator or Representative in Congress, or elector of President and Vice-President, or hold any office, civil or military, under the United States, or under any State, who, having previously taken an oath, as a member of Congress, or as an officer of the United States, or as a member of any State legislature, or as an executive or judicial officer of any State, to support the Constitution of the United States, shall have engaged in insurrection or rebellion against the same, or given aid or comfort to the enemies thereof. But Congress may by a vote of two-thirds of each House, remove such disability.

Section 4

[WHAT PUBLIC DEBTS ARE VALID]

The validity of the public debt of the United States, authorized by law, including debts incurred for payment of pensions and bounties for services in suppressing insurrection or rebellion, shall not be questioned. But neither the United States nor any State shall assume or pay any debt or obligation incurred in aid of insurrection or rebellion against the United States, or any claim for the loss or emancipation of any slave; but all such debts, obligations and claims shall be held illegal and void.

Section 5

[POWER TO ENFORCE THIS ARTICLE]

The Congress shall have power to enforce, by appropriate legislation, the provisions of this article.

AMENDMENT XV

[PROPOSED BY CONGRESS ON FEBRUARY 26, 1869; DECLARED RATIFIED ON MARCH 30, 1870.]

Section 1

[NEGRO SUFFRAGE]

The right of citizens of the United States to vote shall not be denied or abridged by the United States or by any State on account of race, color, or previous condition of servitude.

Section 2

[POWER TO ENFORCE THIS ARTICLE]

The Congress shall have power to enforce this article by appropriate legislation.

AMENDMENT XVI

[PROPOSED BY CONGRESS ON JULY 12, 1909; DECLARED RATIFIED ON FEBRUARY 25, 1913.]

[AUTHORIZING INCOME TAXES]

The Congress shall have power to lay and collect taxes on incomes, from whatever source derived, without apportionment among the several States, and without regard to any census or enumeration.

AMENDMENT XVII

[PROPOSED BY CONGRESS ON MAY 13, 1912; DECLARED RATIFIED ON MAY 31, 1913.]

[POPULAR ELECTION OF SENATORS]

The Senate of the United States shall be composed of two Senators from each State, elected by the people thereof, for six years; and each Senator shall have one vote. The electors in each State shall have the qualifications requisite for electors of the most numerous branch of the State legislatures.

When vacancies happen in the representation of any State in the Senate, the executive authority of such State shall issue writs of election to fill such vacancies: *Provided*, That the legislature of any State may empower the executive thereof to make temporary appointments until the people fill the vacancies by election as the legislature may direct.

This amendment shall not be so construed as to affect the election or term of any Senator chosen before it becomes valid as part of the Constitution.

AMENDMENT XVIII

[PROPOSED BY CONGRESS ON DECEMBER 18, 1917; DECLARED RATIFIED ON JANUARY 16, 1919.]

Section 1

[NATIONAL LIQUOR PROHIBITION]

After one year from the ratification of this article the manufacture, sale, or transportation of intoxicating liquors within, the importation thereof into, or the exportation thereof from the United States and all territory subject to the jurisdiction thereof for beverage purposes is hereby prohibited.

Section 2

[POWER TO ENFORCE THIS ARTICLE]

The Congress and the several States shall have concurrent power to enforce this article by appropriate legislation.

Section 3

[RATIFICATION WITHIN SEVEN YEARS]

This article shall be inoperative unless it shall have been ratified as an amendment to the Constitution by the legislatures of the several States, as provided in the Constitution, within seven years from the date of the submission hereof to the States by the Congress.

AMENDMENT XIX

[PROPOSED BY CONGRESS ON JUNE 4, 1919; DECLARED RATIFIED ON AUGUST 26, 1920.]

[WOMAN SUFFRAGE]

The right of citizens of the United States to vote shall not be denied or abridged by the United States or by any State on account of sex.

Congress shall have power to enforce this article by appropriate legislation.

AMENDMENT XX

[PROPOSED BY CONGRESS ON MARCH 2, 1932; DECLARED RATIFIED ON FEBRUARY 6, 1933.]

Section 1

[TERMS OF OFFICE]

The terms of the President and Vice-President shall end at noon on the 20th day of January, and the terms of Senators and Representatives at noon on the 3rd day of January, of the years in which such terms would have ended if this article had not been ratified; and the terms of their successors shall then begin.

Section 2

[TIME OF CONVENING CONGRESS]

The Congress shall assemble at least once in every year, and such meeting shall begin at noon on the 3rd day of January, unless they shall by law appoint a different day.

Section 3

[DEATH OF PRESIDENT ELECT]

If, at the time fixed for the beginning of the term of the President, the President elect shall have died, the Vice-President elect shall become President. If a President shall not have been chosen before the time fixed for the beginning of his term, or if the President elect shall have failed to qualify, then the Vice-President elect shall act as President until a President shall have qualified; and the Congress may by law provide for the case wherein neither a President elect nor a Vice-President elect shall have qualified, declaring who shall then act as President, or the manner in which one who is to act shall be selected, and such person shall act accordingly until a President or Vice-President shall have qualified.

Section 4

[ELECTION OF THE PRESIDENT]

The Congress may by law provide for the case

Year	Candidates	Party	Popular vote	Electoral vote
1932	***Franklin D. Roosevelt***	Democratic	22,809,638 (57.3%)	472
	Herbert C. Hoover	Republican	15,758,901 (39.6%)	59
	Norman Thomas	Socialist	881,951 (2.2%)	
1936	***Franklin D. Roosevelt***	Democratic	27,751,612 (60.7%)	523
	Alfred M. Landon	Republican	16,681,913 (36.4%)	8
	William Lemke	Union	891,858 (1.9%)	
1940	***Franklin D. Roosevelt***	Democratic	27,243,466 (54.7%)	449
	Wendell L. Willkie	Republican	22,304,755 (44.8%)	82
1944	***Franklin D. Roosevelt*** ***(Harry S Truman, 1945)***	Democratic	25,602,505 (52.8%)	432
	Thomas E. Dewey	Republican	22,006,278 (44.5%)	99
1948	***Harry S Truman***	Democratic	24,105,812 (49.5%)	303
	Thomas E. Dewey	Republican	21,970,065 (45.1%)	189
	J. Strom Thurmond	States' Rights	1,169,063 (2.4%)	39
	Henry A. Wallace	Progressive	1,157,172 (2.4%)	
1952	***Dwight D. Eisenhower***	Republican	33,936,234 (55.2%)	442
	Adlai E. Stevenson	Democratic	27,314,992 (44.5%)	89
1956	***Dwight D. Eisenhower***	Republican	35,590,472 (57.4%)	457
	Adlai E. Stevenson	Democratic	26,022,752 (42.0%)	73
1960	***John F. Kennedy*** ***(Lyndon B. Johnson, 1963)***	Democratic	34,227,096 (49.9%)	303
	Richard M. Nixon	Republican	34,108,546 (49.6%)	219
1964	***Lyndon B. Johnson***	Democratic	43,126,233 (61.1%)	486
	Barry M. Goldwater	Republican	27,174,989 (38.5%)	52
1968	***Richard M. Nixon***	Republican	31,783,783 (43.4%)	301
	Hubert H. Humphrey	Democratic	31,271,839 (42.7%)	191
	George C. Wallace	American Independent	9,899,557 (13.5%)	46
1972	***Richard M. Nixon*** ***(Gerald Ford, 1974)***	Republican	46,631,189 (61.3%)	521
	George McGovern	Democratic	28,422,015 (37.3%)	17
1976	***James E. Carter***	Democratic	40,173,854 (51%)*	297
	Gerald Ford	Republican	38,429,988 (48%)	241
	Eugene J. McCarthy	Independent	654,770 (1%)	

Note: Because only the leading candidates are listed, popular-vote percentages do not always total 100. The elections of 1880 and 1824, in which no candidate received an electoral-vote majority, were decided in the House of Representatives.
* Total reported as of November 3, 1976.

GLOSSARY

adjudication The process by which a judgment or decision is made by law; adversary proceedings in a court of law.

affirmative action The hiring of members of a minority group in order to make up for previous discrimination against that group.

agenda The list of items to be considered at a meeting or legislative session; more generally, the politically relevant issues.

amendment A change in or addition to a bill, motion, or constitution. A constitutional amendment is usually proposed by a two-thirds vote of both houses of Congress. To be ratified, it must be approved by the legislatures of three-fourths of the states.

amicus curiae brief Literally, a brief filed by a "friend of the court"; thus a brief filed by a person who is not a party to a lawsuit but who may be affected by its outcome.

appeal A legal proceeding in which a case is carried from a lower court to a higher court for review or reexamination.

appellate jurisdiction The right to try cases on appeal from lower courts. The Supreme Court usually hears cases on appeal from lower federal courts or state supreme courts.

appropriation A bill granting the actual funds for a program that has been authorized by Congress.

authorization Congressional legislation prescribing a particular program and putting limits on spending for that program.

checks and balances The system under which each branch of the government has the power to limit the activities of the other branches. An example is the President's power to veto acts of Congress.

circuit court (of appeals) A federal court with appellate jurisdiction assigned to one of the eleven judicial circuits, or regions, in the United States.

civil liberties Liberties guaranteed to the individual by the First Amendment to the Constitution: freedom of speech, press, and assembly.

coalition A political union containing a variety of political groups. American political parties, for example, are coalitions; the Democratic party includes both southern conservatives and northern liberals.

collective good A benefit, such as a public park or highway, available to all citizens whether or not they have worked to create that benefit.

communal activity Political activity in which citizens act as a group to pressure the government. Such activity is carried on by both formal and informal organizations.

comprehensive planning A form of planning in which all possible ways of solving a problem are considered (cf. incremental planning).

concurrent majority The idea that a majority of the citizens of the United States cannot determine the policy followed within a particular region.

confederation A form of government in which the central government is subordinate to the state governments (cf. federation, unitary government).

conference committee A committee formed to resolve the differences between the versions of a bill passed by the Senate and the House of Representatives. It usually consists of senior members of the House and Senate committees sponsoring the bill.

congressional caucus A meeting of the members of one political party in the Senate or the

House of Representatives in which various decisions are made such as the choice of congressional party leaders.

Connecticut Compromise An agreement reached during original debates over the Constitution deciding that Congress would consist of two houses: the House of Representatives, in which the number of representatives from each state would be determined by population, and the Senate, in which each state would be represented equally.

conservative A political position that favors maintaining a stable society and stresses the need for strong political and social institutions. Conservatives often stress the need to maintain the status quo (cf. liberal).

constituency The district represented by a legislator; in broader terms, the interests represented by a governmental unit such as a congressional committee or an executive agency.

constituent A person who lives in a legislative district. A resident of Brooklyn is a constituent of the members of Congress representing Brooklyn.

constitutionalism Belief in government according to a basic law, or constitution, against which all other laws are measured.

cooperative federalism The system in which government powers are shared across the various levels of government—federal, state, and local (cf. dual federalism).

de facto segregation Segregation that results from housing patterns in which different social groups, e.g., blacks and whites, live in separate neighborhoods. Not supported in law.

defendant The defending party in a court case; the person sued or accused (cf. plaintiff).

depletion allowance A tax reduction that may be taken by owners of oil and gas wells and other minerals, supposedly to stimulate exploration for such natural resources (cf. tax deduction).

deviating election An election that temporarily changes the balance of political forces (cf. maintaining election, realigning election).

district court A federal court of original jurisdiction. There are ninety district courts in the federal court system.

documentary research The use of records kept by the government, as well as records published by other sources, in conducting research on political questions.

dual federalism The doctrine that the states and the nation have separate areas of responsibility (cf. cooperative federalism).

due process of law The guarantee, contained in the Fifth and Fourteenth Amendments to the Constitution, that an individual cannot be deprived of life, liberty, or property by an arbitrary act of government.

elector A member of the Electoral College. Each state's electors are chosen by the voters in the November election. They usually vote as a unit for the candidate who won the greatest number of votes in that state.

Electoral College The group of electors, representing all the states, who actually choose the new President and Vice-President. The candidates who receive the majority of the electoral votes need not be the same ones who won the plurality of the popular vote, though in practice this has almost always been the case.

ethnic group A group whose members share characteristics such as national background, religion, customs, or language. They often share a sense of *ethnicity,* or a fundamental feeling of group identity.

executive agreement An international agreement signed by the President that does not need Senate approval.

federalism A system of government in which power is shared between a central government and state or regional governments.

Federalist Papers A series of essays written by Alexander Hamilton, James Madison, and John Jay to defend the new Constitution.

federation A union of states in which each member agrees to subordinate its power to the central authority in common affairs while retaining authority on other matters. (cf. confederation, unitary government).

filibuster A delaying tactic used in the Senate in which a small group can "talk a bill to death" under the rule of unlimited debate.

fiscal policy Government efforts to manage the economy through adjustments in taxes and government spending.

floor leaders Party leaders, one from each party in each house of Congress, responsible for keeping party members informed and active in legislative battles.

grandfather clause A law used by southern states to allow whites to vote even when they were disqualified by literacy tests or property rules. Under this clause a person could vote if he or a direct ancestor had been able to vote on January 1, 1867. Ruled unconstitutional.

grant-in-aid A grant of funds by the federal government to a state or local government (or by a state government to a local government) to be used for a particular purpose.

House minority leader The leader of the minority party in the House of Representatives.

impeachment A formal accusation of a public official for misconduct in office, made by the lower house of a legislature. The President may be impeached by the House of Representatives for "high crimes and misdemeanors." The Senate decides by a two-thirds vote whether or not to convict.

implied powers The doctrine that Congress isn't limited to the powers listed in the Constitution but has all the powers necessary to carry out those that are listed.

impoundment Literally, seizing and holding in legal custody; politically, refusal by the President to spend funds appropriated by Congress.

incremental planning A form of planning in which problems are approached one step at a time (cf. comprehensive planning).

independent regulatory commission An agency set up outside the executive branch and responsible for regulating a particular part of the economy. An example is the Securities and Exchange Commission, which regulates the stock market.

injunction A court order prohibiting a person or group from carrying out a particular action.

interest group Organized group that uses various techniques to influence government policy; also referred to as "pressure group" or "lobby."

Jim Crow laws Laws passed by southern states requiring segregation of blacks and whites.

legitimacy of government The belief that the government is legitimate—that public officials deserve support and that the law must be obeyed.

liberal A political position that supports political, social, and economic changes in order to improve the well-being of the individual (cf. conservative).

lobby A group of professionals that tries to influence the decisions of legislative and executive agencies in Washington and the state capitals in favor of a particular interest group.

maintaining election An election that maintains the existing balance of political forces (cf. deviating election, realigning election).

majority A number over 50 percent. In a democracy the majority rules in choosing public officials and making political decisions (cf. plurality).

midterm election The national election that takes place midway between two Presidential elections. All members of the House of Representatives and one-third of the members of the Senate are elected in a midterm election, as are many officials of state governments.

monetary policy Government efforts to manage the economy through changes in the money supply and interest rates.

monopoly An economic situation in which a single corporation has so much power that it can fix prices and eliminate competition.

oligopoly An economic situation in which a few corporations have so much power that they can fix prices and reduce competition in a particular part of the economy.

original jurisdiction The right to try a case for the first time; in other words, a case "originates" in a court that has original jurisdiction.

party identification The feeling that one belongs to a particular political party the way one belongs to a particular religion.

plaintiff A person who brings a suit in a court of law; the challenger (cf. defendant).

platform A political party's statement of principles and policies. Each party's platform is drawn up at its Presidential nominating convention.

plurality The largest number of votes. When more than two strong candidates run for a particular office, the winner usually gets a plurality rather than a majority of the votes (cf. majority).

pocket veto The President's power to veto a bill by holding it for ten days without either signing it or vetoing it; if Congress adjourns during that time the bill does not become law.

political efficacy One's belief that he or she has a voice in the government and can influence its actions.

president protempore The presiding officer of the Senate when the Vice-President is absent (always a member of the party holding a majority of the seats in the Senate).

primary election An election held by a political party to determine which of its members should be nominated for public office.

public-opinion poll A survey that finds out the opinions of a representative sample of the public in order to get a picture of general public opinion.

realigning election An election in which the party that had more faithful identifiers and supporters than the second party loses its advantage and becomes the minority party. This happens when many new voters identify with what had previously been the minority party or when numbers of voters change party allegiances (cf. deviating election, maintaining election).

revenue sharing A program in which the federal government distributes funds to state and local governments to spend where they are needed most.

roll-call vote A vote in Congress in which each legislator's vote is put on record.

Senate majority leader The leader of the majority party in the Senate (also the recognized leader of the Senate).

Senate minority leader The leader of the minority party in the Senate.

seniority rule The congressional rule under which the member of the majority party who has served longest on a committee chairs that committee.

separation of powers The principle under which government power is shared by the three branches of government—legislative, executive, and judicial.

Speaker of the House The presiding officer of the House of Representatives and the leader of the majority party.

special district A local government unit created to provide a single service such as park maintenance or mosquito abatement.

split ticket A ballot on which the voter has chosen candidates from different parties for different offices (cf. straight ticket).

standing committee A permanent committee in the Senate or the House of Representatives. Examples are the House Ways and Means Committee and the Senate Foreign Relations Committee.

state capitalism An economic system under which the government is heavily involved in economic affairs but most of the economy is privately owned.

State of the Union Address An annual speech to Congress in which the President discusses the problems facing the nation and presents a legislative program to deal with those problems.

straight ticket A ballot on which the voter has chosen candidates from the same party for different offices (cf. split ticket).

tariff A tax on imports that protects products made in this country from foreign competition by raising the prices of foreign products.

tax deduction A subtraction, for example, the amount of medical payments or interest on a mortgage, reducing the amount of income that can be taxed. This in turn reduces the amount paid in taxes.

tax exemption Income that is not taxed, such as interest on municipal bonds.

unit rule The rule by which the candidate who gets the greatest number of votes in a primary election wins all of that state's delegate votes at the nominating convention.

unitary government A form of government in which all state and local governments are subordinate to the central government (cf. confederation, federation).

whip An assistant floor leader who acts as a liaison between party leaders and party members and makes sure party members are present for important votes.

writ of certiorari A request from a higher court to a lower court for the record of a case for review.

writ of mandamus A court order requiring an individual, corporation, or public official to perform some duty.

INDEX

77 78 79 80 10 9 8 7 6 5 4 3 2 1